UNIVERSITY CASEBOOK SERIES®

DOING BUSINESS IN EMERGING MARKETS

A TRANSACTIONAL COURSE

SECOND EDITION

by

RICHARD N. DEAN
Partner, Baker & McKenzie

JAMES W. SKELTON, JR.
Attorney at Law, International Legal Consultant and
Adjunct Professor of Law, University of Houston Law Center

PAUL B. STEPHAN
John C. Jeffries, Jr., Distinguished Professor of Law
Elizabeth D. and Richard A. Merrill Professor of Law
University of Virginia

FOUNDATION
PRESS

University Casebook Series is a trademark registered in the U.S. Patent and Trademark Office.

© 2010 by THOMSON REUTERS/FOUNDATION PRESS
© 2015 LEG, Inc. d/b/a West Academic
    444 Cedar Street, Suite 700
    St. Paul, MN 55101
    1-877-888-1330

Printed in the United States of America

ISBN: 978-1-62810-017-4

Mat #41609592

PREFACE

The three of us have, on a combined basis, over 100 years of experience working in, and teaching about, emerging markets. Our enthusiasm for the subject reflects two complementary interests. Idealistically, we believe that lawyers have an ethical obligation to make the world a better place, and that the struggle of developing countries to reform their economic, political and legal systems deserves our support and involvement. Practically, we know that transactional lawyers get paid to spend a lot of time working on investments in emerging markets. The course thus gives students an opportunity to prepare themselves to do good as they do well.

In our course, the country that served as the model for an emerging market has been Russia. This was partly personal: Dean and Stephan acquired graduate degrees in Russian studies before or during our legal training, and the former Soviet Union and its successor states have taken up a great deal of our time and energy throughout our careers, and Skelton devoted a large portion of an 18 year span of his career working on a variety of transactions in Russia. But a good case can be made for this focus, our personal and professional commitments aside. Russia has vast natural resources that are traded internationally and a highly educated work force. For almost two decades now the stated policy of successive governments has been to encourage foreign investment. Yet the obstacles to successful business transactions have been great and the number and scale of failed investments have been many. This juxtaposition of potential and failure compels the attention of lawyers. Were there no potential, there would be no practical reason for a lawyer to care about Russia. Were there no obstacles, a lawyer would not add much value to the transactions contemplated. For the last quarter century, Russia has provided an ideal environment for lawyers to grapple with serious difficulties confounding potentially important and lucrative business deals.

In these materials we continue to look at Russia, but we also bring in China and India, countries where foreign commerce and investment have played a growing role in recent years. We also cover other markets in Asia, Latin American, the Middle East and Africa. The point throughout is not to learn how to solve a particular problem in a particular country, but rather to acquire insights and skills that can translate across the range of emerging markets. The modern transactional lawyer typically works closely with colleagues who have extensive local knowledge and makes a distinct contribution by bringing to bear talents and experience that apply in any emerging market. Putting it simply, emerging markets may vary considerably but still have enough in common to justify a general, thematic approach to the subject.

We have never required our students to take any course as a prerequisite for ours, but that is not to say that traditional law school courses are not relevant to our subject. Some understanding of business law, including courses such as corporations, secured transactions, bankruptcy, intellectual property, antitrust, taxation and securities regulation is essential. A good general course on international business transactions helps enormously. However, we believe that the foundational private law courses of the first year are sufficient.

The materials we use, like the subject, are transactional. Our course is organized around an extended role-playing exercise in which students are assigned particular tasks in a complex negotiation. We take the students through each stage of the negotiating process, showing how the deal takes shape stage-by-stage. This allows us to demonstrate how decisions made early on in the process constrain the choices that follow, which allows the student to appreciate the ramifications of seemingly straightforward choices. Each chapter except the first begins or ends with a problem that provides a context for the materials that follow. The instructor is free to skip or modify these exercises, but our experience suggests that students both enjoy and derive considerable value from the role-playing.

In preparing these materials we have accumulated many debts that we can only partly acknowledge here. Robert E. Scott, John C. Jeffries, Jr., and Paul G. Mahoney, successive as well as successful Deans at Virginia who have supported us generously while remaining close and valued friends, deserve special mention. In addition, Interim Dean Richard Alderman and Associate Dean Lonny Hoffman have supported Jim Skelton in making this course a part of the curriculum at the University of Houston Law Center. The research librarians at the Arthur J. Morris Law Library, in particular Xinh Luu, have provided us with wonderful support, as have Rich Dean's colleagues at Coudert Brothers and Baker & McKenzie. We are grateful to Gene Theroux for his many suggestions and support. The many students who have taken our course have taught us a great deal through their enthusiastic participation and carefully crafted research papers. Our greatest thanks, however, must go to our spouses, Susan Dean, Merrilyn Skelton and Pamela Clark, who have long put up with our work and travels as well as forgiving our many other husbandly deficiencies.

RICHARD N. DEAN
JAMES W. SKELTON, JR.
PAUL B. STEPHAN

August 2014

SUMMARY OF CONTENTS

TABLE OF CASES

The principal cases are in bold type.

UNIVERSITY CASEBOOK SERIES®

DOING BUSINESS IN EMERGING MARKETS

A TRANSACTIONAL COURSE

SECOND EDITION

CHAPTER 1

THE CHALLENGES OF BUSINESS TRANSACTIONS IN EMERGING MARKETS

What precisely is an emerging market and why should lawyers care? One on-line dictionary speaks of "the world's poor countries, also known, often optimistically, as emerging economies."[1] This is too crude. First, "poor" is relative: The BRICs (Brazil, Russia, India and China), which are among the world's ten largest national economies as measured by the World Bank, are emerging markets. Each of those countries contains many holders of great wealth, although they also have vast numbers of the poor as well. Second, the term implies a process rather than a status. We are interested in trade and investment involving those countries that have changed their economic policies from extreme protection to some degree of openness to foreign investors and business partners. The point is one of transition. In particular, it is the uncertainty and challenge of change, risk and opportunity that attracts lawyers as well as business people to emerging markets.[2]

What explains the transition on which the concept of emerging markets rests? Consider the explanation of Anne Krueger, one of the world's leading development economists and formerly the chief economist at the International Monetary Fund:

> [During the quarter century after World War II all] of the industrial countries were growing at sustained rates higher than ever in world economic history, with Japan growing at the fastest rate. In the 1950s, economic development textbooks classified countries as developed or underdeveloped (as the term then was), and often noted that Japan was halfway in between. The country experienced growth rates of around 8 to 9 percent from 1959 to the 1970s, by which time there was no doubt as to Japan's status.
>
> But largely unnoticed by industrial countries' businessmen and policy makers, a few relatively small developing countries shifted policies. The first group to do so, and one that attracted great attention subsequently, was the East Asian Tigers (as they were then called)—Hong Kong, Singapore, South Korea, and Taiwan. These four economies became outer-oriented, shedding most of their protection for domestic industries, and shifting to reliance upon what came to be called export-led growth.
>
> Starting from an incredibly low base, all four economies experienced unheard-of rates of economic growth and poverty

---

[1] Economics A–Z, http://www.economist.com/research/Economics/alphabetic.cfm?term= developingcountries #developingcountries.

[2] Ashoka Mody, *What Is an Emerging Market?* 35 GEO. J. INT'L L. 641 (2004).

reduction. At first, most observers believed these high growth rates to be a short-run, unsustainable phenomenon, but as time passed, and growth persisted, or even accelerated, it came to be recognized that these four were achieving long-lasting results.

It is worth pointing out that South Korea, probably the most successful of the four (although the Taiwanese would argue with that), was one of the poorest countries in Asia, and the world, in the 1950s. The country had followed the same inner-oriented policies as other developing countries and, despite the devastation of the Korean War (and the aftermath of hyperinflation in the late 1940s), annual growth rates did not even average 5 percent, with population growth of over 2 percent. South Korea's per capita income in 1960 was estimated to be about the same as that of Ghana, and below that of a number of Sub-Saharan countries. The country had the highest rate of inflation in the world, multiple exchange rates, a huge fiscal deficit, and much more. Most observers viewed the prospects for growth of the South Korean economy as dismal— with the U.S. Congress even passing a resolution stating that there was no hope for growth and that there should be foreign aid to support consumption levels only.

Taiwan had also opened up the economy in the mid-1950s, and the two both began growing rapidly after their policy shifts. The move toward an outer-oriented trade strategy in both cases was accompanied and supported by a number of other key policy reforms, including fiscal consolidation with sharply reduced inflation; infrastructure and educational investments; and greatly reduced protection for import-competing producers.

For South Korea and Taiwan, as well as Singapore and Hong Kong, the subsequent period until the second half of the 1990s witnessed an economic transformation that had previously been regarded as unthinkable. Economists in the 1960s thought that 6 to 7 percent was the highest possible sustainable rate of economic growth for a poor developing country, yet all four economies exceeded that range with double-digit growth rates in the first part of the period. To give an idea of the orders of magnitude, South Korea is estimated to have realized an annual 8 percent growth rate of real wages from 1964 to 1995; exports grew at an average annual rate of over 40 percent for several decades (during which world prices were fairly stable), so that they rose from about 3 percent of South Korean GDP in 1960 to around 40 percent by the late 1980s (and was last year the 8th largest exporting nation globally). Domestic savings rose from approximately 0 percent in 1960 to about 37 percent by the late 1980s. And there was much else, including rising educational attainments and a sharp drop in the rate of growth of population. The achievements were similar in the other three Asian Tigers.

As the success of the East Asian Tigers became increasingly evident, policy-makers in other countries began altering their development strategies. Some adopted the sorts of policies undertaken in the Asian Tigers wholeheartedly, while many others at least reduced their trade barriers and moderated other economic policies that were deleterious to growth.

The four East Asian Tigers are now regarded as industrial economies. But for purposes of understanding the BRICs and the shift in the global economy, two other points are crucial. First, that the four East Asian Tigers would be the first to shift toward an open economy, for a successful development strategy was not predicted. Many observers credited India with the greatest chances of success, and regarded Brazil's and the Philippines' prospects as relatively bright. Indeed, the four were each seen to have significant problems: the size of the two city-states, Taiwan's diplomatic isolation, and South Korea's poverty. . . .

The second point is that it was the success of the four East Asian Tigers that induced others to try the same policy mix. Although I shall focus on the growth of the BRICs, it should be noted that a number of other countries, such as Chile, Mexico, and Turkey, have also been successful in accelerating their growth and increasing their participation in the international economy.

The BRICs are the largest of them. China abandoned her policies of economic isolation in the early 1980s; India began her economic reforms in 1991 in response to a crisis. Of course, the fate of the Soviet Union stemmed largely from the failure of central planning, giving yet further impetus to the policy shifts in other countries. Russia's growth has again hinged on policy reforms, although the oil and natural gas sector has been very important. Brazil's emergence was somewhat different, in that there was a period of rapid growth in the 1950s, another one in the late 1960s and early 1970s, with more sustained growth since 2002.

Despite the fact that Chinese exports began rising rapidly after that country's policy reforms, which started in the early 1980s, China's participation in the international economy had been so small that high growth from that small base did not constitute a major shift in the global economic structure until around the turn of the century. India's policy reforms came almost a decade later, so that India, like China, still had a relatively small share of world trade until very recent years. Indeed, Brazil, China, and India together accounted for only 3.29 percent of world exports in 1990, and 5.45 percent in 2000— contrasted with 4.52 percent in 1960 (they had lost share in between). By 2010, the same three accounted for 13.3 percent of world exports (I leave Russia out because there are no data available from the IMF for 1990 and before, and Russia's share was only 2.6 percent in 2010, mostly oil and gas).

Thus, until the last decade, the success of the emerging markets that had adopted more realistic growth strategies was an important phenomenon from the viewpoint of their people's welfare. But this did not constitute a very significant shift in the structure of the global economy.

But the past decade marked a watershed. Not only had the BRICs become important, but other emerging markets—the East Asian Tigers, Mexico, Turkey, Chile, and others—had also altered policies and become more important participants in the international economy. As late as 1970, all developing countries accounted for only 25 percent of world exports; by 2010, their exports were 39 percent of the world total, up from 25.4 percent only ten years earlier—a huge shift!

Anne O. Krueger, *The Rise of the Emerging Markets*, 18 LAW AND BUSINESS REVIEW OF THE AMERICAS 445, 447–49 (2012).

Political changes also played a role. The winding down of the Cold War produced profound economic changes throughout the world. From the late 1970s to the mid-1990s many countries that previously had embraced extensive government ownership or control of the economy, coupled with a protectionist or even xenophobic stance toward international economic relations, changed their approach to foreigners. Among the large socialist countries, China under Teng Hsiao Ping began this process in 1979, followed by Mikhail Gorbachev's Soviet Union in 1986 and democratic India in the 1990s. The dismantling of right wing military regimes in Europe in the 1970s and the Western Hemisphere in the 1980s and of apartheid in South Africa complemented these transformations. Much differed from place to place, but in general liberalization consisted of opening up sectors of the economy to private actors, reducing the scale and scope of government regulation of the economy, and authorizing foreigners to take part as investors and traders. To some extent these reforms also took place in the rich world, but the emerging markets were those which had not known much private or foreign economic activity in prior decades.

The reforms, however, were not straightforward. Even countries that formally mandated exclusive state ownership of most economic resources often had a "second economy" in which clandestine transactions took place. At the most fundamental level, what the reforms aspired to do was to replace illegal behavior resting on bribery and embezzlement with law-based (and taxpaying) commerce. Related to this goal was the attraction of foreign capital, technology and know-how that would increase the value of local resources, both physical and human. But it would be wrong to assume that every government that experimented with liberalization did so to improve economic and social conditions.

The Origins of Economic and Political "Reforms"

It is easy enough to understand why political leaders in democratic countries such as India felt the need to experiment with new policies to improve the lives of the people to whom they were accountable. But what about the many countries in the 1970s and 1980s where democratic accountability played little or no role? The enduring puzzle is why the rulers of closed economies rejected the status quo and launched on changes that had the potential for destroying the basis of their power. The extreme example is the old Soviet Union, where economic and political reforms led to the dissolution of the Soviet state and the destruction of the political and economic controls of the Communist Party. In many of these countries the rulers lived well and enjoyed considerable job security. They may have lost the capacity to hold out their systems as shining examples of the pathway to the future, but doubtlessly they could have strung out their economic and political decline over decades. Why did they risk everything on sweeping and unsettling changes in the economy, politics and the law?

First we must understand the nature of the systems that were reformed.[3] Most scholars who studied the behavior of ruling groups in Soviet-type societies—and especially observers within those societies, once they obtained the freedom to publish without censorship—saw the fundamental organizing principal of the system as the extraction of benefits for the "new class" of economic decision-makers at the expense of the general welfare. Membership in this "new class" rested on unstated but widely understood rules and conditions. The group tended towards cohesion, in the sense that members understood that they did well when the group as a whole benefited; the principal incentive to belong to the group was the power to dispose of economic assets through the issuance of orders in what was called a command economy; and within the group there existed a clear hierarchy, with economic power increasing as one rose up the hierarchy. This at least was the idea behind the system, and for many of these countries for much of their history the idea captured a lot of the reality.

Some analysts use the business concept of a cartel as a metaphor for this system. A cartel involves an agreement among producers of a good to act in concert to maximize their joint welfare. Think of oil and gas, much of which is produced by a small number of state-owned companies organized through the Organization of Petroleum Exporting Countries (OPEC). Members of a cartel cooperate by accepting limits on individual production to achieve higher prices, resulting in what economists call monopoly rents or superprofits that they then divide among themselves. In the Soviet-style "new class" system, members of the ruling élite—the people authorized to manage the economy—would abide by the rules of the system to the advantage of their class as a whole. In principle, this meant accepting the allocation of discretionary authority over the economy—the right to command in a command economy. By doing this, rather than competing for the authority to make economic decisions, the people who ran the command economy maximized their own welfare, even though—as in a cartel—society as a whole suffered from the inefficient allocations of investments, goods and services that resulted.

The system, which emerged in the Soviet Union and later was adopted in China and the various states that came under the sway of those two superpowers, made an explicit connection between group membership and economic authority. Further, it specified both whether an individual occupied a position within the economic hierarchy, and what that position was. Job security and stable succession patterns gave individuals within the hierarchy a reason to identify with the group. Members of the élite had many opportunities to convert public discretionary authority into material private benefits such as higher quality residences, food, educational opportunities for children, freedom to travel abroad, etc. In India, which adopted Soviet-style central planning along with western-style political democracy, the pattern was

---

[3] For more on these questions, see Paul B. Stephan, *Toward a Positive Theory of Privatization—Lessons from Soviet-Type Economies*, 16 INT'L REV. L. & ECON. 173 (1996).

complex, but the advantages of belonging to the managerial class were similar and a strong link existed between political power and economic management.

Practice in Soviet-type systems manifested what one would expect from a cohesive interest group inclined to sacrifice the general welfare for its own benefit. Decision-makers refused to permit price changes long after the need for revision became apparent. The planners assigned unusually long useful lives to industrial plant, relative to accounting practices in the West. Central authorities generally imposed barriers to the introduction of new production methods. Innovating firms faced higher production targets if successful, but got no relief from prior targets if their experiments failed, and personnel who developed successful innovations had to be loaned out to other firms without compensation. Intellectual property as such did not exist; rather, the state awarded prizes to innovators, with the amount of the award not connected to the extent of the innovation's exploitation. All of these features dampened productivity-enhancing adaptations, but each protected the central authorities at the top of the hierarchy from opportunistic behavior by firm managers at the bottom.

The cartel metaphor provides a plausible explanation as to why the leaders in Soviet-type societies maintained an economically inefficient system as long as they did, but in its simplest form it does not explain why the leadership undertook to tear down the structure that seemed to provide them with such desirable rents. A possible refinement comes from cartel theory itself. This literature predicts that over time cartels will erode if the cost of detecting member chiseling is relatively high. Members will produce more than their quota to exploit the high monopoly price; if enough do so in sufficient quantities, the price drops to a level that would exist in the absence of the cartel's collusion.

Factors that affect the cost of policing a cartel include the difficulty of measuring output, the ease of assigning particular customers to producers, the extent of customer turnover, and the cost of discovering actual prices paid by buyers. Many economists have argued that OPEC, for example, has failed to control production levels at a level that a monopolist would dictate because the market for petroleum products has these characteristics. And if policing is inadequate, cartel members will cheat by producing more than their quota of the cartelized good—in the case of command economies, the authority to influence economic outcomes—until the price of the good—here, loosely measured in units of tribute—drops to a point where the cost of rule violations, discounted by the likelihood of detection, equals the marginal return from additional "sales." But as the price of the cartelized good declines due to increases in supply, monopoly rents dissipate. In simple terms, the payoff from membership in the "new class" drops, and people within the ruling élite look for other alternatives to pursue wealth and power.

This theory helps to make sense out of the way economic liberalization proceeded in those countries that sought to dismantle a Soviet-type system. In most of these countries, decentralization was rather disorderly, suggesting an unraveling of economic institutions rather than a deliberate adaptation in the light of new experience. For many economic actors the collapse of the administrative apparatus did not lead to the emergence of a "civil economy" based on open and legal markets bolstered through state enforcement of private contracts and property rights. Rather, managers and localities found themselves facing a new dilemma: As long as they retained possession of assets, they had a relatively free hand to do what they wished with them, but if they sought to trade or otherwise dispose of their property, they could not rely on a stable or credible set of legal rights to define and protect their interests. For the same reasons that they obtained freedom from the formal and informal hierarchies, they could not trust any other economic actors to behave cooperatively.

In these countries, informal economies flourished. These included both premodern exchange relations, in which households and firms barter for goods and services, and the illegal economy, which in some cases developed sophisticated institutions. Inflation and shrinkage in the supply of social services contributed to the growth of the premodern economy, while a breakdown of formal social organizations (including police protection) fueled the illegal sector. The absence of effective tax systems further helped the illegal economy, although causal links were complex. Some entrepreneurs, mindful of widespread corruption, feared that organized crime gangs could use tax records for extortion. On the other hand, in some instances the coercive authority of these gangs appeared greater than that of the state, in which case entrepreneurs paid tribute to them in lieu of taxes. In some extreme cases, the informal structures simply displaced the state, offering security and dispute resolution services that the state no longer could provide in return for payments that take the place of taxes that the state no longer could collect.

The privatization process in particular experienced many difficulties. In some countries, debates over restitution to prerevolutionary property-holders complicated the settlement of rights in land and other assets; in many other countries the presence of national minorities (especially Russians outside of Russia) blocked the development of private rights in land. Many countries transferred ownership of small retail firms to the private sector, although claims to particular firms' assets (such as leaseholds) sometimes remained unsettled. But in many countries, large industrial firms and agrobusinesses that accounted for the lion's share of employment remained state-owned for a much longer period. The lack of progress in privatization was linked to political instability, although again distinguishing cause from effect is difficult.

Some of these phenomena may be inevitable in any economic transition, and would have occurred even under political leadership that was fully committed to the public welfare. But several of these aspects seem suspicious, in the sense that opportunistic behavior by influential decision-makers provides a plausible explanation for their occurrence. Of particular significance have been the difficulties over privatization.

The conventional privatization transaction—that which the United Kingdom and France pioneered in the early 1980s and which has become popular in both the developed and developing world since then—involves an open sale of assets in which particular state organs that have an indisputable right to convey the assets transfer an unambiguous bundle of ownership rights in those assets to persons in the private sector. A substantial body of evidence suggests that many of these sales represent a rational response to the inadequacies of governmental bureaucracies as economic managers. Perhaps more to the point, the transparency of the process makes it easier to detect whether transferees paid an adequate price for the assets, which serves to discipline the decision-makers that choose to privatize.

One can contrast this "open" type of privatization with what some call "spurious" privatization. Spurious privatization mimics the form of an open transaction, in that an organ of the state purports to transfer rights over certain assets to entities or persons in the private sector. But the transaction is incomplete, because transparency and due process are lacking, the legal capacity of the transferor to convey the rights is uncertain, and the ability of the transferee to maintain its rights is unclear. Spuriousness devalues privatization transactions: Transferors receive a lower return both in the form of outright payment and through future tax revenues, and transferees get less in the way of enforceable entitlements.

Spuriousness produces a deadweight loss shared by transferors and transferees. Although some of this loss may be unavoidable—a nation that recently regarded private production as a criminal offense might have difficulty giving credible assurances that it respects private property rights—a public-regarding leadership could avoid a significant portion of it by developing and implementing techniques to guarantee ownership. The inability to resolve conflicts that cloud rights growing out of the privatization process, by contrast, suggests the existence of opportunistic, rather than public-regarding, behavior by groups seeking to promote their ability to control particular assets.

A simple example drawn from our experience in Russia illustrates the dysfunctions associated with spurious privatization. In the early 1990s, a Russian executive of a state-owned company undergoing privatization contacted our client, a U.S. manufacturer, to request a loan—not a commercial loan, but a personal loan. Why? To buy privatization vouchers, which had been given to the Russian company's employees, so that he could acquire control of the privatized entity. Security for the loan? No problem: he offered to pledge the assets of the company to secure his personal debt. This failure to observe the differences between corporate and personal interests, and the exploitation of conflicts of interest, plague Russian commerce to this day.

Why the mess? One hypothesis is that in these transition systems, those who benefited from chaos had greater influence than those who might have preferred the creation of clear and reliable ownership rights. Presumably, if the old Soviet-style élites could have acted in their collective self-interest, they would have preserved the system of administrative control and raised the cost of undermining their authority. Yet they failed to do so. It seems implausible that the same people could agree on the allocation of stable ownership rights in a post-Soviet world when they could not stake out clear administrative authority in the *ancien regime*. Rather, it seems reasonable to surmise that those who could seize assets would prefer to exercise control without the protection of state-enforced property rights, rather than see such rights fall into the hands of their rivals. Thus, the prevalence of spurious privatization suggests not only the work of opportunists among the old managerial class, but also the inability of such persons to reach a consensus as to their collective welfare.

A large portion of the privatization transactions in the former Soviet-type societies has been spurious. In general, the more valuable the asset, or the greater the ease of converting it through the informal economy, the more likely has been a delay in privatization or in providing an inadequate specification of rights that a private holder can acquire from a particular state organ. One can observe this pattern both in the more reform-oriented countries (the Czech Republic, Hungary, and Poland) and the least liberal (Belarus, Kazakhstan, Russia, Turkmenistan, Ukraine, and Uzbekistan).

Consider first the difficulty of specifying which state organ has a right to convey which assets. Problems can arise either because of conflicts among state bodies as to ownership of assets, or because the new regimes might recognize some claims of owners who held property before its seizure by a Soviet-type state. Although it may be tempting to set aside disputes stemming from restitution as a special case, even these do not lack elements of opportunism. Expatriates who benefit from restitution have special clout due to their overseas associations, especially in those countries that most fear a resurgent Russia (which is where restitution has been most popular). And conflicts among state bodies over the control of the privatization of particular assets seem singularly motivated by the desire of special interests to profit from the process.

Illustrative is the case of privatization in Moscow. Immediately after the dissolution of the Soviet Union, city officials received special authority from President Yeltsin to accelerate transfers of property to the private sector; most of the assets involved realty, much of it capable of generating hard currency revenues. In the spring of 1993, the Russian Constitutional Court, in the midst of a struggle that had erupted between the President and the legislature, declared that this decree violated the Constitution. The decision cast a cloud on almost all privatization that had occurred in Russia's most important city, as third parties acquired the right to challenge particular transactions. Yeltsin's suspension of the Court six months later in turn added to the uncertainty by raising doubts about the validity of the court decree. Decades later, the security of real estate interests in Moscow remains low relative to their value in the market.

Other conflicts in Russia, both between the executive and the legislature and between the center and the localities, impeded privatization. The energy sector is only the most notorious instance where the inability of the various authorities to agree on the terms under which they would permit investment stymied desirable infusions of foreign technology and capital. Observers noted similar problems in the Czech Republic, Hungary, and Poland, where disputes among various branches of the state thwarted the transfer of commercial realty into private hands. And in many cases the intensity of the conflict was directly related to the value of the assets awaiting privatization. Local resistance to the Russian Federation's authority, for example, has been strongest in those parts of the country that have readily marketable hard currency assets such as energy reserves.

Consider next the lack of rules specifying what transferees get when they participate in privatization. In many of the former Soviet states, the legal concepts that enable complex organizations to hold and to dispose of property remained inchoate at best. Many states have promulgated vague and contradictory laws governing private land use.

The problem runs deeper than the simple absence of technical legal concepts. To be sure, almost all the Soviet-type states carried on their books a version of the Civil Code that corresponded fairly closely to that in effect in Germany. Russia's was enacted in 1921. But these laws had few practical consequences, because most significant assets either were disposed of by the state, which for the most part disregarded civil law in favor of administrative fiat, or in the informal economy, which operated outside the formal legal system. As a result, the former Soviet-type societies largely lack either a sense as to how civil-law rules apply in practical situations or a belief that reference to these rules can inform property-holders as to the extent of their freedom of action.

An especially important lacuna in private law involves concepts of corporate opportunity and conflict of interest. In the former system, where all decision-makers theoretically responded to common, centrally determined goals, rules that presupposed opposing economic interests and conflicting loyalties were subversive and therefore avoided. While this system has ended, the new authorities have not yet addressed this legal vacuum. To be sure, many countries adopted statutes, often at the behest of Western advisors, that purported to specify impermissible conflicts of interest. But weak courts and other legal actors, largely inherited from the *ancient regime*, permit manipulation of these rules for the benefit of the politically well connected.

These legal gaps contribute to the spuriousness of privatization. Transferees may have to defend their acquisitions against charges of corruption without having clear rules as to what does and does not constitute impermissible self-dealing. They also have to worry that even with the law on their side, courts may distort the facts to produce surprising outcomes.

Closely related is the problem of "spontaneous privatizations" that arose in the extractive, industrial and agro-industrial sectors, especially in the former states of the Soviet Union. These transactions, roughly analogous to leveraged buyouts in the West, involve the organization of a private company by managers of state-owned firms, often collaborating with local political authorities, followed by that company's acquisition of the state firm's most valuable assets. The work force as a collective body normally received a substantial share of the new firm's stock, but the managers typically retained voting control. In the process little attention was paid to the rights of residual claimholders in the transferor state firm, whether industrial ministries or local governments.

These spontaneous privatizations performed the necessary first step of terminating state ownership, but they did not leave the new owners with readily defensible claims to the assets over which they have acquired possession. The owners' insecurity in turn raised their cost of capital, as it both prevented the collateralization of the firm's property and discouraged new equity investors. Yet a substantial number of firm managers have preferred taking what they can as quickly as possible, rather than waiting for mechanisms that might leave them with more valuable ownership rights at the end of the process.

Another example involves intellectual property. Under Soviet-type systems intellectual property rights had no value, because the state monopolized production. Such rewards as inventors and authors received represented the state's largesse, not compensation based on value created. The creation of patents, trademarks, and copyrights therefore would not displace interests that existed under the former regime. It should not come as a surprise, then, that most of the former Soviet-type countries have established intellectual property regimes that at least in form do not differ significantly from those found in Western Europe. But one area of significant ambiguity remains in this body of law: When the employee of a firm produces an invention or discovers a trade secret, do rights in the discovery accrue to the employee or the firm? If employees and employers could divide the returns to the patent through bargaining, any definite answer would increase the overall value of future inventive activity. But the failure of the new rules to resolve this issue is consistent with a conflict between scientists, especially in the former defense sector, who wish to market their existing discoveries for hard currency and managers of those firms where the scientists worked.

A final point suggesting the presence of opportunism in the privatization process is the erection of special barriers to foreign investors. In theory the former Soviet-type economies should prefer foreign investment. Domestic financial capital was nearly nonexistent at the time that the command system ended, and firms receiving foreign finance are more likely to benefit from foreign technological and managerial learning. Moreover, for the most part foreigners already operate under legal regimes that require an accounting for profits on a worldwide basis, making more credible their commitments to pay taxes on the returns generated by their investments. By contrast, domestic entrepreneurs in these countries are notoriously poor taxpayers. Yet virtually all of the former Soviet-type states have created special obstacles to foreign investment, including additional licensing requirements and outright bans on foreign ownership of stakes in particular industries such as natural resource exploitation.

Foreign investment, unlike foreign purchases of marketable commodities, comes with strings attached. Most foreigners, accustomed to operating in systems that specify residual ownership rights, will insist on some minimum level of reassurance as to the nature of the claims obtained through their investment. In particular, they would tend to resist spurious privatization because such transactions create unattractive candidates for investment. Seen in this light, state-imposed restrictions on foreign investment might work as a means of forestalling pressure to restrict rent-seeking opportunities by bringing more openness into the privatization process.

None of these arguments is conclusive, but their cumulative effect is to suggest that interest groups in former Soviet-type societies have good reasons to undermine the privatization process by promoting disputes among state organs and obstructing the specification of private property rights. A remaining issue is the extent, as opposed to the existence, of opportunism in the former Soviet-type countries' privatization process. It seems plausible to hypothesize a relationship between the value of the rents that interest groups seek to appropriate and the amount they are willing to invest in procuring them. To the extent that these investments include obstructing openness in the privatization process, one should expect a higher degree of spuriousness in those countries that present the greatest opportunities for rent seekers.

The Ongoing Effects of Political and Economic Transition

As the term "emerging" implies, the category is fluid rather than stable. Since the late 1970s, all but a handful of countries have dabbled with liberalization. Much has changed since then. On the one hand, some countries have enjoyed enough success to vault (at least provisionally) into the rank of advanced economies. Of the former Soviet satellites, for example, four Central European countries (the Czech Republic, Hungary, Poland and Slovakia) now belong to the Organization for Economic Cooperation and Development, traditionally the club of the most developed countries, while those four plus Bulgaria, Croatia, Romania, Slovenia and the three Baltic former Soviet republics are full members of the European Union (EU). The International Monetary Fund still counts these ten countries in the emerging market category, but in many respects they seem to a transactional lawyer broadly similar to the other poorer members of the EU, such as Greece and Portugal.

On the other hand, the Asian financial crisis of 1997 and the precipitous increase in the world price of energy resources in the mid-2000s have both generated some skepticism about the benefits of liberalization and provided some energy-exporting countries with an economic cushion to roll back reform (Russian and Venezuela being prominent examples). The broad points are that a risk of backsliding accompanies any experiment with liberalization and that efforts to imitate advanced economies come with no guarantee of success. From the perspective of private business people, the issue is one of risk, not only opportunity.

In particular, the experiments with reform and liberalization soon made apparent that none of these efforts could do much good without effective legal institutions. No amount of legislation specifying the applicable legal rules can mean anything without a means of implementing those rules. Private economic transactions are worth little unless both stable property rights and a means of enforcing contractual promises work in practice, not just on the law books. Stability of property means at a minimum that mechanisms exist to deter people from taking the property of others as well as that there exist reasonably clear rules as to who can claim which entitlement. There are many ways of determining property rights and enforcing promises, informal as well as formal, but there are some situations where a neutral third party with the capacity to gather evidence and enforce its orders with meaningful punishment works best.

One challenge that many countries have faced is developing adequate legal institutions to carry out these fundamental tasks. Many began the liberalization process with poorly trained, badly compensated and pervasively corrupt police and judges; for some, this remains true today. Moreover, the population had come to expect public officials to be corrupt, both in the sense that they would sell their services to the highest bidder and that they did not take published law seriously.

Convincing them that things would be different in the future presents a challenge.

A difficult question, then, is why corruption and weak public institutions persist, if a society can become wealthier by eliminating these pathologies? No clear answers present themselves.[4] One response asserts that in many places and in many instances, corruption represents a successful adaptation to the world in which people find themselves. In particular, much of what we decry as corruption in the former socialist states represents a rational response to a certain social environment. Behaviors that seem self-defeating to outsiders make sense to people who grew up in these societies and learned how to cope with the conditions of their world. Changing these behaviors would require two difficult, if not impossible, achievements. Most obviously, these countries would have to alter the incentives and deterrents that currently make corrupt behavior reasonable. But in addition, they would have to convince their populations that these conditions have changed and that the break with the past will endure. Some of the former socialist countries have taken a stab at this project, but many have not.

The story begins with the Soviet-style system, implemented with many variations across Europe, Asia, Africa and Latin America but still retaining certain fundamental characteristics. The rulers largely suppressed private ownership of the means of production and subjected the entire economy to a command-and-control regime based on centrally determined planning targets. Managers achieved advancement and preferment through recognition of their success in meeting these targets, which in turn depended largely on their ability either to procure low output quotas and high input allotments or to persuade superiors to accept false reports of output. Managers succeeded at these tasks by forming alliances with persons within some combination of four groups: (1) superiors in the bureaucratic hierarchy devoted to their industrial sector; (2) local political leaders; (3) officials in the police and security organs responsible for overseeing their compliance with the law, especially accounting rules; and (4) persons working as intermediaries in the informal economy (in Russian, *tolkachi* or "pushers"). These alliances had something of the character of feudal bonds, with the vassal manager paying tribute to the lord ally, who in turn reciprocated with protection and support.

As the Soviet-type economies became more complex, and as the penalties for violations of economic law became less draconian, the value of these various alliances changed. In Russia, a large, diverse country with an abundance of natural resources that could be sold in raw form on thick world markets, the relationships between managers, on the one hand, and local political leaders and intermediaries in the informal economy, on the other hand, grew in value relative to the other alliances. Efforts by the central political authorities to break down the existing quasi-feudal ties and to strengthen their control over the economy invariably produced perverse outcomes.

The typical consumer responded to this environment by learning to hoard and to trade. Whether they needed them or not, people would

---

⁴   For more on the subject, see Paul B. Stephan, *Rationality and Corruption in the Post-Socialist World*, 14 CONN. J. INT'L L. 101 (1999).

obtain goods thought to be desirable and hold them for exchange with other hoarders. Because most things of value belonged to the state, successful hoarders had to learn how to grab hold of state property. Restaurant workers would steal food, office workers time, railroad workers cargo. The pervasiveness of this behavior made serious social or criminal sanctions impracticable, although policemen and inspectors did demand kickbacks as the price of their complicity in the kleptomaniacal free-for-all.

These developments took place against a background of strong official campaigns against lawlessness. The authorities, which had a monopoly over public space—television, radio, billboards, newspapers, magazines—would condemn petty corruption and link loose morals to erosion of the national fiber in the face of grave external threats. Occasionally the states announced an increase in the sanctions for these crimes, and well-publicized arrests would take place. But the overwhelming social norm remained one of grabbing anything one could as often as possible.

The operative, as opposed to nominal, rules of society reinforced this norm. Except in privileged sectors, the official economy kept producers and consumers alike on short rations, taking for granted that they would make up the difference through informal transactions. Superiors and law enforcement officials both assumed the existence of these transactions and as a matter of course demanded kickbacks from anyone under their authority, further increasing the incentive to pilfer and embezzle. Neither the resources devoted to enforcement, nor the sanctions imposed on those unfortunate enough to find themselves in situations they could not bribe their way out of, indicated a serious commitment to the formal rules allocating ownership and control. Instead, in most cases control over assets constituted a kind of ownership, whether one was the manager of a collective farm or a worker in a factory.

This system did not teach people only to disregard formal property rights. The sharp contradiction between the professed principles and goals of the system and the working rules of society taught an even deeper lesson: One should regard with deep skepticism formal pronouncements from public authorities, and especially appeals to social solidarity. Whatever the truth about the destruction of social ties and the rise of the culture of narcissism in advanced capitalist societies, Soviet-type societies presented the extreme case of a place where the public space had been stripped of ideals and human connections. The filthy and untended parks, the empty ceremonies that attended every public event, the arid when not banal programming on television and radio all bespoke an emptiness that permeated public, and particularly official, life. The tragedy of the commons never seemed more evident than in these societies' capacious areas of public domain.

On the one hand, the norms of behavior that evolved under socialism have blocked investments that plausibly might increase overall welfare. But, on the other hand, the pervasiveness of corruption, distrust and noncooperation in these societies also have exerted a profoundly conservative force. In those countries where change suggests catastrophe rather than progress, these norms may help the large numbers of people who will lose out through restructuring to buy time, if nothing else.

The Stakes

The absence of reliable legal institutions in the country where a foreigner intends to do business does not render the transactional lawyer irrelevant. To the contrary, these projects force the lawyer to develop creative approaches that overcome or work around these obstacles. External law enforcement institutions, including banks, arbitration, and foreign courts, can regulate some of the risks, and careful contracting can contain others. We will explore the possibilities throughout this text.

What are the stakes? Some numbers may shed light on the size of emerging markets, even though potential transactions may matter more than those that already have gone forward. According to the International Monetary Fund (IMF), the 35 richest countries generated 50.4% of the world's gross domestic product (GDP) in 2012; the remaining 154 countries account for the balance, including Brazil at 2.8%, China at 14.7%, India at 5.7%, and Russia at 3%. (Large is not the same as rich, of course, because China and India have huge populations that make their per capita GDP relatively low, below even Russia's.) Looking at exports, the rich 35 accounted for 61.0% of the world total in 2012, Brazil at 1.3%, China 10.0%, India 2.0%, and Russia 2.6%.[5]

For a deeper analysis of the status of emerging markets today, focusing on the BRICs, let us return to Anne Krueger:

> While the industrial countries have experienced a reduced relative importance, the BRICs still have a long way to go to reach industrial country status. And each has a number of challenges to meet along the away, although they differ among themselves.

> Brazil had a much higher per capita income than the other BRICs thirty or forty years ago, and has the second highest per capita income of the four behind Russia. It has also had the slowest growth of the four in recent years, and its relatively more rapid growth only started in about 2005. It would appear to be challenged even to maintain a 4 to 5 percent growth rate in coming years (growth in 2012 is estimated to have been 3.5 percent, and even that resulted in, or was accompanied by, some overheating). In addition, the government has, in recent months, been undertaking policies that would appear detrimental to growth prospects over the long-run. At least as a partial offset, the discovery of oil offshore may lead to a significant windfall in income and significant policy challenges to manage it successfully.

> Russia has the highest per capita income of the group, and experienced fairly high growth until the recent recession. In Russia's case, however, the heavy dependence on natural resources, and especially on gas and oil, leaves the economy challenged to provide economically efficient incentives for the development of non-natural resource activities. Russia's human capital is very good, and with appropriate policies growth could accelerate, but in the short to medium-term, the prices of

---

[5] The figures come from the statistical appendix to the IMF WORLD ECONOMIC OUTLOOK—OCTOBER 2013 at 139.

Russia's major commodity exports will be a significant determinant of economic growth. Russia is also confronted with a demographic challenge: population has fallen in recent years, and it is not clear whether, and how, that can be reversed.

So the two of the BRICs with the highest per capita incomes also face the biggest challenges in maintaining or accelerating economic growth. India, with the lowest per capita income of the group, has grown more rapidly than almost any other sizeable country, except China, in the past decade. Most economists agree that attaining better fiscal balance, developing infrastructure, increasing flexibility in the labor market, and further removing the heavy hand of bureaucracy from economic activity, will be needed to maintain the rate of acceleration of economic growth. In the short-run, prospects for these needed reforms do not appear promising, especially as the government is mired in political challenges that will probably stalemate reform.

India may potentially have a demographic dividend over the next several decades, as her labor force will grow significantly more rapidly than the total population. But to benefit from that, major labor market reforms will be needed. India still has a very large population of very poor people. Despite success to date, the need for rapid growth of a kind that enables improvement in the living standards of the poor is urgent.

China, the largest of the four BRICs by far, had the highest growth rate of the group throughout the last decade. Its track record over the past three decades is impressive because the authorities have been able to find appropriate policy responses to all of the challenges that they have been confronted with, given such rapid change. The leadership appears to accept that growth must slow down somewhat, with a stated target for 2012 of 8.5 percent. If that were achieved, China would continue to be the most rapidly growing BRIC nation. But questions arise as to inflationary pressure, the sustainability of the export drive, environmental sustainability, and more.

Moreover, China has relied on export-led growth for the past three decades. Domestic consumption is around 35 percent of GDP, and there is considerable evidence that there is wasteful government investment as efforts have been made to maintain the growth rate. The Chinese authorities clearly recognize that they must undertake policies that will result in an increase in domestic demand and raise its contribution to growth. Doing so is clearly a priority for them, but also presents a number of challenges. Going forward, China also faces a demographic challenge similar to that in the industrial countries. The legacy of the one-child policy is that new entrants to the labor force are already falling, and there is not a demographic dividend, which India can potentially use to good effect.

Although the BRICs have been very successful to date, each faces a number of challenges going forward. For Russia, the key challenge lies in removing the legacy of the Soviet era, and finding ways to improve the business climate for nontraditional activities. For Brazil, financial liberalization and reducing government intervention will be a key. For India, finding the political will to carry out major reforms in the bureaucracy and the rule of law to accelerate infrastructure development and reform labor market regulations (to enable more rapid employment growth), constitutes a significant challenge. The Chinese are confronted with the need to prevent further overheating of the economy while simultaneously shifting reliance for growth from exporting to domestic demand.

Anne O. Krueger, *The Rise of the Emerging Markets*, 18 LAW AND BUSINESS REVIEW OF THE AMERICAS 445, 450–52 (2012).

One also may make a case for emerging markets in East Africa, especially with respect to the burgeoning oil and gas industry there. This industry did not hold much attraction for foreign investors until the past few years. Now, however, it has achieved such a complete turnaround that international consultants have hailed East Africa the new frontier in the industry:

> After decades operating in the shadow of North and West Africa, East Africa is finally emerging as one of the most significant players in the continent's oil and gas industry. Large oil discoveries around Uganda's Lake Albert in 2006 and subsequent gas discoveries offshore Mozambique have dramatically altered perceptions of East Africa, transforming it into an up-and-coming destination for extractive industry investment. Companies that previously only gave the region a passing glance before turning their attention to areas such as the Gulf of Guinea are now rapidly coming to terms with the Rift Valley's potentially vast, untapped reserves.

> Exploration has been underway in East Africa for several decades, but the extent of the potential has only become apparent in the last few years. Uganda looks set to become one of the five largest oil producers on the continent, with its Lake Albert oil fields potentially capable of producing 200,000–350,000 barrels per day (bpd). News of fresh discoveries in neighbouring Kenya has boosted onshore exploration in that country, though commercial viability is still being established. South Sudan already has vast reserves and is increasingly looking to East Africa rather than to its hostile northern neighbour to export its oil. Meanwhile, there are hopes that both oil and gas could be discovered in Ethiopia in commercially viable quantities.

> Offshore, the picture is even more promising. The waters of the Indian Ocean are proving a rich hunting ground for natural-gas exploration. The US Geological Survey estimates that coastal areas of Mozambique and Tanzania alone could harbour more than 250 trillion cubic feet of gas in addition to a further 14.5bn barrels of oil. The success rate of companies looking for gas offshore is phenomenal: of the 27 wells drilled in the last two years offshore Tanzania and Mozambique, 24 have yielded discoveries. Compared with the heavily explored areas elsewhere on the continent, East Africa is practically virgin

territory: by 2010, only 600 wells had been drilled, compared with 14,000 and 20,000 in West and North Africa respectively.

A New Frontier: Oil and Gas in East Africa, 1 Control Risks Group Limited, London 2012, www.controlrisks.com.

The reality is, of course, that East Africa's counterpart governments and national oil companies (NOCs) in West Africa and North Africa have decades of the kind of negotiating and operational experience that the governments in East Africa have yet to acquire. As a consequence, both the governments of the East African countries and the international oil companies (IOCs) have a multitude of issues to deal with in connection with the maturation of the industry.

One of the main issues is the lack of the type of infrastructure that would be able to support the industry's development and growth. For instance, there are no pipelines and no refineries in Uganda and there is only one refinery in Kenya. In addition, the petroleum laws and regulations in the area are for the most part outdated and inadequate, and there is a clear tendency for the local communities and national governments to compete politically.

It also appears that a new wave of resource nationalism has taken hold, as indicated by the level of hostility on the part of the governments/NOCs with respect to their dealings with the IOCs:

> Engagement with regional governments is one of the main challenges facing investors in the East African oil and gas sector. As the industry develops and companies seek to move from exploration to production, relations with host governments have come under increasing strain. Suspicion and, in some cases, barely disguised hostility have characterised the attitude of many officials in the Ugandan and Tanzanian governments towards companies. This wariness during contract negotiations stems from recognition on the part of governments of their inexperience in the sector. Several governments have dispatched official delegations on fact-finding missions to established oil and gas-producing states such as Norway, where they can glean fresh insights. However, such superficial efforts cannot substitute for the decades of collective industry experience they face on the other side of the negotiating table.

> Even where model agreements provide a rigid structure, companies continue to encounter underlying resistance and pressure from governments and NGOs. Contracts come under scrutiny from NGOs and civil-society groups anxious to keep track of where revenues are going. This in turn reinforces the defensive stance of officials who are desperate to avoid appearing weak or ill-informed. The overall effect is to create a trust barrier between companies and host governments that is proving hard to breach.

> This barrier tends to be much stronger in countries where commercially viable deposits are already known to exist. While the Kenyan government is anxious to attract further exploration by granting companies the freedom they need, in Uganda the move from exploration to production has been acrimonious. A bitter dispute between companies and the government over tax

liabilities has frustrated attempts to start oil production at Lake Albert. In Tanzania, the legacy of the former socialist government can still be felt. Although the government publicly embraces free-market principles, some of the key decision-makers, themselves stalwarts of the old regime, have struggled to shake off the deeply engrained statist ethos. The government keeps its cards close to its chest when interacting with companies, and mutual suspicion persists.

A cultural shift is needed on the part of government officials in the region to recognise the importance of transparent and positive engagement with companies, not just when awarding exploration licences, but through the entire industry cycle to include the mid and downstream production chain. All too often there is a chasm between the few ministerial technocrats who understand the nuances of negotiations with oil and gas companies, and their political masters and senior civil servants. Moreover, expertise at a ministerial level tends to wane rapidly as countries move from exploration to production. Where there is existing expertise it tends to be in geology rather than other technical or commercial areas that become more significant once initial discoveries have been made.

A New Frontier: Oil and Gas in East Africa, 2 Control Risks Group Limited, London 2012, www.controlrisks.com.

Finally, there is the issue of intraregional competition among three of the five members of the East African Community (EAC), namely, Kenya, Uganda and Tanzania, plus the non-member, Mozambique. While the oil and gas industry in all four of these countries has recently reported major discoveries, none of them has begun producing oil or gas yet. Although one or more of them may be poised to embark on a significant, new form of revenue-raising, it is not clear which country may be in the lead.

The financial crisis of 2008 also had its effects. Among the emerging markets, some countries experienced financial as well as political disruption, with Hungary and Latvia as prominent examples. Others weathered the storm relatively well. Note that one result of the crisis was growth in the influence of larger emerging market countries, especially China and India, in international financial cooperation. How this influence gets exercised, and its impact on the development of international institutions, remains a topic of great interest.

In addition to the international capital markets as a disembodied institution, there exist specific international institutions that work directly with governments to regulate their access to foreign investment. The most prominent is the IMF, which, among other things, provides capital to national central banks faced with shortages of foreign currency. Countries that borrow from the IMF typically must comply with certain conditions regarding the management of their economy to increase the likelihood of repayment. IMF conditionality in turn rests on a commitment to liberalization and transparency. In addition, the International Bank for Reconstruction and Development (more commonly known as the World Bank) provides long-term finance to countries and imposes various conditions on these loans. In recent years the World Bank has promoted anticorruption efforts as a central part of its program. The various regional international financial institutions—the African Development Bank, the Asian Development Bank, the European Bank for Reconstruction and Development, and the Latin American Development Bank, among others—fulfill similar functions.

Finally, home country governments can pressure countries that disappoint their investors. In additional to the traditional array of diplomatic tools, the richer countries have (more or less) independent agencies that provide finance and other services to their citizens engaged in foreign commerce. In the United States, for example, the Overseas Private Investment Corporation (OPIC) and the Export-Import Bank (Eximbank) offer finance, insurance, and technical assistance on favorable terms. These agencies, by withholding their services, can punish countries that create a hostile environment for foreign investors.

At the end of the day, however, business transactions in emerging markets present distinctive challenges to the lawyer. Unstable laws and legal institutions, the necessity of considerable investments, the risk of host country reconsideration of its policy, and a background culture of corruption are constant concerns. Careful planning and negotiation can manage the inevitable risks, but they cannot eliminate them. What a lawyer can do is present the client with a balanced assessment of the possible problems and the means available to address them. The client, informed by the lawyer's best judgment, ultimately must make the decision as to whether the rewards justify the risks.

Supplemental Reading

Law and Development

Anders Åslund, HOW RUSSIA BECAME A MARKET ECONOMY (Brookings Institution Press: Washington, 1995)

Jagdish N. Bhagwati, INDIA IN TRANSITION: FREEING THE ECONOMY (Clarendon Press: Oxford, 1993)

Olivier Blanchard, THE ECONOMICS OF POST-COMMUNIST TRANSITION (Oxford University Press: Oxford, 1997)

Edgardo Buscaglia, THE LAW AND ECONOMICS OF DEVELOPMENT (JAI Press: Greenwich, CT, 1997)

Paul Seabright (ed.), THE VANISHING ROUBLE: BARTER NETWORKS AND NON-MONETARY TRANSACTIONS IN POST-SOVIET SOCIETIES (Cambridge: Cambridge University Press, 2000)

Joseph E. Stiglitz, FAIR TRADE FOR ALL: HOW TRADE CAN PROMOTE DEVELOPMENT (Oxford University Press: Oxford, 2005)

Bernard S. Black & Anna S. Tarassova, *Institutional Reform in Transition: A Case Study of Russia*, 10 SUP. CT. ECON. REV. 211 (2003)

Donald C. Clarke, *Economic Development and the Rights Hypothesis: The China Problem*, 51 AM. J. COMP. L. 89 (2003)

Paul B. Stephan, *Toward a Positive Theory of Privatization—Lessons from Soviet-Type Economies*, 16 INT'L REV. L. & ECON. 173 (1996)

Globalization

Jagdish N. Bhagwati, IN DEFENSE OF GLOBALIZATION (Oxford University Press: Oxford, 2004)

Amy Chua, WORLD ON FIRE: HOW EXPORTING MARKET DEMOCRACY BREEDS ETHNIC HATRED AND GLOBAL INSTABILITY (Anchor Books: New York, 2004)

Joseph E. Stiglitz, MAKING GLOBALIZATION WORK (W.W. Norton & Co.: New York, 2006)

Jedediah Purdy, *A World of Passions: How to Think About Globalization Now*, 11 IND. J. GLOB. LEGAL STUD. 1 (2004)

Corruption

Edgardo Buscaglia, JUDICIAL CORRUPTION IN DEVELOPING COUNTRIES: ITS CAUSES AND ECONOMIC CONSEQUENCES (Hoover Institution on War, Revolution and Peace: Stanford, 1999)

Stephen Handelman, COMRADE CRIMINAL: RUSSIA'S NEW MAFIYA (Yale University Press: New Haven, 1995)

János Kornai, CREATING SOCIAL TRUST IN POST-SOCIALIST TRANSITION (Palgrave Macmillan: New York, 2004)

Susan Rose-Ackerman, CORRUPTION AND GOVERNMENT: CAUSES, CONSEQUENCES, AND REFORM (Cambridge University Press: Cambridge, 1999)

Susan Rose-Ackerman (ed.), INTERNATIONAL HANDBOOK OF THE ECONOMICS OF CORRUPTION (Edgar Elgar: Cheltenham, 2006)

Kenneth W. Abbott & Duncan Snidal, *Values and Interests: International Legalization in the Fight Against Corruption*, 31 J. LEGAL STUD. 141 (2002)

Philip M. Nichols, *Corruption as an Assurance Problem*, 19 AM U. INT'L L. REV. 1307 (2004)

Andrei Shleifer & Robert W. Vishny, *Corruption*, 108 Q. J. ECON. 599 (1993)

Paul B. Stephan, *Rationality and Corruption in the Post-Socialist World*, 14 CONN. J. INT'L L. 101 (1999)

CHAPTER 2

HOME STATE REGULATION— CORRUPTION AND HUMAN RIGHTS

Many of the legal risks associated with business transactions in emerging markets involve something happening (or not) in the host country. But the foreign transactor's home state also may affect overseas business activity. Even though modern regulation usually has a territorial dimension—a state normally has undisputed authority to lay down the rules for conduct occurring within its territory—other bases for regulatory (or "prescriptive") jurisdiction exist. A state traditionally has the authority to govern the behavior of its subjects, wherever that conduct occurs. More controversially, some modern states, first and foremost the United States, assert the authority to regulate conduct by foreign subjects taking place outside of the regulating state's territory if that conduct has a direct, substantial and intended effect on people or things within the territory of the regulating state.

It goes without saying that, to the extent a business carries out activities in its home state, it must comply with all applicable laws (including, for example, those governing its accounting practices and tax obligations as well as those regulating its competitive practices and access to finance). What extraterritoriality means as a practical matter is that someone undertaking a business transaction in an emerging market must comply with both the local law of the host country and those rules of his or her home country that apply to the transaction. For people and firms with a sufficient connection to the United States, this means in particular that the transactor must obey U.S. rules forbidding corrupt payments to foreign officials and violations of human rights standards.

Why corruption and human rights? A short response is that the United States has a longer history of prohibiting corrupt payments to foreign officials than does any other rich country, and that the legal means for enforcing human rights obligations, in particular civil suits for damages, do not have counterparts in other countries. Of course, the reasons are more complex and rooted in how Americans view themselves and their responsibilities in the world. In particular, policy makers, law enforcement officials and private parties have sought to use the U.S. legal system to address actions that have been—and continue to be—widely regarded as wrongful, even at the expense of the advancement of U.S. commercial activity in emerging markets.

Is the U.S. approach unique? At least with respect to corruption, the United States has succeeded through the OECD in "persuading" its members, which constitute virtually all of the developed economies of the world, to enact legislation that criminalizes the payment of bribes to foreign officials. Enforcement of such laws by OECD members against their home state companies has been uneven, but the OECD conducts a rigorous review process to hold its members accountable to increase enforcement. Multiple international conventions support this broad-based attack on corruption in commercial transactions.

The bodies of law addressing corruption and human rights concerns are significant, distinctive and evolving. We can only outline their basic dimensions here.

A. CORRUPTION AND THE SCOPE OF THE FOREIGN CORRUPT PRACTICES ACT

A PROBLEM

Petro Inc. (Petro), a major U.S. oil company with corporate headquarters in New York and stock traded on the New York Stock Exchange, is embarking on a project in Russia's Far East. It is negotiating an arrangement with a government-owned oil company, Vostokneftegaz, a Russian company with its headquarters in Yuzhno-Sakhalinsk. The project involves the development of offshore oil and gas reserves in the Sea of Okhotsk, constructing a liquid natural gas (LNG) facility on the coast of Sakhalin island and building a 150 mile pipeline to a port from which the LNG can be exported. Ivan Ivanovich Prikazy, a former senior official in the Russian Ministry of Natural Resources who enjoys a close relationship with the top management of Vostokneftegaz, introduced Petro to the project. The LNG facility and pipeline will be located in remote areas of Russia, populated only by indigenous ethnic groups whose collective right to occupy the land enjoys the protection of Russian constitutional law and other legislation. Petro and Vostokneftegaz contemplate the creation of a Russian company to implement the project.

Petro wishes to retain Prikazy as a consultant to advise it on the implementation of the project. The Deputy General Director of Vostokneftegaz, Voinivich, has in turn approached Prikazy about being retained in a consulting role to provide special services to the project. Prikazy is a petroleum engineer with long experience in the Russian oil and gas industry. He no longer occupies his former post in the highest echelons of the Ministry, but in addition to his consulting business he heads an institute that advises the Ministry on technical standards applicable to natural resource development. These standards in turn determine what kinds of equipment and engineering practices can be used in energy development projects.

Is there any reason why Petro should not retain Prikazy? He has skills and experience of direct relevance to the project, and Petro needs all the local help it can get. Is this simply a business decision, or are there other concerns? May Petro also retain Voinivich?

Review the Foreign Corrupt Practices Act (FCPA), in the Documents Supplement. Note first that Petro is an issuer within the meaning of 15 U.S.C. § 78dd–1(a) and (g). Is Prikazy or Voinivich a "foreign official" within the meaning of § 1(f)(1)(A)? If not, might there still be problems under § 1(a)(3)? What kind of "act or decision of [a] foreign official in his official capacity" might be implicated here? Is an offer of employment potentially "anything of value" within the meaning of § 1(a)?

Consider the following case, which provides some of the background to the FCPA.

United States of America v. David Kay

United States Court of Appeals for the Fifth Circuit
359 F.3d 738 (2004)

■ WIENER, CIRCUIT JUDGE:

Plaintiff-appellant, the United States of America ("government") appeals the district court's grant of the motion of defendants-appellees David Kay and Douglas Murphy ("defendants") to dismiss the Superseding Indictment ("indictment") that charged them with bribery of foreign officials in violation of the Foreign Corrupt Practices Act ("FCPA"). In their dismissal motion, defendants contended that the indictment failed to state an offense against them. The principal dispute in this case is whether, if proved beyond a reasonable doubt, the conduct that the indictment ascribed to defendants in connection with the alleged bribery of Haitian officials to understate customs duties and sales taxes on rice shipped to Haiti to assist American Rice, Inc. in obtaining or retaining business was sufficient to constitute an offense under the FCPA. Underlying this question of sufficiency of the contents of the indictment is the preliminary task of ascertaining the scope of the FCPA, which in turn requires us to construe the statute.

The district court concluded that, as a matter of law, an indictment alleging illicit payments to foreign officials for the purpose of avoiding substantial portions of customs duties and sales taxes to obtain or retain business are not the kind of bribes that the FCPA criminalizes. We disagree with this assessment of the scope of the FCPA and hold that such bribes could (but do not necessarily) come within the ambit of the statute. . . .

I.   FACTS AND PROCEEDINGS

American Rice, Inc. ("ARI") is a Houston-based company that exports rice to foreign countries, including Haiti. Rice Corporation of Haiti ("RCH"), a wholly owned subsidiary of ARI, was incorporated in Haiti to represent ARI's interests and deal with third parties there. As an aspect of Haiti's standard importation procedure, its customs officials assess duties based on the quantity and value of rice imported into the country. Haiti also requires businesses that deliver rice there to remit an advance deposit against Haitian sales taxes, based on the value of that rice, for which deposit a credit is eventually allowed on Haitian sales tax returns when filed.

In 2001, a grand jury charged Kay with violating the FCPA and subsequently returned the indictment, which charges both Kay and Murphy with 12 counts of FCPA violations. As is readily apparent on its face, the indictment contains detailed factual allegations about (1) the timing and purposes of Congress's enactment of the FCPA, (2) ARI and its status as an "issuer" under the FCPA, (3) RCH and its status as a wholly owned subsidiary and "service corporation" of ARI, representing ARI's interest in Haiti, and (4) defendants' citizenship, their positions as officers of ARI, and their status as "issuers" and "domestic concerns" under the FCPA. The indictment also spells out in detail how Kay and Murphy allegedly orchestrated the bribing of Haitian customs officials to accept false bills of lading and other documentation that intentionally understated by one-third the quantity of rice shipped to Haiti, thereby significantly reducing ARI's customs duties and sales taxes. In this regard, the indictment alleges the details of the bribery scheme's machinations, including the preparation of duplicate documentation, the calculation of bribes as a percentage of the value of the rice not reported, the surreptitious payment of monthly retainers to Haitian officials, and the defendants' purported authorization of withdrawals of funds from ARI's bank accounts with which to pay the Haitian officials, either directly or through intermediaries all to produce substantially reduced Haitian customs and tax costs to ARI. Further, the indictment alleges discrete facts regarding ARI's domestic incorporation and place of business, as well as the particular instrumentalities of interstate and foreign commerce that defendants used or caused to be used in carrying out the purported bribery.

In contrast, without any factual allegations, the indictment merely paraphrases the one element of the statute that is central to this appeal, only conclusionally accusing defendants of causing payments to be made to Haitian customs officials:

> for purposes of influencing acts and decisions of such foreign officials in their official capacities, inducing such foreign officials to do and omit to do acts in violation of their lawful duty, and to obtain an improper advantage, in order to assist American Rice, Inc. in obtaining and retaining business for, and directing business to American Rice, Inc. and Rice Corporation of Haiti.

Although it recites in great detail the discrete facts that the government intends to prove to satisfy each other element of an FCPA violation, the indictment recites no particularized facts that, if proved, would satisfy the "assist" aspect of the business nexus element of the statute, i.e., the nexus between the illicit tax savings produced by the bribery and the assistance such savings provided or were intended to provide in obtaining or retaining business for ARI and RCH. Neither does the indictment contain any factual allegations whatsoever to identify just what business in Haiti (presumably some rice-related commercial activity) the illicit customs and tax savings assisted (or were intended to assist) in obtaining or retaining, or just how these savings were supposed to assist in such efforts. In other words, the indictment recites no facts that could demonstrate an actual or intended cause-and-effect nexus between reduced taxes and obtaining identified business or retaining identified business opportunities.

In granting defendants' motion to dismiss the indictment for failure to state an offense, the district court held that, as a matter of law, bribes paid to obtain favorable tax treatment are not payments made to "obtain or retain business" within the intendment of the FCPA, and thus are not within the scope of that statute's proscription of foreign bribery. The government timely filed a notice of appeal.

. . .

None contend [sic] that the FCPA criminalizes every payment to a foreign official: It criminalizes only those payments that are intended to (1) influence a foreign official to act or make a decision in his official capacity, or (2) induce such an official to perform or refrain from performing some act in violation of his duty, or (3) secure some wrongful advantage to the payor. And even then, the FCPA criminalizes these kinds of payments only if the result they are intended to produce their quid pro quo will assist (or is intended to assist) the payor in efforts to get or keep some business for or with "any person." Thus, the first question of statutory interpretation presented in this appeal is whether payments made to foreign officials to obtain unlawfully reduced customs duties or sales tax liabilities can ever fall within the scope of the FCPA, i.e., whether the illicit payments made to obtain a reduction of revenue liabilities can ever constitute the kind of bribery that is proscribed by the FCPA. The district court answered this question in the negative; only if we answer it in the affirmative will we need to analyze the sufficiency of the factual allegations of the indictment as to the one element of the crime contested here.

The principal thrust of the defendants' argument is that the business nexus element, i.e., the "assist . . . in obtaining or retaining business" element, narrowly limits the statute's applicability to those payments that are intended to obtain a foreign official's approval of a bid for a new government contract or the renewal of an existing government contract. In contrast, the government insists that, in addition to payments to officials that lead directly to getting or renewing business contracts, the statute covers payments that indirectly advance ("assist") the payor's goal of obtaining or retaining foreign business with or for some person. The government reasons that paying reduced customs duties and sales taxes on imports, as is purported to have occurred in this case, is the type of "improper advantage" that always will assist in obtaining or retaining business in a foreign country, and thus is always covered by the FCPA.

. . .

C. FCPA Legislative History

As the statutory language itself is amenable to more than one reasonable interpretation, it is ambiguous as a matter of law. We turn therefore to legislative history in our effort to ascertain Congress's true intentions.

1. 1977 Legislative History

Congress enacted the FCPA in 1977, in response to recently discovered but widespread bribery of foreign officials by United States business interests. Congress resolved to interdict such bribery, not just because it is morally and economically suspect, but also because it was causing foreign policy problems for the United States. In particular, these concerns arose from revelations that United States defense contractors and oil companies had made large payments to high government officials in Japan, the Netherlands, and Italy. Congress also discovered that more than 400 corporations had made questionable or illegal payments in excess of $300 million to foreign officials for a wide range of favorable actions on behalf of the companies.

In deciding to criminalize this type of commercial bribery, the House and Senate each proposed similarly far-reaching, but non-identical, legislation. In its bill, the House intended "broadly [to] prohibit[ ] transactions that are corruptly intended to induce the recipient to use his or her influence to affect any act or decision of a foreign official. . . ." Thus, the House bill contained no limiting "business nexus" element. Reflecting a somewhat narrower purpose, the Senate expressed its desire to ban payments made for the purpose of inducing foreign officials to act "so as to direct business to any person, maintain an established business opportunity with any person, divert any business opportunity from any person or influence the enactment or promulgation of legislation or regulations of that government or instrumentality."

At conference, compromise language "clarified the scope of the prohibition by requiring that the purpose of the payment must be to influence any act or decision of a foreign official . . . so as to assist an issuer in obtaining, retaining or directing business to any person." In the end, then, Congress adopted the Senate's proposal to prohibit only those payments designed to induce a foreign official to act in a way that is intended to facilitate ("assist") in obtaining or retaining of business.

Congress expressly emphasized that it did not intend to prohibit "so-called grease or facilitating payments," such as "payments for expediting shipments through customs or placing a transatlantic telephone call, securing required permits, or obtaining adequate police protection, transactions which may involve even the proper performance of duties." Instead of making an express textual exception for these types of non-covered payments, the respective committees of the two chambers sought to distinguish permissible grease payments from prohibited bribery by only prohibiting payments that induce an official to act "corruptly," i.e., actions requiring him "to misuse his official position" and his discretionary authority, not those "essentially ministerial" actions that "merely move a particular matter toward an eventual act or decision or which do not involve any discretionary action."

In short, Congress sought to prohibit the type of bribery that (1) prompts officials to misuse their discretionary authority and (2) disrupts market efficiency and United States foreign relations, at the same time recognizing that smaller payments intended to expedite ministerial actions should remain outside of the scope of the statute. The Conference Report explanation, on which the district court relied to find a narrow statutory scope, truly offers little insight into the FCPA's precise scope, however; it merely parrots the statutory language itself by stating that the purpose of a payment must be to induce official action "so as to assist an issuer in obtaining, retaining or directing business to any person."

. . .

For purposes of deciding the instant appeal, the question nevertheless remains whether the Senate, and concomitantly Congress, intended this broader statutory scope to encompass the administration of tax, customs, and other laws and regulations affecting the revenue of foreign states. To reach this conclusion, we must ask whether Congress's remaining expressed desire to prohibit bribery aimed at getting assistance in retaining business or maintaining business opportunities was sufficiently broad to include bribes meant to affect the administration of revenue laws. When we do so, we conclude that the legislative intent was so broad.

Congress was obviously distraught not only about high profile bribes to high-ranking foreign officials, but also by the pervasiveness of foreign bribery by United States businesses and businessmen. Congress thus made the decision to clamp down on bribes intended to prompt foreign officials to misuse their discretionary authority for the benefit of a domestic entity's business in that country. This observation is not diminished by Congress's understanding and accepting that relatively small facilitating payments were, at the time, among the accepted costs of doing business in many foreign countries.

In addition, the concern of Congress with the immorality, inefficiency, and unethical character of bribery presumably does not vanish simply because the tainted payments are intended to secure a favorable decision less significant than winning a contract bid. Obviously, a commercial concern that bribes a foreign government official to award a construction, supply, or services contract violates the statute. Yet, there is little difference between this example and that of a corporation's lawfully obtaining a contract from an honest official or agency by submitting the lowest bid, and either before or after doing so bribing a different government official to reduce taxes and thereby ensure that the under-bid venture is nevertheless profitable. Avoiding or lowering taxes reduces operating costs and thus increases profit margins, thereby freeing up funds that the business is otherwise legally obligated to expend. And this, in turn, enables it to take any number of actions to the disadvantage of competitors. Bribing foreign officials to lower taxes and customs duties certainly can provide an unfair advantage over competitors and thereby be of assistance to the payor in obtaining or retaining business. This demonstrates that the question whether the defendants' alleged payments constitute a violation of the FCPA truly turns on whether these bribes were intended to lower ARI's cost of doing business in Haiti enough to have a sufficient nexus to garnering business there or to maintaining or increasing business operations that ARI already had there, so as to come within the scope of the business nexus element as Congress used it in the FCPA. Answering this fact question, then, implicates a matter of proof and thus evidence.

In short, the 1977 legislative history, particularly the Senate's proposal and the SEC Report on which it relied, convinces us that Congress meant to prohibit a range of payments wider than only those that directly influence the acquisition or retention of government contracts or similar commercial or industrial arrangements. On the other end of the spectrum, this history also demonstrates that Congress explicitly excluded facilitating payments (the grease exception). In thus limiting the exceptions to the type of bribery covered by the FCPA to this narrow category, Congress's intention to cast an otherwise wide net over foreign bribery suggests that Congress intended for the FCPA to prohibit all other illicit payments that are intended to influence non-trivial official foreign action in an effort to aid in obtaining or retaining business for some person. The congressional target was bribery paid to engender assistance in improving the business opportunities of the payor or his beneficiary, irrespective of whether that assistance be direct or indirect, and irrespective of whether it be related to administering the law, awarding, extending, or renewing a contract, or executing or preserving an agreement. In light of our reading of the 1977 legislative history, the subsequent 1988 and 1998 legislative history is only important to our analysis to the extent it confirms or conflicts with our initial conclusions about the scope of the statute.

2. 1988 Legislative History

After the FCPA's enactment, United States business entities and executives experienced difficulty in discerning a clear line between prohibited bribes and permissible facilitating payments. As a result,

Congress amended the FCPA in 1988, expressly to clarify its original intent in enacting the statute. Both houses insisted that their proposed amendments only clarified ambiguities "without changing the basic intent or effectiveness of the law."

In this effort to crystallize the scope of the FCPA's prohibitions on bribery, Congress chose to identify carefully two types of payments that are not proscribed by the statute. It expressly excepted payments made to procure "routine governmental action" (again, the grease exception), and it incorporated an affirmative defense for payments that are legal in the country in which they are offered or that constitute bona fide expenditures directly relating to promotion of products or services, or to the execution or performance of a contract with a foreign government or agency.

We agree with the position of the government that these 1988 amendments illustrate an intention by Congress to identify very limited exceptions to the kinds of bribes to which the FCPA does not apply. A brief review of the types of routine governmental actions enumerated by Congress shows how limited Congress wanted to make the grease exceptions. Routine governmental action, for instance, includes "obtaining permits, licenses, or other official documents to qualify a person to do business in a foreign country," and "scheduling inspections associated with contract performance or inspections related to transit of goods across country." Therefore, routine governmental action does not include the issuance of every official document or every inspection, but only (1) documentation that qualifies a party to do business and (2) scheduling an inspection—very narrow categories of largely non-discretionary, ministerial activities performed by mid- or low-level foreign functionaries. In contrast, the FCPA uses broad, general language in prohibiting payments to procure assistance for the payor in obtaining or retaining business, instead of employing similarly detailed language, such as applying the statute only to payments that attempt to secure or renew particular government contracts. Indeed, Congress had the opportunity to adopt narrower language in 1977 from the SEC Report, but chose not to do so.

. . .

3.   1998 Legislative History

In 1998, Congress made its most recent adjustments to the FCPA when the Senate ratified and Congress implemented the Organization of Economic Cooperation and Development's Convention on Combating Bribery of Foreign Public Officials in International Business Transactions (the "Convention"). Article 1.1 of the Convention prohibits payments to a foreign public official to induce him to "act or refrain from acting in relation to the performance of official duties, in order to obtain or retain business or other improper advantage in the conduct of international business." When Congress amended the language of the FCPA, however, rather than inserting "any improper advantage" immediately following "obtaining or retaining business" within the business nexus requirement (as does the Convention), it chose to add the "improper advantage" provision to the original list of abuses of discretion in consideration for bribes that the statute proscribes. Thus, as amended, the statute now prohibits payments to foreign officials not just to buy any act or decision, and not just to induce the doing or omitting of an official function "to assist . . . in obtaining or retaining business for or with, or directing business to, any person," but also the making of a payment to such a foreign official to secure an "improper advantage" that will assist in obtaining or retaining business.

The district court concluded, and defendants argue on appeal, that merely by adding the "improper advantage" language to the two existing kinds of prohibited acts acquired in consideration for bribes paid, Congress "again declined to amend the 'obtain or retain' business language in the FCPA." In contrast, the government responds that Congress's choice to place the Convention language elsewhere merely shows that Congress already intended for the business nexus requirement to apply broadly, and thus declined to be redundant.

The Convention's broad prohibition of bribery of foreign officials likely includes the types of payments that comprise defendants' alleged conduct. The commentaries to the Convention explain that " 'other improper advantage' refers to something to which the company concerned was not clearly entitled, for example, an operating permit for a factory which fails to meet the statutory requirements." Unlawfully reducing the taxes and customs duties at issue here to a level substantially below that which ARI was legally obligated to pay surely constitutes "something [ARI] was not clearly entitled to," and was thus potentially an "improper advantage" under the Convention.

As we have demonstrated, the 1977 and 1988 legislative histor[ies] already make clear that the business nexus requirement is not to be interpreted unduly narrowly. We therefore agree with the government that there really was no need for Congress to add "or other improper advantage" to the requirement. In fact, such an amendment might have inadvertently swept grease payments into the statutory ambit or at least created new confusion as to whether these types of payments were prohibited even though this category of payments was excluded by Congress in 1977 and remained excluded in 1988; and even though Congress showed no intention of adding this category when adopting its 1998 amendments. That the Convention, which the Senate ratified without reservation and Congress implemented, would also appear to prohibit the types of payments at issue in this case only bolsters our conclusion that the kind of conduct allegedly engaged in by defendants can be violative of the statute.

4. Summary

Given the foregoing analysis of the statute's legislative history, we cannot hold as a matter of law that Congress meant to limit the FCPA's applicability to cover only bribes that lead directly to the award or renewal of contracts. Instead, we hold that Congress intended for the FCPA to apply broadly to payments intended to assist the payor, either directly or indirectly, in obtaining or retaining business for some person, and that bribes paid to foreign tax officials to secure illegally reduced customs and tax liability constitute a type of payment that can fall within this broad coverage. In 1977, Congress was motivated to prohibit rampant foreign bribery by domestic business entities, but nevertheless understood the pragmatic need to exclude innocuous grease payments from the scope of its proposals. The FCPA's legislative history instructs that Congress was concerned about both the kind of bribery that leads to discrete contractual arrangements and the kind that more generally helps a domestic payor obtain or retain business for some person in a foreign country; and that Congress was aware that this type includes illicit payments made to officials to obtain favorable but unlawful tax treatment.

Furthermore, by narrowly defining exceptions and affirmative defenses against a backdrop of broad applicability, Congress reaffirmed its intention for the statute to apply to payments that even indirectly assist in obtaining business or maintaining existing business operations in a foreign country. Finally, Congress's intention to implement the Convention, a treaty that indisputably prohibits any bribes that give an advantage to which a business entity is not fully entitled, further supports our determination of the extent of the FCPA's scope.

Thus, in diametric opposition to the district court, we conclude that bribes paid to foreign officials in consideration for unlawful evasion of customs duties and sales taxes could fall within the purview of the FCPA's proscription. We hasten to add, however, that this conduct does not automatically constitute a violation of the FCPA: It still must be shown that the bribery was intended to produce an effect here, through tax savings that would "assist in obtaining or retaining business."

. . .

NOTES

1. The *Kay* opinion provides an extensive history of the FCPA, including its two revisions. Note the background of the two amendments. The 1988 amendments, adopted as part of an omnibus trade bill, mostly codified rules that previously had rested on the legislative history of the original Act. The necessity of conforming the FCPA to the OECD Convention prompted the 1998 amendments. We discuss this Convention below. After remand from the decision in text, a jury convicted the accused, and the Fifth Circuit affirmed. 513 F.3d 432 (2007), *rehearing en banc denied*, 513 F.3d 461 (2008), *cert. denied*, 555 U.S. 813 (2008).

2. ◦Does *Kay*'s discussion of the business nexus requirement make you more or less comfortable about Petro's proposed relationship with Prikazy? What kind of benefits might a prosecutor accuse Petro of seeking from or through Prikazy?

3. Suppose you could determine that Russian law expressly permitted someone in Prikazy's position to undertake consulting work while heading his institute. Does that solve the problem? Note that the FCPA provides an affirmative defense for payments that are "lawful under the written laws and regulations" of the country of the recipient. 15 U.S.C. §§ 78dd–1(c)(1), –2(c)(1), –3(c)(1). Does the lawfulness of consulting work necessarily mean that the contemplated transaction would be lawful?

4. Only one court so far has dealt with the scope of the "lawful" defense. The case involved payments to Azeri officials. Azerbaijan, like most of the former Soviet republics, has a provision in its criminal code that states that the payer of a bribe is "freed from criminal responsibility" if the payment resulted from extortion. In *United States v. Kozeny*, 582 F. Supp. 2d 535 (S.D.N.Y. 2008), the court interpreted this provision as excusing the payment but not as rendering it legal. The court noted, however, that proof of extortion could nullify the requisite corrupt intent under the FCPA itself and thus negate an element of the offense.

5.   If there is a concern about Prikazy's capacity as a foreign official, does the facilitation or "grease" payment exception under the FCPA ameliorate that concern? Why not?

6.   Suppose that Petro is adamant that it will hire Prikazy. Suppose it already has. What can be done to minimize the risk that this relationship will be characterized as a violation of the FCPA? Focus on the language of § 78dd–1(a) and (g), which requires that an act must be done "corruptly" to constitute a violation of the statute. What steps can Petro take (and require Prikazy to take) to avoid the imputation of corruption to their relationship?

7.   "Corruptly" has been understood, based on the legislative history of the FCPA, to mean intending to cause an official to misuse his or her official position in order to wrongfully direct business to the payor, or his client, to obtain preferential legislation or a favorable regulation. S. Rep. No. 95–114 (1977). In *Kay*, the jury was instructed that a corrupt act is one court stated that is "done voluntarily and intentionally, and with a bad purpose or evil motive, an unlawful end or result, or a method or means." *United States v. Kay*, 513 F. 3d 432, 446 (5th Cir. 2007).

8.   One of the vexing issues under the FCPA is just who qualifies as a "foreign official"? The FCPA contains no definition, referring only to "an officer or employee of a foreign government or any department, agency or instrumentality thereof". The question therefore is what is an "instrumentality"? Much commentary and a couple of lower court opinions added to the uncertainty. In *United States v. Esquenazi*, 752 F.3d 912 (11th Cir. 2014), the Eleventh Circuit defined instrumentality under the FCPA as "an entity controlled by the government of a foreign country that performs a function the controlling government treats as its own". What impact might this definition have on FCPA enforcement? What if, for example, a company pays a bribe to the general manager of a hotel in Beijing to win a tender to install equipment at the hotel? Evidence shows that the hotel is owned by a Chinese municipality but operates under the brand of a major international hotelier.

9.   Is the government required to introduce evidence of improper payments in order to bring an FCPA case? Consider SEC v. Oracle Corporation, No. 12-CV-4310 (N.D. Cal. Aug. 16, 2012) (Complaint) (at http://www.sec.gov/litigation/complaints/2012/comp-pr2012-158.pdf), where the evidence indicated that Oracle India had arranged with its Indian distributors to manipulate pricing to create a slush fund at the distributor level, off of the books of Oracle India. The SEC in its complaint listed no instances of the use of those funds to pay bribes but simply stated that the slush funds created the opportunity for such payments to be made. Should that be sufficient to justify an enforcement action?

10.   U.S. companies cannot permit their employees to pay bribes to foreign officials. How far should the responsibility of U.S. companies extend? What obligations does a U.S. company (and its executives) have to ensure that the company's agents, representatives or distributors in emerging markets do not pay bribes? Consider the following case brought by the SEC against a U.S. company under the accounting provisions of the FCPA, as distinct from the anti-bribery provisions that were the focus of *Kay*.

In the Matter of GE InVision, Inc. (formerly known as InVision Technologies, Inc.)

Respondent Admin. Proc. File No. 3–11827 Securities and Exchange Commission
February 14, 2005

ORDER INSTITUTING CEASE-AND-DESIST PROCEEDINGS, MAKING FINDINGS, AND IMPOSING A CEASE-AND-DESIST ORDER PURSUANT TO SECTION 21C OF THE SECURITIES EXCHANGE ACT OF 1934

I.

The Securities and Exchange Commission ("Commission") deems it appropriate that cease-and-desist proceedings be, and hereby are, instituted pursuant to Section 21C of the Securities Exchange Act of 1934 ("Exchange Act"), against GE InVision, Inc., formerly known as InVision Technologies, Inc. ("InVision" or "Respondent").

II.

In anticipation of the institution of these proceedings, Respondent has submitted an Offer of Settlement (the "Offer") which the Commission has determined to accept. Solely for the purpose of these proceedings and any other proceedings brought by or on behalf of the Commission, or to which the Commission is a party, and without admitting or denying the findings herein, except as to the Commission's jurisdiction over it and the subject matter of these proceedings, which are admitted, Respondent consents to the entry of this Order Instituting Cease-and-Desist Proceedings, Making Findings, and Imposing a Cease-and-Desist Order Pursuant to Section 21C of the Securities Exchange Act of 1934 ("Order"), as set forth below.

III.

On the basis of this Order and Respondent's Offer, the Commission finds that:

Summary

1.   This proceeding involves violations of the Foreign Corrupt Practices Act ("FCPA") by InVision, a California-based manufacturer of explosives detection systems used by airports. From at least June 2002 through June 2004, InVision, through its employees, sales agents and distributors, engaged in transactions in violation of the FCPA in three countries: the People's Republic of China, the Republic of the Philippines and the Kingdom of Thailand. In each of the transactions, InVision was aware of a high probability that its foreign sales agents or distributors paid or offered to pay something of value to government officials in order to obtain or retain business for InVision. Despite this, InVision authorized improper payments to the agents or distributors, or allowed them to proceed with transactions on InVision's behalf, in violation of the FCPA. During this period, InVision improperly accounted for certain payments to its agents and distributors in its books and records in violation of the FCPA, and failed to devise and maintain a system of internal controls with respect to foreign sales sufficient to assure compliance with the FCPA.

Respondent

2.   InVision, incorporated in Delaware and headquartered in Newark, California, designs and manufactures advanced explosives detection systems to scan checked baggage by airport security personnel in the United States and other countries. At the time of the conduct described below, InVision's common stock was registered with the Commission pursuant to Section 12(g) of the Exchange Act and was listed on the NASDAQ National Market. InVision filed reports with the Commission pursuant to Section 13 of the Exchange Act.

Facts

3.   To facilitate its sales abroad, InVision retained local sales agents and distributors who were familiar with the business practices and customs of their respective countries. The sales agents and distributors negotiated with InVision's customers, including governmental aviation authorities, and typically reported to InVision through an InVision Regional Sales Manager. The Regional Sales Managers reported directly to an InVision senior sales executive (the "Senior Executive").

A.   China

4.   In November 2002, InVision agreed to sell two explosives detection machines for use at an airport under construction in Guangzhou, China. The airport is owned and controlled by the government of China. The sale to the airport was conducted through InVision's local distributor in China, which purchased the two machines from InVision for approximately $2.8 million. The distributor, in turn, negotiated the re-sale of the machines and was InVision's primary representative to the airport and associated governmental agencies.

5.   Under the terms of the transaction, InVision was obligated to deliver the two machines by mid-2003. Due to problems in obtaining an export license from the United States government, however, InVision did not deliver the machines until October 2003. During the delay, the distributor in China informed the responsible Regional Sales Manager and the Senior Executive that the airport intended to impose a financial penalty on InVision. The distributor advised the Regional Sales Manager that, in order to avoid this penalty, it intended to offer foreign travel and other benefits to airport officials. The Regional Sales Manager notified the Senior Executive of the distributor's intention.

6.   The distributor requested financial compensation from InVision to pay for penalties and costs that, it claimed, would be incurred as a result of the delay in shipment. The distributor's request included compensation for benefits that the distributor intended to offer to airport officials. In October 2003, the Senior Executive agreed to pay the distributor $95,000. Based on information provided by the Senior Executive and the Regional Sales Manager, InVision's finance department subsequently authorized the payment, which was completed in April 2004. At the time of the payment, based on the information provided to the Regional Sales Manager and the Senior Executive, InVision was aware of a high probability that the distributor intended to use part of the funds it received from InVision to pay for foreign travel and other benefits for airport officials.

7.   InVision improperly recorded the payment in its books as a cost of goods sold. InVision realized profits of approximately $589,000 from the sale of the two machines in China.

B.   Philippines

8.   InVision sold two explosives detection machines for use in an airport in the Philippines in November 2001. Although InVision had retained a sales agent in the Philippines since at least 1996, the sale was made directly by InVision to the subcontractor responsible for building the airport terminal baggage handling system.

9.   Beginning at about the time of the November 2001 sale, InVision received repeated requests for a commission on the sale from its sales agent in the Philippines. At the same time, in communications with both the responsible Regional Sales Manager and the Senior Executive, the agent indicated that it was negotiating for additional sales of InVision products to other airports owned and controlled by the government of the Philippines. The agent indicated that it intended to use part of any commission it obtained in connection with the November 2001 sale to make gifts or pay cash to government officials in order to influence their decision to purchase additional InVision products.

10.   In December 2001, the Senior Executive agreed to pay the Filipino sales agent a commission in the amount of approximately $108,000 in connection with the November 2001 sale. Based on information provided by the Regional Sales Manager and Senior Executive, InVision's finance department subsequently authorized the payment, which was completed in July 2002. At the time of the payment, based on the information provided to the Regional Sales Manager and the Senior Executive, InVision was aware of a high probability that the sales agent intended to use part of the commission to make gifts or pay cash to influence Filipino government officials to purchase InVision products. InVision improperly recorded the payment in its books as a sales commission. The Filipino agent did not complete any additional sales on behalf of InVision.

C.   Thailand

11.   Beginning no later than 2002, InVision competed for the right to supply explosives detection machines to an airport under construction in Bangkok, Thailand. Construction of the airport is overseen by a corporation controlled by the government of Thailand. InVision retained a distributor in Thailand to lobby the airport corporation and the Thai government on InVision's behalf. Under the terms of the transaction, the distributor would purchase the explosives detection machines from InVision and then make its profit by reselling them at a higher price for use by the airport. The distributor was InVision's primary representative to the airport and associated governmental agencies.

12.   From at least January 2003 through April 2004, in communications with the responsible Regional Sales Manager and the Senior Executive, the distributor indicated that it had offered to make gifts or payments to officials with influence over the airport corporation. Based on the information provided to the Regional Sales Manager and the Senior Executive, InVision was aware of a high probability that the distributor intended to fund any such gifts or offers out of the difference between the price the distributor paid InVision to acquire the machines

and the price for which the distributor was able to resell them. Despite this awareness, InVision authorized the distributor to continue to pursue the transaction.

13. In or about April 2004, the airport corporation, through its general contractor, agreed to purchase 26 of InVision's explosive detection machines from the InVision distributor in a sale InVision valued at approximately $35.8 million. Consummation of the transaction was deferred after InVision received notification of possible FCPA violations. InVision has not recognized any revenue from the transaction and has agreed that the transaction will proceed, if at all, only as a sale directly to the airport corporation or another Thai governmental entity.

D. InVision's Lack of Internal Controls

14. During the period of the foreign transactions described above, InVision failed to develop an adequate process to select and train its sales agents and distributors employed outside the United States. In choosing foreign sales agents and distributors, InVision primarily relied on introductions by other American companies. InVision conducted little, if any, investigation into the backgrounds of its foreign sales agents and distributors.

15. InVision's standard agreement with its foreign agents and distributors contained a clause prohibiting violations of the FCPA. Beyond the contractual provision, however, InVision provided no formal training or education to its employees (including its Regional Sales Managers) or its sales agents and distributors regarding the requirements of the FCPA.

16. InVision also failed to establish a program to monitor its foreign agents and distributors for compliance with the FCPA. For example, InVision did not have a regular practice of periodically updating background checks or other information regarding foreign agents and distributors. With respect to the transactions described above, InVision failed to establish an internal system sufficient to prevent and detect violations of the FCPA.

Legal Analysis

. . .

17. In each of the transactions described above, based on the information provided to the responsible Regional Sales Manager and the Senior Executive, InVision was aware of the high probability that its foreign sales agents and distributors intended to make gifts or payments in order to obtain or retain business for InVision. In each instance, by proceeding with the transactions, InVision made or authorized the making of illegal payments to foreign officials, in violation of Section 30A. InVision violated Section 13(b)(2)(A) by improperly recording in its books and records payments it made in the transactions involving its distributor in China and its sales agent in the Philippines. Finally, InVision violated Section 13(b)(2)(B) by failing to devise and maintain an effective system of internal controls to prevent and detect violations of the FCPA.

. . .

Undertakings

InVision and its corporate parent General Electric undertake to:

18. Incorporate InVision into General Electric's corporate compliance program, including its program designed to detect and prevent violations of the FCPA.

19. Retain and pay for an Independent Consultant not unacceptable to the staff of the Commission and the Department of Justice within 60 calendar days of the issuance of this Order.

20. Require the Independent Consultant to:

a. Evaluate the efficacy of the integration by General Electric of InVision into General Electric's existing FCPA compliance program, including but not limited to the implementation of FCPA training for appropriate InVision employees; and

b. Within 180 days of the issuance of this Order, report to the staff of the Commission (with a copy of any such written report being provided to General Electric) regarding General Electric's efforts to comply with Paragraph 23(a), above.

21. Cooperate fully with the Independent Consultant and provide the Independent Consultant with access to its files, books, records and personnel as reasonably requested for the Independent Consultant's evaluation.

22. Require the Independent Consultant to enter into an agreement that provides that for the period of engagement, and for a period of two years from completion of the engagement, the Independent Consultant shall not enter into any employment, consultant, attorney-client, auditing or other professional relationship with InVision, its successor-in-interest GE InVision, Inc., GE Security, Inc., General Electric, or any of these entities' present or former affiliates, directors, officers, employees, or agents acting in their capacity. The agreement will also provide that the Independent Consultant shall require that any firm with which the Independent Consultant is affiliated or of which Independent Consultant is a member, and any person engaged to assist the Independent Consultant in performance of Independent Consultant's duties under the Order memorializing the terms of this Offer, shall not, without prior written consent of the staff of the Commission's San Francisco District Office, enter into any employment, consultant, attorney-client, auditing or other professional relationship with InVision, its successor-in-interest GE InVision, Inc., GE Security, Inc., or any of these entities' present or former subsidiaries, directors, officers, employees, or agents acting in their capacity as such for the period of the engagement and for a period of two years after the engagement.

IV.

In view of the foregoing, the Commission deems it appropriate to impose the sanctions agreed to in Respondent's Offer.

Accordingly, it is hereby ORDERED that:

A. Respondent cease and desist from committing or causing any violations and any future violations of Sections 13(b)(2)(A), 13(b)(2)(B), and 30A of the Exchange Act.

B. Respondent shall comply with the undertakings enumerated in Section III, above.

C.   IT IS FURTHER ORDERED that Respondent shall, within ten days of the entry of this Order, pay disgorgement of $589,000 plus prejudgment interest of $28,703.57, for a total amount of $617,703.57 to the United States Treasury.

NOTES

1.   The SEC brought a separate proceeding against David M. Pillor, InVision's Senior Vice President for Sales and Marketing and a member of the company's board of directors. He was the Senior Executive mentioned in the SEC order. The SEC did not allege that Pillor directed any of his subordinates to engage in proscribed conduct, but he did receive reports of illicit payments and did not act to stop them. The SEC charged Pillor with violating the "books and records" requirements of Section 13(b)(2)(A) by creating false records of payments and with aiding and abetting InVision's violations of the international controls provisions of Section 13(b)(2)(B).

2.   How much did InVision do, as opposed to let happen? How onerous are the obligations the SEC imposes (due diligence, training and oversight)? Was it fair to lay InVision's failure at the feet of David Pillor? The facts in his case indicated that he had failed to respond to emails and had insisted that a distributor present an itemization of expenses for which it was seeking reimbursement. The SEC charged Pillor because he failed to obtain actual evidence supporting that itemization. Is this too great a burden for a corporate executive to meet? Once a firm learns that a bribe may occur, what steps must it take to prevent the payment from happening?

3.   Note that *GE InVision* involved the SEC's civil enforcement authority, while *Kay* was a criminal prosecution brought by the Justice Department. Only "issuers" face SEC sanctions. The SEC faces a lower burden of proof in its proceedings, because the criminal standard of beyond a reasonable doubt does not apply. Just as important, the cost to a company of complying with an SEC order usually is not as great as that entailed in a criminal conviction. Typically the company will consent to an order forbidding future violations, pay a fine or agree to disgorgement of illicit profits, improve its controls over its intermediaries and relationships with government officials, and institute training programs to increase employee sensitivity to the requirements of the FCPA. Indirect consequences may include a decline in the price of public traded stock, thereby increasing the firm's cost of capital at least temporarily. But no one goes to jail and the company does not run the risk of losing government contracting privileges and regulatory licenses, which may happen after a criminal conviction.

4.   What advantages does the U.S. government have in prosecuting bribery through the SEC's civil enforcement authority? Why did the SEC, rather than the Justice Department, prosecute David Pillor?

5.   The InVision and Pillor cases raise the distinction between criminal prosecution under the anti-bribery provisions of the FCPA and civil prosecution under the accounting provisions. In the latter, the SEC does not have to establish scienter. The enforcement of the accounting provisions are generally viewed as imposing strict liability: Books and records are either accurate or they are not; internal controls are adequate or not. This standard, of course, facilitates prosecution in cases where the proof of knowledge, actual or constructive, of a wrongful act may be lacking. This is particularly complicated where intermediaries are used to pay bribes.

Consider the standards for proving knowledge under the anti-bribery provisions. The definition of knowledge is contained in 15 U.S.C. §§ 78dd–1(f)(2)(B), 78dd–2(h)(3)(B), and 78dd–3(f)(3)(B):

> (A) A person's state of mind is "knowing" with respect to conduct, a circumstance, or a result if—
>
> (i) such person is aware that such person is engaging in such conduct, that such circumstance exists, or that such result is substantially certain to occur; or
>
> (ii) such person has a firm belief that such circumstance exists or that such result is substantially certain to occur.
>
> (B) When knowledge of the existence of a particular circumstance is required for an offense, such knowledge is established if a person is aware of a high probability of the existence of such circumstance, unless the person actually believes that such circumstance does not exist.

Below is the relevant part of the House Conference Report No. 100–576 to the Omnibus Trade and Competitiveness Act of (1988), at 920:

> . . . Thus the "knowing" standard adopted covers both prohibited actions that are taken with "actual knowledge" of intended results as well as other actions that, while falling short of what the law terms "positive knowledge," nevertheless evidence a conscience disregard or deliberate ignorance of known circumstances that should reasonably alert one to the high probability of violations of the Act.
>
> In clarifying the existing foreign anti-bribery standard of liability under the Act as passed in 1977, the Conferees agreed that "simple negligence" or "mere foolishness" should not be the basis for liability. However, the Conferees also agreed that the so called "head-in-the-sand" problem—variously described in the pertinent authorities as "conscious disregard," "willful blindness" or "deliberate ignorance"—should be covered so that management officials could not take refuge from the act's prohibition by their unwarranted obliviousness to any action (or inaction), language or other "signaling device" that should reasonably alert them of the "high probability" of an FCPA violation.

The "head-in-the-sand" problem is not unique to this area of criminal law and occurs in a variety of contexts, perhaps the most common being the situation where a person acquires property under "suspicious" circumstances and is charged with "knowledge" that it is stolen. Courts and commentators have considered such behavior to be "distinct from, but equally culpable as actual knowledge." See G. Williams, Criminal Law: The General Part, sec. 57 at 157 (2d ed. 1961).

Consider the following excerpts from the Statement of Facts in the Alcoa FCPA case addressing the question of what constitutes knowledge. Alcoa involved a long term relationship with an agent who later became a distributor ("Consultant A") of alumina for resale to Alba, the smelter controlled by the Bahraini government. Alumet, AAAC and ULESCO are companies owned by Consultant A.

United States v. Alcoa World Alumina LLC

No. 14-CR-00007 (W.D. Penn. Jan. 9, 2014)
(Plea Agreement, Statement of Facts)
http://www.justice.gov/criminal/fraud/fcpa/cases/alcoa-world-alumina/01-
09-2014plea-agreement.pdf

The Corruption Scheme in Bahrain

Background

17. From 1989 to approximately 1996, Alcoa of Australia managed its long term supply relationship with Alba. As part of that relationship, Alcoa of Australia retained Consultant A to assist in long-term contract negotiations with Alba and Bahraini government officials. By 2000, when Alcoa World Alumina LLC assumed direct oversight of the Alba relationship, Consultant A was playing a significant role in the relationship between Alcoa of Australia and Alba. Executive A, who inherited the Alba oversight relationship as part of his duties at Alcoa World Alumina LLC, became the primary liaison with Consultant A regarding the Alba relationship.

Overview

18. In or around 2002, Alcoa World Alumina LLC, through Executive A, caused Alcoa of Australia to enter into a purported distributorship for the sale of approximately one million tons of alumina annually to Alba through Consultant A's shell companies, Alumet and AAAC.

19. In or around 2004, Alcoa World Alumina LLC, through Executive A, coordinated another purported distribution agreement that involved the sale of up to 1.78 million tons of alumina to Alba every year through Alumet and AAAC. This corrupt arrangement lasted through on or about December 31, 2009.

20. As part of the 2002 and 2004 purported distributorship agreements, Consultant A imposed a mark-up on Alumet's and AAAC's purported sales of alumina to Alba and used the mark-up from those sales to enrich himself and pay bribes to senior government officials of Bahrain. Alcoa World Alumina LLC, through Executive A, consciously disregarded the fact that Consultant A would pay bribes to senior government officials from the mark-up on alumina sales to Alba.

I.   Alcoa World Alumina LLC, Through Executive A, Enlarged Consultant A's Role in the Alumina Supply Relationship

21. By 2000, Executive A, who was then based in Alcoa World Alumina LLC's offices in Pittsburgh, had assumed direct responsibility for managing the Alba relationship.

22. From April to December 2001, Executive A took a series of steps to cause Alumet and AAAC to become Alcoa of Australia's purported distributors for all of its sales of alumina to Alba.

23. On or about April 12, 2001, Executive A wrote to Official C to advise him that "Alcoa wishes" to extend the "present supply contract [with Alba] for three years to December 31, 2004."

24. On or around August 15, 2001, after receiving a request from Alba to continue the existing supply arrangements through December

2003, Executive A facilitated Alba's entering into an extension of the existing alumina supply arrangement through December 2003.

25. On or about February 14, 2002, Executive A caused Alcoa of Australia to enter into a purported distribution agreement with Alumet and AAAC for the supply of approximately one million tons of alumina intended for sale to Alba.

26. Executive A knew that Alcoa of Australia would continue to ship alumina directly to Alba. Executive A consciously disregarded the fact that the purported contractual arrangement he crafted with Consultant A would permit Alumet and/or AAAC to mark-up sales to Alba of alumina from Alcoa of Australia. In or around February 2002, Alcoa of Australia ceased to invoice Alba directly for shipments of alumina.

The Mark-Up and Commission Payments from 2002 Through 2004

27. From 2002 to 2004, Executive A, acting on behalf of Alcoa World Alumina LLC, caused AAAC to receive in excess of $79 million in mark-ups on alumina sales to Alba.

28. AAAC also received a commission under the terms of the 2002 distribution agreement. The purported 2002 distribution agreement provided for a commission of 0.125% of all payments made by AAAC to Alcoa of Australia for alumina. From 2002 to 2004, Alcoa of Australia paid AAAC a commission of $493,509.

Consultant A Channeled Corrupt Payments to Government Officials from 2002 Through 2004

29. From 2002 through 2004, Consultant A made corrupt payments to Officials B and C from bank accounts at RBC in Guernsey held in the name of Alumet and ULECO.

II. Executive A Retained Consultant A for Joint Venture Negotiations Between Alcoa and Alba

30. In 2002, Alcoa was attempting to negotiate a joint venture with Alba, in which Alcoa would supply Alba with alumina from the AWAC system's smelters, and, in exchange, Alba would supply Alcoa with aluminium. Executive A participated in the negotiations for Alcoa and retained Consultant A to privately lobby Official C on behalf of Alcoa's position. On or about April 27, 2002, Executive A caused Alcoa to enter a consulting agreement with Consultant A pursuant to which Consultant A would receive an $8 million "success fee" based on limited specified negotiation "advice and assistance to Alcoa" if the joint venture were successful.

31. As part of the negotiations, Executive A proposed a joint venture structure that contemplated supplying alumina to Alba through a distributor.

32. On or about March 26, 2003, an in-house attorney in Alcoa's legal department sent an email asking Executive A to explain the role of the distributor. On or about March 27, 2003, Executive A responded that "[t]he Distributorship rol[e] is something the Bahrain Government wants" and that Alcoa "shouldn't get too involved with how the Distributor and the Government interact. We are currently selling the alumna we supply to Alba through a Distributor." In response, the in-

house attorney wrote that "we will need to understand the Distributor's role completely . . . for Foreign Corrupt Practice Act purposes."

33. On September 15, 2003, Alcoa and Alba agreed to a Memorandum of Understanding ("MOU") outlining an equity investment by Alcoa in Alba and providing for alumina to be sold to the Government of Bahrain, as majority shareholder of Alba, "directly or through an associated company of Alcoa satisfactory to GoB [Government of Bahrain] and Alcoa." The MOU was approved by Official C on behalf of Alba. However, the joint venture negotiations fell through, and Consultant A was never paid the $8 million success fee.

34. Within 17 days of the signing of the MOU, Consultant A transferred $2 million to Official C's account at Deutsche Bank in Geneva, Switzerland, from a ULECO bank account at RBC in Guernsey.

III. Alcoa World Alumina LLC, Through Executive A, Caused Alcoa of Australia to Secure a 2005 Long-Term Alumina Supply Deal with Alba

35. By the summer of 2004, Alcoa of Australia was supplying approximately one million metric tons of alumina annually to Alba, but was invoicing Alba indirectly through Consultant A's companies. Alba's obligations under pre-existing supply arrangements with Alcoa of Australia were set to expire at the end of 2004.

36. In the summer of 2004, Executive A and one of his supervisors, another senior member of Alcoa World Alumina LLC's global alumina sales department, sought to secure a new long term alumina supply agreement with Alba. On or around August 5, 2004, Executive A and his supervisor were advised by a former senior Alcoa executive who had a relationship with Consultant A that if they attempted to negotiate a direct contractual relationship between Alcoa of Australia and Alba, rather than negotiate a supply arrangement through Consultant A and one of his companies, some or all of Alba's business could be lost to another alumina supplier.

37. On or about August 19, 2004, Executive A and his supervisor met with Consultant A at Consultant A's London Office to discuss using Consultant A's companies "as Alcoa's exclusive distributor in the region."

38. On or about August 22, 2004, Executive A sent an email to his supervisor documenting with more specificity certain items that were discussed at the meeting. Among them, Executive A noted that "[w]e agreed to supply [Consultant A] with pricing indications for supply to [AAAC] by 8/24 so he can have these for his meeting [in Bahrain] with [Official C]. We mentioned pricing close to 14%." Executive A's email also noted that "[Official C] is holding on to publishing [Alba's] alumina tender [to the market] until he has further discussions with [Consultant A] on 8/29." The pricing terms per metric ton of alumina that Executive A quoted to Consultant A at the meeting in London were less than the pricing terms for Alba that Executive A had quoted to Official C approximately one month earlier.

39. On or around September 29, 2004, Executive A facilitated AAAC's tendering a bid to supply Alba up to 1.6 million tons of alumina for ten years commencing in 2005.

40. On or about October 8, 2004, Attorney 1, the in-house attorney responsible for supporting the alumina business, suggested terminating the consulting agreement that Alcoa had entered with Consultant A, as "the terms of [Consultant A's] current engagement created a lot of anxiety in the organization." Executive A advised that the consultancy agreement should not be terminated until Alcoa had secured a new long-term alumina supply agreement with Alba.

41. On or about November, 1, Official C caused Alba to accept AAAC's tender offer for a ten-year supply of alumina.

42. On or about December 31, 2004, Executive A caused Alcoa of Australia to enter a purported ten-year distributorship agreement with Alumet and AAAC to purportedly supply them with up to 1.78 million tons of alumina for sale to Alba from 2005 to 2014. From 2005 to 2009, the price term was 13.9% of LME minus $0.25 per ton of alumina. From 2010 to 2014, the price decreased to 13.5% of LME minus $0.25 per ton of alumina. Executive A consciously disregarded the fact that Alcoa of Australia would continue to supply alumina directly to Alba that was purportedly being "distributed" through Alumet and AAAC.

43. On or about March 4, 2005, a representative of Consultant A sent the CEO of Alba a final, unexecuted contract for the purported supply agreement between AAAC and Alba.

44. On or about June 8, 2005, the final agreement negotiated between AAAC and Alba was signed by Alba's CEO on behalf of Alba. The agreement's effective date was January 1, 2005, and its term was through December 31, 2014. The agreement provided that AAAC would supply Alba with 1.508 million metric tons of alumina in 2005, and 1.6 million metric tons of alumina thereafter for each remaining contract year. From 2005 to 2009, the price formula in the agreement resulted in an average price to Alba of 14.98% of LME per metric ton of alumina. From 2010 through 2014, the price formula in the agreement resulted in an average price to Alba of 14.42% of LME per metric ton of alumina. Alba was required to bear the cost of shipping and insurance.

Consultant A's Mark-Up on Alumina Sales From 2005 to 2009

45. As a result of Alcoa World Alumina LLC's conduct, through Executive A, from 2005 through 2009, Alumet and AAAC received in excess of $188 million on the mark-up of alumina sales to Alba. This money was transferred from the initial accounts in which payment from Alba was received through various bank accounts controlled by Consultant A, including accounts in the name of shell entities Alumet and ULECO at RBC in Guernsey.

Additional Corrupt Payments to Official C

46. From 2005 through 2006, Consultant A made millions in corrupt payments from the account of ULECO at RBC in Guernsey through the account of La Fosca in Luxembourg to accounts that were beneficially owned by Official C under client code names at ABN AMRO Bank in Luxembourg and LGT Bank in Liechtenstein.

47. Under these circumstances, Alcoa World Alumina LLC, through Executive A, consciously disregarded the fact that the mark-up imposed by Consultant A on Alumet and AAAC's sales of alumina to Alba was

facilitating corrupt payments to government officials who controlled Alba's tender process.

IV. *Alcoa World Alumina LLC Caused Alcoa to Extend Materially Significant Lines of Credit to Consultant A*

48. Consultant A sought a line of credit from Alcoa to cover the cost of alumina shipments to Alba until Alba remitted payment to Alumet and AAAC. Consultant A, however, refused to provide financial statements for Alumet or AAAC to Alcoa's credit department, which was normally required for a significant extension of credit to a third-party. Notwithstanding this, in or around December 2004, Alcoa World Alumina LLC, through Executive A, sought and received approval to extend credit to Consultant A's companies and thereby caused Alcoa's credit department to extend a $23 million line of credit to Alumet and AAAC.

49. Thereafter, in each of contract years 2005 through 2009, Alcoa continued to grant business unit overrides to extend materially increasing credit lines to Consultant A's purported distributorships. By 2007, Alcoa was extending a credit line of $58 million to Alumet and AAAC. During this period, Alcoa granted Alumet and AAAC credit lines that were significantly greater than those granted by Alcoa to any other third-party.

50. By facilitating the extension of credit to Consultant A, Executive A enabled the purported distributorship scheme by allowing Consultant A to defer paying Alcoa of Australia for the multi-million dollar shipments of alumina to Alba until Alumet and AAAC received payment from Alba.

NOTES

1. Consider the implications of paragraphs 20, 26 and 42. Is the Justice Department suggesting that Executive A has violated the FCPA because the distributor could mark up its prices to Alba, thus creating a fund from which bribes could be paid? What duty should a company have to monitor the prices its distributors charge to an end user of the company's products? What collateral concerns does the imposition of such a duty create?

2. In paragraphs 31–33, why does the Justice Department highlight the role of the distributor in the proposed joint venture? Why does it matter that the Bahrain Government wants the distributorship as part of the joint venture?

3. Of what relevance to the Justice Department's case is the extension of lines of credit to Consultant A? The Justice Department is concerned that Consultant A refused to provide financial statements to Alcoa, but that Alcoa still chose to extend credit to Consultant A. Is this a red flag? If so, would the red flag be resolved by evidence that Consultant A paid his invoices in full on a timely basis and therefore was considered an excellent credit risk?

4. What is your assessment of the factual allegations made by the Justice Department? Do they clearly make out "knowledge" by Alcoa World Alumina and therefore support an FCPA violation?

5. Managing the risks associated with using third party intermediaries is the greatest challenge global companies face. Most bribe schemes depend upon the use of such companies, yet global companies are frequently

dependent upon a broad range of intermediaries—distributors, agents, consultants, etc.—to conduct their business in emerging markets. The InVision case, in paragraph 14–16 of the Cease and Desist Order, imposed new due diligence, training and oversight requirements. In November 2012, the SEC and Department of Justice published the Resource Guide to the FCPA which amplified those requirements.

The Justice Department and SEC's FCPA enforcement actions demonstrate that third parties, including agents, consultants, and distributors, are commonly used to conceal the payment of bribes to foreign officials in international business transactions. Risk-based due diligence is particularly important with third parties and will also be considered by the Justice Department and SEC in assessing the effectiveness of a company's compliance program.

Although the degree of appropriate due diligence may vary based on industry, country, size and nature of the transactions, and historical relationship with the third-party, some guiding principles always apply.

First, as part of risk-based due diligence, companies should understand the qualifications and associations of its third-party partners, including its business reputation, and relationship, if any, with foreign officials. The degree of scrutiny should increase as red flags surface.

Second, companies should have an understanding of the business rationale for including the third party in the transaction. Among other things, the company should understand the role of and need for the third party and ensure that the contract terms specifically describe the services to be performed. Additional considerations include payment terms and how those payment terms compare to typical terms in that industry and country, as well as the timing of the third party's introduction to the business. Moreover, companies may want to confirm and document that the third party is actually performing the work for which it is being paid and that its compensation is commensurate with the work being provided.

Third, companies should undertake some form of ongoing monitoring of third-party relationships. Where appropriate, this may include updating due diligence periodically, exercising audit rights, providing periodic training, and requesting annual compliance certifications by the third party.

In addition to considering a company's due diligence on third parties, the Justice Department and SEC also assess whether the company has informed third parties of the company's compliance program and commitment to ethical and lawful business practices and, where appropriate, whether it has sought assurances from third parties, through certifications and otherwise, of reciprocal commitments. These can be meaningful ways to mitigate third-party risk.

2012 FCPA Guide at 60–61.

How does the Guide alter the InVision requirements? Why is a focus on the "business purpose" for using a third party intermediary important?

6.   What prophylactic compliance responsibilities does the FCPA place upon U.S. companies? Consider the following attachments to the Deferred Prosecution Agreement entered into in April 2011 between the Department of Justice and Johnson & Johnson related to the latter's FCPA violations:

United States v. Johnson & Johnson (Depuy)

No. 11-CR-00099 (D.D.C. Apr. 8, 2011)
(Deferred Prosecution Agreement, Attachments C and D)
http://www.justice.gov/criminal/fraud/fcpa/cases/depuy-inc/04-08-11depuy-dpa.pdf

Corporate Compliance Program

In order to address deficiencies in its internal controls, policies, and procedures regarding compliance with the Foreign Corrupt Practices Act ("FCPA"), 15 U.S.C. §§ 78dd–1, et seq., and other applicable anticorruption laws, Johnson & Johnson and its subsidiaries and operating companies (collectively, "J&J") agree to continue to conduct, in a manner consistent with all of its obligations under this Agreement, appropriate reviews of its existing internal controls, policies, and procedures.

Where necessary and appropriate, J&J agrees to adopt new or to modify existing internal controls, policies, and procedures in order to ensure that it maintains: (a) a system of internal accounting controls designed to ensure that J&J makes and keeps fair and accurate books, records, and accounts; and (b) a rigorous anticorruption compliance code, standards, and procedures designed to detect and deter violations of the FCPA and 'other applicable anticorruption laws. At a minimum, this should include, but not be limited to, the following elements:

1.   A clearly articulated corporate policy against violations of the FCPA, including its anti-bribery, books and records, and internal controls provisions, and other applicable counterparts (collectively, the "anticorruption laws").

2.   Promulgation of compliance standards and procedures designed to reduce the prospect of violations of the anticorruption laws and J&J's compliance code. These standards and procedures shall apply to all directors, officers, and employees and, where necessary and appropriate, outside parties acting on behalf of J&J in a foreign jurisdiction, including but not limited to, agents, consultants, representatives, distributors, teaming partners, and joint venture partners (collectively, "agents and business partners");

3.   The assignment of responsibility to one or more senior corporate executives of J&J for the implementation and oversight of compliance with policies, standards, and procedures 'regarding the anticorruption laws. Such corporate official(s) shall have the authority to report matters directly to J&J's Board of Directors or any appropriate committee of the Board of Directors;

4.   Mechanisms designed to ensure that the policies, standards, and procedures of J&J regarding the anticorruption laws are effectively communicated to all directors, officers, employees, and, where appropriate, agents and business partners. These mechanisms shall

include: (a) periodic training for all directors, officers, and employees, and, where necessary and appropriate, agents and business partners; and (b) annual certifications by all such directors, officers, and employees, and, where necessary and appropriate, agents, and business partners, certifying compliance with the training requirements;

5.   An effective system for reporting suspected criminal conduct and/or violations of the compliance policies, standards, and procedures regarding the anticorruption laws for directors, officers, employees, and, where necessary and appropriate, agents and business partners;

6.   Appropriate disciplinary procedures to address, among other things, violations of the anticorruption laws and J&J's compliance code by J&J's directors, officers, and employees;

7.   Appropriate due diligence requirements pertaining to the retention and oversight of agents and business partners;

8.   Standard provisions in agreements, contracts, and renewals thereof with all agents and business partners that are reasonably calculated to prevent violations of the anticorruption laws, which may, depending upon the circumstances, include: (a) anticorruption representations and undertakings relating to compliance with the anticorruption laws; (b) rights to conduct audits of the books and records of the agent or business partner to ensure compliance with the foregoing; and (c) rights to terminate an agent or business partner as a result of any breach of anticorruption laws, and regulations or representations and undertakings related to such matters; and

9.   Periodic testing of the compliance code, standards, and procedures designed to evaluate their effectiveness in detecting and reducing violations of anticorruption laws and J&J's compliance code.

ENHANCED COMPLIANCE OBLIGATIONS

In addition to and building upon the commitments enumerated in [Items 1–9 above], Johnson & Johnson and its subsidiaries and operating companies (collectively, "J&J") agree that they have or will undertake the following, at a minimum, for the duration of this Agreement:

General

1.   J&J will:

a.   Appoint a senior corporate executive with significant experience with compliance with the FCPA, including its anti-bribery, books and records, and internal controls provisions, as well as other applicable anticorruption laws and regulations (hereinafter "anticorruption laws and regulations") to serve as Chief Compliance Officer. The Chief Compliance Officer will have reporting obligations directly to the Audit Committee of the Board of Directors.

b.   Appoint heads of compliance within each business sector and corporate function. These compliance heads will have reporting obligations to the Chief Compliance Officer and the Audit Committee.

c.   Maintain a global compliance leadership team, including regional compliance leaders and business segment compliance leaders, with responsibility for overseeing its company-wide compliance program. That leadership team will have reporting obligations directly to the Chief Compliance Officer.

2.   J&J shall institute gifts, hospitality, and travel policies and procedures in each jurisdiction that are appropriately designed to prevent violations of the anticorruption laws and regulations. At a minimum, these policies shall contain the following restrictions regarding government officials, including but not limited to public health care providers, administrators, and regulators:

a.   Gifts must be modest in value, appropriate under the circumstances, and given in accordance with anticorruption laws and regulations, including those of the government official's home country;

b.   Hospitality shall be limited to reasonably priced meals, accommodations, and incidental expenses that are part of product education and training programs, professional training, and conferences or business meetings;

c.   Travel shall be limited to product education and training programs, professional training, and conferences or business meetings; and

d.   Gifts, hospitality, and travel shall not include expenses for anyone other than the official.

Complaints, Reports, and Compliance Issues

3.   J&J shall maintain its mechanisms for making and handling reports and complaints related to potential violations of anticorruption laws and regulations, including referral for review and response to a standing committee that includes internal audit, legal, and compliance personnel, and will ensure that reasonable access is provided to an anonymous, toll-free hotline as well as to an anonymous electronic complaint form, where anonymous reporting is legally permissible.

4.   J&J will ensure that its Sensitive Issue Triage Committee reviews and responds to FCPA and corruption issues promptly and consistently; this Triage Committee will include members from J&J's internal audit, legal, and compliance functions.

Risk Assessments and Audits

5.   J&J will conduct risk assessments of markets where J&J has government customers and/or other anticorruption compliance risks on a staggered, periodic basis. Such risk assessments shall occur at reasonable intervals and include a review of trends in interactions with government officials, including health care providers, to identify new risk areas. On the basis of those assessments, as needed, J&J will modify compliance implementation to minimize risks observed through the risk assessment process.

6.   J&J will conduct periodic audits specific to the detection of violations of anticorruption laws and regulations ("FCPA Audits"). Specifically, J&J will identify no less than five operating companies that are high risk for corruption because of their sector and location and will conduct FCPA Audits of those operating companies at least once every three years. High risk operating companies shall be identified based on J&J's risk assessment process in consultation with the Chief Compliance Officer,

sector compliance leaders, corporate internal audit, and the Law Department, taking into account multiple risk factors including, but not limited to: a high degree of interaction with government officials; the existence of internal reports of potential corruption risk; a high corruption risk based on certain corruption indexes; and financial audit results. The list of high risk operating companies shall be reviewed annually and updated as necessary. FCPA Audits of other operating companies that pose corruption risks shall occur no less than once every five years. Each FCPA Audit shall include:

     a.   On-site visits by an audit team comprised of qualified auditors who have received FCPA and anticorruption training;

     b.   Where appropriate, participation in the on-site visits by personnel from the compliance and legal functions;

     c.   Review of a statistically representative sample appropriately adjusted for the risks of the market, of contracts with and payments to individual health care providers;

     d.   Creation of action plans resulting from issues identified during audits; these action plans will be shared with appropriate senior management, including the Chief Compliance Officer, and will contain mandatory undertakings designed to enhance anticorruption compliance, repair process weaknesses, and deter violations; and

     e.   Where appropriate, feasible, and permissible under local law, review of the books and records of distributors which, in the view of the audit team, may present corruption risk.

Acquisitions

7.   J&J will ensure that new business entities are only acquired after thorough FCPA and anticorruption due diligence by legal, accounting, and compliance personnel. Where such anticorruption due diligence is not practicable prior to acquisition of a new business for reasons beyond J&J's control, or due to any applicable law, rule, or regulation, J&J will conduct FCPA and anticorruption due diligence subsequent to the acquisition and report to the Department any corrupt payments, falsified books and records, or inadequate internal controls as required by Paragraph 11 of the Deferred Prosecution Agreement.

8.   J&J will ensure that J&J's policies and procedures regarding the anticorruption laws and regulations apply as quickly as is practicable, but in any event no less than one year post-closing, to newly-acquired businesses, and will promptly:

     a.   Train directors, officers, employees, agents, consultants, representatives, distributors, joint venture partners, and relevant employees thereof, who present corruption risk to J&J, on the anticorruption laws and regulations and J&J's related policies and procedures; and

     b.   Conduct an FCPA-specific audit of all newly-acquired businesses within 18 months of acquisition.

Relationships with Third Parties

9. J&J will conduct due diligence reviews of sales intermediaries, including agents, consultants, representatives, distributors, and joint venture partners. At a minimum, such due diligence shall include:

    a. A review of the qualifications and business reputation of the sales intermediaries;

    b. A rationale for the use of the sales intermediary; and

    c. A review of FCPA risk areas.

10. Such due diligence will be conducted by local businesses and reviewed by local healthcare compliance officers. New intermediaries that have not worked for the company prior to the date of this agreement, or where due diligence raises any red flags, shall be reviewed by a regional compliance officer with specific knowledge of and responsibility for anticorruption due diligence of sales intermediaries. Due diligence will be conducted prior to retention of any new agent, consultant, representative, distributor, or joint venture partner and for all such intermediaries will be updated no less than once every three years.

11. Where necessary and appropriate and where permitted by applicable law, J & J shall include standard provisions designed to prevent violations of the FCPA and other applicable anticorruption laws and regulations in agreements, contracts, grants, and renewals thereof with agents, distributors, and business partners, including:

    a. Anticorruption representations and undertakings relating to compliance with the anticorruption laws and regulations;

    b. Rights to conduct audits of the books and records of the agent, distributor, or business partner that are related to their business with J&J; and

    c. Rights to terminate the agent, distributor, or business partner as a result of any breach of anticorruption laws and regulations or representations and undertakings related to such anticorruption laws and regulations.

Training

12. J&J shall provide:

    a. Annual training on anticorruption laws and regulations to directors, officers, executives, and employees who could present corruption risk to J&J.

    b. Enhanced and in-depth FCPA training for all internal audit, financial, and legal personnel involved in FCPA audits, due diligence reviews, and acquisition of new businesses.

    c. Training as necessary based on risk profiles to relevant third parties acting on the company's behalf that may interact with government officials at least once every three years.

13. J&J shall implement a system of annual certifications from senior managers in each of J&J's corporate-level functions, divisions, and business units in each foreign country confirming that their local standard operating procedures adequately implement J&J's anticorruption policies and procedures, including training requirements,

and that they are not aware of any FCPA or other corruption issues that have not already been reported to corporate compliance.

NOTES

1. In light of these materials, what precaution should Petro take if they wish to hire Prikazy? What about Prikazy's hiring of Voinivich, the Deputy General Director of Vostokneftegaz? At the end of the day, can Petro guarantee that its relationship with Vostokneftegaz will not create problems under the FCPA? If not, should it still go ahead?

2. Why might Petro hire Prikazy in spite of the risk that, in hindsight, the SEC or the Justice Department might question the relationship? Is there a good business case to be made for taking on such relationships in emerging markets? Does the business case help or hinder the legal problem?

3. Johnson & Johnson had a detailed compliance program in place before the resolution of its case with the Justice Department and the SEC in 2011, which entailed one of the largest settlements, $70 million, at that time. As the Justice Department noted in the Deferred Prosecution Agreement, "J&J had a pre-existing compliance and ethics program that was effective and the majority of problematic operations globally resulted from insufficient implementation of the J&J compliance and ethics program in acquired companies." How far should the regulators be permitted to go in imposing additional compliance requirements on companies like J&J? At what point do these requirements interfere with legitimate business activities?

B. INTERNATIONAL ANTICORRUPTION COOPERATION

If corruption is pervasive in high risk emerging markets, do U.S. firms face an unfair burden when doing business there as a result of their FCPA obligations? Or should all rich-country firms equally face the same restrictions on improper payments?

Until 1998, the United State was unique in forbidding the bribery of foreign officials. Indeed, some countries allowed their taxpayers to treat such bribes as a deductible business expenses for tax purposes. In that year, the Organization for Economic Cooperation and Development, the Paris-based international institution that coordinates economic policy among the richer countries, promulgated an international agreement to induce all its members to take equivalent steps against improper payments. The following article, authored by the person within the Clinton Administration most responsible for this achievement, reports on the results.

Daniel K. Tarullo, The Limits of Institutional
Design: Implementing the OECD
Anti-Bribery Convention

44 VA. J. INT'L L. 665 (2004)

A decade ago there were no significant international agreements pertaining to government corruption. Today such agreements are in force in three major regional organizations: the Convention on Combating Bribery of Foreign Public Officials in the Organization for Economic

Cooperation and Development (OECD Convention); the Inter-American Convention Against Corruption negotiated in the Organization of American States; and both Criminal and Civil Law Conventions on Corruption in the Council of Europe. A United Nations Convention Against Corruption, on which negotiations recently concluded, is awaiting ratification. Meanwhile, anti-corruption or "good governance" initiatives have been adopted by the World Bank and other multilateral lending institutions. Despite this impressive institutionalization of anti-corruption obligations and programs, however, there is little evidence of any diminution in the incidence of corruption in, and by nationals of, the participating countries. Of more immediate interest, implementation of the relevant international agreements has been limited at best, precluding an assessment of whether vigorous enforcement of the new international obligations would in fact curb at least some forms of corruption.

. . .

The story of the unexpectedly rapid negotiation of the OECD Convention has been well recounted by legal and international relations scholars. This scholarship properly poses the question of why five years of desultory negotiations in the OECD suddenly gave way to three years of progress, culminating in the signing of the Convention. The answer that emerges from these accounts, though not phrased as such, is in its essence a combination of realist and liberal explanations: Because of shifts in the preferences of domestic interest groups and the government in power, the United States became more committed to an international agreement and then used its power, assisted by domestic political forces in some of the states, to press an agreement upon the rest of the OECD member states.

There are, of course, numerous forms of corruption that may be practiced by government officials, and thus numerous corresponding forms of overseas bribes that may be offered by multinational companies. Most attention has focused on what is sometimes called "grand corruption"—instances of large bribes paid to government officials influential in awarding contracts for large procurements such as power plants, defense purchases, and civil aircraft. Though there is little systematic documentation of practices in this shadowy world, it appears that there is frequently a "going rate" of perhaps five percent of the value of the contract paid as a bribe by a successful bidder.

. . .

Once the U.S. government decided to elevate the issue in the fall of 1993, it needed to find ways to change the assessment of the payoff structure of the overseas bribery game by other governments. It had ruled out the most obvious move, which was to permit U.S. firms to meet bribery with bribery, in a kind of tit-for-tat strategy within the iterated game of international contracts. . . . But this device was precluded by ethical, legal, reputational, and foreign policy considerations, and never considered. Instead, the U.S. government adopted the familiar game theoretic course of offering rewards and punishments to alter the payoff calculus of key OECD governments. As is often the case in international relations, the conditional strategic moves used were largely outside the "game" of international bribery as narrowly defined.

One U.S. move was to communicate to its OECD negotiating partners the message that progress on matters of interest to them would be less likely absent progress on the anti-bribery effort. Although no issue linkage or reciprocity was ever articulated explicitly, the message was conveyed by the very prominence of the issue in meetings involving senior officials of the State Department, Treasury Department, Commerce Department, and Office of the U.S. Trade Representative. In effect, U.S. officials were saying, "We care a lot about this issue, your government has been obstructionist, and we are not going to be very helpful on some issues of interest to you until progress is made at the OECD." A game theorist might classify this move as an implicit promise to be helpful once the bribery issue was addressed (i.e., increasing the payoff for cooperation), though it also had the flavor of a threat to withhold cooperation that would otherwise have been forthcoming. A more clear-cut use of threats occurred when the Trade Representative's office hinted darkly that, if progress was not forthcoming in the OECD, the United States might turn the issue into a trade policy matter, with the further hint of trade sanctions against countries whose companies paid bribes that hurt the business prospects of their U.S. competitors.

An additional source of leverage became apparent to U.S. officials only after they began their campaign for progress in the OECD negotiations. Domestic bribery scandals in several European countries had sensitized the European press and, by extension, publics to the foreign corruption issue. Transparency International, which is based in Berlin, reinforced the message from a non-American perspective. Although there does not seem to have been much direct public pressure on European governments with respect to overseas bribery as such, European officials reacted in anticipation of such pressures developing. Attention to overseas bribery might further have complicated efforts to contain the harm from domestic bribery scandals that were at that time commanding such media and public attention. U.S. officials thus learned that they were, unwittingly at first, affecting the domestic political situation in France, Germany, Britain, and other countries that had resisted international obligations to limit overseas bribery. Having learned of this effect, they added a new move to their tactical repertoire. The European press showed great interest in the U.S. initiative, resulting in numerous newspaper articles and even a lengthy segment on a British television program. U.S. officials engaged in more "public diplomacy" by granting interviews and giving speeches on the topic. Thus, in a turn of events that seems very far from today's world, efforts of the United States to exercise its power in pursuit of an international arrangement elicited a favorable reaction from European publics and, in accordance with liberal explanations for international behavior, helped shift the positions taken by European governments which, until that point, had been recalcitrant.

One additional factor was the emergence of the foreign bribery issue as a point of concern for some developing-country governments, particularly those elected in the surge of democratization that had recently occurred around the world. Anti-corruption efforts were, at the behest of several South American countries, a focal point of the 1994 Summit of the Americas, an eventual byproduct of which was the Inter-American Convention Against Corruption. During OECD "outreach" efforts with representatives of developing countries, officials of the latter repeatedly acknowledged their chronic problems with government corruption. More to the point, they went on to suggest that governments of developed countries had, by failing to act against foreign bribery by their own multinationals, become complicit in that bribery. This charge was vexing to many other OECD member governments, which have often tried to expand their influence in multilateral institutions by taking positions more sympathetic to developing countries, on issues such as development assistance, than those adopted by the United States. Preservation of that advantage may not have required a shift in position on the foreign bribery issue, but it certainly argued for one by revealing additional costs to continued bribery-permissive policies.

The extended tactical maneuvers of the mid-1990s that eventually resulted in the OECD Convention are less important for present purposes than the foregoing identification of the basic factors that explain why countries that had resisted an international anti-bribery arrangement eventually yielded. Just as important is the absence of a factor frequently associated with the creation of a new international arrangement. This was not a case where various countries each valued an agreement by others to take, or forbear from, certain actions. On the contrary, many OECD members were satisfied with the status quo, in which U.S. companies were forbidden by their domestic laws from bribing foreign officials but European and other companies were not. There is little doubt that these other governments would gladly have allowed the issue to fade into obscurity, but for the persistence of the United States and the links drawn between domestic and foreign bribery in journalistic and public discourse.

While some of these government officials may have been "converted" to the U.S. view during the negotiations, others quite clearly signed the Convention as the least-cost way of moving the problem out of the public eye. This hypothesis is consistent with the rational choice premises of game theory. The variation on the typical game is that here the payoff structure was significantly affected by factors outside the narrow bounds of the bribery "game." Realist and liberal theories of international relations offer ready explanations of how the factors described earlier convinced governments to enter into an international agreement, but nothing in these explanations or in game theory suggests that these governments intended the resulting Convention actually to repress overseas bribery.

. . .

The OECD Convention on Combating Bribery of Foreign Public Officials in International Business Transactions was adopted by an OECD negotiating conference on November 21, 1997, and entered into force on February 15, 1999, following the requisite number of ratifications. The Convention's core legal obligation is set forth in Article 1:

> Each party shall take such measures as may be necessary to establish that it is a criminal offence under its law for any person intentionally to offer, promise or give any undue pecuniary or other advantage . . . to a foreign public official . . . in order that the official act or refrain from acting in relation to the performance of official duties, in order to obtain or retain

business or other improper advantage in the conduct of international business.

Article 8 requires signatories to implement certain accounting standards to combat efforts by companies to conceal overseas bribes. Most of the remainder of the relatively brief convention elaborates upon the scope of the criminalization obligation. There is no explicit obligation to prosecute bribe-payers, although it is implicit in the articles dealing with sanctions, jurisdiction, and enforcement. The only institutional provision is Article 12, which states that the "[p]arties shall co-operate in carrying out a programme of systematic follow-up to monitor and promote the full implementation" of the Convention. The Convention creates no other mechanisms for enforcement of the signatories' obligations, dispute settlement, or related matters.

The Convention, which deals only with transnational bribery, is the exemplary case of an arrangement addressing the "supply-side" of bribery. It obliges signatories to criminalize bribery of foreign officials but does not address the taking of bribes by their own officials. Thus, it covers only the impact of bribery by one country's residents (including corporations) upon the government of another country. As noted earlier, it aims to effect a "level playing field" among foreign companies operating in a country, by assuring that none will gain a competitive advantage through bribery. In prisoner's dilemma terms, the criminalization requirement is a commitment to cooperation.

. . .

NOTES

1.   Although OECD member countries have been slow to prosecute bribery of foreign officials, the trend is beginning with numerous investigations underway in France, Germany and Italy. The mechanisms for evaluating the implementation and enforcement of national legislation under the OECD Convention are both formal and informal. For the formal aspects of OECD review see http://www.oecd.org. The informal aspects involve the growing network of prosecutors and law enforcement officials who share information about cases where overlapping jurisdiction exists and parallel prosecutions possible.

2.   How might foreign prosecution of corrupt payments affect U.S. companies? One possibility is that foreign prosecutors will go after U.S. companies that might be seen as too close to the government. A French investigation into Halliburton for alleged violations of the new French law that resulted from the OECD Convention gives some support to this hypothesis. Symmetrically, U.S. prosecutors might pursue foreign firms that enjoy the status at home of national champions or U.S. prosecution of foreign companies may induce the prosecutors in the jurisdictions of those companies to proceed against them. With respect to persons that are neither U.S. issuers nor nationals, what nexus with the United States is sufficient to justify a prosecution under the FCPA?

3.   One of the functions of the OECD Convention is to create a mechanism for prosecutors to meet regularly to discuss the efforts to attack corrupt payments by companies within their jurisdiction. Knowing that these channels of communication exists, how might a firm cope with a pattern of potentially criminal activity over which more than one country has jurisdiction? Can a company obtain protection from prosecution in one jurisdiction by cooperating with prosecutors in another?

4. How might the OECD Convention affect the ability of a company to bring political pressure to bear on anticorruption prosecutors in its home country? In December 2006 the United Kingdom's Serious Fraud Office announced that it would terminate an investigation to allegations that the British firm BAE paid bribes to government officials in Saudi Arabia to procure the sale of weapons systems to that country. Prime Minister Blair defended this decision as consistent with interests of national security as well as necessary to protect British jobs. The OECD in turn announced that it would review the British action, and the U.S. Department of Justice looked into the matter and ultimately prosecuted BAE.

5. On the heels of the OECD Convention, the United Nations presided over another multilateral treaty designed to harmonize the international approach to corruption. The General Assembly endorsed the Convention Against Corruption in 2003, which entered into force two years later. The United States joined this Convention in 2006. Like the OECD Convention, the UN Convention does not have direct effect in U.S. law; the U.S. made a declaration at the time that it joined that the Convention would not be self-executing in its domestic law. The United States also exercised its option under the Convention not to submit to the jurisdiction of the International Court of Justice (ICJ) in the event of any dispute between it and another party over the interpretation or application of the treaty. Many of the other countries that have joined also have eschewed ICJ jurisdiction. If this Convention does not have direct legal effect, what work does it do?

The Siemens *Case: International Cooperation at Work*

At the end of 2008, the U.S. and German authorities settled the largest case every brought under anticorruption law, and the first to involve coordinated and substantial penalties paid to multiple sovereigns. Siemens AG, a multinational company based in Germany, agreed to pay fines and penalties amounting to $1.6 billion, divided roughly equally between the United States and Germany. The following statement of facts, taken from the plea agreement between Siemens and the U.S. Department of Justice, indicates the nature of the conduct involved.

United States v. Siemens Aktiengesellschaft

No. 08-CR-367 (D.D.C. Dec. 12, 2008) (Statement of Offense)
http://www.justice.gov/criminal/fraud/fcpa/cases/siemens/12-15-08siemens-statement.pdf

Siemens' Historical Failure to Maintain Sufficient Internal Anti-Corruption Controls

Pre-1999

32. By the late nineteenth century, Siemens and its subsidiaries had become known as an international company, with over half of their employees outside of Germany. After World War II, with most of its facilities destroyed, its material assets and trademark patents confiscated, and its business prospects in the developed world weakened. Siemens began to focus on developing markets. By the mid-1950s,

Siemens was handling major infrastructure projects in South America, the Middle East, and Africa. By the mid-1990s, Siemens became the first foreign corporation to have a holding company in China.

33. Until in or about February 1999, Siemens operated in a largely unregulated environment with respect to international business practices, in which (a) German law did not prohibit overseas bribery and permitted tax deductions for bribe payments to foreign officials; (b) Siemens was not yet listed on the NYSE; and (c) Siemens operated in many countries where corruption was endemic.

34. Until in or about February 1999, Siemens' project cost calculation sheets sometimes reflected "nützliche aufwendungen" ("NAs"), a common tax term literally translated as "useful expenditures" but partly understood by many Siemens employees to mean "bribes."

35. Until in or about February 1999, certain systems existed within Siemens that allowed for corrupt payments as necessary to win business. For example, there were multiple "cash desks" housed within Siemens offices where employees could withdraw large sums of cash, up to and including one million Euros at a time. In addition, in the 1990s, very large sums of money—more than one billion Euros—were withdrawn for questionable business purposes from off-books accounts in Austria, Switzerland, Liechtenstein, and elsewhere. Siemens also relied heavily on purported "business consultants," in many cases for the sole purpose of passing along corrupt payments from Siemens to foreign government officials responsible for awarding business.

1999–2004

36. Over the period from in or about February 1999 to in or about July 2004, certain Siemens ZV members became aware of changes in the regulatory environment. While foreign anti-corruption circulars and policies were promulgated, that "paper program" was largely ineffective at changing Siemens' historical, pervasive corrupt business practices.

37. On or about February 15, 1999, the German law implementing the OECD Convention on Combating Bribery of Foreign Public Officials in International Business Transactions (the "OECD Convention"), which generally required signatory countries to implement antibribery laws similar to the FCPA, came into force. On the same day. Officer A made a presentation at a high-level Siemens executive meeting expressing "concern at the number of criminal and other investigations into members of the company," further noting the new German law prohibiting foreign bribery and that "[a]s the Board could possibly be held responsible for various offenses, it was important to take protective measures."

38. In or about March 1999, the Siemens ZV issued a Z Circular, a company-wide policy, reminding employees of the general need to observe laws and regulations.

39. On or about April 25, 2000, Officer B issued a report to the Siemens ZV recommending the creation of a company-wide list of agents and consultants and a committee to review these relationships.

40. On or about April 25, 2000, during the Siemens ZV meeting, a debate ensued regarding whether to promulgate company-wide uniform guidelines for consultants, but meeting minutes indicate that the

Siemens ZV rejected the concept of instituting such guidelines due to "different business practices" in each division.

41. In or about June 2000, Siemens' lawyers sent memoranda to Officer C and a Supervisory Board member warning of the potential criminal and civil implications of maintaining off-books accounts for cash payments in light of Siemens' upcoming listing on the NYSE. Specifically, the memoranda identified "three bank accounts in Switzerland which are run as trust accounts for Siemens AG and for which confiscation was ordered by the Swiss courts."

42. On or about July 5, 2000, Siemens issued a Z Circular requiring operating groups and regional companies to ensure that the following anti-corruption clause would be included in all contracts with agents, consultants, brokers, or other third parties: "The agent shall strictly comply with all laws and regulations regarding the performance of the activities applicable to the agent. Without limitation, the Agent agrees to comply with the requirements of the anticorruption laws applicable to the Parties."

43. In or about September 2000, Officer B forwarded to Officer C a letter regarding a foreign public prosecutor's investigation into bribes to a former Nigerian dictator allegedly paid from Siemens' off-books accounts. Officer B's handwritten note on the letter said "for info—particulars verbally."

44. On or about September 12, 2000, in connection with an investigation, Austrian authorities froze assets in at least one Austrian bank account used by Siemens. On or about February 7, 2001, in connection with the Nigeria investigation, an Austrian judge granted a Swiss prosecutor's request for judicial assistance concerning that account and another off-books Austrian bank account used by Siemens for improper payments.

45. On or about March 12, 2001, Siemens became listed on the NYSE. At the time of listing. Siemens and its subsidiaries had over 400,000 employees and operated in 190 countries.

46. On or about July 18, 2001, Siemens issued Business Conduct Guidelines that included the following anti-corruption provision: "No employee may directly or indirectly offer or grant unjustified advantages to others in connection with business dealings, neither in monetary form nor as some other advantage." The guidelines also provided that gifts to business partners should "avoid the appearance of bad faith or impropriety," that no gifts should be made to "public officials or other civil servants," and that employees entering into contracts with consultants or agents must see to it that those parties also offered no "unjustified advantages."

47. In or about July 2001, Siemens established a new position for a Corporate Officer for Compliance and expanded the existing antitrust compliance system to cover anticorruption issues. The Corporate Officer for Compliance worked on compliance issues part-time due to other job duties and, until 2004, had a staff of only two lawyers.

48. On or about October 18, 2001—nearly seven months after Siemens became an issuer—the Swiss off-books accounts were still active, despite knowledge by certain individuals at the highest levels of

Siemens of the legal concerns surrounding these accounts raised in or about June 2000.

49. On or about October 18, 2001, Officer A testified about the Swiss off-books accounts before a German parliamentary committee investigating donations to a political party. Officer A confirmed the existence of the accounts and testified that they were not used for cash payments to German political parties, but rather for business consultant commissions in foreign countries.

50. On or about June 13, 2002, Siemens issued principles and recommendations, but not mandatory policies, regarding business-related internal controls and agreements with business consultants, including that such agreements should be in writing, transparent, and as detailed as possible. These non-binding recommendations were largely ineffective. They contained no discussion of how to conduct due diligence on consultants or agents, and although Siemens employees often reduced consulting agreements to writing, they frequently did so only after Siemens won a contract and needed documentary support for a payment. Many written consulting agreements were form agreements containing no substance particular to the engagement, and most called for success fee payments.

51. In or about July 2003, *The Financial Times* reported that the Milan, Italy public prosecutor's office was investigating payments by Siemens to managers of the Italian energy company, Enel. The Milan investigation focused on €6 million in bribes that PG managers had arranged to be paid to managers of Enel so that PG could win two power plant projects. The payments to the Enel managers were routed through slush funds in Liechtenstein and through an account at Emirates Bank.

52. In or about July 2003, the Darmstadt, Germany public prosecutor's office also publicly announced an investigation into the Enel matter.

53. In or about August 2003, Siemens engaged a U.S. law firm for advice on how to respond to the Enel cases.

54. On or about September 9, 2003, the U.S. law firm submitted to Siemens a memorandum, received by several Siemens ZV members including Officer A, Officer C, Officer D, and Officer E, concluding that there was an "ample basis for either the [Securities and Exchange Commission] or [Department of Justice] to start at least an informal investigation of a company's role in such a matter." In addition, the U.S. law firm informed Siemens that U.S. enforcement officials would expect an internal investigation to be carried out on behalf of senior management and Siemens ZV. Finally, the U.S. law firm suggested that Siemens immediately review and assure proper functioning of its FCPA compliance program, report on those findings to the Siemens ZV, and discipline the employees involved in wrongdoing.

55. On or about September 30, 2003, Siemens engaged a local law firm in Erlangen, Germany to investigate some of the facts underlying the Enel allegations.

56. In or about October 2003, Siemens' outside auditors discovered that €4,120,000 in cash had been brought to Nigeria by COM personnel and flagged the issue for additional review. A Siemens compliance lawyer conducted a one-day investigation and wrote a report warning of

numerous possible violations of German law, including antibribery laws, in connection with cash payments to purported business consultants. Officer C received the report, which identified as playing prominently in the scheme several COM employees later arrested by the Munich public prosecutor's office in 2006. Further, the compliance lawyer's report indicated that based on interviews with employees, the issue investigated was not an isolated incident. Officer C asked the CFO of COM to take care of the problem, but no follow-up was conducted on whether any action was taken. The report itself was not circulated to the Vorstand as a whole or to the Audit Committee, and the employees involved were not disciplined.

57. In or about November 2003, to comply with the Sarbanes-Oxley Act of 2002, Siemens issued a Code of Ethics for Financial Matters, which, among other things, required Chief Financial Officers and business heads to act responsibly and with integrity.

58. In or about November 2003, at a meeting of Siemens financial officers, Officer C reported on "unpleasant topics regarding Business Conduct which emerged in the past weeks of the Financial Statement," and reminded the financial officers of their duties to adhere to the Business Conduct Guidelines.

59. In or about November 2003, a compliance lawyer, at Officer B's request, wrote a memorandum describing the standards for an effective compliance organization under both German and United States law, and highlighting deficiencies in Siemens' compliance organization.

60. In or about November 2003, Officer B forwarded to Officer C the memorandum outlining deficiencies in Siemens' compliance organization, with a request to circulate the memorandum to other members of the Siemens ZV. The subject of compliance was taken off the agenda for the Siemens ZV meeting that immediately followed the drafting of the memorandum, and was also not discussed at the subsequent Siemens ZV meeting in or about December 2003.

61. From in or about February 1999 to in or about July 2004, notwithstanding the promulgation of some written policies, Siemens senior management provided little corresponding guidance on how to conduct business lawfully in countries where Siemens had been paying bribes historically. The Siemens ZV provided few strong messages regarding anti-corruption. Senior management made no clear statement that Siemens would rather lose business than obtain it illegally, and employees were still under tremendous pressure to meet their sales goals.

2004–2006

62. From in or about mid-2004 to in or about 2006, the Siemens ZV grew increasingly alarmed at developments in the Enel corruption cases and adopted more robust—but still imperfect—compliance measures in response. Certain Siemens ZV members began to recognize the serious legal risks in both the United States and Europe that Siemens faced for bribery.

63. On or about April 24, 2004, the Milan, Italy investigating judge issued a written opinion stating that the evidence in the Enel case indicated that Siemens, as a company, saw bribery "at least as a possible business strategy." The judge further opined that the existence of the

Liechtenstein and Emirates Bank accounts had been "disguised deliberately" and that such conduct "creates the danger that cases of corruption will recur." Finally, the judge noted that Siemens was not cooperating with the investigation, as evidenced by its concealment of the accounts.

64. On or about May 4, 2004, several members of the Siemens ZV. Including Officer A. Officer C, Officer D, Officer E, and Officer F received a memorandum outlining the Milan, Italy investigating judge's ruling.

65. On or about June 1, 2004, the Erlangen law firm Siemens engaged to investigate the Enel matter issued the first report of its findings to Officer B, who shared the report with Officer A, Officer C, and Officer D. The report discussed the Milan prosecutor's allegations that various Siemens employees had paid bribes to Enel officials through purported business consultants. In the report, the Erlangen law firm indicated that several key Siemens employees had refused to submit to interviews. None of these key Siemens employees was ever disciplined as a result of the failure to submit to interviews by Siemens' Erlangen lawyer regarding the Enel corruption allegations.

66. On or about July 2004, Officer C delivered a speech to the Siemens ZV and high-level business managers entitled "Tone from the Top," which was the first time a member of Siemens ZV strongly and directly sent a message to a large group of employees that corruption would not be tolerated and was contrary to Siemens' principles of integrity. In this speech, Officer C proposed that in order to impose more control over consulting agreements and "offset the[ir] danger," such agreements should be reviewed and signed by the chairmen of the divisional boards. Officer C also suggested implementing more stringent disciplinary penalties for employees who violate internal controls and fail to cooperate with investigations. He explained that in U.S. companies, "whenever employees refuse to cooperate with the authorities, they are immediately dismissed irrespective of their position on the corporate ladder."

67. On or about August 4, 2004, Siemens promulgated its first Company-wide, comprehensive policy on the use of bank accounts and external payment orders. The policy. among other things, restricted the use of bank accounts controlled by Siemens employees or third parties, a mechanism that had previously been heavily used by certain operating groups, particularly COM, to make improper payments on behalf of Siemens.

68. On or about September 7, 2004, Officer C sent an email to Siemens ZV members Officer A and Officer E stating that divisional chairmen did not consider his July 2004 compliance speech as mandatory and requesting a Z Circular regarding agreements with business consultants.

69. On or about November 4, 2004, the Erlangen law firm Siemens engaged to investigate the Enel case issued its second report, and the full Siemens ZV received a briefing about the contents of the report. The report highlighted questionable payments from Siemens to a Dubai-based business consultant and to certain off-books accounts in Liechtenstein.

70. On or about November 5, 2004, the Siemens ZV received a written report identifying by name the Dubai-based purported business consultant as the conduit for the payments through Emirates Bank in the Enel matter. Nevertheless, no action was taken to investigate the broader implications of this report.

71. On or about January 26, 2005, at an Audit Committee meeting in which the Enel case was discussed, a member of the Audit Committee asked Officer C "whether pointers could be drawn from this regarding gaps in the internal control system." In response. Officer C said "the existing rules were comprehensive and clearly written down," despite the fact that he and other senior executives were aware by that time of significant control weaknesses.

72. On or about April 25, 2005, at an Audit Committee meeting in which the offbooks accounts in Liechtenstein were mentioned, a member of the Audit committee asked Officer C whether "an inference might be drawn from existing knowledge that cash deposits might exist outside Siemens AG." Despite his knowledge that such cash deposits did exist, Officer C replied that "no indication existed of any [such] accounts which may be attributable to the company and in the case that any such indication existed, the company would look into this."

73. On or about May 4, 2005, the Erlangen law firm engaged by Siemens to investigate the Enel case issued the final report of its findings to several Siemens ZV members.

74. On or about May 31, 2005, the full Siemens ZV learned at a meeting that the final report of the Enel investigation submitted by the Erlangen lawyer had discovered 126 payments totaling €190 million to Liechtenstein accounts from 1997 to 1999 for which recipients could not be identified. At the same meeting, Siemens ZV received a report that Liechtenstein authorities were investigating a former ICN employee accused of siphoning money from Siemens through sham consulting agreements. The report identified five off-books accounts in Liechtenstein that were seized. Despite striking similarities between the facts of the two reports, Siemens ZV members took no action to investigate the payments or accounts further. Similarly, Siemens ZV made no attempt to determine whether the former ICN employee had in fact embezzled company money. At the same Siemens ZV meeting, Officer B including the following statements in his presentation:

> The most important thing in each Compliance programme is the absolute commitment of management: Adherence to the laws is for us the most important commandment. Offences are not tolerated and are punished consistently and without exception. *In the Enel case, the investigating Frankfurt chief prosecutor said to a counsel for the defence of the former Siemens employees that he considered the Siemens Compliance programme to exist only on paper.* (Emphasis added.)

75. On or about July 27, 2005, Officer B made a presentation to the Audit Committee, during which he told the Audit Committee that "an investigation by an external [accountant] of unclarified payments to a bank in Liechtenstein had become necessary. This has revealed that the recipient of 126 payments totaling EUR 190 million in 1997 to 1999 could not be identified." Officer B said the information had been given to the

auditors and that [two] Z Circulars . . . had added new rules on external payments and bank accounts, which would make it possible in the future to identify payment recipients. During the same meeting, Officer B included in his presentation statements regarding the compliance and adherence to the laws that were identical to those he had made at the May 31, 2005 Siemens ZV meeting, but he removed the final sentence regarding the Frankfurt prosecutor's statement that Siemens' compliance program existed only on paper.

76. On or about July 26, 2005, the Corporate Compliance Office, at Officer G's request, completed a written benchmarking analysis comparing Siemens' compliance program and infrastructure with that of General Electric Company ("GE"). The analysis, which was distributed to Officer E and Officer G, showed serious deficiencies in Siemens' resourcing and infrastructure when compared to GE's. In particular, the analysis noted, "[t]he Compliance Office team is extremely small (six lawyers) in relation to the number of employees, and understaffed in comparison with GE." which had 300 "ombudsmen." The memorandum further pointed out that GE's program "seem[ed] more efficient than Siemens' at diffusing Compliance principles throughout the entire company." Siemens took no action to augment compliance resources in response to the benchmarking memorandum apart from Officer G ordering an audit of the compliance organization, which remained in draft form until as late as November 2006.

77. In or about July 2005, Siemens redistributed the Business Conduct Guidelines, with a new foreword by Officer G.

78. On or about June 29, 2005—nine months after Officer C's email request for consulting agreement guidelines—Siemens enacted a Z Circular containing mandatory guidelines regarding agreements with business consultants. The guidelines prohibited success fees and required relevant compliance officers to sign off on consulting agreements and attached a due diligence questionnaire.

79. On or about November 23, 2005, in his report to the Siemens ZV, Officer B commented on the lack of effectiveness of the Regional Compliance Officers. Officer B noted that when Siemens attempted to collect business consulting agreements from the regions after the June 29, 2005 Z Circular, most Regional Compliance Officers had reported that "either such agreements [did] not exist, or that the possible infringements of the laws of the Business Conduct Guidelines [were] not visible." Officer B went on to comment that "[t]aking into account the known business environments in, for example, the Asiatic territories, the correctness of this statement [had] to be questioned. It also [shed] some doubt as to the quality of the [Regional Compliance Officers]." Notwithstanding Officer B's explicit doubts that existing consulting agreements had been produced by regions as requested, there was no follow-up to seek the missing documents.

80. On or about December 7, 2005, during his presentation to the Audit Committee, Officer B made no mention of the questions he had raised at the November 23, 2005 Siemens ZV meeting regarding the Regional Compliance Officers' quality and their truthfulness in reporting on the status of business consulting agreements.

81. In or about March 2006, in the course of a compliance investigation, a Siemens Greece COM manager admitted to the Corporate Compliance Office and Internal Audit that he had received substantial funds to make "bonus payments" to managers at the Greek national telephone company, OTE. Neither the Siemens ZV nor the Corporate Compliance Office undertook a comprehensive investigation aimed at discovering the full extent of corruption in Greece or in the COM business more broadly.

82. In or about April 2006, in response to a special audit request by Intercom's board of directors, Siemens' outside auditors reported at least 250 suspicious payments made through Intercom to companies in foreign jurisdictions on behalf of COM ICM and Siemens' Italian subsidiary. The audit report was provided to the board of directors of Intercom, as well as to certain members of the Siemens ZV and the Corporate Compliance Office. Neither the Siemens ZV nor the Corporate Compliance Office made any attempt to investigate these facts, or explore whether they were related to other similar instances of wrongdoing.

83. From in or about 2004 to in or about 2006. in addition to learning of the corruption issues involving Siemens in Nigeria, Italy, Greece, Liechtenstein, and elsewhere, Siemens' senior management became aware of government investigations into corruption by Siemens in Israel. Hungary. Azerbaijan, Taiwan, and China. Nevertheless. Siemens ZV members and other senior management failed to adequately investigate or follow up on any of these issues. Siemens ZV also failed to take effective disciplinary measures with respect to any of the employees implicated in the various investigations. For example, the three PG managers implicated in the Enel cases each received a severance package standard for early retirees, despite the fact that certain Siemens ZV members knew that at least two of the PG managers had already admitted to paying bribes at the time of their retirement.

84. From in or about 2004 to in or about 2006, the Corporate Compliance Office continued to lack resources, and there was an inherent conflict in its mandate, which included both defending the company against prosecutorial investigations and preventing and punishing compliance breaches. In addition, there were extremely limited internal audit resources to support compliance efforts. All of these factors undermined the improved policies because violations were difficult to detect and remedy, and resources were insufficient to train business people in anti-corruption compliance.

85. From in or about 2004 to in or about 2006 there was a consistent failure on the part of certain members of management to alert the Audit Committee to the significance of the compliance failures discovered within Siemens. Reports to the Audit Committee by the Chief Compliance Officer were principally status reports on prosecutorial investigations and often conveyed incomplete information. In some instances, management provided inaccurate information in response to Audit Committee inquiries. At no time did management convey to the Audit Committee a sense of alarm or growing crisis.

NOTES

1. Other facts admitted by Siemens included its payment of kickbacks to Iraqi officials between 2000 and 2002 as part of the UN-administered "Food for Oil" program. The program, ostensibly designed to ease the burden of UN-imposed economic sanctions on the Iraqi general population without reducing the supposed pressure on the Iraqi regime to comply with weapons inspections requirements, became a means of enriching the Iraqi leadership as well as persons in the United Nations and various Western countries whom the leadership wished to reward. Siemens admitted to paying kickbacks of over $1.7 million and earning a gross profit of $38 million on these transactions.

2. Facing multiple investigations in Europe and the United States, Siemens replaced its top leadership and entered into negotiations that produced a plea bargain and the historic fines. The possibility of criminal prosecution of Siemens' former officials in Germany remains open, as do possible prosecutions in several other countries in which Siemens paid bribes.

3. Did coordination of the investigations by the German and U.S. authorities make it more likely that Siemens would come to grips with its past practices? Why did Siemens delay as long as it did in unwinding its corruption mechanisms?

4. While the OECD members have enacted legislation similar to the FCPA, the U.K. Bribery Act ("UKBA") has received the most attention. See the Documents Supplement for the texts of the UKBA and the UKBA Guidance. The UKBA provides new robust offenses, enhanced sentencing powers for the courts and wide jurisdictional powers to replace the antiquated UK anti-bribery legislation which dates back to 1889. The UKBA criminalizes the offences of offering or receiving bribes, as well as the bribery of foreign public officials.

The UKBA also introduces a strict liability criminal "corporate offense" that is committed where a commercial organization fails to prevent a bribe being paid on its behalf by "associated persons." It also establishes a statutory defense where a commercial organization can show "that despite a particular case of bribery it nevertheless had adequate procedures in place to prevent persons associated with it from bribing."

The UKBA Guidance, issued by the Ministry of Justice as part of the implementation of the UKBA, is not prescriptive as to the nature of systems and procedures that firms should implement to meet the "adequate procedures" standards. It maintains that a one-size-fits-all approach is simply not possible. It instead articulates six principles of bribery prevention that apply generally.

The principles should inform companies' implementation of adequate procedures; however, they remain quite high level and further definition will develop through case law. "The onus will remain on the organisation, in any case when it seeks to rely on the defense, to prove that it had adequate procedures in place to prevent bribery."

5. How does the UKBA differ from the FCPA? Is strict liability, coupled with an "adequate procedures" defense, a fairer way to treat companies whose employees engage in bribery?

C. THE INSTITUTIONALIZATION AND EXTENSION OF THE FCPA

The Department of Justice and the SEC Resource Guide seeks to provide guidance to companies and individuals on the U.S. government's enforcement policies and on how to comply with the FCPA. The Guide has contributed to a better understanding of how these U.S. government agencies enforce the FCPA. For the last several years, the threat of FCPA enforcement constituted the leading compliance risk for global companies with businesses linked to the United States. The broad discretion these agencies possess, coupled with the lack of judicial oversight because no major company was willing to litigate against the DOJ or SEC, contributed to increasingly aggressive interpretations of the law. U.S. businesses largely through trade associations, such as the U.S. Chamber of Commerce, pressed the U.S. authorities for more guidance on how those authorities interpret and apply the FCPA.

The Guide represents the U.S. authorities' response to such criticism. It serves as a useful compilation of FCPA case resolutions and will enable global companies to understand the FCPA's enforcement history. This understanding may also permit companies to predict with greater accuracy how the FCPA will be applied. The Guide clarifies certain issues and provides important direction regarding the interpretation of certain parts of the FCPA. The Guide lays out what the authorities expect regarding effective anti-corruption compliance programs and what criteria they apply in deciding to initiate enforcement actions. These contributions are sufficient to justify the issuance of the Guide and underscore the importance of this initiative.

However, there are important caveats to keep in mind in understanding the Guide. It is very much a statement of how the DOJ and SEC interpret the law in settling enforcement cases; it should not be seen as a statement of what the law actually is in many areas. Moreover, the Guide does not effectively reflect how the DOJ and SEC actually approach the investigation of facts and the resolution of cases. Although the Guide states that authorities credit a company's disclosure and cooperation with the government's investigation, U.S. authorities have yet to give explicit details as to how that is measured. How much credit to extend to a company for its cooperation is still left to the individual prosecutors who make those decisions, subject to only very general criteria.

Through the use of many examples the Guide explains certain key concepts in FCPA enforcement such as "anything of value", "corruptly" and the business purpose test. It presents an approach to defining a "foreign official" that is more nuanced than that which the government for many years had been willing to endorse. Unlike much of the Guide, these nuances have been developed by judges in litigation where individual defendants have challenged the government's broad definition of "instrumentality" as applied to foreign commercial entities. In contrast, the explanations of "facilitation payments" and the defenses available under the FCPA, the virtually useless "local law" defense and the critically important "promotional expenses" defense, offer no surprises. Nonetheless, the explanations themselves and the accompanying examples are helpful.

The Guide covers certain provisions of the FCPA that are well-known in practice. In almost textbook fashion it states the jurisdictional requirements for an FCPA case. Two points are significant. First, the Guide appears to concede that the language in the statute that requires a person not otherwise subject to the FCPA's jurisdiction, such as a foreign national, to "commit any act in furtherance of a corrupt payment while on the territory of the United States" means a physical presence, as opposed to sending an email or making a telephone call into the United States. Of course, the Guide takes that concession back by also noting that a foreign national or entity may be liable as an agent, aider and abettor or co-conspirator even if they have taken no action in the United States. Since these various legal theories give the government broad charging authority, the government, as a practical matter, will assert broad jurisdictional powers despite any limitations contained in the statute.

Second, practitioners know very well that no FCPA case before the U.S. authorities begins with a discussion of jurisdiction. The DOJ and SEC will allow a case to progress for many months before any meaningful discussion of jurisdictional limits occurs. Jurisdiction is rarely a limiting factor in an FCPA case involving a global company whose shares are listed on a U.S. stock exchange, especially because of the SEC's ability to hold parent companies strictly liable for the misconduct of their overseas subsidiaries, as reflected by deficiencies in their books and records and internal controls, even if there is no connection between the misconduct and the United States.

Certain portions of the Guide reinforce how aggressively the DOJ and SEC interpret the law. In its discussion of successor liability under the FCPA, the Guide claims that as a general matter when a company acquires another company it assumes the liabilities of the latter. Such an unqualified statement cuts too far and fails accurately to reflect basic principles of corporate law and the myriad ways that companies can structure transactions directly. To assume that every acquisition brings with it all the liabilities of the acquired company disregards commercial realities and well-established principles of limited liability. The lack of substantive discussion in the Guide of these differences illustrates how little regard the DOJ and SEC pay to corporate formalities in their approach to enforcement. This is certainly an issue on which companies can, and should, meaningfully contest the government's approach.

The Guide also assumes that a subsidiary can and, in certain circumstances, should be treated as an agent of its parent in seeking to apply the anti-bribery provisions of the FCPA to reach the misconduct of a foreign subsidiary. The approach focuses on the amount of control the parent exercises over the subsidiary as a basis for arguing that the parent should be liable for the actions of its subsidiary under an agency theory. This approach again seems to ignore the traditional principle of limited liability so critical to corporate law. While this principle is of course limited by circumstances in which the affairs of the parent and subsidiary are so intermingled that "piercing the corporate veil" and holding the parent responsible for the liabilities of the subsidiary is appropriate, such limitations are not discussed in the Guide. Established case law identifying when a company can actually be held liable for the actions of its subsidiary uses a far more rigorous analysis than the DOJ and SEC seem willing to apply. Because most FCPA cases against companies will never be litigated, the government's refusal to respect corporate distinctions has not been tested. Most important, the DOJ's apparent reluctance to acknowledge parent-subsidiary distinctions in discussing criminal liability in the Guidance gives parent companies scant comfort that they will be able to avoid prosecution even if the parent lacked knowledge of the subsidiary's criminal activities. Again, the lack of judicial oversight resonates in this portion of the Guide.

The Guide is useful to inform how the DOJ and the SEC enforce the FCPA and how these enforcement agencies hope courts will rule on their theories of enforcement, particularly in successor liability and parent-subsidiary relationships. However, the lack of substantive detail regarding these issues in the Guide reinforces the importance of careful analysis to protect the rights of companies and individuals who find themselves under the glaring light of continued aggressive enforcement.

NOTE

Consider the following excerpts from the Ralph Lauren ("RLC") FCPA case.

1.   RLC was headquartered in New York, New York and incorporated in Delaware. RLC issued and maintained a class of publicly traded securities registered pursuant to Section 12(b) of the Securities Exchange Act of 1934 (15 U.S.C. § 781), which traded on the New York Stock Exchange and, therefore, was an "issuer" within the meaning of the Foreign Corrupt Practices Act ("FCPA"), 15 U.S.C. § 78dd–1(a). RLC was in the business of design, marketing, and distribution of apparel, accessories, and other products in many countries around the world, including Argentina.

2.   PRL S.R.L. was an indirect wholly-owned subsidiary of RLC headquartered and incorporated in Argentina. PRL S.R.L. marketed and sold RLC merchandise, including merchandise that was imported from outside Argentina.

3.   General Manager A was a dual U.S. and Argentine citizen, and thus a "domestic concern," as that term is used in the FCPA, Title 15, United States Code, Section 78dd–2(h)(1)(A). General Manager A was hired by RLC to manage the business of PRL S.R.L. and from in or around 2003 until in or around 2009, General Manager A was the General Manager of PRL S.R.L., and thus was an employee and agent of an issuer, as that term is used in the FCPA, Title 15, United States Code, Section 78dd–1(a).

4.   Agent 1 was a customs clearance agency that was retained by PRL S.R.L. to assist with customs clearance issues in Argentina.

5.   From in or around 2004, and continuing through in or around 2009, PRL S.R.L. and its employees, including General Manager A, together with Agent 1 and others, conspired to make unlawful payments to foreign officials to use the officials' influence with foreign government agencies and instrumentalities in order to assist PRL S.R.L. in obtaining and retaining business for and with, and directing business to PRL S.R.L.

3-2

Section D

problem 71-72

Problem #

①

③

)ort licenses and
rted into Argentina.
customs clearance

hers at PRL S.R.L.
officials to assist in
for goods to clear
1out the necessary
bited items, and to
routine government
Code, Section 78dd–

thers at PRL S.R.L.
2ed to pay bribes to
by which the bribes
called the offices of
1eed to make bribe
poke with General

Manager A or the Area Manager of PRL S.R.L.

9.   General Manager A, Agent 1, and others disguised the bribe payments by having Agent 1 include the payments in Agent 1's invoices as "Loading and Delivery Expenses" and "Stamp Tax/Label Tax." General Manager A and others at PRL S.R.L. knew of the true purpose of these expenses and nonetheless approved reimbursement to Agent 1.

10.   For example, on April 14, 2009, Agent 1 submitted an invoice to PRL S.R.L. for General Manager A's approval that contained a line item for "Loading and Delivery Expenses" in the amount of $4,315 and a line item for "Stamp Tax/Label Tax" in the amount of $1,984.

11.   On April 21, 2009, Agent 1 submitted an invoice to PRL S.R.L. for General Manager A's approval that contained a line item for "Loading and Delivery Expenses" in the amount of $1,986 and a line item for "Stamp Tax/Label Tax" in the amount of $750.

12.   On May 19, 2009, Agent 1 submitted an invoice to PRL S.R.L. for General Manager A's approval that contained a line item for "Loading and Delivery Expenses" in the amount of $3,847 and a line item for "Stamp Tax/Label Tax" in the amount of $1,936.

13.   On May 28, 2009, Agent 1 submitted an invoice to PRL S.R.L. for General Manager A's approval that contained a line item for "Loading and Delivery Expenses" in the amount of $2,986 and a line item for "Stamp Tax/Label Tax" in the amount of $2,740.

14.   On or about September 22, 2009, Agent 1 sent a letter to PRL S.R.L. describing new customs-related implementations that could result in "complications" and "major delays" in importing goods, but that "we have adopted a strategy together with you to successfully cope with this situation, thus, achieving a reduction in delays and the impact on the Company."

15.   In the five years that General Manager A, Agent 1, and others at PRL S.R.L. carried out this scheme, RLC did not have an

anti-corruption program and did not provide any anti-corruption training or oversight with respect to PRL S.R.L.

16.   In total, General Manager A and PRL S.R.L. paid roughly $580,000 to Agent 1 for the purpose of paying bribes to customs officials in order to obtain improper customs clearance of merchandise.

The Justice Department did not have to prove that it had jurisdiction over the misconduct in Argentina, because RLC, like virtually all companies facing FCPA violations, settled with the Justice Department. However, what is the basis for the Justice Department's assertion of jurisdiction? Note how the Justice Department treats the General Manager of Ralph Lauren's Argentinian subsidiary. Should an employee of a foreign subsidiary be considered an agent of the parent? Under what circumstances should the subsidiary itself be considered an agent of the parent? Does the Justice Department's approach to this issue create, in essence, strict liability for parent corporations for the criminal acts of their subsidiaries? Consider Philip Urofsky's thoughtful analyses in "The Ralph Lauren Case: Are There Any Limits to Parent Corporation Liability? (Bloomberg Law, May 13, 2013).

D. FRAUD AND MONEY LAUNDERING

The FCPA remains the principal federal statute dealing with corruption. Are there others? What about participation in transactions that conceal the origins of criminal activity, including bribery of foreign government officials? Corrupt payments by their nature involve secrecy and an exchange of benefits. It seems plausible that secret deals that enrich some at the expense of others also constitute fraud. Furthermore, otherwise straightforward financial transactions—the sale of an interest in a business or other property—might constitute money laundering, if the business or property represents the proceeds of criminal activity. Here we explore the extent to which federal statutes criminalizing fraud and money laundering may reach emerging market transactions.

A PROBLEM

The General Director of Vostokneftegaz wishes to invest $1,000,000 of his own money in the joint venture company that Petro and Vostokneftegaz intend to form. The money would be invested by an offshore entity located in a Caribbean tax haven, in which entity the General Director apparently has a controlling interest. He wants to receive a 5% interest in the joint venture company in return for his investment and other services to be rendered by him.

1.   What problems, if any, might Petro have under the U.S. Foreign Corrupt Practices Act?

2.   Does it matter if it comes to light that the General Director's wealth reflects oil trading activities in which he buys cheap oil from state firms and then sells the product at high international prices?

3.   The General Director is later removed from office. Petro would like to buy out his interest. What problems might arise?

Review 18 U.S.C. § 1956 in the Documents Supplement. Would embezzlement of money by a foreign official from the Russian government constitute a "specified offense" within the meaning of § 1856(c)(7)? If the money invested by the offshore entity constitutes the proceeds of a specified offense, what legal risks would Petro face in buying out that interest? What steps could it take to ameliorate that risk? Focus on the intent requirements of § 1856(a).

The overlap between fraud subject to U.S. criminal prosecution and corrupt payments to foreign officials is a matter of controversy. Consider the following case (the facts of which inspired, in the most elastic sense of that word, the popular film *Syriana*). Ultimately Giffen pleaded guilty to a misdemeanor tax charge and received no jail time or probation.

United States of America v. James H. Giffen

United States District Court for the Southern District of New York

326 F. Supp. 2d 497 (2004)

■ WILLIAM H. PAULEY III, DISTRICT JUDGE:

The defendant, James H. Giffen ("Defendant" or "Giffen"), moves to dismiss portions of the 62-count indictment against him. The indictment charges Giffen with making unlawful payments totaling more than $78 million to Nurlan Balgimaev, the former Prime Minister and Oil Minister of the Republic of Kazakhstan, and Nursultan Nazarbaev, the current President of Kazakhstan (collectively, "senior Kazakh officials") in violation of the Foreign Corrupt Practices Act (the "FCPA"), 15 U.S.C. § 78dd–2 et seq., mail and wire fraud statutes, 18 U.S.C. §§ 1341, 1343, 1346, money laundering statutes, 18 U.S.C. §§ 1956, 1957, and the federal income tax laws. 26 U.S.C. §§ 7206, 7212.

Giffen moves to dismiss: (1) Counts One through Fifty-Nine on the ground that they are precluded by the act of state doctrine; and (2) those portions of Counts Fifteen through Twenty-Three that allege a scheme to deprive the citizens of Kazakhstan of the honest services of their government officials.

For the reasons set forth below, Giffen's motion to dismiss is granted in part and denied in part.

BACKGROUND

The indictment alleges that between 1995 and 1999, Giffen made unlawful payments totaling $78 million to senior Kazakh officials to obtain business for his New York-headquartered company Mercator Corporation ("Mercator"). From the business obtained by Mercator, Giffen directed millions of dollars in unreported compensation to a Mobil Oil executive, a Mercator employee and himself. The Indictment alleges a series of complex financial transactions that enabled Mercator to conceal illicit payments to the senior Kazakh officials.

Kazakhstan, formerly a republic within the Soviet Union, became a sovereign nation in 1991. Kazakhstan has vast oil and gas reserves, which are the property of the Kazakh government. Since its independence, Kazakhstan has sold rights to its oil and gas reserves to international oil companies. The Kazakh government hired Mercator to advise it regarding these oil and gas transactions.

The indictment alleges that on or about August 1, 1995, Giffen was named a Counselor to the President of Kazakhstan. The Counselor position was a semi-official title that enabled Giffen to effect numerous oil and gas transactions. In December 1994, Mercator entered into an agreement with the Kazakh Ministry of Oil and Gas Industries to assist the Ministry in developing a strategy for foreign investment in Kazakhstan's natural resources. The agreement further provided that Mercator would receive substantial success fees if the oil and gas transactions were completed.

Between 1995 and 2000, Mercator received nearly $67 million in success fees from the Kazakh government for its work on the Tengiz oil fields, the Karachaganak oil and gas fields, the Caspian Pipeline, the Karachaganak Production Sharing Agreement, the Offshore Kazakhstan International Operating Company, and the Kazakh oil transactions.

Apart from Mercator's success fees on these transactions, Giffen deposited approximately $70 million into escrow accounts at Banque Indosuez and its successor, Credit Agricole Indosuez, located in Switzerland. According to the indictment, Giffen then diverted these escrow monies into the Swiss bank accounts of several different offshore entities to conceal the fact that they were benefitting the senior Kazakh officials.

In total, the Government contends that Giffen funneled more than $78 million in cash and luxury items to the senior Kazakh officials for their personal benefit. For example, Giffen purportedly paid $36,000 of Balgimbaev's personal bills, and gifted an $80,000 speedboat to Nazarbaev. According to the indictment, the senior Kazakh officials had the power to help obtain and retain "lucrative business as advisors and counselors to the government of Kazakhstan." The illegal payments thus ensured that Giffen and Mercator "remained in a position from which they could divert large sums from oil transactions into accounts for the benefit of senior Kazakh officials and Giffen personally."

Based on these allegations, the indictment charges Giffen with numerous federal crimes, including, inter alia, (i) conspiracy to violate the FCPA and substantive FCPA crimes; (ii) conspiracy to defraud Kazakhstan of "tens of millions of dollars" and substantive counts of mail and wire fraud; and (iii) conspiracy to participate in a scheme to "deprive the citizens of Kazakhstan of their intangible right to the honest services of their political leaders" and substantive counts of mail and wire fraud.

. . .

III. Deprivation of Honest Services

The indictment alleges that Giffen's actions violated 18 U.S.C. § 1346 by depriving the citizens of Kazakhstan of the honest services of their government officials. Giffen asserts that application of the honest services theory of Section 1346 to Kazakhstan impermissibly extends the mail and wire fraud statutes to cover activities beyond Congress' original intent. He also argues that Section 1346 is unconstitutionally vague as applied to him, and that it violates fundamental principles of international comity.

Notably, Giffen does not challenge the indictment's reliance on the mail and wire fraud statutes to criminalize schemes that deprive foreign victims of money or property. Thus, Giffen does not seek dismissal of Counts Fifteen through Twenty-Three to the extent they rely on the mail and wire fraud statutes.

A.   Section 1346's Scope

Section 1346 provides: "For the purposes of this chapter, the term 'scheme or artifice to defraud' includes a scheme or artifice to deprive another of the intangible right of honest services." 18 U.S.C. § 1346. In 1988, Congress enacted Section 1346 to overrule *McNally v. United States*, 483 U.S. 350, 358 (1987), and reinstate the intangible rights theory. In *McNally*, the Supreme Court held that the then-existing mail fraud statute did not criminalize schemes "designed to deprive individuals, the people, or the government of intangible rights, such as the right to have public officials perform their duties honestly." As such, under *McNally*, schemes to deprive others of their intangible rights to good government and honest services were beyond the mail and wire fraud proscriptions.

"When [Congress] enacted . . . [Section 1346] Congress was recriminalizing mail- and wire-fraud schemes to deprive others of that 'intangible right of honest services,' which had been protected before *McNally*." Accordingly, this Court must examine pre-*McNally* precedent to determine whether the honest services theory is applicable to a United States citizen for deprivation of honest services by foreign government officials to foreign nationals.

The Government argues that pre-*McNally* jurisprudence applied the wire and mail fraud statutes to criminalize deprivation of honest services to foreign citizens by their own governments. However, the Government offers the slenderest of reeds to support its expansive interpretation; namely, an indictment in this district in 1978 and another the same year in the District of Columbia. At argument, the Government conceded that there were no court decisions addressing the validity of the two 25-year old indictments. Nor could the Government point to any decision where a court upheld application of the honest services theory in an international setting involving a foreign government and its citizens.

Of more recent vintage, the Government alluded to United States v. Lazarenko, No. CR 00–0284 (MJJ), pending in the Northern District of California. There, the defendant, a former president of the Republic of Ukraine, was charged with depriving Ukrainian citizens of the honest services of their government officials. Tellingly, the district court dismissed the honest services charge at the close of the evidence, because the government failed to prove that the defendant violated any provision of Ukrainian law analogous to Section 1346. Notably, the *Lazarenko* court required the Government to show the existence of a law in Ukraine analogous to Section 1346 that was violated by the defendant. Here, however, the Government makes no allegation regarding any Kazakh law, much less a Kazakh statute, analogous to Section 1346. In fact, the Government noted that it did not intend to provide the jury with any Kazakh law on this issue.

That three different United States Attorneys in three different districts over a twenty-five year time span obtained indictments under an intangible rights theory, grounded between a foreign government and its citizenry, is not the kind or quality of precedent this Court need consider. The Government has not unearthed any published decision on this issue. The question appears to be one of first impression.

The touchstone is whether any pre-*McNally* precedent supports prosecution of American citizens for depriving foreign nationals of the honest services of their own government officials. In view of the total absence of pre-*McNally* precedent supporting the Government's overseas application of the intangible rights theory, this Court concludes that in enacting Section 1346 Congress was merely recriminalizing the deprivation of the intangible right to honest services as it existed before *McNally*. As a corollary, this Court holds that Section 1346 did not criminalize deprivations of "all intangible rights of honest services, whatever they might be thought to be." In fact, "there is no reason to think that Congress sought to grant carte blanche to federal prosecutors, judges and juries to define 'honest services' from case to case for themselves."

The Government also argues that Congress' 1988 amendments to the FCPA considered and rejected the notion that mail and wire fraud statutes should not reach bribery of foreign government officials. From this, the Government draws two conclusions: (1) Congress was aware that foreign bribery violated the mail and wire fraud statutes as they existed in 1988; and (2) Congress was comfortable with that result. The Government's contention is not persuasive. Subsequent legislative history does not provide a reasonable platform to interpret an original statute's text or legislative history. Indeed, discarded legislative proposals are seldom useful in interpreting an existing statute.

Accordingly, this Court finds that Congress did not intend that the intangible right to honest services encompass bribery of foreign officials in foreign countries.

. . .

C. International Comity

Finally, Giffen contends that the application of the intangible rights theory to him presents a "non-justiciable" controversy. Giffen argues that "there can be no violation of Section 1346 in a public corruption case unless a government official owed a duty of honest services to the public." He further contends that while the scope of "honest services" is well understood in the United States, it is obscure and ambiguous in a developing nation, like Kazakhstan.

The concept of the Kazakh people's intangible right to honest services by their government officials requires definition. The indictment does not allege any facts or law regarding the meaning of honest services by Kazakh officials to the Kazakh people. The Government's argument that "the notion that government officials owe a duty to provide honest services to the public is not so idiosyncratically American as to have no application at all to Kazakhstan" is inapposite and begs the question. In a jarring disconnect, the Government acknowledges that "Kazakhstan has sought to derail the investigation and eventual prosecution of this matter by numerous appeals to officials . . . in the executive branch including . . . [the] Departments of State and Justice." Implicit in the Government's observation is the suggestion that Kazakhstan itself is unable to define "honest services" within its own polity.

In effect, the Government urges that American notions of honesty in public service developed over two centuries be engrafted on Kazakh jurisprudence. "While admittedly some . . . countries do not take their [anti-corruption] responsibilities seriously, the correct answer to such a situation is not the extraterritorial application of United States law but rather cooperation between [the appropriate] home and host country . . . authorities." "An argument in favor of the export of United States law represents not only a form of legal imperialism but also embodies the essence of sanctimonious chauvinism." While well intentioned, the Government's suggestion that American legal standards be exported to Kazakhstan is simply a bridge too far.

> . . .

NOTES

1. The holding of the *Giffen* court on comity (but not its interpretation of Section 1346) is inconsistent with the reasoning of the subsequent Supreme Court decision *Pasquantino v. United States*, 545 U.S. 349 (2005). *Pasquantino* involved a scheme to smuggle cigarettes into Canada to avoid paying Canadian taxes. The Court ruled that Canada's right to tax imported cigarettes constituted a property right within the meaning the federal antifraud provisions. The Court further held that Congress had not incorporated a strong form of the common-law revenue rule into these provisions. Under the revenue rule, one sovereign does not enforce the penal laws of another, but the Court ruled that "enforcement" was subject to multiple interpretations. Canada was not using the U.S. court directly to collect its taxes; rather, the United States was imposing criminal sanctions on the evader of foreign taxes. The Court asserted that whatever policy concerns derived from comity considerations might apply were not for the judiciary to consider; the Executive branch took them into account in deciding to prosecute, and its calculus is not subject to judicial review.

2. Suppose Petro hires Prikazy, after taking appropriate steps to prevent him from improperly influencing Russian government decisions. Suppose that Prikazy insists on receiving his compensation through a Cayman Islands bank account. Further suppose that Russian law forbids Russian citizens from receiving payment in foreign currency for rendering services in Russia, and also forbids Russian citizens from holding foreign currency in foreign bank accounts without a license from the Central Bank. Presumably the Russian authorities impose these rules to prevent taxpayers from hiding taxable income. By making payments to the Cayman Islands account, does Petro facilitate the evasion of Russian financial and tax laws? If so, could Petro be guilty of wire fraud?

3. Bribery at its heart involves secret ("corrupt") payments made to procure special treatment. Money laundering also involves corrupt payments, but the goal is to conceal the source of the proceeds used to make the payment. Wire fraud and money laundering may overlap, if the money obtained by fraud then is used in a subsequent transaction that has as its purpose concealment of the prior fraud. Working with the *Giffen* facts, suppose that Banque Indosuez had transferred the money deposited by Giffen into a brokerage account, which the corrupt Kazakh officials then used to buy stock. Suppose that Banque Indosuez officials had reason to know where the money had come from. Could 18 U.S.C. § 1956 apply?

4. Wire fraud and money laundering are criminal offenses. Can they also result in civil liability? Consider the following case.

Kensington International Limited v. Société Nationale des Pétroles du Congo

United States District Court for the Southern District of New York
2006 WL 846351

■ Loretta A. Preska, United States District Judge:

Kensington International Limited ("Plaintiff") brings this action against Société Nationale Des Pétroles Du Congo, Bruno Jean-Richard Itoua, BNP [Paribas] S.A. (collectively, "Defendants") under the civil RICO statute alleging a conspiracy to misappropriate the resources, including oil, of the Republic of Congo ("Congo") for the private use of allegedly corrupt public officials and to facilitate and conceal that misappropriation, all at the expense of the Congolese people and of legitimate creditors like Kensington. Defendants now move to dismiss for, *inter alia*, failure to state a RICO claim and a variety of jurisdictional infirmities. For the reasons set forth below, Defendants' motions are denied.

BACKGROUND

Plaintiff, a corporation organized and existing under the laws of the Cayman Islands, purchases foreign debt instruments issued by U.S. and foreign entities. Kensington is managed by Elliott International Capital Advisors, Inc., a Delaware corporation with its principal place of business in New York City. From 1996 to 2001, Plaintiff obtained the "right, title and interest" as lender under various Congo loan agreements of which Congo is in default. Defendant Société Nationale Des Petroles Du Congo ("SNPC"), which was created by statute in 1998, is Congo's principal state oil company. Defendant Bruno Jean-Richard Itoua ("Itoua") was SNPC's Chief Executive during the relevant time period. Defendant BNP Paribas S.A. ("BNP") is a French bank with a branch office in New York City. Following its investigation, Plaintiff alleges that it discovered a money laundering scheme by Defendants to keep funds earned from oil revenues from creditors through the management of SNPC and through "complex, convoluted and unconventionally structured" Prepayment Agreements.

Plaintiff alleges that it has been unable to collect on its rights as a creditor because Defendants have transported stolen oil in foreign commerce and sold those goods in the United States in violation of 18 U.S.C. §§ 2314, 2315. Plaintiff alleges that Defendants worked through the SNPC and Prepayment Enterprises, to create a system of Prepayment Agreements using "straw men," or sham intermediaries, to misappropriate Congo's oil and oil revenues. According to the Complaint, BNP loaned Congo about $650 million, and SNPC pledged about $1.4 billion in oil sales in an "excessive over collateralization [that] served to shield a substantial portion of Congo's oil revenues from both oversight and attachment by creditors." Plaintiff alleges that Defendants sold at least eleven shipments of stolen oil totaling 9,210,221 barrels to United States purchasers. After the oil was sold, proceeds from at least one sale were deposited into BNP's New York branch.

Defendants move to dismiss the complaints against them on several grounds. First, SNPC and BNP contend that this Court does not have subject matter jurisdiction over RICO claims. Second, Itoua and SNPC contend that the Court does not have personal jurisdiction over them.

Further, Itoua contends—in his reply brief—that he was improperly served. Third, BNP and Itoua argue forum non conveniens. Fourth, SNPC, BNP, and Itoua argue that Plaintiff has failed to state a RICO claim, including that Plaintiff lacks standing to maintain a RICO claim. Fifth, SNPC and Itoua contend that they are immune under the Foreign Sovereign Immunities Act.

DISCUSSION

. . .

I. *Subject Matter Jurisdiction*

SNPC and BNP argue that this Court does not have subject matter jurisdiction over RICO claims. Subject matter exists in federal district court if the action involves a federal question. 28 U.S.C. § 1331. The civil RICO statute, 18 U.S.C. § 1961 *et seq.*, and the money laundering statute, 18 U.S.C. § 1956, invoke federal questions. Defendants urge the Court to find that the alleged fraud occurred outside the United States and thus to apply the Court of Appeals' conduct or effects test to determine jurisdiction." However, where racketeering activities . . . occur within the United States, it is unnecessary to apply any test for determining the extraterritorial reach of the Statute." This Court has jurisdiction where there were "domestic communications or negotiations that were material to the completion of the alleged fraud," or "RICO predicate acts occurred primarily in the United States."

Here, Kensington has alleged numerous predicate acts that occurred in the United States as part of Defendants' alleged money-laundering scheme, including selling eleven shipments of stolen oil totaling 9,210,221 barrels to United States purchasers, and SNPC's paying multimillion dollar option premium payments to BNP's New York branch, It is not necessary to apply the Court of Appeals' conduct or effects test to determine jurisdiction because a sufficient amount of activity is alleged to have occurred domestically. Thus, Defendants SNPC and BNP's motion to dismiss for lack of subject matter jurisdiction is denied.

[The court's discussion of personal jurisdiction and forum non conveniens is omitted.]

IV. *Failure to State a RICO Claim*

Defendants move pursuant to 12(b)(6) of the Federal Rules of Civil Procedure on the ground that Plaintiff has failed to state a RICO claim. "Dismissal of a civil RICO complaint for failure to state a claim is appropriate only when 'it is clear that no relief could be granted under any set of facts that could be proved consistent with [plaintiff's] allegations.' "

A. *Standing to Maintain a RICO Claim*

To begin, Defendants argue that Plaintiff lacks standing to maintain a RICO claim. The statute provides as follows: "Any person injured in his business or property by reason of a violation of section 1962 of this chapter may sue therefor in any appropriate United States district court." 18 U.S.C. § 1964(c). The Court of Appeals has explained the three elements that a plaintiff must plead to demonstrate standing: " '(1) the defendant's violation of [§] 1962, (2) an injury to the plaintiff's business or property, and (3) causation of the injury by the defendant's violation.

This third requirement is satisfied if the defendant's injurious conduct is both the factual and the proximate cause of the injury alleged.' "

The first two standing factors were clearly pleaded; the issue here is whether proximate cause was properly pleaded. I must analyze a two-part test for proximate causation:

> First, the plaintiff's injury must have been "proximately caused by a pattern of racketeering activity violating [18 U.S.C. §] 1962 or by individual RICO predicate acts." . . . Second, the plaintiff must have suffered a direct injury that was foreseeable: "Central to the notion of proximate cause [under RICO] is the idea that a person is not liable to all those who may have been injured by his conduct, but only to those with respect to whom his acts were 'a substantial factor in the sequence of responsible causation,' and whose injury was 'reasonably foreseeable or anticipated as a natural consequence.' "

As to the first part of the test, I must determine if Plaintiff's injury was proximately caused by a pattern of racketeering activity or by individual RICO predicate acts. The Court of Appeals generally has found creditors' injuries to be derivative and not proximately caused by the RICO violations. The Court of Appeals, however, has recognized "a narrow exception to the general rule denying creditors standing" when the creditors of a bankrupt company sustained a "direct injury." . . . Plaintiff alleges a direct injury of having been defrauded as a creditor as part of the scheme to hide proceeds of the oil shipments. As discussed below, Plaintiff has sufficiently alleged Defendants' racketeering pattern of money laundering through what Plaintiff calls the "SNPC Enterprise" and the "Prepayment Enterprise." Thus, Plaintiff has met the first part of the proximate cause test to establish standing.

As to the second part of the test,

> the foreseeability component of proximate cause is established where the plaintiff was a "target[ ]" and "intended victim[ ] of the racketeering enterprise," even if he was not the primary target or victim, and . . . "no precedent suggests that a racketeering enterprise may have only one 'target,' or that only a primary target has standing."

. . . In this case, . . . the scheme that Plaintiff alleges is that the three Defendants acted intentionally to hide the oil proceeds, precisely to avoid their creditors. Plaintiff alleges that BNP and SNPC were involved in an "excessive over collateralization [that] served to shield a substantial portion of Congo's oil revenues from both oversight and attachment by creditors" by pledging about "$1.4 billion in oil sales" to BNP to support about $650 million in loans. Further, Plaintiff alleges that "when legal actions by Congo's creditors threatened to disrupt the Prepayment Agreements, these arrangements were deliberately modified [by Defendants] to provide greater obscurity for the transactions and greater protection from attachment for SNPC's assets." Then, Plaintiff alleges, "In October 2002, BNP Paribas, SNPC, and their lawyers met to consider ways of restructuring the Prepayment Agreements to evade creditor's legal actions." Also, Plaintiff alleges, "In December 2002, BNP Paribas granted a new Prepayment Agreement to SNPC, with modifications explicitly intended to further shield the lending arrangement from other creditors." Thus, Plaintiff also has met the second part of the proximate cause test and has established standing, and thus Defendants' motions to dismiss for lack of standing are denied.

B.   *Pleading the Elements of the Predicate Offense*

. . . At issue in this case is whether there was an "enterprise" and whether there was "racketeering activity."

The RICO statute defines "enterprise" as "any individual, partnership, corporation, association, or other legal entity, and any union or group of individuals associated in fact although not a legal entity." 18 U.S.C. § 1961(4). The Court of Appeals has noted the Supreme Court's explanation of a RICO enterprise as " 'a group of persons associated together for a common purpose of engaging in a course of conduct,' the existence of which is proven 'by evidence of an ongoing organization, formal or informal, and by evidence that the various associates function as a continuing unit.' " "The enterprise must be separate from the pattern of racketeering activity and distinct from the person conducting the affairs of the enterprise." The Court of Appeals explained that RICO requirements are "most easily satisfied when the enterprise is a formal legal entity" but stated that "an enterprise may be found where there is simply a 'discrete economic association existing separately from the racketeering activity.' " [The Court of Appeals] goes on to state that the Court "further requires that a nexus exist between the enterprise and the racketeering activity that is being conducted."

Here, Plaintiff alleges the existence of one "corporation enterprise," the "SNPC Enterprise," allegedly consisting of SNPC, Itoua, and BNP, and one "association-in-fact enterprise," the "Prepayment Enterprise," consisting of SNPC, Itoua, and BNP. Plaintiff alleges that BNP associated with these enterprises since their inception, and that BNP is "the originator," "major facilitator," and "financier" of the mechanisms used by the enterprises to carry out their "illegal activities." Further, Plaintiff alleges that BNP worked with SNPC to restructure and modify the Prepayment Agreements in 2002 and 2003, and then to "keep[ ] SNPC in a state of permanent indebtedness and retain[ ] management and control over SNPC's principal assets and revenues" by providing loans that exceeded the value of any single oil cargo. For purposes of pleading "a short and plain statement," Plaintiff's allegations of enterprise are sufficient as to each Defendant—particularly in the case of the "SNPC Enterprise." . . .

As to the "racketeering activity," acts of money laundering indictable under 18 U.S.C. § 1956 and transport of stolen property indictable under 18 U.S.C. §§ 2314, 2315 are among the predicate acts enumerated in 18 U.S.C. § 1961(1). Plaintiff alleges that Defendants committed acts of money laundering and transportation of stolen oil in foreign commerce, constituting the predicate acts for the RICO claims. For example, as to SNPC, Plaintiff alleges several times that "SNPC did not make full payment to Congo for the oil" in transactions in 2001, 2002, and 2004–05, and that "the transactions in which [SNPC] was involved were highly unusual and outside normal and legitimate business arrangements," done in secrecy to help divert the funds from Congo. As to BNP, Plaintiff alleges that the unusual structure and complexity of the Prepayment Agreements was explicitly intended to enable BNP Paribas to deliver Congo's oil into the hands of international buyers and deliver the sales proceeds back to the Sassou-Nguesso regime without interference from Congo's unpaid creditors and without oversight from anyone outside the regime's inner circle. . . . The substantial, above-market fees collected by BNP Paribas for the numerous elements of these complex transactions effectively constitute the premium charged for laundering both oil sales and cash revenues for the regime.

As to Itoua, Plaintiff alleges that

Itoua, as President and General Manager of SNPC, was aware that SNPC obtained oil from Congo without full compensation and that he personally received a portion of the oil revenues. He was aware that the Prepayment Agreements were carried out in secret to facilitate those illegal transactions and to conceal the source and ultimate disposition of the proceeds. . . . He personally signed all documents comprising the Prepayment Agreements on behalf of SNPC.

For purposes of pleading "a short and plain statement," Plaintiff's allegations of racketeering activity are sufficient as to each Defendant.

[The court's discussion of the Foreign Sovereign Immunities Act is omitted.]

NOTES

1.   On appeal, the Second Circuit ruled that SNPC enjoyed immunity under the Foreign Sovereign Immunities Act, and remanded the case to the district court to reconsider Itoua's claim to immunity. 505 F.3d 147 (2d Cir. 2007).

2.   Focus on the allegations against BNP. How does its conduct fit within the money laundering statute? What steps could it take to minimize its liability?

3.   Note that RICO does not create a new substantive offense, but rather increases penalties and creates a basis for a civil suit in situations where conduct criminalized under other statutes also satisfies its "criminal enterprise" requirements. Where it applies, RICO both enhances criminal penalties and permits private lawsuits pursuant to which the plaintiff may collect treble damages.

4.   What about exposure to civil suits under the FCPA? The principal legal risk faced by a firm that makes corrupt payments is criminal prosecution, with SEC administrative sanctions also a possibility. Private civil suits for the moment do not seem to present a significant problem. One court of appeals has ruled that persons injured by FCPA violations do not have an implied right to recover damages under that statute, which does not expressly provide for any private relief. *Lamb v. Phillip Morris, Inc.*, 915 F.2d 1024 (6th Cir. 1990). Nor are violations of the FCPA covered by the Racketeering Influenced and Corrupt Organizations Act (RICO), which does authorize the recovery of treble damages in civil suits. But if an FCPA violation also comes within the ambit of one of RICO's specified offenses, such as wire or mail fraud, then a "pattern" of bribe paying may constitute a RICO violation and open the bribe payer up to a civil suit. *Environmental*

Tectonics v. W.S. Kirkpatrick, Inc., 847 F.2d 1052 (3rd Cir. 1988), *aff'd on other grounds*, 493 U.S. 400 (1990).

5. Normally only a business competitor who loses an opportunity because of a bribe or a foreign government that overpaid for goods or services would have standing to sue under RICO. *See, e.g., Oceanic Exploration Co. v. ConocoPhillips, Inc.*, 2008 WL 1777003 (S.D. Tex. 2008) (dismissing claim for failure to plead proximate causation between bribe and injury). How does Kensington have standing under RICO?

6. Anticorruption rules do not exhaust the problem of home country regulation of transactions undertaken by firms in emerging markets. Suppose a firm seeks to extract resources in a region beset by civil conflict. Further suppose that the only effective authority in the region where this firm operates is a paramilitary organization that acts independently of the host government. Also suppose that the Secretary of State has designated the effectively ruling entity as a "foreign terrorist organization" (FTO) pursuant to 8 U.S.C. § 1189. Were our hypothetical firm to compensate the ruling entity for providing security and other services, would these payments constitute a violation of the Global Terrorism Sanctions Regulations? *See* 50 U.S.C. § 1705(b) (the International Emergency Economic Powers Act); 31 C.F.R. § 594.204 (regulations implementing post-911 sanctions on terrorist organizations). In March 2007, Chiquita Brands International pled guilty to violating these rules, because its Colombian subsidiary had paid the AUC, a right-wing paramilitary organization designated as a FTO, for providing security to its banana-growing operations. The subsidiary believed that the AUC would have organized attacks on its property and employees if it had not made these payments. As part of the settlement, Chiquita paid a $25 million fine. The senior executives with knowledge of this transaction were not subjected to sanctions. (Interestingly, Chiquita Brands' lawyer in this case, Eric Holder, is now Attorney General of the United States). The Eleventh Circuit dismissed a subsequent civil suit on behalf of persons alleged to have suffered torture and murder in Colombia. *Cardona v. Chiquita Brands Intern., Inc.*, 2014 WL 3638854 (11th Cir. 2014).

E. CIVIL LIABILITY FOR HUMAN RIGHTS VIOLATIONS

With respect to human rights violations, the corrupt-payments pattern of significant criminal law risk and uncertain civil liability is reversed. The criminal risk under U.S. law is uncertain, as most of the relevant statutes focus on misconduct by government officials, not private actors. But the Judiciary Act of 1789, the first enactment constituting the federal courts of the United States, contained a provision today codified at 28 U.S.C. § 1350. It states, in full, that: "The district courts shall have original jurisdiction of any civil action by an alien for a tort only, committed in violation of the law of nations or a treaty of the United States." For most of the nation's history, litigants ignored this provision. It seemed only to provide for jurisdiction over certain kinds of suits, rather than extending the enforcement mechanism that might apply to international law violations. But then a court of appeals, urged on by the Carter Administration, discovered what now is called the Alien Tort Statute or the Alien Tort Claims Act and gave birth to a new subject of litigation, namely violations of international human rights. *Filartiga v. Peña-Irala*, 630 F.2d 876 (2nd Cir. 1980).

Filartiga involved allegations that the defendant, a Paraguayan police official who had come to the United States, had tortured and killed the plaintiffs' son and brother. As the defendant had no assets and already was in the process of being expelled from the United States for violating the conditions of his visa, the judgment was not expected to produce any compensation, but the court believed it important that the United States go on record as opposing torture. Congress later enacted a law expressly providing for a right of compensation for victims of torture and extrajudicial killings. Torture Victims Protection Act of 1991, Pub. L. No. 102–256, 106 Stat. 73 (1992) (codified at 28 U.S.C. § 1350 note).

These events left open what constitutes a tort in "violation of the law of nations." The 1991 legislation also did not indicate the legal basis of civil suits based on claims other than torture or extrajudicial killing, or what concepts of complicity would extend liability beyond those who directly carried out the offending conduct. Since 1991, an increasing number of cases have involved multinational firms operating in emerging markets. The cases are vexing because of the indefinite nature of international human rights law, which in any event does not expressly create civil remedies.

In 2004, the Supreme Court for the first time took up the issue of the meaning of § 1350. *Sosa v. Alvarez-Machain*, 542 U.S 692 (2004). The case involved a claim for damages against a Mexican police official who had assisted U.S. Drug Enforcement Agency officials in seizing a suspected murderer in Mexico and transporting him to the United States. An earlier decision of the Court had held that the fact of this informal rendition did not provide a basis for throwing out the murder prosecution. *United States v. Alvarez-Machain*, 504 U.S. 655 (1992). In *Sosa*, the Court refused to recognize a customary international law norm forbidding arbitrary detention and thus threw out the lawsuit. A majority of the Court asserted, however, that victims of some violations of international law could bring suits under Section 1350, but only if the international norms alleged to have been transgressed were well established. It cited as examples piracy, violations of safe conducts and offenses against ambassadors, the illegality of which under international law would (the Court argued) have seemed settled at the time of the adoption of the Judiciary Act.

A PROBLEM

Petro is concerned about the costs associated with the direct and extended presence of its personnel in remote parts of Russia in the early phases of the project. It proposes to have Vostokneftegaz handle the preparatory work, including acquisition of the land rights necessary for the building and the operation of the LNG facility and the pipeline. Recall that this involves an area populated only by indigenous ethnic groups whose collective right to occupy the land enjoys the protection of Russian constitutional law and other legislation. During construction of these facilities, Vostokneftegaz also will work with local authorities to provide security for the project.

Can Petro safely allow Vostokneftegaz to undertake these tasks without any restrictions on how to achieve the desired results? What responsibility does Petro have for any actions commissioned or procured by Vostokneftegaz? The following materials may help you frame your answers.

Kiobel v. Royal Dutch Petroleum Co.

Supreme Court of the United States

133 S. Ct. 1659 (2013)

Petitioners, a group of Nigerian nationals residing in the United States, filed suit in federal court against certain Dutch, British, and Nigerian corporations. Petitioners sued under the Alien Tort Statute, 28 U.S.C. § 1350, alleging that the corporations aided and abetted the Nigerian Government in committing violations of the law of nations in Nigeria. The question presented is whether and under what circumstances courts may recognize a cause of action under the Alien Tort Statute, for violations of the law of nations occurring within the territory of a sovereign other than the United States.

I

Petitioners were residents of Ogoniland, an area of 250 square miles located in the Niger delta area of Nigeria and populated by roughly half a million people. When the complaint was filed, respondents Royal Dutch Petroleum Company and Shell Transport and Trading Company, p.l.c., were holding companies incorporated in the Netherlands and England, respectively. Their joint subsidiary, respondent Shell Petroleum Development Company of Nigeria, Ltd. (SPDC), was incorporated in Nigeria, and engaged in oil exploration and production in Ogoniland. According to the complaint, after concerned residents of Ogoniland began protesting the environmental effects of SPDC's practices, respondents enlisted the Nigerian Government to violently suppress the burgeoning demonstrations. Throughout the early 1990's, the complaint alleges, Nigerian military and police forces attacked Ogoni villages, beating, raping, killing, and arresting residents and destroying or looting property. Petitioners further allege that respondents aided and abetted these atrocities by, among other things, providing the Nigerian forces with food, transportation, and compensation, as well as by allowing the Nigerian military to use respondents' property as a staging ground for attacks.

Following the alleged atrocities, petitioners moved to the United States where they have been granted political asylum and now reside as legal residents. They filed suit in the United States District Court for the Southern District of New York, alleging jurisdiction under the Alien Tort Statute and requesting relief under customary international law. The ATS provides, in full, that "[t]he district courts shall have original jurisdiction of any civil action by an alien for a tort only, committed in violation of the law of nations or a treaty of the United States." 28 U.S.C. § 1350. According to petitioners, respondents violated the law of nations by aiding and abetting the Nigerian Government in committing (1) extrajudicial killings; (2) crimes against humanity; (3) torture and cruel treatment; (4) arbitrary arrest and detention; (5) violations of the rights to life, liberty, security, and association; (6) forced exile; and (7) property destruction. The District Court dismissed the first, fifth, sixth, and seventh claims, reasoning that the facts alleged to support those claims did not give rise to a violation of the law of nations. The court denied respondents' motion to dismiss with respect to the remaining claims, but certified its order for interlocutory appeal pursuant to § 1292(b).

The Second Circuit dismissed the entire complaint, reasoning that the law of nations does not recognize corporate liability. We granted certiorari to consider that question. After oral argument, we directed the parties to file supplemental briefs addressing an additional question: "Whether and under what circumstances the [ATS] allows courts to recognize a cause of action for violations of the law of nations occurring within the territory of a sovereign other than the United States." We heard oral argument again and now affirm the judgment below, based on our answer to the second question.

II

Passed as part of the Judiciary Act of 1789, the ATS was invoked twice in the late 18th century, but then only once more over the next 167 years. Act of Sept. 24, 1789, § 9, 1 Stat. 77; *see Moxon v. The Fanny*, 17 F. Cas. 942 (No. 9,895) (D.C. Pa.1793); *Bolchos v. Darrel*, 3 F. Cas. 810 (No. 1,607) (D.C.S.C.1795); *O'Reilly de Camara v. Brooke*, 209 U.S. 45 (1908); *Khedivial Line, S.A.E. v. Seafarers' Int'l Union*, 278 F.2d 49, 51–52 (C.A.2 1960) (*per curiam*). The statute provides district courts with jurisdiction to hear certain claims, but does not expressly provide any causes of action. We held in *Sosa v. Alvarez-Machain*, 542 U.S. 692, 714 (2004), however, that the First Congress did not intend the provision to be "stillborn." The grant of jurisdiction is instead "best read as having been enacted on the understanding that the common law would provide a cause of action for [a] modest number of international law violations." We thus held that federal courts may "recognize private claims [for such violations] under federal common law." The Court in Sosa rejected the plaintiff's claim in that case for "arbitrary arrest and detention," on the ground that it failed to state a violation of the law of nations with the requisite "definite content and acceptance among civilized nations."

The question here is not whether petitioners have stated a proper claim under the ATS, but whether a claim may reach conduct occurring in the territory of a foreign sovereign. Respondents contend that claims under the ATS do not, relying primarily on a canon of statutory interpretation known as the presumption against extraterritorial application. That canon provides that "[w]hen a statute gives no clear indication of an extraterritorial application, it has none," *Morrison v. National Australia Bank Ltd.*, 561 U.S. 247, ___ (2010), and reflects the "presumption that United States law governs domestically but does not rule the world," *Microsoft Corp. v. AT & T Corp.*, 550 U.S. 437, 454 (2007).

This presumption "serves to protect against unintended clashes between our laws and those of other nations which could result in international discord." *EEOC v. Arabian American Oil Co.*, 499 U.S. 244, 248 (1991) (*Aramco*). As this Court has explained:

> "For us to run interference in . . . a delicate field of international relations there must be present the affirmative intention of the Congress clearly expressed. It alone has the facilities necessary to make fairly such an important policy decision where the possibilities of international discord are so evident and retaliative action so certain." The presumption against extraterritorial application helps ensure that the Judiciary does not erroneously adopt an interpretation of U.S. law that carries foreign policy consequences not clearly intended by the political branches.

We typically apply the presumption to discern whether an Act of Congress regulating conduct applies abroad. The ATS, on the other hand, is "strictly jurisdictional." *Sosa*, 542 U.S., at 713. It does not directly regulate conduct or afford relief. It instead allows federal courts to recognize certain causes of action based on sufficiently definite norms of international law. But we think the principles underlying the canon of interpretation similarly constrain courts considering causes of action that may be brought under the ATS.

Indeed, the danger of unwarranted judicial interference in the conduct of foreign policy is magnified in the context of the ATS, because the question is not what Congress has done but instead what courts may do. This Court in *Sosa* repeatedly stressed the need for judicial caution in considering which claims could be brought under the ATS, in light of foreign policy concerns. As the Court explained, "the potential [foreign policy] implications . . . of recognizing . . . causes [under the ATS] should make courts particularly wary of impinging on the discretion of the Legislative and Executive Branches in managing foreign affairs." . . . These concerns, which are implicated in any case arising under the ATS, are all the more pressing when the question is whether a cause of action under the ATS reaches conduct within the territory of another sovereign.

These concerns are not diminished by the fact that *Sosa* limited federal courts to recognizing causes of action only for alleged violations of international law norms that are "specific, universal, and obligatory." As demonstrated by Congress's enactment of the Torture Victim Protection Act of 1991, 106 Stat. 73, note following 28 U.S.C. § 1350, identifying such a norm is only the beginning of defining a cause of action. Each of these decisions carries with it significant foreign policy implications.

The principles underlying the presumption against extraterritoriality thus constrain courts exercising their power under the ATS.

III

[The Court reviewed and rejected arguments as to why causes of action implied by the ATS should not be subject to the presumption against territoriality.]

We therefore conclude that the presumption against extraterritoriality applies to claims under the ATS, and that nothing in the statute rebuts that presumption. "[T]here is no clear indication of extraterritoriality here,", and petitioners' case seeking relief for violations of the law of nations occurring outside the United States is barred.

IV

On these facts, all the relevant conduct took place outside the United States. And even where the claims touch and concern the territory of the United States, they must do so with sufficient force to displace the presumption against extraterritorial application. Corporations are often present in many countries, and it would reach too far to say that mere corporate presence suffices. If Congress were to determine otherwise, a statute more specific than the ATS would be required.

NOTES

1. In a concurring opinion, Justice Kennedy observed:

> The opinion for the Court is careful to leave open a number of significant questions regarding the reach and interpretation of the Alien Tort Statute. In my view that is a proper disposition. Many serious concerns with respect to human rights abuses committed abroad have been addressed by Congress in statutes such as the Torture Victim Protection Act of 1991 (TVPA), 106 Stat. 73, note following 28 U.S.C. § 1350, and that class of cases will be determined in the future according to the detailed statutory scheme Congress has enacted. Other cases may arise with allegations of serious violations of international law principles protecting persons, cases covered neither by the TVPA nor by the reasoning and holding of today's case; and in those disputes the proper implementation of the presumption against extraterritorial application may require some further elaboration and explanation.

Because Kennedy provided the fifth vote for the *Kiobel* majority, his view matters. What questions remain open? Note that a year earlier, a unanimous Court had held that the TVPA did not authorize lawsuits against legal entities such as corporations. *Mohamad v. Palestinian Authority*, 132 S. Ct. 1702 (2012). As Roberts's opinion noted, the Second Circuit in *Kiobel* had ruled that the ATS also did not apply to corporations. One court of appeals, in a summary ruling and over a strong dissent, interpreted the Supreme Court's decision as implicitly rejecting that holding. *Doe I v. Nestle USA, Inc.*, 738 F.3d 1048 (D.C. Cir. 2013). Another interpreted *Kiobel* as barring suits against U.S. corporations at least where the harms allegedly caused by their conduct occurred outside the United States. *Balintulo v. Daimler AG*, 727 F.3d 174 (2d Cir. 2013). But see *In re Apartheid Litigation*, 2014 WL 1569423 (S.D.N.Y. 2014) (refusing to follow *Balintulo* decision). But another court has reached the opposite conclusion, allowing a suit to proceed against a U.S. company based on alleged misconduct by U.S. citizens hired in the United States. *Al Shimari v. CACI Premier Technology, Inc.*, 2014 758 F.3d 516 (4th Cir. 2014).

2. Why is it necessary for the plaintiffs to establish that Royal Dutch Shell violated a rule of international law? Could they bring a claim against Royal Dutch Shell under Nigerian law? New York law? There may be federal constitutional limits to the application of a State's tort law to regulate conduct occurring in Nigeria. *Home Insurance Co. v. Dick*, 281 U.S. 397 (1930). The issue, however, is far from clear.

3. In many instances, a multinational firm finds itself faced with a civil suit not because it directly carried out human rights violations, but rather because it did business in a country where the government engaged in egregious behavior. The legal question becomes how to determine complicity for purposes of the so-called Alien Tort Statute. The courts of appeals have divided on the issue. Compare *Presbyterian Church of Sudan v. Talisman Energy, Inc.*, 582 F.3d 244 (2d Cir. 2009) (requiring defendant to have purpose of aiding and abetting illegal conduct), with *Doe v. Exxon Mobil Corp.*, 654 F.3d 11 (D.C. Cir. 2011) (mere knowledge of illegal conduct is sufficient).

4. To summarize, *Kiobel* may impose a considerable barrier to torts suits based on federal law against multinational companies, but the dust has not yet settled. Foreign multinationals probably have the strongest defense from federal suits. U.S. firms may be at greater risk if their conduct in the United States caused harm outside the United States, but the courts ultimately may conclude that the place of injury is decisive. Even if U.S. conduct by a U.S. firm is alleged, plaintiffs still must confront the issue of what is necessary to establish aiding-and-abetting liability. Suits under foreign or State law remain a possibility, but questions remain about these as well.

5. Up until now, human rights advocates have focused on bringing civil suits in U.S. courts, perhaps in part because of the historic role of those courts in developing the domestic law of civil rights. As barriers have arisen in the United States, however, advocates have pursued alternatives in foreign courts. *See* Jodie A. Kirshner, *Why Is the U.S. Abdicating Policing of Multinational Corporations to Europe? Extraterritoriality, Sovereignty, and the Alien Tort Statute*, 30 BERKELEY J. INT'L L. 259 (2012). Whether these efforts will succeed in imposing significant liability or otherwise affect corporate behavior remains unclear.

6. Another class of suits against multinational companies involves environmental torts, which may rest on either international or foreign law. In at least two prominent instances, U.S. corporate defendants obtained dismissal of U.S. suits on the grounds of *forum non conveniens*, arguing that the country where the harm occurred had a superior claim on the case. In both instances, populist governments then came to power that supported the plaintiffs, perhaps excessively so. The defendants suffered enormous damages awards and have ended up playing defense to block enforcement of those judgments outside the forum country. *See* Osorio v. Dow Chemical Co., 635 F.3d 1277 (11th Cir. 2011) (refusing to recognize Nicaraguan judgment); *Chevron Corp. v. Donziger*, 974 F. Supp. 2d 362 (S.D.N.Y. 2014) (finding plaintiffs and their lawyers guilty of fraud in procuring foreign judgment for environmental damages and enjoining efforts to collect on Ecuadorian judgment).

7. *Kiobel* rests on a presumption against extraterritorial effect of federal legislation. Applying this presumption can present challenging issues. In a typical case, the transaction in question has both foreign and domestic components. The issue becomes which components trigger the statute. *Morrison v. National Australia Bank, Ltd.*, the case discussed in *Kiobel*, involved allegedly fraudulent efforts to conceal the losses suffered by a U.S. subsidiary of a foreign bank. The purported fraud took place in the United States, but the sales of the foreign bank's securities took place abroad. The Supreme Court ruled that the relevant federal statute regulated the purchase and sale of securities, not fraud, and that the relevant issue therefore was where the sales occurred.

Compare the related issue of what it takes to demonstrate a legislative intent to cover extraterritorial conduct. In *European Community v. RJR Nabisco, Inc.*, 2014 WL 1613878 (2d Cir. 2014), the Court ruled that the extraterritorial effect of the Racketeering Influenced and Corrupt Organizations Act (RICO) depended on the predicate statute to which RICO applied.

Thus, when a RICO claim depends on violations of a predicate statute that manifests an unmistakable congressional intent to apply extraterritorially, RICO will apply to extraterritorial conduct, too, but only to the extent that the predicate would. Conversely, when a RICO claim depends on violations of a predicate statute that does not overcome Morrison's presumption against extraterritoriality, RICO will not apply extraterritorially either.

8.   Independent of civil liability, multinational firms face other sanctions for inattention to human rights standards. An active network of nongovernmental organizations, already suspicious of modern business and globalization, closely monitors the behavior of firms and publicizes accusations of improper practices. The bad publicity in turn can affect both customer choices and governmental relations. Firms that sell branded goods to consumers (think of the apparel industry) fear consumer boycotts. Firms that either contract directly with governments or depend on governments for approvals and protection worry about political backlash.

Consider a UN report on this issue. Then-Secretary General Kofi Annan appointed John Ruggie, a professor of political science at Columbia University, as a Special Representative for Business and Human Rights. His initial reports surveyed strategies for increasing business accountability:

> 82.   The permissive conditions for business-related human rights abuses today are created by a misalignment between economic forces and governance capacity. Only a realignment can fix the problem. In principle, public authorities set the rules within which business operates. But at the national level some governments simply may be unable to take effective action, whether or not the will to do so is present. And in the international arena states themselves compete for access to markets and investments, thus collective action problems may restrict or impede their serving as the international community's "public authority." The most vulnerable people and communities pay the heaviest price for these governance gaps.
>
> 83.   There are lessons to be drawn from earlier periods. The Victorian era of globalization collapsed because governments and business failed to manage its adverse impact on core values of social community. Similarly, the attempt to restore a laissez-faire international economy after World War I barely made it off the ground before degenerating into the destructive political "isms" that ascended from the left and right, and for which history will remember the first half of the twentieth century—all championed in the name of social protection against economic forces controlled by "others." There are few indications that such extreme reactions are taking root today, but this is the dystopia states and businesses need to consider—and avoid—as they assess the current situation and where it might lead. Human rights and the sustainability of globalization are inextricably linked.
>
> 84.   This report has identified areas of fluidity in the business and human rights constellation, which in some respects may be seen as hopeful signs. By far the most consequential legal development is the gradual extension of liability to companies for international crimes, under domestic jurisdiction but reflecting international standards. But this trend is largely an unanticipated by-product of

states' strengthening the legal regime for individuals, and its actual operation will reflect variations in national practice, not an ideal solution for anyone. No comparably consistent hard law developments were found in any other areas of human rights, which leaves large protection gaps for victims as well as predictability gaps for companies—who may still get tried in "courts of public opinion."

85.   Considerable innovation was found in soft law initiatives, both intergovernmental and, even more so, the multi-stakeholder hybrids. In the latter, individual states most directly concerned with a pressing problem collaborate directly with business and civil society to establish voluntary regulatory systems in specific operational contexts. In addition, self-regulation by business through company codes and collective initiatives, often undertaken in collaboration with civil society, also exhibits innovation and policy diffusion. All of these approaches show some potential, despite obvious weaknesses. The biggest challenge is bringing such efforts to a scale where they become truly systemic interventions. For that to occur, states need to more proactively structure business incentives and disincentives, while accountability practices must be more deeply embedded within market mechanisms themselves.

86.   Judging from the treaty body commentaries, and reinforced by the SRSG's questionnaire survey of states, not all state structures as a whole appear to have internalised the full meaning of the state duty to protect, and its implications with regard to preventing and punishing abuses by nonstate actors, including business. Nor do states seem to be taking full advantage of the many legal and policy tools at their disposal to meet their treaty obligations. Insofar as the duty to the protect lies at the very foundation of the international human rights regime, this uncertainty gives rise to concern.

87.   Lack of clarity regarding the implications of the duty to protect also affects how corporate "sphere of influence" is understood. This concept has no legal pedigree beyond fairly direct agency relationships. But in exploring its potential utility as a practical policy tool the SRSG has discovered that it cannot easily be separated operationally from the state duty to protect. Where governments lack capacity or abdicate their duties, the corporate sphere of influence looms large by default, not due to any principled underpinning. Indeed, disputes between governments and businesses over just where the boundaries of their respective responsibilities lie are ending up in courts. The soft law hybrids have made a singular contribution by acknowledging that for some purposes the most sensible solution is to base initiatives on the notion of "shared responsibility" from the start—a conclusion some moral philosophers have also reached with regard to global structural inequities that cannot be solved by individual liability regimes alone. This critical nexus requires greater clarification.

88. The extensive research and consultations conducted for this mandate demonstrate that no single silver bullet can resolve the business and human rights challenge. A broad array of measures is required, by all relevant actors. Mapping existing and emerging standards and practices was an essential first step. What flows logically from the current report is the need for a strategic assessment of the major legal and policy measures that states and other social actors could take, together with views and recommendations about which options or combinations might work best to create effective remedies on the ground. But because the mandate made only 18 months available to the SRSG, it has not been possible for him to build on his work and submit to the Council the "views and recommendations" Resolution 2005/69 invited. Therefore, he would welcome a one-year extension to complete the assignment. As has been his custom throughout, he would continue to hold transparent consultations with all stakeholders during this process and in advance of submitting his views and recommendations in his next (and final) report to the Council.

Implementation of General Assembly Resolution 60/251 of 15 March 2006 Entitled "Human Rights Council," A/HRC/4/035 (2007), at 23–25.

In 2011, the UN Human Rights Council, an intergovernmental body responsible for the promotion and protection of human rights, unanimously endorsed the Guiding Principles on Business and Human Rights. These Principles rest on a three-pillared framework entitled "Protect, Respect and Remedy." These comprise: (1) the State duty to protect against human rights abuses by third parties, including business; (2) the corporate responsibility to respect human rights; and (3) the need for greater access to remedies for victims of business-related abuse.

The principles contained in the second pillar, i.e., the corporation's responsibility to respect human rights, apply to all business enterprises, not just publicly traded companies or companies of a certain size. This means, according to the Guiding Principles, that businesses should (1) avoid infringing on human rights, and (2) address negative or adverse human rights impacts with which they are involved.

The Guiding Principles stipulate that the types of human rights that businesses should respect include at a minimum those contained in what the Commission on Human Rights in 1947 called the International Bill of Human Rights ("IBHR"). The IBHR comprises the Universal Declaration of Human Rights, adopted by the UN General Assembly in 1948, and two international treaties, the International Covenant on Civil and Political Rights, and the International Covenant on Economic, Social and Cultural Rights. Consequently, businesses increasingly have found that the human rights standards contained in these instruments, which by their terms are only legally binding upon states, have become a frame of reference for evaluating their activities.

A key message that emerges from the Guiding Principles is that corporations should institute processes in order to ensure respect for human rights. While it is clear that the Guiding Principles are guidelines and do not represent legally binding obligations, they already have had an effect on corporations.

An excerpt from a recent article provides insight into the Guiding Principles and the consideration that lawyers should give to human rights issues when drafting and negotiating international transactions:

Lawyers should take into account a newly emerging issue when handling international commercial transactions for goods and services—managing human rights risks. Disregarding these risks can have serious financial and reputational consequences for the client, as a number of major corporations have experienced.

Last September [2012], Apple experienced severe media criticism and production delays as a result of working conditions at its Chinese supplier Foxconn, which assembles iPhones. The Swedish retail giant H&M has been pressured to cease using Uzbek cotton due to allegations of forced labor in Uzbekistan's cotton fields. At the end of April [2013], the collapse of a Bangladeshi garment factory, with a death toll of over 1100, drew the world's attention to treatment of workers manufacturing clothing for European and American markets in that country.

Lawyers working on international commercial transactions are already seeing new legislative and regulatory measures that address human rights concerns in a company's supply chain. In 2010, California adopted the California Transparency in Supply Chains Act, which requires companies to disclose information concerning steps taken to ensure the supply chain is free of slavery and human trafficking. The U.S. Dodd-Frank Wall Street Reform and Consumer Protection Act (Dodd-Frank), specifically section 1502, requires companies to carry out due diligence on their supply chains to ensure that they are not sourcing "conflict minerals" from the Democratic Republic of Congo.

Businesses, as well as the lawyers who advise them, will likely witness the increasing predominance of human rights as a part of businesses' risk management and corporate responsibility strategies in coming years. Consequently, lawyers advising purchasers and suppliers of goods and services need to understand the relevance of human rights to international transactions. This article is intended to provide some initial guidance in a rapidly developing and evolving area.

. . .

Understanding the Human Rights Risks Associated with a Transaction

An initial question for lawyers drafting agreements or providing advice on an international transaction for goods or services is, how might the client be associated with adverse human rights impacts. The Guiding Principles articulate three basic ways a business can be involved in an adverse human rights impact.

First, the business may cause the impact through its own activities. An example would be where a company employee conducting an audit of working conditions meets only with male employees of the supplier to obtain information about labor practices and thus acts in a discriminatory manner toward female employees. Second, the business may contribute to the impact, as, for example, where it sets an unreasonable deadline for the manufacture of a component by a supplier and the supplier then requires its workers to work an excessive number of overtime hours in order to meet the company's deadline for the component. The third way in which the business may be involved in adverse human rights is on the basis of its business relationship with another enterprise where the impact is linked to the business's own operations, products, or services. A company that purchases carpets from a supplier that utilizes primary school children to weave the carpets in violation of the terms of the contract would be linked to the human rights infringements because of its relationship with the supplier.

Advising the Client on Human Rights Risks Associated with the Transaction

The role of the lawyer in advising a client on human rights risks associated with a given transaction will vary depending on the specific circumstances of the transaction and the extent to which the client has implemented policies and practices to ensure its respect for human rights. In particular, the client's knowledge of the specific human rights risks of the other party to the proposed transaction will affect the lawyer's advice. For example, the client may already, through its risk management strategies, have identified the general types of risks within the industry sector or country from which the supplier will source the goods or services, or it may have discovered the particular human rights risks associated with the supplier through a pre-qualification assessment. In addition, where the client is aware of its own potential and actual adverse human rights impacts through an ongoing human rights due diligence process, the client will likely be a more attractive supplier or purchaser in an international commercial transaction to other parties that are committed to respecting human rights.

A small or medium-sized business client, however, may not have internal policies or processes in place to identify its own adverse human rights impacts or those of a potential supplier or purchaser. In this case, the lawyer may need to provide more extensive general advice on human rights risks or suggest that the client seek outside expert advice.

Where it appears that the transaction may result in an adverse human rights impact to which the client would contribute, then pursuant to the Guiding Principles, the client should make the necessary changes in order to prevent or mitigate the chance of the impact occurring. For example, where the client's fluctuating demands could result in the supplier requiring employees to work excessive overtime and providing inadequate rest periods during peak demand periods in order to fill the client's order, then the client should discuss scheduling production to avoid infringements of the human rights of the supplier's employees.

However, where the client discovers that the supplier is already demanding excessive hours from its employees, in addition to preventing its own contribution to the infringement of workers' rights, the client should use its leverage to effect changes in the inappropriate working conditions of employees of the supplier. The ability of the client to change the supplier's harmful practice would likely depend upon how much leverage the client has with the supplier. Leverage will vary depending upon factors such as whether the client's business is crucial to the supplier and whether the payments to the supplier are sufficient to allow the supplier to invest in training and safety equipment.

Even where the client would not contribute to a potential or actual adverse human rights impact of the other party, the transaction could still result in the client being directly linked to the adverse human rights impact based on the business relationship through the contract. In this case, according to Guiding Principle 13, the client should use its leverage to encourage the party to prevent or mitigate the impact. For example, where the supplier has monogramming done by hand on sweatshirts in a section of the factory with inadequate lighting that severely affects the sight of the workers, but the production of the sweatshirts is carried out in a more modern section of the factory with good lighting and the client's products do not have monogramming, then the client could use its leverage to encourage the supplier to improve lighting in the area for monogramming.

In this case, the client may need to consider whether it should turn to another business for the transaction. This determination will likely be affected by how crucial the product or service is to the client, whether alternative suppliers or purchasers exist, the severity of the impact, and the influence the client has in ensuring that the other party ceases its adverse human rights impacts.

In either situation, the client's contribution to an adverse human rights impact or its involvement in the impact because of its business relationship with the other party, the contract could be drafted so as to include a reference to the particular negative human rights impacts and the steps that the other party is to take to prevent or mitigate such impacts. The contract could also provide for termination where the other party to the transaction fails to take steps to prevent the identified human risks or to take action to remedy specified rights.

Where the client requires suppliers to sign a code of conduct, it could be modified to incorporate human rights. Monitoring of the supplier, either by the contracting company or an independent third party, could also include compliance with human rights. However, in the case of an existing severe abuse, such as child labor, the client would likely wish to see the abuse addressed before signing the contract.

However, not all human rights risks can be identified during discussions and negotiations with the other party to the transaction. Actual human rights infringements or additional potential risks may be identified during the course of the arrangement. A change in ownership or management of the other party or even a modification of the purchaser's demands could result in an increase in adverse human rights risks. Thus, the lawyer and the client need to be aware that the process of ascertaining human rights risks is an ongoing process that requires awareness, periodic monitoring, and appropriate follow-up.

Corinne Lewis, Don't Overlook Human Rights Risks When Negotiating and Drafting International Commercial Transaction Agreements, 42 International Law News 1 (Summer 2013).

9. Firms fear irresponsible charges that might be used to extort concessions (such as "voluntary" donations to the charging organization). But in many cases they have worked with human rights groups, both transnational and local, to develop a monitoring and compliance program to minimize human rights abuses. In addition, local governments that engage in murder, robbery, slavery and rape probably are not otherwise reliable business partners, and human rights concerns may steer firms away from projects that present all kinds of excessive risks. At the same time, one hears complaints that, as with anticorruption law, "first world" human rights standards may give an advantage to firms from countries with a less scrupulous regard for human rights. *E.g.*, Andrew Brady Spalding, The Irony of International Business Law: U.S. Progressivism and China's New Laissez-Faire, 59 UCLA L. REV. 354 (2011); Andrew Brady Spalding, *Unwitting Sanctions: Understanding Anti-Bribery Legislation as Economic Sanctions Against Emerging Markets*, 62 FLA. L. REV. 351, 371–74 (2010). For a rebuttal, see Paul B. Stephan, *Regulatory Competition and Anticorruption Law*, 53 VA. J. INT'L L. 53, 67–69 (2013).

Supplemental Reading

Foreign Corrupt Practices Act

Kevin E. Davis, *Self-Interest and Altruism in the Deterrence of Transnational Bribery*, 4 AM. L. & ECON. REV. 314 (2002)

Stanley Sporkin, *The Worldwide Banning of Schmiergeld: A Look at the Foreign Corrupt Practices Act on Its Twentieth Birthday*, 18 NW. J. INT'L L. & BUS. 269 (1998)

Symposium: Fighting International Corruption & Bribery in the 21st Century, 33 CORNELL J. INT'L L. 465 (2000)

Paul B. Stephan, *Regulatory Competition and Anticorruption Law*, 53 VA. J. INT'L L. 53, 67–69 (2013)

Daniel K. Tarullo, *The Limits of Institutional Design: Implementing the OECD Anti-Bribery Convention*, 44 VA. J. INT'L L. 665 (2004)

FCPA Blog: http://fcpablog.com/

Fraud and Money Laundering

Marian Hagler, *International Money Laundering and U.S. Law: A Need to "Know-Your-Partner,"* 31 SYRACUSE J. INT'L L. & COMMERCE 227 (2004)

Human Rights Liability of Businesses

Gary Clyde Hufbauer & Nicholas K. Mitrokostas, AWAKENING MONSTER: THE ALIEN TORT STATUTE OF 1789 (Institute for International Economics: Washington, D.C., 2003)

Curtis A. Bradley, Jack L. Goldsmith & David H. Moore, Sosa, *Customary International Law, and the Continuing Relevance of* Erie, 120 HARV. L. REV. 869 (2007)

Steven R. Ratner, *Corporations and Human Rights: A Theory of Legal Responsibility*, 111 YALE L.J. 443 (2001)

Paul B. Stephan, *Human Rights Litigation in the United States After* Kiobel, 1 PEKING U. TRANSNAT'L L. REV. 338 (2013)

CHAPTER 3

ORGANIZATIONAL FORMS FOR FOREIGN INVESTMENT, DUE DILIGENCE AND PROBLEMS OF CORPORATE GOVERNANCE

Businesses enter a new market because they believe they can make money. How they make money, however, may not be so straightforward. They could, of course, sell products—goods or services—at a profit. But, for any number of reasons, they also could enter into transactions that do not bring an immediate return. They may want to test the waters in that market, build relationships with local entrepreneurs and government officials, learn how to operate in a different culture, with the hope of exploiting this knowledge in future business transactions. In some cases, the opening of a store might be worth its cost simply as a form of advertising. The McDonald's first restaurant in Moscow, which opened in 1990 at the end of the Soviet period, initially hemorrhaged money, but the company regarded the expense as worth it initially because of the positive publicity generated by establishing its brand in the homeland of international communism. It was said that the opening of that restaurant was featured on the front page of every major newspaper in the world.

Organizing a business in an emerging market should be seen as a process, not a one-off decision. At first, the business may do nothing more than hold meetings and make contacts. As opportunities increase, it might set up ongoing representation so that it can stay in touch with potential partners and customers. At some point, representation might require the establishment of some kind of legal structure, both to comply with local regulations and to formalize the authority and responsibility of the local representative. As concrete transactions materialize, the foreign business might be called on to devote its resources to, and raise capital for, a specific project. Each stage of this process requires new choices about what legal structure to use.

Organizational issues are hardly the only barrier to entering a new sector in an emerging market. Most countries bar foreigners outright from taking part in some sectors, and a few emerging market countries impose stringent limits on outsiders. Even where foreign participation is legal, the government may tolerate or encourage informal actions that have the effect of exclusion. These are issues for another course, however, in particular one focused on trade and international economic law. We will assume that the business opportunity exists, and look at how a foreign business might pursue it.

A. CHOICE OF FORM

Both the requirements of local law and the structures that local law permits will vary across jurisdictions. But certain basic patterns exist in most jurisdictions, and especially in the larger emerging market countries such as China, India and Russia. Characteristically, emerging market countries have little or no history of offering foreign entrepreneurs an array of choices in how to structure their operations. In most cases, however, they do have newly minted laws that seek to mimic what is available in well established market economies. The law on the books points toward flexibility based on business calculations, but the officials responsible for administering the law often take a different view based on their past experience. Typically they will resist authorizing novel transactions, even if they seem to fit under the newly enacted laws. Businesses will not adopt an organizational form that may be nominally available if local officials create too many obstacles.

1. HISTORICAL BACKGROUND

A sense of history also is important. Most emerging markets involve countries with a sense of injustice and exploitation by outsiders. This sense is not just general, but specific to business forms. People in the host country will have a long memory about past swindles. As a case in point, considering the following case:

Chang Yen-Mao v. Moreing

High Court of Justice Chancery Division
The Times, Mar. 2, 1905, p. 3, also reported at 120 L.T. Jour. 313 (1906)

[Chang, a high ranking Chinese official, and the Chinese Mining and Engineering Company of Tien Tsin (the Chinese Company) sought to nullify a transfer of the Chinese Company's mines and other assets to Moreing, an English company. The petition claimed that Herbert Hoover, acting as an agent of Moreing, induced the Chinese parties to make the transfer to avoid British seizure of the mines as indemnification for injuries by its subjects during the Boxer Rebellion. Chang agreed to put the mines into the Chinese Company and then have that Company transfer them to Moreing. The transfer agreement promised that the Chinese Company would receive 37.5% of the shares of Moreing in return.

[According to the petition, Moreing distributed the remaining 62.5% of its stock to other persons in return for nothing other than "promotional considerations," This decision violated an earlier agreement between the Chinese parties and Hoover, acting on Moreing's behalf, promising that the remaining stock would be sold for not less than $625,000.]

Mr. Justice Joyce said:—This is an action by his Excellency Chang and the Chinese Mining and Engineering Company of Tien-tsin, whom I will call the Chinese Company, asking for a declaration that a certain document called the memorandum of February 19, 1901, is binding on the defendants, and an order for the carrying into effect of the provisions of such memorandum. Alternatively, and in the event of such memorandum being held not to be so binding, for either a declaration that a certain other document called the transfer of February 19, 1901, was obtained by the fraudulent representations and fraud of the defendants or their agents and ought to be set aside, and an order that the same may be set aside accordingly, or a declaration that the defendants are not entitled to retain the benefits of the said transfer, except on the condition of making good to the plaintiffs the obligations imposed by, and performing the provisions contained in, the said memorandum, and such order consequent on such declaration as may be necessary for giving effect thereto.

. . .

[The initial transfer agreement, dated July 30, 1990,] purported to be a grant of an assignment in terms by Detring, as agent and attorney of the Chinese Company, to Hoover, who was the agent of the defendant Moreing, upon trust, of all the property of the Chinese Company, and it was thereby in effect provided, among other things, that Hoover should hold the property as trustee for the contemplated new company when formed. Now, his Excellency Chang, . . . personally objected, and, as it has turned out very wisely, declined positively to execute the transfer when submitted to him because it did not contain any statement of the arrangements for which he had stipulated with respect to, among other things, the constitution and management of the new company into which the Chinese Company was to be transformed. The document did not appear to him adequately to protect his Government or the Chinese shareholders or himself; and in this he was perfectly right. In particular, as I observe, it did not even provide for the 375,000 shares being given or paid to the shareholders of the Chinese Company for the purchase of that company's property.

Between his Excellency and the agents of the defendants, including Mr. White Cooper, which agents also represented the Oriental Syndicate, as I consider, and its creature, the defendant company, there were long and heated discussions extending over four days. Hoover, as he himself admits, went so far as to use various threats to his Excellency. Ultimately his Excellency was induced with difficulty to accede to a proposal of Mr. White Cooper's, that the terms, on account of the absence of which from the transfer he declined to execute, should be embodied in another document, being the memorandum I have already spoken of, to be executed previously to and at the same time with the transfer. Under this arrangement his Excellency was assured by the representatives of the other parties to the transaction that the memorandum would be, as it was expressed to be, the ruling document and to be acted upon, or, in other words, would be binding and be carried into effect. It was upon the faith of and in reliance on these assurances that his Excellency was induced to affix his seal to the two versions of the transfer. The memorandum in two versions, Chinese and English, was executed at the same time in the same manner by Hoover, the agent of the defendant Moreing, De Wouters, who I think may be taken to have represented the Oriental Syndicate and the defendant company and every one interested through them, and it was also executed by his Excellency and Detring.

. . .

[It] appears by a letter of Mr. Hoover of March 22, 1901, that he actually took possession of some of the title deeds of the property by main force. Under the circumstances, I am of opinion that to allow the defendant company, while they insist on retaining the benefits of the transfer, to escape from the obligations of the memorandum upon any such pretext as that Hoover or De Wouters were not authorized to agree to its terms, or that it was impossible for the defendant company to perform some of these terms without altering its constitution, would be contrary to one of the plainest principles of equity. It would be to sanction such a flagrant breach of faith as, in my opinion, could not be tolerated by the law or any country. In this Court a purchaser of real estate, even though he may have obtained possession and an actual conveyance may have been made to him will not be allowed to keep the property without discharging the consideration for the same.

Holding

. . . I hold and declare that the memorandum dated February 19, 1901, is binding as against the defendants, and that the defendant company was not, and is not, entitled to take or retain possession or control of the property comprised in the transfer or the benefits thereof without complying with and performing the provisions and obligations contained in the memorandum. In other words, I am of opinion that, unless within a reasonable time the provisions and obligations of the memorandum be complied with and performed, this Court ought to do what it can to restore to the plaintiffs the mines and property the subject of the transfer, and, probably by injunction if necessary, to prevent the defendant company, its agents and servants, from retaining possession.

. . . The defendant company has all along claimed, and still claims, to have acquired all the property of the Chinese Company by virtue of the transfer of February 19, 1901, expressed to be made in the pursuance of the agreement of July 30, 1900. Nevertheless, by an agreement dated May 2, 1901, nearly three months afterwards, and expressed to be made between the Oriental Syndicate of the one part, and the defendant company of the other, the whole of whose nominal capital was $1,000,000 in $1 shares, the syndicate affected to sell to the company the benefit of the aforesaid agreement of July 30, 1990, for a purchase consideration of 999,993 of these 1,000,000 shares to be allotted as fully paid up to the syndicate or their nominees, and the sum of $2,000 odd in cash, being the amount of the fees paid by the syndicate on the registration of the defendant company. This agreement of May 2, 1901, was sealed at a meeting of the board of the defendant company held on the 25th of the same month of May. At that meeting 50,000 of these shares are allotted as fully paid up to the defendant Moreing and 150,000 as fully paid up to the Oriental Syndicate, and it was resolved that the board agree to allot to the nominees of the Chinese Company 375,000 shares. These, of course, were for the shareholders of the Chinese Company, and then (this is the extraordinary part of it) to the nominees of the Oriental Syndicate 424,993 shares—that is, all the rest of the capital, deducting the seven shares required for the signatories of the memorandum of association. . . . Suppose it be granted that the 50,000, and even the 150,000 (making together 200,000 shares) were to go for promotion profits—if indeed that were allowable—why were 424,993 fully paid-up shares of the company to go among the nominees of the syndicate for no consideration that I have been able to discover?

In short, it appears to me upon the facts that transpired in the course of this trial, that there are at least plausible grounds for contending that the defendant company has been defrauded of nearly 425,000 shares, to the injury and loss of the Chinese shareholders, who were justly entitled to the 375,000 shares. These shares, as I understand, are not of a merely nominal value, but are being or have been sold at a price above par; for the plaintiffs say, and it seems to me with reason, that the value of the 375,000 shares coming to the shareholders of the Chinese Company for the purchase of their property, undoubtedly of great value, is substantially—it may be to the extent of one half-reduced by the issue, for no consideration whatever, of these fully paid-up shares to the promoters or their nominees.

. . . I think perhaps I ought to add one other observation, which is that, in the investigation taken before me of the transactions in question, it has not been shown to me that his Excellency Chang has been guilty of any breach of faith or of any impropriety at all, which is more than I can say for some of the other parties concerned.

NOTES

1. Why did the Chinese company accept foreign investment? At the end of the nineteenth century the European great powers (Great Britain, France, Germany and Russia) and, to a lesser extent, the United States, exercised economic, political and strategic domination over China, which was enfeebled by the weak Manchu dynasty. The anti-foreigner Boxer Rebellion was a product of the debasement and frustration that the imperialist incursions engendered. It ran from the end of 1899 to early 1901 and its suppression resulted in the final humiliation of the Chinese authorities. The Chinese Mining and Engineering Company owned and ran the Kaiping Mines, a rich source of coal and one of a handful of locally owned modern industrial enterprises. The transfer of a stake to foreign investors was both a means of reassuring foreigners (or, put differently, a manifestation of the increased power of the imperialists) as much as a device for raising capital. The document of transfer recites a threat of seizure of the Mines by the European powers as compensation for damages caused during the Rebellion.

2. How did the foreign investors seek to exploit corporate law to inflate their stake in the new company and freeze out the Chinese owners represented by Chang? This case illustrates a classic example of stock watering. The Chinese party thought they were giving up assets worth three-eighths of $1 million in return for three-eighths ownership of a company worth at least $1 million. But the defendants gave themselves the remaining stock for essentially nothing, diminishing the value of the Chinese stake to roughly $106,000. We will encounter further instances of stock watering later in this chapter.

3. This case serves both as a model for predation among business partners in an emerging market and as an instructive reminder that host country opportunism has hardly been the only dysfunctional behavior associated with these investments. The case documents the reasons why host country authorities might well be suspicious of the good faith of foreign investors. By the way, the Hoover involved in this controversy was a young mining engineer named Herbert Hoover, who later became the 31st President of the United States. How well did he behave in this transaction?[1]

---

[1] We are grateful to Professor Brad DeLong, professor of economics at University of California Berkeley, for drawing our attention to the Chinese Mining and Engineering Company case through his excellent blog, Grasping Reality with Both Hands, http://delong.typepad.com. For more on the transaction, see Ellsworth C. Carlson, THE KAIPING MINES, 1877–1912 (1957).

2. FIRST STEPS

Consider the challenge facing Alltel Information Services (AIS) in 2000. This wholly owned subsidiary of the telecommunications giant Alltel provided information technology and data processing services to financial institutions. It wanted to enter the Chinese market. Chinese banks were state-owned and subject to political as much as legal control, but were engaged in increasingly sophisticated and large-scale operations. These banks could achieve enormous savings by applying modern information technology. But AIS, whatever its expertise in information technology, did not have any links to Chinese banks so that it could convince them of the value of its services.

According to complaints filed in state and federal courts, Grace & Digital Information Technology Co. (Grace), a Chinese firm, persuaded AIS that it could facilitate sales of AIS software to the China Construction Bank (CCB), a leading financial institution in China. In June 2001, the complaints allege, Grace contracted to provide AIS with sales and marketing assistance in return for one-third of all software license fees, and 15% of all implementation service fees, obtained by AIS as a result of these services during the next ten years. Grace believes that in the ensuing year it made possible contacts worth $176 million between AIS and CCB. After a change of leadership at the bank, however, AIS changed sales agents. The complaints allege that the new agents persuaded CCB to terminate the existing contracts, thus providing a basis for AIS's refusal to pay Grace any fees, and then substituted new contracts. The heart of Grace's case against AIS, which was purchased by Fidelity National Financial (Fidelity) in 2003, is an allegation that the new sales agents procured these results through bribes paid to the new leadership at CCB and that AIS and then Fidelity knew about these bribes.[2]

3. DUE DILIGENCE ACTIVITIES

The importance of conducting due diligence activities as part of the evaluation of a new business opportunity is a critical factor in the process of deciding whether to invest in an emerging market country in which the investor does not have any prior experience. Due diligence is a pre-investment activity that all companies involved in the international business, for example in the oil and gas industry, conduct, whether they are major international oil companies (IOCs) or small, independent exploration companies, also known as frontier companies. The organizational structure of an IOC is typically large enough to enable them to assign the due diligence activities with respect to the legal, tax and fiscal regime of an emerging market country to its tax, finance or legal department. In comparison, the frontier companies are normally hard pressed to find enough hands on deck to assign separate tasks to specific individuals, and will most likely have to improvise to accomplish the task. In fact, one writer has said about frontier companies that they

---

[2]   The complaints are Grace & Digital Information Technology Co. v. Fidelity Information Services, Inc., Case No. M72515 (Monterey Calif. Super. Ct.), filed Dec. 9, 2004, and Grace & Digital Information Technology Co., Ltd. v. Fidelity National Financial, Civ. No. 06–CV–275 (M.D. Fla.), filed Mar. 6, 2006. [As of this writing, neither court has issued an opinion addressing the merits of these complaints.]

look for investment overseas by "applying their relish for risk and the nimbleness which comes from their small size to undertake preliminary exploration, with a view to discovering a prospect which either may be proven on a shoestring or farmed out to a larger company."[3]

In many cases, the due diligence activity begins with sending a team of professionals to the capital city of the host country to meet their counterparts at the applicable ministry office or that of the national oil company (NOC). Once those initial meetings take place, the scientists usually meet at the ministry or NOC offices for another day or two to review and discuss the geological and geophysical data that the host authorities make available to them. The legal and tax representatives will then interview local law firms and accounting firms to find the best candidates for local assistance, while the business development personnel may meet with potential consultants and representatives of other foreign companies who may be doing business in the host country.

Thereafter, the legal and tax representatives will retain the services of the international firms of their choice with offices in the host country and ask for information regarding the existing laws and regulations, as well as the past practices of the host country government. The responsible department of the investor normally will use the information obtained from such local firms, whether they are accounting or legal firms, in preparing its recommendations to management with respect to anticipated problems and obstacles. Frontier companies, on the other hand, may have to rely on a consultant in the emerging market country to obtain some or most of the information they are looking for, and, due to inherent organizational restrictions, what they are looking for will be somewhat less extensive than what the IOCs expect to uncover.

In its 2003 report on Foreign Direct Investment in Emerging Market Countries, the International Monetary Fund listed several subjects of critical importance to foreign investors in deciding whether to invest in an emerging market country. It states that foreign investors concur "that certain general factors consistently determine which countries attract the most FDI."[4] These include: (i) market size and growth prospects; (ii) wage-adjusted productivity of labor, rather than the cost of labor; (iii) the availability of infrastructure in the project area; (iv) reasonable levels of taxation and overall stability of the tax regime; (v) reasonably stable political environment, as well as conditions that support physical and personal security; (vi) the level of corruption and governance concerns; and (vii) the legal framework and the rule of law.[5] Although all of these factors are important to foreign investors, factors (iii) through (vii) are the most important for decision makers in the international petroleum industry. Items (i) and (ii) may not be as crucial for the international petroleum industry because they are more applicable to retail oriented businesses.

The due diligence process invariably considers these factors. For example, while examining the current legal framework and the extent to

---

[3]   David Ebner, Smaller Exploration Companies on the International Frontier, 37 Natural Res. J. 707, 708 (Summer 1997).

[4]   International Monetary Fund, Foreign Direct Investment in Emerging Market Countries—Report of the Working Group of the Capital Markets Consultative Group, at 3, September 18, 2003, www.imf.org/external/np/cmcg/2003/eng/091803.htm

[5]   Id. at 3–4.

which the rule of law is followed, an IOC or a frontier company will also investigate the history of the laws and regulations in terms of their predictability, stability and enforcement. It would have been critical to know, for example, that the foreign investment law of Russia, which guaranteed an export rate of 100% of production for joint ventures with at least 30% foreign investment, would be totally ignored and disrespected by the authorities, as was the case in Russia in the 1990s.[6] As a consequence, the Customs Service and the Ministry of Energy of Russia were able to dilute the right to export by instituting a new policy that limited access to export pipelines to 30% of production, thereby forcing such joint ventures to sell the majority of their production on the domestic market where the price was more than 20% lower than the world market price.[7] This drastic change in policy caused an immediate decline in cash flow for the joint ventures that had designed their economics, agreements and financing arrangements on the basic guarantee of 100% export rights.[8] Although some investors considered suing the government, they were reluctant to do so because of the transitional stage of the Russian economy at the time, and such factors as the political consequences of litigation for the IOC, thereby rendering the foreign investment law unenforceable.

In terms of the levels of taxation and the stability and predictability thereof, the legal and tax departments of IOCs would consider the laws and regulations in existence, beginning with the constitution, petroleum legislation, and laws covering exchange controls, income tax, customs and corporations and other forms of companies. If necessary, they would retain an outside law firm and/or accounting firm or even a bank with offices in the host country to provide guidance and an opinion regarding the status of the laws and the way in which they would be applied, including the history of their application by the government. These inquiries should include the creditability of local taxes for home-country tax purposes, possible exemptions from income taxation, tax rates based on the type of entity used, tax on contractors and subcontractors, expatriate employees, and other taxes. In addition, the contents of the rights-granting documents, all of the other types of applicable agreements, and financial documentation would be critical elements of the investigation.

In the view of one expert, "the increasing competitiveness among countries seeking exploration and production investment requires specific consideration of applicable tax laws at the time each contract is negotiated."[9] Such tax information could "include income taxes, windfall taxes or additional profit taxes," but "small exploration companies must also give careful attention to customs duties, withholding taxes, turnover and value added taxes, excise taxes and other fees. . . ."[10] "Without a complete analysis of both the contract terms and the effective tax rate, it

---

[6]   Skelton, Arranging Project Financing for Polar Lights Company in Russia, VI Currents Int'l Trade L.J. 3, 7 (Winter 1997).

[7]   Id.

[8]   Id.

[9]   See David Ebner, Smaller Exploration Companies on the International Frontier, supra note 3, at 718.

[10]   Id. at 715.

is simply not possible to determine the attractiveness of a prospective opportunity."[11]

With respect to the political environment and the level of corruption, the due diligence process should closely examine the history and the stability of the host government, as well as its reputation concerning corrupt activities. There are many sources available online for both of these topics, but it is always best to also retain the services of an expert in the host country to provide its opinion from a "hands on" point of view. Once those facts are obtained, it is possible to construct an internal view of the level of political risk, as well as the amount of corruption that may exist in the government and/or in various segments of the economy.

As soon as the analysis of technical data and the detailed report of the due diligence activities are complete, the investigator will give the results to economists for use in the economic model, and prepare and submit a formal report to management. The investor's management and professionals then will organize a seminar-like discussion of the project based on the report, a Power Point presentation and the preliminary economic runs. The discussion will identify the pros and cons of the possible project and propose solutions with respect to the problem areas.

The evaluation process will weigh the significant issues that arise in accordance with their relative importance. For example, if an essential element of the proposed contractual structure is totally out of line with the investor's model contract, such as setting cost recovery oil at the extremely low level of 20%, the evaluation most likely would highlight this issue first. Both the written report and the presentation made to management would emphasize these types of red flags. The process will study closely and assign priority to other basic elements of the fiscal terms and the related tax issues according to the magnitude of the potential problems. Decision makers usually discount the economic analysis somewhat at this stage due to its preliminary nature. They will send the economists back to the drawing board to update, revise and finalize the assumptions and the various outcomes.

The evaluation process will consider other economic factors, including exit costs. If those conducting the evaluation deem any of these factors to be of great importance, they will include them in the overall report and may also provide a supplemental economic analysis to provide management with an additional level of insight into all the variables applicable to the overall decision making procedure.

4. THE FOREIGN PARTNER

Returning to AIS, how does a multinational company with a sophisticated and customer-specific product such as business and systems management software convince potential customers in new markets to purchase services worth many millions of dollars? How can it avoid working with a local partner? If using a local partner is inevitable (and it often is), what risks does it face and how can it protect itself?

Perhaps the single most important issue that a business in AIS's position faces is the selection of its local collaborator. You may think this is simply a matter of business judgment, and some businesses may agree.

---

[11] Id. at 718.

But a wrong choice can have legal consequences, and lawyers can help firms assess and manage these risks. Questions that the client might ask, and for which the lawyer might help obtain answers, include:

- What does the client know about the potential collaborator?
- Who recommends the potential collaborator?
- Has the potential collaborator had legal or financial problems in the past? What is the collaborator's reputation for integrity?
- Does it have a track record of bringing success to similar projects with other partners?
- What is the basis of its expertise?
- What kinds of relationships does the potential collaborator have with potential customers?
- Are the representations of the potential collaborator realistic? (It is important to keep in mind W.C. Fields' powerful insight: "You can't cheat an honest man.")

If the client is satisfied with the potential collaborator, there remains the question of how to structure their relationship. According to the Grace plaintiffs, AIS used a commission contract. The partner would receive compensation based on the amount of business it brought in, much like a royalty from the use of intellectual property or a broker's commission. Such contracts require a number of decisions:

- What is the right base for measuring compensation? (The Grace contract apparently treated all orders received from CCB as eligible.)
- Is it sufficient for a customer to place an order, or must the customer first pay for the goods or services before the collaborator has any right to compensation?
- What events will terminate the payment obligation? (According to Grace, AIS treated CCB's cancelling of the sales as sufficient to justify nonpayment under the contract.)
- What actions or relationships will constitute a forbidden conflict of interest by either party?
- What is the term of the contract, that is, when does it expire?
- Can either or any party terminate the contract, either for cause or without cause?
- What promises should the foreign party require of its collaborator? According to the Grace complaint, the parties modified the initial contract to add a promise not to violate the Foreign Corrupt Practices Act. How do the standards imposed by the *InVision* proceeding, discussed in Chapter 2 above, affect these requirements?

5. REPRESENTATIVE OFFICES

A foreign firm must decide how to organize its presence in the host country. Short of acting only through local partners, the form that entails the least investment and the lowest legal profile is the representative office. Requirements for setting up such an office vary among countries, but consider the rules below as they exist in China.[12]

REPRESENTATIVE OFFICES

Legal Status

Representative offices established in China by foreign companies are regulated by several national regulations, as well as local legislation, which supplement the national regulations. In general, representative offices may not conduct direct business activities. A representative office is permitted only to make business contacts and render services on behalf of its head office. Personnel employed by the representative office of a foreign company should not sign contracts on behalf of either the foreign company or third parties.

Registration

Pursuant to a 2004 State Council decision, it is no longer necessary to obtain approval for establishment of the most common types of representative office. Instead, direct registration with the industry and commerce authorities is permitted. Certain local registration authorities require an applicant company to submit application materials through designated agencies, and different registration authorities may require different documents.

Documents to be submitted generally include:

- a registration form for the representative office;
- a letter of creditworthiness from the foreign company's bank;
- registration forms for the chief representative and any other representatives; and
- copies of the foreign company's incorporation certificate and business registration certificate.

In addition to attending to the above registration, the foreign company must register the representative office and its foreign staff with the local tax bureau, and a number of other government departments including the public security bureau (for residence permits) and with the local customs authority (for importation of personal belongings).

A representative office has no legal capacity, *i.e.*, it cannot enter into contracts or own property on its own behalf. Any engagements that it undertakes therefore will be on behalf of the foreign company itself. Does this present a potential problem?

6. LEGAL PERSONS

There are two general categories of reasons why a foreign business might operate in an emerging market through a locally created legal person (putting aside for the moment the precise characteristics of the forms of legal persons that local law permits). First, a multinational corporation may not want to assume liability for all the obligations created by these operations. To the extent local law recognizes the separate legal personality of the local entity (what U.S. corporate law regards as limited liability), the corporation may succeed in placing only

---

[12]   Baker & McKenzie, Doing Business in China 16 (2005).

its local investment, rather than its world-wide assets, at risk. Second, host-country regulators may believe that they have greater leverage over a local entity, and thus may encourage or even require that the business operate through a local entity. Moreover, national pride and politics might inhibit the embrace of foreign businesses. Requiring that foreigners operate through a local entity with substantial local ownership may respond to this concern. In addition, the foreign business may want to establish manufacturing or direct selling operations activities that, under local law, only local entities can carry out.

Most emerging market countries have laws that permit the formation of domestic legal persons in which foreigners have a full or partial interest. In Russia, for example, the Civil Code provides the basic framework for these entities. Its Chapter 4 provides, *inter alia*, for general partnerships, limited partnerships, limited liability companies, and joint stock companies, as well as various other structures based on state ownership. Detailed laws supplement and embellish these provisions. Consider provisions from the 1995 Federal Law on Joint Stock Companies, as amended multiple times through 2013 and contained in the Documents Supplement.

Consider what aspects of the law governing legal persons are mandatory, and what part is optional. The charter contains many of the optional rules, and persons who invest in or do business with a joint stock company are presumed to know what those rules are. Consider also the three tiers of decisionmaking: the shareholders meeting, the board, and the officers. The allocation of responsibility to these tiers and the procedures with which each tier's decisionmaking must comply constitute the principles of corporate governance, which we will discuss below.

The following case raises many issues, not all of which are germane to this course, but it does expose both the reasons why a multinational company may operate in an emerging market (here India) through a local entity and illustrate how a local entity may operate in practice.

In re: Union Carbide Corporation Gas Plant Disaster at Bhopal, India in December, 1984

United States District Court for the Southern District of New York
634 F. Supp. 842 (1986)

■ John F. Keenan, United States District Judge:

On the night of December 2–3, 1984 the most tragic industrial disaster in history occurred in the city of Bhopal, state of Madhya Pradesh, Union of India. Located there was a chemical plant owned and operated by Union Carbide India Limited ("UCIL"). The plant, situated in the northern sector of the city, had numerous hutments adjacent to it on its southern side which were occupied by impoverished squatters. UCIL manufactured the pesticides Sevin and Temik at the Bhopal plant at the request of, and with the approval of, the Government of India. UCIL was incorporated under Indian law in 1934. 50.9% of its stock is owned by the defendant, Union Carbide Corporation, a New York corporation. Methyl isocyanate (MIC), a highly toxic gas, is an ingredient in the production of both Sevin and Temik. On the night of the tragedy MIC leaked from the plant in substantial quantities for reasons not yet determined.

The prevailing winds on the early morning of December 3, 1984 were from Northwest to Southeast. They blew the deadly gas into the overpopulated hutments adjacent to the plant and into the most densely occupied parts of the city. The results were horrendous. Estimates of deaths directly attributable to the leak range as high as 2,100. No one is sure exactly how many perished. Over 200,000 people suffered injuries— some serious and permanent—some mild and temporary. Livestock were killed and crops damaged. Businesses were interrupted.

On December 7, 1984 the first lawsuit was filed by American lawyers in the United States on behalf of thousands of Indians. Since then 144 additional actions have been commenced in federal courts in the United States. The actions have all been joined and assigned by the Judicial Panel on Multidistrict Litigation to the Southern District of New York by order of February 6, 1985.

The individual federal court complaints have been superseded by a consolidated complaint filed on June 28, 1985.

The Indian Government on March 29, 1985 enacted legislation, the Bhopal Gas Leak Disaster (Processing of Claims) Act (21 of 1985) ("Bhopal Act"), providing that the Government of India has the exclusive right to represent Indian plaintiffs in India and elsewhere in connection with the tragedy. Pursuant to the Bhopal Act, the Union of India, on April 8, 1985, filed a complaint with this Court setting forth claims for relief similar to those in the consolidated complaint of June 28, 1985.

By order of April 25, 1985 this Court established a Plaintiffs' Executive Committee, comprised of F. Lee Bailey and Stanley M. Chesley, Esqs., who represented individual plaintiffs and Michael V. Ciresi, Esq., whose firm represents the Union of India. Jack S. Hoffinger, Esq., who represents individual plaintiffs, was appointed liaison counsel for the Plaintiffs' Executive Committee.

On September 24, 1985, pursuant to the Bhopal Act, the Central Government of India framed a "scheme" for the Registration and Processing of Claims arising out of the disaster. According to the Union of India's counsel, over 487,000 claims have been filed in India pursuant to the "scheme."

There presently are 145 actions filed in the United States District Court for the Southern District of New York under the Judicial Panel for Multidistrict Litigation's order of February 6, 1985, involving approximately 200,000 plaintiffs.

Before this Court is a motion by the defendant Union Carbide Corporation ("Union Carbide") to dismiss the consolidated action on the grounds of *forum non conveniens*.

DISCUSSION

The doctrine of *forum non conveniens* allows a court to decline jurisdiction, even when jurisdiction is authorized by a general venue statute. . . . [The court discussed the leading Supreme Court *forum non conveniens* cases *Gulf Oil Corp. v. Gilbert*, 330 U.S. 501 (1947), and *Piper Aircraft Co. v. Reyno*, 454 U.S. 235 (1981).]

. . .

2.   Private Interest Concerns.

The [Supreme] Court set forth a list of considerations which affect the interests of the specific litigants to an action, and which should be weighed in making a *forum non conveniens* determination. The so-called private interest factors, along with public interest factors discussed below, were not intended to be rigidly applied. . . . [I]t appears that the burdensome effect of a trial in this forum supports a finding that the private interest factors in this case weigh strongly in favor of dismissal.

A.   Sources of Proof.

The first example of a private interest consideration is "relative ease of access to sources of proof." As stated, the analysis of this issue must hinge on the facts. Limited discovery on the issue of *forum non conveniens* has taken place, pursuant to the Court's order of August 14, 1985. The Court can therefore proceed to discuss this question.

Union Carbide argues that virtually all of the evidence which will be relevant at a trial in this case is located in India. Union Carbide's position is that almost all records relating to liability, and without exception, all records relevant to damages, are to be found in and around Bhopal. On the liability question Union Carbide asserts that the Bhopal plant was managed and operated entirely by Indian nationals, who were employed by UCIL. Defendant asserts that the Bhopal plant is part of UCIL's Agricultural Products Division, which has been a separate division of UCIL for at least 15 years, and that the plant had "limited contact" with UCIL's Bombay headquarters, and almost no contact with the United States. Woomer claims to have been the last American employed by UCIL. He departed from Bhopal in 1982.

Woomer describes the structure and organization of the Bhopal facility at the time of the accident. The plant had seven operating units, each headed by a manager or department head, each an Indian national. The managers or department heads each reported either directly to the plant's General Works Manager, or to one of three Assistant Works Managers. Each of these is also an Indian national. Three of the operating units which at this very early stage of inquiry into liability appear to have been potentially involved in the MIC leak are the Carbon Monoxide, MIC/Phosgene and Carbamoylation units. The Carbon Monoxide and MIC/Phosgene units together employed 63 employees, all Indian nationals. The Carbamoylation unit employed 99 Indian nationals. Mr. Woomer states that an inquiry into the cause of the accident would require interviews with at least those employees who were on duty at the Bhopal facility "immediately prior or after the accident;" Mr. Woomer asserts that there are 193 employees, all Indians, who must be interviewed.

In addition to the seven operating units, the Bhopal plant contained seven functional departments which serviced operations. The seven heads of the units reported within the plant much as the department heads did.

The maintenance unit was apparently subdivided into departments including Instrumentation, Mechanical Maintenance, both part of the Agricultural Chemical Maintenance unit, which employed 171 people in total, and Plant Engineering and Formulation Maintenance, which employed 46 people. In addition, the Utilities and Electrical department employed 195 people. According to Mr. Woomer, the various maintenance organizations performed repairs on equipment, provided engineering support, fabricated certain equipment, salvaged other portions, and controlled utilities, temperatures and pressures throughout the plant.

Moreover, according to Mr. Woomer, these UCIL departments also kept daily, weekly and monthly records of plant operations, many of which were purportedly seized by the [Central Bureau of Investigation (CBI)] and selected for copying by CBI immediately after the accident. The records and reports of the various maintenance units would likely be relevant to the question of liability at trial.

Of the additional functional units, it is possible that Quality Control, with 54 employees, Purchasing, with 53, or Stores may have been directly involved in the disaster by virtue of their participation in analyzing plant output, procuring raw materials for the chemical processes of the plant, and maintaining spare parts and certain chemicals. Thus, the records and reports of these three departments may be necessary to an investigation of liability. While examination of members of the Works Office department and Industrial Relations department would likely be less directly useful, information regarding plant budgets and employee histories might be of relevance. Of great importance are the records and reports of the Safety/Medical department, which was responsible for daily auditing of safety performance in all departments, training and testing on safety rules, maintaining safety statistics and planning and implementing safety drills. The 31 Indian employees of this department worked with the Central Safety Committee of the plant, whose members were drawn from plant management, and the Departmental Safety Committees. Operating units were required to monitor plant safety mechanisms weekly, and to keep monthly checklists. The Central Safety Committee met monthly, as did the Departmental Safety Committees. The MIC Unit held monthly safety committee meetings, for example, and issued monthly reports. Quarterly "Measures of Performance" reviews also covered safety issues, and were required of each operating unit. Certainly, interviews of the plant personnel involved in safety reports and audits would be particularly relevant to the investigation of the disaster.

Plaintiffs refer to three occasions upon which Union Carbide, not UCIL, employees conducted safety audits at the Bhopal plant. As defendant correctly argues, these three events constitute a very small fraction of the thousands of safety audits conducted at the Bhopal facility. The three audits, moreover, were conducted in 1979, the fall of 1980 and in May of 1982, many years prior to the accident which is the subject of this lawsuit.[14]

Moreover, Union Carbide states that the Union of India, itself, conducted similar safety audits and made recommendations.

---

[14] The 1982 "Operational Safety Survey" was apparently fairly extensive. It was conducted by three United States employees of Union Carbide, and led to a report which discussed "major" concerns and possibility of "serious personnel exposure." Mr. Woomer asserts, and plaintiffs do not refute, that this Survey was not intended to "serve a policing function," but was performed at the specific request of UCIL. In addition, follow-up responsibility "rested exclusively with UCIL plant management."

Two accidents which occurred previously at the Bhopal plant might also be of relevance to the liability inquiry in this litigation. On December 24, 1981, a phosgene gas leak killed a UCIL maintenance worker. Reports of the fatality were sent to Union Carbide management in the United States. Plaintiffs assert that the accident report called for increased training in Bhopal by United States employees of Union Carbide's Institute, West Virginia, plant. Defendant states that the responsibility for remedying problems in the Bhopal plant rested with the plant itself, and that Union Carbide did not make any recommendations, and was involved only to the extent of receiving a copy of the report which called for its involvement in further training.

The second accident at Bhopal prior to the disaster of December, 1984 took place on February 9, 1982, when a pump seal, perhaps improperly used, failed. Many employees were injured, and at least 25 were hospitalized. Plaintiffs discuss the fact that Robert Oldford, president of Union Carbide Agricultural Products Company ("UCAPC") a wholly-owned subsidiary of Union Carbide headquartered in the United States, was in Bhopal at the time of the February 1982 leak. Union Carbide asserts that Mr. Oldford was visiting UCIL's Research and Development Centre, located several miles from the Bhopal plant for an unrelated purpose, and was only coincidentally in Bhopal when the leak occurred. To the extent that this presence in India in 1982 has any significance, Mr. Oldford, and any other United States employees of Union Carbide who conducted safety audits in Bhopal or were present when accidents occurred there, may be flown to Bhopal for testimony or discovery.

In addition to safety data, two other types of proof may be relevant to a trial of this case on the merits. Information regarding plant design, commissioning and start-up may bear upon the liability question. Information pertinent to employee training should also have significance.

Leaving aside the question of whether the Government of India or UCIL chose the site and product of the Bhopal plant, the Court will evaluate the facts which bear on the issue of relevant records. The findings below concern the location of proof only, and bear solely upon the *forum non conveniens* motion. The Court expressly declines to make findings as to actual liability at this stage of the litigation.

Plaintiffs and defendant agree that in 1973 Union Carbide entered into two agreements with UCIL which were entitled "Design Transfer Agreement" and "Technical Service Agreement." According to plaintiffs, Union Carbide, pursuant to the Design Transfer Agreement, provided a process design to UCIL, the "detailing [of which] was undertaken in India." The process design package consisted of the basic plan of the factory, which was to be fleshed out in the detailing phase. Plaintiffs state that at least nine Union Carbide technicians travelled to India to monitor the progress of the project. Union Carbide also allegedly assigned a "key engineer," John Couvaras, to serve as UCIL Bhopal project manager. Mr. Couvaras allegedly "assumed responsibility for virtually every aspect of the detailing of the process design," and approved detail reports of "not only UCIL but also independent contractors, including Humphreys &

Glasgow Consultants Private Ltd. and Power Gas Limited" of Bombay, India.[15]

Plaintiffs also claim that "no change of any substance was made from Union Carbide's design during the detailing phase." Plaintiffs note that only "one portion" of the process design work provided to UCIL by Union Carbide was not used. In effect, plaintiffs seek to establish that Union Carbide was the creator of the design used in the Bhopal plant, and directed UCIL's relatively minor detailing program. They urge that for the most part relevant proof on this point is located in the United States.

Defendant seeks to refute this contention, with notable success. Turning first to the affidavit of Robert C. Brown, who describes himself as "chief negotiator for Union Carbide Corporation in connection with the two agreements it entered into with . . . UCIL in November, 1973," the Court is struck by the assertion that the two agreements were negotiated at "arms-length" pursuant to Union Carbide corporate policy, and that the Union of India mandated that the Government retain "specific control over the terms of any agreements UCIL made with foreign companies such as Union Carbide Corporation."[16]

Mr. Brown alleges that the Letter of Intent issued by the Union of India in March 1972, pursuant to which construction and design of the plant were allowed to ensue provided, *inter alia*, that:

> (2) Foreign collaboration and import of equipment be settled to the satisfaction of the Government.

Mr. Brown claims, on personal information, that UCIL told him that Union Carbide would not be allowed to be involved in the Bhopal project beyond the provision of process design packages. The Design Transfer Agreement indicates that Union Carbide's duty under the Agreement was to provide process design packages, and that UCIL, not Union Carbide, would be responsible to "detail design, erect and commission the plant." Union Carbide, accordingly, issued limiting warranties with respect to the design packages, detailing of which it would not be involved with.

The nature of UCIL's detail design work is discussed in the affidavit of Ranjit K. Dutta, who has held various positions at UCIL and UCAPC. From 1973 through 1976, Mr. Dutta was employed as General Manager of the Agricultural Products Division of UCIL.

Mr. Dutta asserts that the Bhopal facility was built by UCIL over the eight years from 1972 to 1980. He asserts that Union Carbide's role

---

[15] Plaintiffs assert that Mr. Couvaras exemplifies Union Carbide's "international employee" whose mobility throughout the Union Carbide affiliates causes "any notion of discrete corporate identities [to] blur[ ]."

[16] As support, Mr. Brown points to the Union Carbide Corporate Policy Manual, Section 1.10 which states:

> The "arms-length principle" is a central consideration in transfer and pricing of all technology transactions with affiliates.

> "Arms length" is defined as:

> The principle whereby inter-company transactions between Union Carbide and its affiliates, or between affiliates, will reflect the cost to unrelated parties of the same or similar technology under similar circumstances.

Thus, Mr. Brown argues that Union Carbide related with UCIL much as it would have with an unaffiliated, or even competing company.

in the project was "narrow", and limited to providing "certain process design packages for certain parts of the plant." He continues, stating:

Once it did that, it had no further design or engineering role, and that:

> The process design packages which Union Carbide Corporation provided are nothing more than summary design starting points. . . . They set forth only the general parameters. . . . A plant cannot be constructed from a process design package. The detail design comprises approximately 80 percent of the sum of the man hours involved in the design of any project and transposes the general process design parameters into an actual design which can be used for purchasing equipment and actual construction.

According to Mr. Dutta, during the five years between the date upon which Union Carbide submitted process designs, and the date upon which the plant started-up, there were only four visits to Bhopal by Union Carbide process design engineers. In contrast, he asserts that ten to fifteen UCIL engineers, working primarily out of Bombay, were involved in design detailing. These UCIL engineers oversaw the 55 to 60 Indian engineers employed by the Bombay engineering firm which performed the detail design work. This firm, Humphreys and Glasgow, submitted designs and drawings to the UCIL engineers for approval. Corrected drawings were returned by UCIL to Humphreys and Glasgow for changes, and sent back to UCIL for final approval. Mr. Dutta alleges that "at no time were Union Carbide Corporation engineering personnel from the United States involved in approving the detail design or drawings prepared upon which construction was based. Nor did they receive notices of changes made."

Mr. Dutta expressly states that the MIC storage tank and monitoring instrumentation were fabricated or supplied by two named Indian sub-contractors. The vent gas scrubber is alleged to have been fabricated in the Bhopal plant shop.

Of the 12,000 pages of documents purportedly seized by the CBI regarding design and construction of the Bhopal plant, an asserted 2,000 are design reports of Humphreys and Glasgow, UCIL or other contractors. Defendant claims that blueprints and calculations comprise another 1,700 pages of documents held by the CBI. Five thousand pages of contractors' files, including specifications and contracts are asserted to be in India. In addition, Union Carbide claims that blueprints and diagrams may not reflect final design changes as incorporated into the actual plant, and that the detail design engineers' testimony will be needed to determine the configuration of the actual plant.[18]

One final point bearing on the information regarding liability is contained in the affidavit of Edward Munoz, at a relevant time the General Manager of UCIL's Agricultural Products Division. He later acted as Managing Director of UCIL. Mr. Munoz has submitted an affidavit in which he states that Union Carbide decided to store MIC in

---

[18] Mr. Couvaras, whom plaintiffs assert was a "key engineer" for the project, and enjoyed mobility between Union Carbide and UCIL, is described by Mr. Dutta as primarily a UCIL employee. The "international employee" status he carried is explained as a pension accounting mechanism.

large quantities at the Bhopal plant, despite Mr. Munoz' warnings that MIC should be stored only in small amounts because of safety. Mr. Dutta, for defendant, asserts that there was never any issue of token storage of MIC at Bhopal, as Mr. Munoz states, and that there is no truth to Mr. Munoz' assertion that he was involved in the storage issue. The Court cannot make any determination as to the conflicting affidavits before it. This question, which involves credibility concerns, is left for later in the litigation. To the extent that this particular matter bears upon the relative ease of access to sources of proof, Mr. Munoz and Mr. Dutta both may be called to testify at trial or discovery. Mr. Dutta's home is in Bhopal. The Court is not aware of the whereabouts of Mr. Munoz at this time. Either of the two could travel to either alternative forum.

In addition to design and safety records, material regarding training of Bhopal personnel is likely to be relevant to the question of liability. Plaintiffs state that Warren Woomer supervised the training of UCIL personnel at Union Carbide's Institute, West Virginia plant. According to plaintiffs, 40 UCIL employees were transported to Institute's MIC facility for lengthy training. Mr. Woomer states in reply that the 40 employees thus trained represented a fraction of the over 1,000 employees who were trained exclusively in Bhopal. In addition, Mr. Woomer asserts that the training at Institute was pursuant to an arms-length agreement, that UCIL selected the parties to be trained, and that UCIL paid Union Carbide for the training. Moreover, Mr. Woomer's description of the training provided at Bhopal suggests that each of the plant's employees had lengthy cumulative training, of which the Institute training was but a very small portion. Personnel records, in any event, are located in Bhopal.

The briefs and affidavits contain considerable discussion on the matter of commissioning and start-up of the Bhopal plant. The Court need not resolve the question of who was responsible for these aspects of plant operation. However, the Court determines that the manual regarding start-up was prepared by Indian nationals employed by UCIL.

In the aggregate, it appears to the Court that most of the documentary evidence concerning design, training, safety and start-up, in other words, matters bearing on liability, is to be found in India. Much of the material may be held by the Indian CBI. Material located in this country, such as process design packages and training records of the 40 UCIL employees trained at Institute, constitutes a smaller portion of the bulk of the pertinent data than that found in India. Moreover, while records in this country are in English, a language understood in the courts of India, certain of the records in India are in Hindi or other Indian languages, as well as in English. The Indian language documents would have to be translated to be of use in the United States. The reverse is not true. It is evident to the Court that records concerning the design, manufacture and operation of the Bhopal plant are relatively more accessible in India than in the United States, and that fewer translation problems would face an Indian court than an American court. Since Union Carbide has been directed to submit to discovery in India pursuant to the liberal grant of the American Federal Rules of Civil Procedure, and this opinion is conditioned upon such submission, any records sought by plaintiffs must be made available to them in India. The private interest factor of relative ease of access to sources of proof bearing on liability favors dismissal of the consolidated case.[20] The Indian Government is asserted to have been involved in safety, licensing and other matters relating to liability. Records relating thereto are located in India, as are the records seized by the CBI. Although plaintiffs state that all such records could and would be made available to this Court, it would be easier to review them in India. Transmittal and translation problems would thereby be avoided.

. . .

B. The Interests of India and the United States.

Plaintiffs, and especially *amicus curiae* emphasize this point of argument in opposition to the motion to dismiss. Concerned with the asserted possibility of developing a "double-standard" of liability for multinational corporations, plaintiffs urge that American courts should administer justice to the victims of the Bhopal disaster as they would to potential American victims of industrial accidents. The public interest is served, plaintiffs and *amicus* argue, when United States corporations assume responsibility for accidents occurring on foreign soil. "To abandon that responsibility," *amicus* asserts, "would both injure our standing in the world community and betray the spirit of fairness inherent in the American character." The specific American interests allegedly to be served by this Court's retention of the case include the opportunity of creating precedent which will "bind all American multinationals henceforward," promotion of "international cooperation," avoidance of an asserted "double standard" of liability, and the prevention of "economic blackmail of hazardous industries which would extract concessions on health and environmental standards as the price of continuing operations in the United States." An additional American public interest ostensibly to be served by retention of the litigation in this forum is advanced by plaintiffs themselves. They assert that the deterrent effect of this case can be distinguished from the situation in *Piper*, where the Court rejected the argument that "American citizens have an interest in ensuring that American manufacturers are deterred from producing defective products, and that additional deterrence might be obtained if Piper and [its co-defendant] were tried in the United States, where they could be sued on the basis of both negligence and strict liability." The Court stated that:

> The incremental deterrence that would be gained if this trial were held in an American court is likely to be insignificant. The American interest in this accident is simply not sufficient to justify the enormous commitment of judicial time and

---

[20] Union Carbide asserts throughout its briefs and affidavits that evidence relevant to the question of damages is located in India, as well. Certainly the victims themselves, and, for the most part, their medical records, are found in or near Bhopal. However, as plaintiffs argue, a "head count" of witnesses is not dispositive of a *forum non conveniens* motion. Not all of the victims would need to be transported to the United States to describe their injuries. The Bhopal "scheme" provides a mechanism for evaluating each individual's claim. Only representative plaintiffs need testify as to damages. This Court would not countenance the impractical and time-consuming process of calling each of the approximately 200,000 victims at a trial in this country. Evidence on damages, as well as liability, is found in India, but not to the overwhelming extent contended by defendant. Moreover, the Court is concerned with the policy effect of allowing the number of foreign victims to affect directly the *forum non conveniens* determination. If carried to the extreme, this "head count" doctrine would mean that the more people hurt, the less likely a suit in this country would be.

resources that would inevitably be required if the case were to be tried here.

According to plaintiffs, the potential for greater deterrence in this case is "self-evident."

The opposing interest of India is argued to be ill-served by sending this litigation to India. Pointing to the fact that the Union of India chose this forum, plaintiffs state that there can be "no question as to the public interest of India." Union Carbide's statements regarding the interests of India in this litigation are summarily dismissed by the plaintiffs, who state that "Union Carbide, whose actions caused the suffering of an entire city, has no standing to assert this belated concern for the welfare of the Indian populace."

Union Carbide, not surprisingly, argues that the public interest of the United States in this litigation is very slight, and that India's interest is great. In the main, the Court agrees with the defendant.

As noted, Robert C. Brown states in his affidavit on behalf of Union Carbide that the Indian Government preserved the right to approve foreign collaboration and import of equipment to be used in connection with the plant. In addition, Mr. Brown quoted excerpts from the 1972 Letter of Intent entered into by the Union of India and UCIL, one term of which required that "the purchase of only such design and consultancy services from abroad as are not available within the country" would be allowed. Ranjit K. Dutta states that the Indian Government, in a process of "Indianization," restricted the amount of foreign materials and foreign consultants' time which could be contributed to the project, and mandated the use of Indian materials and experts whenever possible. In an alleged ongoing attempt to minimize foreign exchange losses through imports, the Union of India insisted on approving equipment to be purchased abroad, through the mechanism of a "capital goods license."

The Indian Government, through its Ministry of Petroleum and Chemicals, allegedly required information from UCIL regarding all aspects of the Bhopal facility during construction in 1972 and 1973, including "information on toxicity" of chemicals. The Ministry required progress reports throughout the course of the construction project. These reports were required by the Secretariat for Industrial Approvals, the Director General of Technical Development and the Director of Industries of Madhya Pradesh. Moreover, UCIL was ultimately required to obtain numerous licenses during development, construction and operation of the facility. The list of licenses obtained fills five pages.[21]

The Indian Government regulated the Bhopal plant indirectly under a series of environmental laws, enforced by numerous agencies, much as the Occupational Safety and Health Administration, the Environmental Protection Agency and state and local agencies regulate the chemical industry in the United States. Emissions from the facility were monitored by a state water pollution board, for example. In addition, state officials periodically inspected the fully-constructed plant.[22] A

---

[21] Indian federal and municipal officials also allegedly conducted on-site inspections resulting in approvals for portions of the construction, including approvals for the flare tower, MIC layout and storage, unit refrigeration and MIC/Phosgene structure.

[22] One such regular inspection appears to have taken place approximately two weeks before the MIC disaster.

detailed inquiry into the plant's operations was conducted by the Indian Government in the aftermath of the December, 1981 fatality at the MIC unit and the February, 1982 incident involving a pump seal. Numerous federal, state and local commissions, obviously, investigated the most tragic incident of all, the MIC leak of December, 1984.

The recital above demonstrates the immense interest of various Indian governmental agencies in the creation, operation, licensing and regulation, and investigation of the plant. Thus, regardless of the extent of Union Carbide's own involvement in the UCIL plant in Bhopal, or even of its asserted "control" over the plant, the facility was within the sphere of regulation of Indian laws and agencies, at all levels. . . .

The Indian government, which regulated the Bhopal facility, has an extensive and deep interest in ensuring that its standards for safety are complied with. As regulators, the Indian government and individual citizens even have an interest in knowing whether extant regulations are adequate. This Court, sitting in a foreign country, has considered the extent of regulation by Indian agencies of the Bhopal plant. It finds that this is not the appropriate tribunal to determine whether the Indian regulations were breached, or whether the laws themselves were sufficient to protect Indian citizens from harm. It would be sadly paternalistic, if not misguided, of this Court to attempt to evaluate the regulations and standards imposed in a foreign country. . . . India no doubt evaluated its need for a pesticide plant against the risks inherent in such development. Its conclusions regarding "questions as to the safety of [products] marketed" or manufactured in India were "properly the concern of that country." This is particularly true where, as here, the interests of the regulators were possibly drastically different from concerns of American regulators. The Court is well aware of the moral danger of creating the "double-standard" feared by plaintiffs and *amicus curiae*. However, when an industry is as regulated as the chemical industry is in India, the failure to acknowledge inherent differences in the aims and concerns of Indian, as compared to American citizens would be naive, and unfair to defendant. . . .

The Indian interest in creating standards of care, enforcing them or even extending them, and of protecting its citizens from ill-use is significantly stronger than the local interest in deterring multinationals from exporting allegedly dangerous technology. The supposed "blackmail" effect of dismissal by which plaintiffs are troubled is not a significant interest of the American population, either. Surely, there will be no relaxing of regulatory standards by the responsible legislators of the United States as a response to lower standards abroad. Other concerns than bald fear of potential liability, such as convenience or tax benefits, bear on decisions regarding where to locate a plant. Moreover, the purported public interest of seizing this chance to create new law is no real interest at all. This Court would exceed its authority were it to rule otherwise when restraint was in order.

The Court concludes that the public interest of India in this litigation far outweighs the public interest of the United States. This litigation offers a developing nation the opportunity to vindicate the suffering of its own people within the framework of a legitimate legal system. This interest is of paramount importance.

NOTES

1. To what extent did using Union Carbide India Limited (UCIL) cap the parent company's exposure to liability for the disaster? The plaintiffs sought to portray UCIL as a passive, pass-through agent of the parent and also sought to attribute the disaster to actions and inactions by the parent (faulty design, inadequate supervision) rather than to conduct of the persons who directly operated the plant. Does the availability of these theories undercut the function of limited liability, or would Union Carbide's exposure be even greater absent UCIL?

2. Following litigation in India, Union Carbide made a substantial payment to the Government of India in settlement of all claims. On appeal, the Second Circuit upheld the decision to dismiss this suit in favor of legal proceedings in India. *In re Union Carbide Corp. Gas Plant Disaster at Bhopal*, 809 F.2d 195 (2d Cir. 1987). Subsequent efforts in the United States to bring claims on behalf of individual victims, some of whom alleged that they never saw any of the money that India collected, have failed. *Bano v. Union Carbide Corp.*, 273 F.3d 120 (2d Cir. 2001); *Bi v. Union Carbide Chemicals & Plastics Co.*, 984 F.2d 592 (2d Cir. 1993).

3. Note the reference to the host country's policy of "Indianization." This is a common theme in emerging market countries. Two interrelated but distinct forces often apply. First, countries with a history of imperialist domination and exploitation respond with barriers meant to prevent the recurrence of these evils. Distrust of foreigners, especially those associated with former colonial powers, is great. The host government may suspect that the foreign investor will seek to evade its laws, cheat local suppliers and employees, and avoid its fiscal obligations. Recall the *Chang* case above. Second, the government seeks to develop skills and expertise among its nationals. The first is a barrier to trade and investment, but the second may not be. Foreign businesses as much as host countries want to develop local skills, as expatriate employees generally are much more costly. The conflict in interests is more subtle: The foreign investor would want the local employees whom it trains to remain with its business and not become its competitors, while the host government would like to see as broad a diffusion of skills and know-how throughout its economy as possible.

4. The Bhopal case raises the possibility of catastrophic consequences from which the foreign party cannot fully protect itself even if it operates through a local entity. Consider the following case as an illustration of the more pedestrian legal risks a foreign company faces when operating in an emerging market with a local partner.

Amco Ukrservice & Prompriladamco v. American Meter Company

312 F.Supp.2d 681 (E.D. Pa. 2004)

■ DALZELL, DISTRICT JUDGE.

Plaintiffs Amco Ukrservice and PrompriladAmco are Ukrainian corporations seeking over $200 million in damages for the breach of two joint venture agreements that, they contend, obligated defendant American Meter Company to provide them with all of the gas meters and related piping they could sell in republics of the former Soviet Union.

I. *Factual and Procedural History*

The origins of this action lie in the collapse of the Soviet Union and the newly-independent Ukraine's fitful transition to a market economy. American Meter began to explore the possibility of selling its products in the former Soviet Union in the early 1990s, and in 1992 it named [C. Douglas] Prendergast as Director of Operations of C.I.S. [Commonwealth of Independent States] Projects. Sometime in 1996, a Ukrainian-born American citizen named Simon Friedman approached Prendergast about the possibility of marketing American Meter products in Ukraine.

Ukraine was a potentially appealing market for American Meter at that time. During and immediately after the Soviet era, Ukrainian utilities had not charged consumers for their actual consumption of natural gas but instead had allocated charges on the basis of total deliveries to a given area. That system penalized consumers for their neighbors' wastefulness and saddled them with the cost of leakage losses. In 1997, the Ukrainian government enacted legislation requiring utilities to shift toward a usage-based billing system. Prendergast's early prediction was that implementation of the legislation would require the installation of gas meters in millions of homes and apartment buildings.

After some investigation, Prendergast and his superiors at American Meter concluded they could best penetrate the Ukrainian market by forming a joint venture with a local manufacturer. To this end, American Meter Vice-President Andrew Watson authorized Friedman on June 24, 1997 to engage in discussions and negotiations with Ukrainian organizations, and the corporation also hired a former vice-president, Peter Russo, to consult on the project. Prendergast, Russo, and Friedman began to identify potential joint venture partners, and by late 1997, they had selected Promprilad, a Ukrainian manufacturer of commercial and industrial meters based in Ivano-Frankivsk, the industrial capital of western Ukraine. On December 11, 1997, Prendergast (representing American Meter), Friedman (representing his firm, Joseph Friedman & Sons, International, Inc.), and representatives of Promprilad and American-Ukrainian Business Consultants, L.P. ("AUBC") met in Kyiv (the current preferred transliteration of "Kiev") and entered into the first of the agreements at issue here.

The agreement provided for the establishment of a joint venture company, to be called PrompriladAmco, in which the four signatories would become shareholders. PrompriladAmco would work in conjunction with its principals to develop the market for American Meter products in the former Soviet Union and, most important for the purposes of this action, the agreement committed American Meter to the following obligations:

> 9. AMCO shall grant Joint Venture PrompryladAmco exclusive rights to manufacture and install Meters within the former Soviet Union. . . .

> 10. AMCO shall grant Joint Venture PrompryladAmco exclusive rights to distribute the products manufactured by PrompryladAmco and all products manufactured by AMCO in the former Soviet Union. . . .

> 13. AMCO will deliver components and parts for Meters taking into account 90% assembly.

14. PrompryladAmco (at the first stage) shall perform 10% of the work required to assembl[e] the Meters using components and parts delivered by AMCO.

15. AMCO will deliver the components and parts for Meters by lots in containers, payments for the delivery being subject to at least a 90-day grace period.

16. The number of the components and parts for Meters to be delivered to Ukraine shall be based on demand in the former Soviet Union.

17. Orders for the components and parts for Meters, with the quantities and prices according to paragraph 16 above shall be an integral part of this Agreement.

After executing the agreement, the parties incorporated PrompriladAmco in Ukraine, and Friedman became its Chief Executive Officer. The new corporation set out to obtain Ukrainian regulatory approval for American Meter products, which required bringing Ukrainian officials to the United States to inspect American Meter's manufacturing process, and it sponsored a legislative measure that would give those products a competitive advantage in the Ukrainian market.

On April 20, 1998, Friedman and a representative of AUBC executed a second joint venture agreement for the purpose of marketing the gas piping products of Perfection Corporation, a wholly-owned subsidiary of American Meter. Again, the parties agreed to create and fund a corporation, this one to be called Amco Ukrservice, and American Meter committed itself to deliver, on credit, a level of goods based on demand in the former Soviet Union. The parties duly formed Amco Ukrservice, and Friedman became its Chief Executive Officer.

By early summer, PrompriladAmco and Amco Ukrservice had begun submitting product orders to American Meter. In late June or early July, however, American Meter President Harry Skilton effectively terminated the joint ventures by stopping a shipment of goods that was on its way to Ukraine and by refusing to extend credit to either PrompriladAmco or Amco Ukrservice. Finally, at a meeting on October 27, 1998, American Meter Vice-President Alex Tyshovnytsky informed Friedman that the corporation had decided to withdraw from Ukraine "due to unstable business conditions and eroding investment confidence in that country."

On May 23, 2000, PrompriladAmco and Amco Ukrservice filed parallel complaints claiming that American Meter had breached the relevant joint venture agreement by refusing to deliver the meters and parts that the plaintiffs could sell in the former Soviet Union. PrompriladAmco's complaint alleges that the breach caused it to lose $143,179,913 in profits between 1998 and 2003, and Amco Ukrservice claims lost profits of $88,812,000 for the same period. We consolidated the actions on August 18, 2000.

II. *American Meter's Motion for Summary Judgment*

American Meter argues that summary judgment is warranted here because the joint venture agreements are invalid under the CISG and Ukrainian law. It also contends that it is entitled to summary judgment because the plaintiffs' claims for damages are based on nothing but "rank speculation." We consider each of these arguments in turn.

[The court concluded that the Convention on Contracts for the International Sale of Goods does not apply to distributorship agreements as such.]

B. *Ukrainian Law*

In the alternative, American Meter argues that the joint venture agreements are unenforceable because they violate a number of Ukrainian laws on the form of contracts for the sale and supply of goods. To resolve this question, we must first determine whether Ukrainian law indeed controls the validity of these agreements under Pennsylvania's choice of law rules, which are applicable here pursuant to *Klaxon Co. v. Stentor Electric Mfg. Co.*, 313 U.S. 487 (1941).

. . .

2. *Sources of Law*

While the plaintiffs and American Meter agree that ordinary breach of contract principles would govern the plaintiffs' claims under Pennsylvania law, they dispute whether the joint venture agreements are invalid under Ukrainian law and, if so, what governmental interests any invalidating laws would serve. We therefore begin with a discussion of Pennsylvania's interest in this action and then turn to the more difficult problems that Ukrainian law presents, first examining the statutes that American Meter has identified and then predicting whether a Ukrainian court would apply them in this case. Finally, after we have isolated any applicable statutory provisions, we will consider Ukraine's interest in their enforcement. . . .

Not only does Pennsylvania have significant contacts with both the parties and the joint ventures, but enforcement of the joint venture agreements would advance the Commonwealth's general interests. As American Meter grudgingly concedes, the vindication of contractual parties' legitimate expectations creates a stable business environment and thereby helps the Commonwealth achieve its commercial potential. Finally, although American Meter asserts that the plaintiffs' claims for damages are too speculative, it does not dispute that, as an abstract proposition, the joint venture agreements create enforceable obligations under Pennsylvania law.

(b) *Ukrainian Law*

In the years since it achieved independence, Ukraine has developed a complex and, from an outsider's perspective, exceptionally murky body of law governing the form and content of international commercial agreements. American Meter contends that the joint venture agreements are invalid under three separate statutory schemes and that each advances identifiable and significant state interests.

1. *"Regulations on the Supply of Industrial Goods" (1988)*

On July 25, 1988, the USSR Council of Ministers promulgated "Regulations on the Supply of Industrial Goods," which remained effective in Ukraine after the collapse of the Soviet Union pursuant to a general reception statute that the Verkovna Rada, the Ukrainian Parliament, enacted in 1991. Under Paragraph 19 of the Regulations, a contract for the supply of goods must identify the goods to be delivered, the time of delivery, and their price, quantity, and quality. American Meter's Ukrainian legal expert has opined that the Regulations were still in force in 1998 and that the joint venture agreements are invalid because their supply provisions lack the terms detailed in Paragraph 19. The plaintiffs' legal expert, however, contends that the Regulations have no relevance here because they were enacted to regulate the Soviet Union's internal market and, in any event, never applied to joint venture agreements. In support of this interpretation, the plaintiffs' expert points to Paragraph 2, which provides that the Regulations cover the relations among state-owned and cooperative and other social organizations regarding the supply of goods (including the supply of . . . imported products in the internal market, unless otherwise provided by law). . . ."

Although American Meter solicited a supplemental affidavit from its Ukrainian expert, he declined to challenge the plaintiffs' expert's views on the Regulations. In view of the fact that the plaintiffs' contentions appear to have textual support and in the absence of a counter-argument from American Meter we must conclude that the plaintiffs' view carries the day on this issue and that the Regulations are inapplicable here.

2. *"Provisions on the Form of Foreign Economic Agreements" (1995)*

American Meter's legal expert has also brought to our attention the "Provisions on the Form of Foreign Economic Agreements," which the Ukrainian Ministry of Foreign Economic Relations and Trade enacted in 1995. The Provisions' preamble states that they "are applicable when concluding sale (purchase) agreements on goods (services, performance of work) and barter agreements among Ukrainian and foreign economic subjects irrespective of their property form and type of activities."

Agreements governed by the Provisions must, *inter alia*, identify the goods to be sold and specify their quantity and quality. Provisions § 1.3 American Meter contends that the joint venture agreements are invalid under the Provisions because they manifestly do not satisfy these requirements. However, as the plaintiffs' legal expert has contended, the Provisions offer no textual support for American Meter's position. Indeed, the text of the Provisions suggests that they do not regulate joint venture agreements and were instead enacted to regularize contracts for the sale of goods and provision of services. Not only does the preamble state that the Provisions are applicable to sale and barter agreements, but several sections of Part One clearly contemplate that its requirements will apply to contracts for goods and services. *See*, e.g., § 1.3 providing that the "Subject of Agreement" section of a contract must "define what goods (services, works) one of the counterparts is required to supply"; §§ 1.5 & 1.8 (mandating that a contract specify "basic conditions of goods supply (acceptance of performed works or services)" and "conditions of acceptance (handing-over) of goods (works, services)").

Finally, the plaintiffs' construction of the Provisions gains support from the framers' apparent intention that they be read *in pari materia* with Ukraine's Foreign Economic Activities Law ("FEAL"). *See* Preamble (providing that foreign economic agreements must be made pursuant to the FEAL); § 3 (listing the FEAL among "legal and normative acts of Ukraine, which regulate the form, procedures of conclusion and performance of foreign economic agreements (contracts)"). Because the

FEAL recognizes joint venture agreements, *see* FEAL art. 6 para. 12 (providing that "[a] foreign economic agreement (contract) on joint venture creation shall be governed by the law of the country in which the joint venture is created and officially registered"), it is improbable that the Foreign Ministry intended the 1995 enactment to invalidate such agreements, which create long-term relationships and are unlikely to contain price, quantity, and delivery terms that would be sufficiently precise to satisfy the Provisions.

In view of this textual evidence, we conclude that although the Provisions would likely govern a particular sales contract executed pursuant to a joint venture agreement, they do not bear on the validity of the joint venture agreement itself.

3. *Foreign Economic Activity Law (1991)*

Finally, American Meter invites us to consider whether the Ukrainian courts would invalidate the joint venture agreements under Article 6 of the FEAL. At the time the parties entered into these agreements, Article 6 required any contract between a Ukrainian entity and a foreign entity to be executed by two representatives of the Ukrainian signatory, and neither Promprilad nor AUBC complied with this rule.

Ukraine's two-signature rule was the final incarnation of a policy with deep roots in the history of the Soviet command economy. According to a Stalin-era decree, any contract between a foreign entity and a Soviet foreign trade organization ("FTO") that was executed in Moscow required the signatures of the FTO's chairman or deputy as well as a person possessing the chairman's power of attorney. Contracts executed abroad required the signatures of two persons with powers of attorney. The government published the names of FTO officials with the power to sign such agreements in a foreign trade journal. A 1978 enactment of the USSR Council of Ministers, "On the Procedure for Signing Foreign Trade Transactions," retained the two-signature rule, and according to a late Soviet court decision, failure to comply with the rule rendered the contract voidable at the instance of the FTO.

One writer has suggested that the purpose of the two-signature rule was "to protect foreign trade organizations from being bound by improvident contracts concluded by junior officials in return for kickbacks." The plaintiffs' legal expert has offered the more sinister, but not incompatible, explanation that the role of the second signatory generally was to exercise control over the first signatory in the interests of the KGB."

Whatever its purpose may have been, one might have thought that the two-signature rule would have disappeared after 1990 along with the other legal trappings of the Soviet economy. In 1991, however, the Verkovna Rada enshrined the two-signature rule in the FEAL:

> In the event that the foreign economic agreement is signed by an individual, signature of such individual shall be required. The foreign economic agreement shall be signed on behalf of other subjects of economic activity by two persons: one person who is authorized to sign by virtue of his/her position, in accordance with his/her founding documents, and another person who is solely authorized to sign on the basis of the power

of attorney issued under the hand of the directors of the subject of foreign economic activity, unless otherwise provided by founding documents.

FEAL art. 6 para. 2.

Ukrainian businesses, however, did not always comply with the two-signature rule, and a dispute between a Ukrainian pharmaceutical firm and its American trading partner soon forced the courts and Verkovna Rada to clarify the rule's place in Ukrainian commercial law. Armor Pharmaceutical filed a claim in the Ukrainian Arbitration Court against Lubnipharm for the return of partially unpaid pharmaceuticals. On November 22, 1996, the Supreme Arbitration Court of Ukraine ("SACU") invalidated the original contracts on the ground that two representatives of Lubnipharm did not execute them, but on January 11, 1997 the Arbitration Board of the SACU declared that failure to comply with the two-signature rule was not automatic grounds for invalidation and overturned the decision of November 22nd. The Plenary Meeting of the SACU upheld the Arbitration Board's decision, and the dispute ultimately landed in the Constitutional Court of Ukraine. In a decision dated November 26, 1998, the Court somewhat ambiguously stated that the two-signature rule was "obligatory" but also held that failure to comply "*may* be the basis for invalidation of the foreign economic agreement in court as not meeting the requirements of laws or international agreements of Ukraine." *Id.* (emphasis added).

The Verkovna Rada and SACU swiftly acted to blunt the Constitutional Court's ruling. The Deputy Prosecutor General of Ukraine filed a submission in the Supreme Arbitration Court to review the Lubnipharm case, but in a ruling issued June 11, 1999, the SACU affirmed its earlier decision to uphold the Lubnipharm contracts. Seizing upon the Constitutional Court's statement that failure to comply with the two-signature rule *may* be a basis for invalidating a contract, the Court concluded that it retained the discretion to affirm non-conforming contracts and that invalidation would be inappropriate in the Lubnipharm case because both parties had actually performed under the contracts. The Court also noted that, in any event, the Constitutional Court's decision did not state whether it had retroactive effect. Four months later, the Verkovna Rada at last repealed the two-signature rule.

Apparently, however, neither the SACU's narrow construction of the Constitutional Court's ruling nor the amendment to Article 6 has dimmed the lower court's willingness to invoke the two-signature rule in cases involving contracts executed before the repeal. In 2001, for example, Judge Zyrnov of the Kyiv City Commercial Court relied upon the rule to nullify a lease and credit agreement between a Ukrainian corporation and Fortis Bank of the Netherlands, despite the fact that the Bank had rendered performance.

Predicting another judicial system's resolution of an issue is always a perilous business, but we must conclude there is at least a possibility that a Ukrainian court would invalidate the joint venture agreements on the ground that the Ukrainian parties did not comply with the two-signature rule. The Constitutional Court has confirmed that the courts may invalidate a contract for failure to comply with the rule, and while the SACU has shown its willingness to uphold contracts where (as here) there has been performance, the Fortis Bank decision shows that the lower courts are still prepared to enforce the rule even in circumstances where the SACU might demur.

4.   *Characterization of the Conflict of Law Problem*

Our conclusion that the courts of Pennsylvania and Ukraine might diverge in their treatment of the joint venture agreements merely poses the conflict of law problem without resolving it. In order to determine whether this case involves a false or true conflict, we must first determine what, if any, governmental interests the two-signature rule advances.

American Meter contends that Ukraine has an interest in the retroactive enforcement of the rule because it protects Ukrainians who enter into contracts with foreigners and promotes certainty, predictability, and uniformity in commercial relationships. American Meter's "argument from paternalism" would bear close scrutiny if we were resolving this conflict of law problem in 1992. After all, the plaintiffs' legal expert had stated that the Verkovna Rada included the rule in the FEAL as a sop to legislators who opposed economic liberalization, and perhaps its proponents believed that requiring two signatures on contracts would protect Ukrainian naifs from more commercially sophisticated (and capitalism-hardened) foreigners. Now that the Verkovna Rada has repealed the two-signature rule, however, we cannot conclude on the record before us that its continued enforcement advances any *current* social, political, or economic interest of Ukraine.

Turning to American Meter's "argument from commercial certainty," we note that this articulation of Ukraine's interest in the rule remains plausible despite the repeal. A hard-and-fast policy that all foreign economic agreements executed between the enactment of the FEAL and the statute's 1999 amendment must comply with the two-signature rule would like any bright-line rule have the advantage of letting parties know exactly where they stand. But as the recent decisions of the SACU and Kyiv Commercial Court underscore, the difficulty with this argument is that the two-signature rule is not so much a bright-line rule as it is a controversial repository of judicial discretion that allows courts to invalidate contracts for any reason or perhaps for no reason at all. Under these circumstances, we cannot discern how the two-signature rule advances any of the procedural or commercial advantages that Ukraine would derive from a predictable body of law governing the validity of contracts.

To summarize, we have concluded that Pennsylvania and Ukraine both have significant relationships with the parties and the transactions. Moreover, we have found that Pennsylvania has a general interest in the enforcement of contracts, and it goes without saying that this interest would be compromised if a Pennsylvania corporation could defeat the expectations of its trading partners in the manner American Meter has proposed here. Finally, we have concluded that American Meter has not identified any governmental interest of Ukraine in the continued enforcement of the repealed two-signature rule.

Because our analysis reveals that Pennsylvania's interest would be harmed by applying Ukraine's law, but that no identified Ukrainian interest will be impaired by enforcing these contracts, this case presents a false conflict. Under the Pennsylvania choice-of-law regime,

Pennsylvania law therefore governs the plaintiffs' claims, and American Meter is not entitled to summary judgment on the ground that the contracts are invalid under Ukrainian law.

C. *Compensatory Damages*

American Meter finally argues that, even if the joint venture agreements are enforceable, the plaintiffs' claims for damages are too speculative to warrant submission to a jury because they are nothing more than extrapolations from sales agreements that were never valid under Ukrainian law.

In Pennsylvania, a plaintiff seeking damages for anticipated lost profits must offer evidence providing a basis for estimating them with reasonable certainty. Although a new business with no record of profitability cannot usually satisfy this standard, the Pennsylvania Superior Court has carved out an exception for a new business that can show a "significant interest" in its product or service before the contract breach occurred. Moreover, the Superior Court has cautioned that "it is better that the jury hear the evidence of future lost profits and decide its weight than allow the court to exclude the evidence entirely."

There is no question that PrompriladAmco and Amco Ukrservice were new businesses operating in an unstable commercial environment, but for summary judgment purposes the record sufficiently shows that Ukrainian purchasers demonstrated their interest in American Meter's products during the brief lifespan of the joint ventures. Russo and representatives of PrompriladAmco attended an industrial trade show in Kyiv in July of 1998, and Prendergast reported that interest in American Meter's products at the trade show was "overwhelming."

Moreover, the plaintiffs entered into six sales contracts with Ukrainian municipalities and gas companies in June and July of 1998. American Meter argues that these agreements have no evidentiary value because they violated a 1997 decree of the Ukraine Cabinet of Ministers granting a state firm, Ukrgas, the exclusive right to purchase and produce gas meters. However, the plaintiffs' legal expert has declared that on July 30, 1998, the Council of Ministers rescinded the decree, thereby making it possible for purchasers and suppliers to re-execute any agreements entered during the pendency of the decree.

Viewing this record in the light most favorable to the plaintiffs, we conclude that summary judgment would be premature because there remain material issues of fact concerning the demand for American Meter's products and the extrapolative value of the six sales contracts.

III. *PrompriladAmco's Partial Motion for Summary Judgment*

American Meter's president, Harry Skilton, has candidly acknowledged that he terminated the Ukrainian project in 1998 after refusing to extend credit or ship goods. On the basis of this admission, Prompriladamco contends that it is entitled to summary judgment on the issue of liability because there is no genuine issue of material fact as to whether American Meter breached the joint venture agreements. American Meter responds that even if its conduct would constitute a breach of the agreement there remains a genuine issue of material fact as to whether Prendergast had actual or apparent authority to execute such a contract in his capacity as the corporation's agent.

A. *Prendergast's Actual Agency Authority*

We begin with Prendergast's actual agency authority. Pennsylvania law recognizes two forms of actual authority: express and implied. Express actual authority is "directly granted by the principal to bind the principal as to certain matters," while implied actual authority exists where the agent's acts are necessary, proper and usual in the exercise of the agent's express authority."

While it is true that Prendergast was actively identifying and then negotiating with potential Ukrainian partners in 1997, Harry Skilton has averred that he never approved or was even aware of the Prompriladamco agreement. He also claims that, pursuant to a longstanding resolution of the Board of Directors, neither Prendergast nor Watson (Prendergast's immediate supervisor) could have made the multimillion dollar commitment contemplated in the agreement without Board approval. At his deposition, moreover, Skilton stated that he had only authorized Watson and Prendergast to secure certification for American Meter's products and create "standby" or "cubbyhole" joint ventures with local companies that could have become active if the corporation had decided to move forward with the Ukrainian project.

Jim Diasio, who gradually assumed Watson's responsibilities as Chief Financial Officer in 1998, acknowledges that he was aware of Friedman's and AUBC's lobbying and marketing efforts and that he knew PrompriladAmco and American Meter had created a "standby" joint venture company. However, he denies any knowledge of the joint venture agreement, and he claims that there was not even a copy of the agreement in Watson's files.

Finally, American Meter's Assistant Secretary and custodian of corporate seals, C. Kelsey Brown, avers that the rubber stamp Prendergast used to authenticate his signature on the agreement is not an official corporate seal, that he never issued it to Prendergast, and that he has never even seen it. Viewed in the light most favorable to American Meter, this record shows that there is a genuine issue of material fact as to whether Prendergast had actual authority to enter into the joint venture agreement.

B. *Prendergast's Apparent Agency Authority*

American Meter also argues that there is a disputed question of fact as to whether Prendergast had apparent authority to execute the Prompriladamco agreement. Apparent authority exists under Pennsylvania law where a principal, by words or conduct, leads people with whom the alleged agent deals to believe that the principal has granted the agent the authority he or she purports to exercise. The third party is entitled to believe the agent has the authority he purports to exercise only where a person of ordinary prudence, diligence and discretion would so believe. Thus, a third party can rely on the apparent authority of an agent when this is a reasonable interpretation of the manifestations of the principal.

Whether the doctrine of apparent authority applies in a given case is almost never suited for summary judgment because it closely turns on both the principal's manifestations and the reasonableness of the third party's beliefs. The only person involved in this action who conceivably could have been deceived into thinking that Prendergast could sign the joint venture agreement was Simon Friedman, and what he knew about Prendergast's authority is very much an open question. Prendergast testified that he told Friedman he had authority to negotiate and execute the joint venture agreements, but American Meter plausibly counters that Friedman's own correspondence with Diasio betrays his awareness that Prendergast was not unilaterally calling the shots at American Meter.

On this record, therefore, summary judgment would be inappropriate because Prendergast's apparent authority is a highly consequential question of disputed fact that must await trial.

NOTES

1. Much of the court's attention focuses on the conflicts of law issues, and its elaborate discussion underscores the importance of resolving this issue in the contract itself rather than having to resort to the courts. How do lawyers typically avoid such disputes through the contract drafting process? Why is the choice of law to govern a contract such an important issue? Why might a lawyer seek to specifically exclude the application of the CISG in a contract?

2. What does the dispute over Prendergast's authority teach about taking steps to ensure you are dealing with a party with proper authority? How do companies solve such a problem?

3. Note the grants of exclusive rights to manufacture and distribute the metering equipment. Efforts to obtain such exclusive rights in emerging markets are common. Why do companies seek such rights? The answer may be, in part, because they can, but what are the consequences for such companies and for the local markets?

A PROBLEM

Our client, the multinational energy conglomerate Petro America Inc., a Delaware corporation, wishes to begin activities in Russia. Initially, Petro would like to sell pipeline repair equipment to Transneft, the Russian state organization responsible for the domestic transport of oil via pipeline operators. As we discuss Petro's plans for the Russian market, we learn that they also are interested in oil and gas exploration opportunities in the Far East, and will establish contacts with appropriate Russian oil companies that may be interested in forming joint ventures. Within the next year or so, Petro plans to station a representative in Moscow to follow developments in the oil and gas sector, and may seek to hire Russian employees as support staff in Moscow.

Petro also mentions to you that they have been introduced to Geodata, a recently formed Russian enterprise, which purports to have available geological data of interest to Petro and which has among its employees a number of senior officials of the Russian Ministry of Fuel and Energy. Geodata suggests that Petro form a joint venture to develop and market geological data and eventually to explore for and produce oil and gas. Geodata currently has extra office space that it is prepared to make available to Petro. Eager to gain a foothold (and useful contacts) in the Russian oil and gas industries, Petro is seriously considering Geodata's proposal.

Among the questions on which Petro seeks advice are the following:

1.   What type of presence does Petro need in Moscow to seek customers and to enter into contracts for the sale of their equipment and technology? How would you structure this "presence"?

2.   Should Petro form a Russian subsidiary that it can own directly? What are the advantages and disadvantages of forming a subsidiary now? If you do not think it appropriate for them to form a subsidiary at this time, under what circumstances would such an action be appropriate?

3.   Would it be advisable to form a joint venture with Geodata? What issues should concern Petro and how would you propose to deal with them?

4.   What issues are raised by Geodata's proposal to make available office space to Petro?

B. CORPORATE GOVERNANCE AND THE PITFALLS OF EMERGING MARKET INVESTMENTS

The legal structure of a business is meant to solve, or at least address, two fundamental problems. First, the structure allocates decisionmaking authority in a way that, ideally, maximizes the chances that the project will create rather than destroy value. Participants come to an enterprise with different assets and expectations. The structure seeks to create a way for them to work out their differences without hurting the business. Second, the structure identifies rights that the different participants have and thus sets boundaries on what the parties can do. If an investor expects to be robbed, the investment will not occur. In theory, the creation of basic rights benefits all parties by making complex cooperative business operations possible.

The effectiveness of legal rights, however, may not work out as expected. Even investors with some experience and competent counsel may find themselves surprised by how the legal system treats their rights.

In the Documents Supplement you will find the Russian Federation's Law on Joint Stock Companies. Review its provisions. What kinds of protection do minority shareholders have against exploitation by the majority? What kind of control does the governing board have over the management of a company? What provisions are mandatory, and what can be modified by contract?

The Law on Joint Stock Companies is significant, among other reasons, because prominent U.S. law professors played a central role in its conception and drafting. Consider their explanation of the statute, published soon after its adoption.

Bernard Black & Reinier Kraakman,
A Self-Enforcing Model of
Corporate Law

109 HARV. L. REV. 1911 (1996)

In this Article, we sketch the basic elements of a "self-enforcing" model of corporate law, designed for an emerging economy. The model is grounded in a case study: the effort, in which we participated, to develop a new corporate law for Russia. We begin with three central claims. First, effective corporate law is context-specific, even if the problems it must address are universal. The law that works for a developed economy, when transplanted to an emerging economy, will not achieve a sensible balance among company managers' need for flexibility to meet rapidly changing business conditions, companies' need for low-transaction-cost access to capital markets, large investors' need to monitor what managers do with the investors' money, and small investors' need for protection against self-dealing by managers and large investors. The defects in the law will increase the cost of capital and reduce its availability.

In developed countries, corporate law combines with other legal, market, and cultural constraints on the actions of corporate managers and controlling shareholders to achieve a sensible balance among these sometimes competing needs. Corporate law plays a relatively small, even "trivial" role. In emerging economies, these other constraints are weak or absent, so corporate law is a much more central tool for motivating managers and large shareholders to create social value rather than simply transfer wealth to themselves from others. The "market" cannot fill the regulatory gaps that an American-style "enabling" corporate law leaves behind.

Further, corporate law in developed countries evolved in tandem with supporting legal institutions. For example, the United States relies on expert judges to assess the reasonableness of takeover defenses and the fairness of transactions in which managers have a conflict of interest. When necessary, these judges make decisions literally overnight to ensure that judicial delay does not kill a challenged transaction. A company law that depends on fast and reliable judicial decisions is simply out of the question in many emerging markets. In Russia, for example, courts function slowly if at all, some judges are corrupt, and many are Soviet-era holdovers who neither understand business nor care to learn. Better judges and courts will emerge only over several decades, as the old judges die or retire. In the meantime, Russian corporate law must rely on courts as little as possible.

More generally, every emerging economy has some legal and market institutions, some norms of behavior, some distribution of share ownership, and some financial institutions. Corporate law must reflect these background facts. For example, if (as in Russia) employees often own large stakes in their companies, but are vulnerable to having their votes controlled by corporate managers, company law needs special rules that safeguard the rights of employee-shareholders. Company law must also limit the influence of dysfunctional background features, such as widespread corruption.

Our second central claim is that despite the context-specificity of effective corporate law, there is a large class of emerging capitalist economies (including formerly Communist countries) that are sufficiently similar to permit generalization about the type of corporate law that will be useful for them. Russia is perhaps an extreme case, but it is hardly alone in having insider-controlled companies, malfunctioning courts, weak and sometimes corrupt regulators, and poorly developed capital markets. For example, an acute problem in Russia is protecting minority investors against exploitation by managers or controlling shareholders. Protection of minority investors has also emerged as a central political issue in the most successful post-Communist economy, the Czech Republic, and is at the core of recent reforms in Israeli corporate law.

Our third claim is that our task is not impossible. Despite weak markets and institutions, one can design a company law that prevents a significant fraction of the corporate governance failures that would otherwise occur. Even developed country corporate governance systems fail with uncomfortable frequency. We can expect still more failures in emerging markets. Nonetheless, it is possible to design a law that works tolerably well—that vests substantial decisionmaking power in large outside shareholders, who have incentives to make good decisions; that reduces, though it cannot eliminate, fraud and self-dealing by corporate insiders; that minimizes, though it cannot altogether avoid, the need for official enforcement through courts; that gives managers and controlling shareholders incentives to obey the rules even when they could often get away with ignoring them; that reinforces desirable cultural attitudes about proper managerial behavior; and that still leaves managers with the flexibility they need to take risks and make quick decisions. Such a law can add far more value than corporate law adds in developed economies, precisely because other institutions that could shape corporate behavior are weak in developing economies.

The central features of our "self-enforcing" model of corporate law are:

(i) Enforcement, as much as possible, through actions by direct participants in the corporate enterprise (shareholders, directors, and managers), rather than indirect participants (judges, regulators, legal and accounting professionals, and the financial press).

(ii) Greater protection of outside shareholders than is common in developed economies, to respond to a high incidence of insider-controlled companies, the weakness of other constraints on self-dealing by managers and controlling shareholders, and the need to control self-dealing to strengthen the political credibility of a market economy.

(iii) Reliance on procedural protections—such as transaction approval by independent directors, independent shareholders, or both—rather than on flat prohibitions of suspect categories of transactions. The use of procedural devices balances the need for shareholder protection against the need for business flexibility.

(iv) Whenever possible, use of bright-line rules, rather than standards, to define proper and improper behavior. Bright-line rules can be understood by those who must comply with them and have a better chance of being enforced. Standards, in contrast, require judicial interpretation, which is often unavailable in emerging markets, and presume a shared cultural understanding of the regulatory policy that underlies the standards, which may also be absent.

(v) Strong legal remedies on paper, to compensate for the low probability that the sanctions will be applied in fact.

Enforcement takes place primarily through a combination of voting rules and transactional rights. The central voting elements include: shareholder approval (including in some cases supermajority approval or approval by a majority of outside shareholders) for broad classes of major transactions and self-interested transactions; approval of self-interested transactions by a majority of outside directors; mandatory cumulative voting for directors, which empowers large minority shareholders to select directors (this power is protected by requirements of one common share, one vote; minimum board size; and no staggering of board terms); and a unitary ballot on which both managers and large shareholders can nominate directors. The honesty of the vote is protected through confidential voting and independent vote tabulation, while the quality of voting decisions is buttressed by mandatory disclosure rules.

Shareholders also receive transactional rights (put and call options) triggered by specified corporate actions. These include preemptive rights when a company issues new shares; appraisal rights for shareholders who do not approve major transactions; and takeout rights when a controlling stake in the firm is acquired (that is, minority shareholder rights to sell their shares to the new controlling shareholder).

The self-enforcing model seeks to build legal norms that managers and large shareholders will see as reasonable and comply with voluntarily. The need to induce voluntary compliance reinforces our preference for procedural rather than substantive protections. For example, managers may evade a flat ban on self-interested transactions, yet comply with a procedural requirement for shareholder approval because they think that they can obtain approval. Once they decide to obtain shareholder approval, the managers may make the transaction more favorable to shareholders, to ensure approval and avoid embarrassment. The model often relies not only on bright-line rules, but also on relatively simple rules. Managers can't comply with, and judges can't enforce, rules that they don't understand. Nor will managers respect an unduly complex statute.

. . .

The self-enforcing model is designed to harness the monitoring ability of large, albeit still minority, outside shareholders. Collective action problems preclude effective monitoring by small shareholders. But large shareholders, in defending their own self-interest, will often defend the interests of small shareholders as well. Many companies are likely to have large outside blockholders, in part because sophisticated investors understand all too well the weak position of a small outside shareholder and thus prefer to hold an influential block of a company's stock, if they own its shares at all.

Corporate law and investor preferences interact: the more influence that the law gives to large outside investors, the more likely investors are to choose to hold large stakes—and to use the influence that these stakes provide. In terms of Albert Hirschman's dichotomy between exit and voice as monitoring mechanisms, thin capital markets eliminate exit as an available option in emerging economies. Investors therefore look to maximize their voice, and the self-enforcing model empowers them to do so.

1. *Structural Constraints.*—The structural constraints that define the self-enforcing model operate both at the shareholder level and at the level of the board of directors. At the shareholder level, these constraints typically involve shareholder voting requirements or transactional rights (put and call options) triggered by specific corporate actions.

With regard to voting rules, a self-enforcing statute can require supermajority shareholder approval for central business decisions such as mergers, rather than the simple majority approval of the enabling approach. It can also require shareholder approval for a broader range of corporate actions than an enabling statute would, such as decisions to issue significant amounts of new equity or to purchase or sell major assets. For self-interested transactions between the company and its directors, officers, or large shareholders, a self-enforcing statute replaces the permissiveness of the enabling approach (loosely policed by courts) and the ban of the prohibitory model with approval by independent directors, a majority of noninterested shareholders, or both. The voting decisions of large shareholders, if obtained through fair voting procedures and with adequate disclosure, are a more fine-grained way to distinguish between good and bad transactions than substantive prohibitions could possibly be.

To safeguard the voting mechanism, the self-enforcing statute can include a one share, one vote rule to prevent insiders from acquiring voting power disproportionate to their economic interest in the company, as well as procedures to ensure honest voting, such as use of an independent registrar to record share transfers, confidential voting, and independent vote tabulation. Outside shareholders' influence can be increased through use of a universal ballot that lets them cheaply place director nominations and other proposals on the voting agenda. Good voting decisions require good information, but the quality of shareholders' information can be improved by mandatory disclosure rules and by cumulative voting, which enhances large blockholders' access to information about the company.

Voting mechanisms, which by their nature must be exercised collectively, can be supplemented with transactional rights that individual shareholders can exercise. A self-enforcing law can convey appraisal rights (put options) to unhappy shareholders for a broader range of corporate actions than a typical enabling statute would. Exercise of appraisal rights can be made simpler, and low-ball repurchase offers chilled, by requiring a company, when it solicits shareholder approval for an action that will trigger appraisal rights, to publish an offer price that will be binding on the company if the appraisal rights are exercised. The law can convey mandatory preemptive rights (call options) to acquire shares in proportion to one's ownership stake, as protection against underpriced stock issues. It can give shareholders takeout rights (put options) to sell their shares to a new controlling shareholder, as protection against transfer of control from known (and presumably trusted) hands to less trusted ones.

The voting rights and transactional rights approaches can be combined, with voting used to define the extent of the transactional rights. For example, preemptive rights can be made waivable *ex ante* by shareholder vote, and takeout rights can be made waivable by a majority vote of shareholders other than the new controlling shareholder.

A self-enforcing statute also introduces structural constraints at the level of the board of directors. For example, it can require that a certain proportion of a company's board of directors be independent, and then vest these independent directors with authority over key corporate decisions—such as approval of self-interested transactions. It can mandate board structures, such as an audit committee, that amplify the power of independent directors but are optional under enabling statutes.

A critical feature of the self-enforcing model, linking shareholder level and board level constraints, is a cumulative voting rule for election of directors, buttressed by a mandatory minimum board size and a ban on staggered terms of office. Cumulative voting allows large outside shareholders to elect representatives to the board. As long as outside shareholders hold stakes large enough to elect their own representatives, cumulative voting enhances information flow and ensures that at least some directors will be true shareholder representatives. An insider majority will still control non-related-party transactions under this rule, but outside representation makes it harder for insiders to ignore or deceive minority shareholders. Although other voting rules, such as class voting, can also ensure minority representation on the board of directors, a cumulative voting rule is flexible enough to encompass a wide variety of ownership structures.

2. Simple, Bright-Line Rules and Strong Remedies.—The self-enforcing model compensates for the weakness of formal enforcement through a combination of relatively simple, bright-line rules governing when its structural constraints apply, rules that insiders will often comply with voluntarily, and strong sanctions for violating the rules. The self-enforcing model might, for example, require a shareholder vote for a purchase or sale of assets that equals 50% or more of the book value of the firm's assets. To be sure, book value is an imperfect measure of a transaction's importance. Moreover, a percentage threshold will be overinclusive in some cases (hindering transactions by requiring a shareholder vote without sufficient reason) and underinclusive in others (failing to reach transactions that could seriously affect shareholder value). But this rule is far clearer in application than the familiar enabling law requirement of shareholder approval for a sale of "substantially all" assets.

When a pure bright-line rule is unavailable, the self-enforcing approach uses more concrete standards than are often found in developed markets. Compare, for example, the following alternative instructions to directors who must decide whether to approve a transaction between a company and one of its directors:

> (i) a self-interested transaction must be either ratified by shareholders or approved by the noninterested directors acting

in the best interests of the company, or else is subject to "entire fairness" review by the courts;

(ii) a transaction between the company and a director or top manager must be approved by noninterested directors, who should grant approval only if the transaction is fair to the company;

(iii) a transaction between the company and a director must be approved by noninterested directors, who should grant approval only if the company receives consideration, in exchange for property or services delivered by the company, that is worth no less than the market value of the property or services, and the company pays consideration, in exchange for property or services, that does not exceed the market value of the property or services.

The first approach, with some judicial gloss, is essentially the legal rule today in the United States and Great Britain. In an emerging economy, it offers meager guidance to directors. The second approach borrows from current best practice in the United States by vesting the decision in noninterested directors who are instructed to review the "fairness" of the transaction. In the United States, this best practice rests on a cultural understanding that "fairness" turns largely on price, relative to market price. But in an emerging economy, directors and judges may not know what it means for a transaction to be "fair."

We favor the third approach in an emerging economy. Enforcement is still scarcely automatic, but even an unsophisticated judge can understand that the company's sale of property to a manager, who promptly resells it for thrice the price that he paid, was not at market value. A corrupt judge who nonetheless blesses such a transaction advertises his corruption to all. Sunshine is an imperfect disinfectant, but an important one nonetheless.

The third approach also tells directors how they ought to behave. Over time, the norms that a company's transactions with insiders should be at market prices and should be reviewed by noninterested directors may become part of corporate culture. The cost of this more precise approach is that it fails to reach situations where a transaction, although at a "market" price, is nonetheless unfair to the company—perhaps because the price was toward the low end of a broad range of plausible "market" prices.

. . .

The self-enforcing approach further encourages managers to comply with its rules through relatively severe sanctions for noncompliance, which compensate in part for the low probability of enforcement. For example, the remedy for failure to obtain advance approval of a self-interested transaction can be automatic forfeit to the company of the self-interested person's profit from the transaction. This contrasts with the enabling approach, in which an interested party generally can defend a transaction on the grounds that it was substantively fair.

A statute can rely heavily on rules (rather than standards) and still be so complex that managers and judges can't understand it, and managers soon give up in disgust and stop trying. Every additional rule and nuance adds to the law's overall complexity and detracts from its overall effectiveness. This is a kind of externality—the direct benefits from tailoring the law more closely to fit discrete situations must be balanced against the indirect costs of complexity. To combat this problem, a bias in favor of simplicity must overlay every discrete decision embedded in a self-enforcing law.

. . .

The self-enforcement model is designed to minimize reliance on official enforcement. But how effective can the law be if judicial enforcement is as weak, corruption as widespread, and organized crime as strong as is currently the case in Russia? Are all efforts to control private behavior within the corporate form doomed to failure without some minimum level of enforcement capability?

To explore these questions, let us imagine, counterfactually, a world with no official enforcement—no government organ that can enforce the official corporate rules. If the self-enforcing approach can elicit partial compliance in this hypothetical world, then it can only work better—though still imperfectly—in the more realistic case where official enforcement is weak but not wholly absent.

The concept of rules without official enforcement is not new. Robert Ellickson has explored situations in which norms of conduct emerge without official enforcement, including conflict between whaling vessels in international waters, and situations where official rules are so out of touch with practical needs that a public consensus develops around informal norms. Here, we consider the potential for rules to function without official enforcement in the specific context of corporate law. For example, suppose that company directors can ignore all shareholder voting rules without fear of official intervention. What recourse is open to a 20% shareholder who loses a board seat because the company erases him from the shareholder register, refuses to provide cumulative voting, or conveniently loses his ballot?

One answer is that the question is posed too starkly. Even without official sanctions, many companies will not resort to such tactics. Some managers will comply with the written law simply because it is both written and reasonable; some will comply because their peers do; others will comply so as not to risk embarrassing news stories. Companies that need capital will comply with the rules to build a reputation for honest behavior, and companies that plan to enter long-term contractual relations must safeguard their reputation for honesty and fair dealing.

Without official enforcement, the entire corporate law (including its nominally "mandatory" terms) becomes a set of default rules from which the participants in the corporate enterprise can depart, jointly or unilaterally. But, as with any set of default rules, it will be costly to ignore them or contract around them.

There may also be penalties harsher than loss of reputation for breaking the rules. A world without official enforcement will surely develop unofficial enforcement. Suppose, plausibly, that some shareholders are willing and able to resort to violence if their rights are violated, and that company directors are not sure which shareholders may react this way. Fear of these few can cause directors to behave properly toward all shareholders.

Few shareholders are likely to shoot a director just for making a bad business decision. That would be foolish: it is unlikely to encourage better decisions in the future and risks retaliation in kind. But the situation is very different if the directors break a clear rule conferring voting rights. Now a wrong has been committed, and directors will face personal liability of a tangible kind if some shareholders feel they must respond. Thus, few directors will blatantly disregard the written law. At the very least, they will take seriously a 20% shareholder's demand for board representation by weighing the personal risks from rejecting the demand against the benefits, much as if official enforcement of shareholder rights were in prospect. The more blatantly shareholder rights are violated, the more likely a shareholder is to take extralegal action, and thus the greater the expected sanction will be. For example, removing a shareholder from the share register is more likely to provoke a violent response than refusing to use the required procedures for approving a self-interested transaction.

We do not suggest that unofficial enforcement is anything near ideal. Some directors will be shot for imagined wrongs or, as at Krasnoyarsk Aluminum, as part of a quite literal takeover "battle." Shareholders, too, will be at risk if they complain too loudly when a company is looted. Large shareholders may succeed in extorting private benefits from companies when these can be hidden from other shareholders. But on the whole, men with guns will often be polite to each other, especially if, as is common for corporate enterprises, they expect to meet again. Repeated interaction magnifies both the importance of reputation and the risk of retaliation for misbehavior. Unofficial yet still organized enforcement may arise and coalesce around the written law. In sum, a corporate law that defines norms of politeness in ways that the participants perceive as reasonable can be partially effective even without official enforcement.

An example: our model law limits the right of insolvent companies to distribute assets to shareholders or to sell assets for less than equivalent value. In a developed country, these "fraudulent conveyance" rules are enforced by courts and bankruptcy trustees, who chase and often retrieve improperly transferred assets. In Russia, creditors cannot rely on this kind of official enforcement. But there is a substitute already in place: creditors often threaten, and not infrequently shoot, debtors who haven't repaid their debts. The corporate law can help private actors to distinguish situations when an asset distribution was proper, even though the business later couldn't pay its debts, from situations when the asset distribution was improper when made. If the rules of conduct are clearer, borrowers with good investment opportunities will be more willing to risk borrowing money to finance these investments. The effective cost of capital will decline.

Once we reinstate the possibility of some recourse to courts, even corrupt courts, the self-enforcing model's effectiveness quickly increases. A corrupt judge can twist a "reasonableness" standard to reach the decision he was paid to reach, but cannot so easily twist a requirement that the company provide cumulative voting or appraisal rights. If the judge finds an exception on some spurious ground, it will be obvious to all. Yet few corrupt officials want to admit their corruption in public. Such a judge will also risk personal retaliation, much as corporate managers do, at the hands of private enforcers.

Moreover, over the longer term, blatant violation of reasonable norms can create a constituency for enforcement. Shareholders will bring political pressure to strengthen enforcement capability and will have obvious abuses to point to. News stories will highlight scandals, bringing further pressure for enforcement. Test cases, even if they fail in corrupt or incompetent courts, will form a basis for public opinion—and repeat players in financial markets may be willing to underwrite the costs of such test cases.

Finally, even if official enforcement is weak today, it may be stronger tomorrow. The prospect that future enforcement may threaten their gains will make corporate actors reluctant to presume nonenforcement, especially if the official sanctions, if imposed, are likely to be severe. For example, managers may prefer to seek shareholder approval of a self-interested transaction if they believe that approval is likely, rather than run even a small risk of facing a future lawsuit to disgorge profit or have the transaction unwound.

In short, the claim that corporate law can do much to shape private behavior even under conditions of weak official enforcement is not as strange as it may first appear to be. And even law with no official enforcement is not an oxymoron.

. . .

Transactions by a company that personally benefit directors, managers, or large shareholders (all of whom we call insiders, recognizing that the description may not be accurate for large shareholders) are inherently suspect because the insider has both the incentive and the ability to cause the company to enter into the transaction on unfair terms. Yet sometimes these transactions are advantageous to the company. Outright prohibition, in our judgment, is justified only when experience discloses both little business justification for a transaction type and a particularly high risk of abuse. We identify two such cases: loans by the company to insiders, and payments (kickbacks) by another person to an insider in connection with a transaction between the company and the other person. For other self-interested transactions, the self-enforcement model relies on a rigorous set of procedural protections, which apply in addition to any other board or shareholder approval requirements for particular transactions, such as mergers.

The principal procedural protections are (i) approval by noninterested directors (directors who don't have a financial interest in the transaction); and (ii) for sizeable transactions (our threshold for Russia was 2% of the book value of the company's assets or 2% of annual revenues), approval by noninterested shareholders. Even noninterested directors will often not act independently. Nevertheless, directors who are elected by minority shareholders through cumulative voting are likely to be genuinely independent. Thus, the cumulative voting rules interact importantly with the rules on self-interested transactions. The size threshold balances the risk that the cost and delay of a shareholder vote will block good transactions against the need to block large bad transactions. Noninterested directors can cheaply review all self-interested transactions; only large transactions should require the costly additional step of shareholder approval.

The self-enforcement model instructs the noninterested directors to approve a self-interested transaction only if they conclude that the company will receive value, in property or services, at least equal to the market value of the property or services the company gives up. This required finding informs the directors as to how to exercise their review power, gives directors who want to reject a transaction a basis for doing so, and provides a norm around which actual review practices may gradually coalesce. This standard may also provide a basis for a court challenge to especially egregious transactions, where the required finding was manifestly not made in good faith.

Sometimes, of course, insiders will hide their interest in a transaction. But in some transactions, the insiders' interests cannot be concealed; in others the insiders will obtain an honest vote to protect the transaction against later attack in the courts; and managers who think of themselves as honest will voluntarily follow the rules. When self-interested transactions are disclosed, shareholders or noninterested directors can vote down some of the worst transactions, while the "sunshine" requirement that transactions be disclosed to shareholders will deter others.

NOTES

1. Self-enforcement of rules is the subject of a rich and extensive theoretical literature. Rarely, however, does one encounter states of complete anarchy, where no formal institutions operate at all. Rather, formal institutions may be weak or impaired but still capable of having some influence on behavior. Where this is true (and in much of the emerging-market world, it is) there is a subtle but significant interrelationship between legal institutions and self-enforcement mechanisms. Self-enforcement strategies that operate in the context of strong legal systems (Robert Ellickson famously studied disputes among dairy farmers in the United States) may not perform as well where the institutions are weak or impaired. As you consider the cases below, reflect on well the self-enforcing model works in actual context.

2. Focus particularly on the interested-party rules. To what extent do they protect shareholders? To what extent do they allow interested persons to undo valuable and legitimate transactions? What is the role of the courts in enforcing these rules?

3. The following excerpt illustrates this problem. Compare its account of how things worked out under the law with the authors' earlier expectations:

**Bernard Black, Reinier Kraakman &
Anna Tarassova, Russian Privatization and
Corporate Governance: What Went Wrong?**
52 STAN. L. REV. 1731 (2000)

Company managers soon learned that they could plunder their firms with negligible risk of prosecution. For example, it's been two years since the 1998 ruble collapse exposed self-dealing at Russian banks and prompted a race to strip the assets that remained. Yet not a single bank official has been charged with anything. Khodorkovski's Bank Menatep offers an example of how the bankers behaved. After Bank Menatep collapsed in mid-1998, Khodorkovski transferred its good assets to a new bank, Menatep-St. Petersburg, leaving depositors and creditors to pick at the old bank's carcass. To ensure that the transactions couldn't be traced, Khodorkovski arranged for a truck containing most of Bank Menatep's records for the last several years to be driven off a bridge into the Dybna river. Where presumably they will remain.

Russia's core problem today is less lack of decent laws than lack of the infrastructure and political will to enforce them. For example, the company law prohibits much of the rampant self-dealing by managers and large shareholders that occurs every day. But the courts respect only documentary evidence, which is rarely available given limited discovery and managers' skill in covering their tracks.

Moreover, a shareholder who sues a major company will usually lose at trial and first-level appeal, because of home-court bias, judicial corruption, or both. A shareholder with a strong case has a decent chance of getting an honest decision on further appeal, but that will take years. And judgments must be enforced (or, often, not enforced) by the same biased or corrupt lower court where the case began.

A recent example: the bankruptcy proceedings for Sidanko, an oil holding company owned by kleptocrat Vladimir Potanin, and Chernogoneft and Kondpetroleum, two key Sidanko subsidiaries. Chernogoneft and Kondpetroleum went bankrupt after selling oil to Sidanko, which failed to pay for the oil and was itself looted so severely that it went bankrupt. In the Chernogoneft bankruptcy proceedings, 98% of the creditors voted for one external manager, but the local judge appointed a different manager with ties to Tyumen Oil, owned by kleptocrat Mikhail Fridman, which wanted to acquire Chernogoneft cheap. The court also rejected a Chernogoneft offer to pay all creditors in full! Tyumen was able to buy Chernogoneft for $176 million and Kondpetroleum for $52 million (a small fraction of actual value), in what Potanin publicly called "an atmosphere of unprecedented pressure on the court system." Which apparently means that Tyumen didn't merely bribe judges (Sidanko could have offered its own bribes), but threatened them as well. Indeed, a judge who issued an early ruling against Tyumen was beaten for his troubles.

Sidanko's bankruptcy was marked by similar irregularities, some reflecting a battle between Potanin and Fridman for control of the proceedings. Other prominent bankruptcy cases were also rigged by insiders, with the cooperation of the courts and (for bankrupt banks) the Central Bank.

Prosecutors are no better than judges. The reported price to stall a criminal investigation into, say, a business-related Mafia hit: $50,000 in Moscow; less elsewhere.

. . .

Privatization proponents argued that privatization would put control of Russia's major companies in the hands of competent businessmen, who had incentives to restructure these enterprises, replace managers who couldn't make the transition to a market economy, and make the investments needed to improve productivity. The kleptocrats devoted themselves instead to skimming profits from their companies; starving them of funds (to the point where many were unable to pay their workers or their tax bills, let alone invest in new equipment); replacing managers who resisted the skimming (or threatening/bribing them into submission); and shooting managers and local government officials who resisted too strongly.

This story can only be told through anecdotes. We offer five below— hopefully enough to convince the reader that our strong words are justified. For the first four, we have firsthand knowledge of the shenanigans. The fifth, Gazprom, is simply too big to be left out.

Khodorkovski/Yukos. We recounted above the example of Yukos, whose reported 1996 oil revenues were $8.60 per barrel, about $4 below what they should have been, with the rest presumably skimmed. But this was only part of Yukos' activity. Yukos owned several operating subsidiaries, each of which had large minority interests. Yukos purchased oil from these subsidiaries at even lower prices, averaging around $7.50 per barrel—low enough so that these subsidiaries, with combined pretax profits of around $1 billion before Yukos acquired control, were soon reporting minimal profits or outright losses, and defaulting on their tax payments. Yukos had bled them of whatever cash they had. The subsidiaries' sale of oil to Yukos, without approval by the subsidiaries' minority shareholders, was a flagrant violation of the company law, but no matter. No one sued, and if they had, well, judges could be bought or their decisions ignored. The transactions were flagrant enough to prompt the Russian Securities Commission to investigate the dealings between Yukos and its subsidiaries. But the investigation went nowhere, perhaps because the Commission didn't have the staff to pursue it, or because it was warned off by Khodorkovski's government allies.

Khodorkovski's ambition exceeded his reach, however. In 1997 and 1998, he borrowed heavily from Western banks, using Yukos shares and guarantees from Yukos' subsidiaries as collateral. When the Russian ruble collapsed in mid-1998, Khodorkovski's Bank Menatep, like most major banks, suffered heavy losses on ruble-denominated Russian government bonds. If one counts his offshore wealth, Khodorkovski surely could have weathered this storm, but he chose instead to let Menatep and Yukos sink. Yukos defaulted on its loan payments, which meant that 30% of its shares would soon be seized by Western lenders. But Khodorkovski still controlled Yukos for the moment, and he used that control to strip Yukos of its real value—ownership of its oil producing subsidiaries.

At each major subsidiary—Tomskneft, Yuganskneftegaz, and Samaraneftegaz—each worth many billions of dollars based on their oil reserves—Yukos proposed for shareholder approval the following package of proposals, with minor variations:

(i) A massive new share issuance to obscure offshore companies, at prices that valued the companies at 1% or less of their true value, and perhaps 10% of their depressed trading prices. Even that modest amount would be paid not in cash but in promissory notes issued by other Yukos subsidiaries, of dubious legality and even more dubious value. Enough shares were to be issued (between 194% and 243% of the previously outstanding shares) to transfer control from Yukos to the offshore companies.

(ii) A multiyear agreement obligating the subsidiary to sell its output to the offshore companies at the laughable price of 250 rubles per ton (around $1.30 per barrel at mid-1999 exchange rates, and headed lower as the ruble depreciates against the dollar).

(iii) Shareholder approval of large asset transfers to still other obscure companies, including both past and unidentified future transactions.

Shareholders who opposed these proposals were given the opportunity to sell their shares back to the company at prices that valued the three companies, with proven oil and gas reserves of around 13 billion barrels of oil equivalent, at a total of $33 million-$.0025 per barrel of proven reserves. No, this is not a misprint.

To be sure, Yukos needed shareholder approval for this raw theft. Yukos owned only 51% of the shares in the subsidiaries, and needed 75% of the votes of the shareholders who participated in a shareholder meeting to authorize the share issuance (plus a majority of the votes of noninterested shareholders). Khodorkovski's solution was bold, if not exactly legal: The day before the subsidiaries' shareholder meetings, Yukos arranged for a compliant judge to declare that the minority shareholders were acting in concert, in violation of the Antimonopoly Law. The judge disqualified everyone but Yukos and its affiliated shareholders from voting. When minority shareholders arrived at the meetings, they were greeted by armed guards; most were barred from voting or attending on the basis of this court order. Yukos' shares were voted and were counted as noninterested; the proposals all passed. Having used Yukos' voting power to ram through these proposals, Khodorkovski then transferred Yukos' remaining shares in two of the three oil-producing subsidiaries to still other offshore companies.

Maybe, if oil prices stay strong, Khodorkovski will put Yukos back together. Maybe in a few years, an appellate court will rule that all this was illegal. But the initial lawsuits have been abandoned. And in the meantime, Khodorkovski will have stolen billions through below-market sales of the subsidiaries' oil.

Besides, opposing Yukos can be bad for one's health. The mayor of Nefteyugansk was murdered in 1998, shortly after he publicly demanded that Yukos subsidiary Yuganskneftegaz pay its local taxes and back wages. In March 1999, Yevgeni Rubin, the head of a company which had won a lawsuit against Yukos, had his car blown up near his home, with armed attackers waiting to finish off anyone who survived the bomb. By chance, he wasn't inside, but his bodyguards were less fortunate.

Khodorkovski's behavior didn't trouble senior Russian officials. In the middle of the scandal, he accompanied then Prime Minister Yevgeni Primakov on a trip to meet President Clinton. It did trouble the Securities Commission, which launched an investigation. But the outcome of that investigation was hardly promising. The Chairman of the Securities Commission resigned in disgust, after failing to get the cooperation he needed from other government agencies to bring a court action; the Commission's remaining members approved the share issuances.

Berezovski/Sibneft. Sibneft is another major Russian oil holding company. So far as anyone can tell, it is controlled by Boris Berezovski and his partner Roman Abramovich (and perhaps also by Aleksandr Smolenski). But no one knows for sure, because Berezovski rarely owns shares in his own name, and operates through obscure intermediary companies. Sibneft's main production subsidiary is Noyabrskneftegaz, which in 1997 was 61% owned by Sibneft. In round numbers, Noyabrskneftegaz earned $600 million in 1996, before Berezovski acquired control of Sibneft, and $0 in 1997. Most of the missing $600 million showed up as Sibneft profit, even though under the company law, transactions between parent and subsidiary require approval by the subsidiary's minority shareholders, which was never obtained.

Simply appropriating Noyabrsk's profits didn't satisfy Berezovski. At the 1998 Noyabrsk annual general meeting, shareholders were asked to approve a new charter and a proposal to increase the number of "announced" common shares that could be issued by decision of the board of directors. Management announced at the shareholder meeting that it proposed new announced shares equal to an astounding 1963 times the current number of issued shares. Virtually no shareholder other than Sibneft voted to authorize these shares, but the authorization squeaked through with the necessary support from 75% of the shareholders who showed up and voted, perhaps because Sibneft hadn't previously disclosed how many shares it proposed to authorize and some minority shareholders didn't attend the meeting.

Noyabrsk's charter provided for preemptive rights, which let all shareholders buy newly issued shares in proportion to their current holdings. Thereafter, Noyabrsk's management ignored its charter and issued shares at roughly half of Noyabrsk's trading price (already severely depressed by Sibneft's expropriation of Noyabrsk's profits) to four purchasers with close relationships to Sibneft, ignoring along the way the company law requirements that shares be issued at "market value" and that any transaction with a 20% shareholder or its affiliated persons be approved by noninterested shareholders.

These actions enhanced Sibneft's trading price at the same time that they depressed Noyabrsk's trading price. Sibneft then announced an exchange offer to swap four Sibneft shares for each Noyabrskneftegaz share held by Noyabrsk's minority shareholders. This exchange rate was around 4% of the relative value of Noyabrsk and Sibneft before this sorry saga started. Most minority shareholders accepted the offer—the alternative was no more attractive. One shareholder who sued found the local courts unreceptive. The local appellate court rejected the shareholder's appeal on the astonishing grounds that the lawyer's signature on the appeal papers differed from the signature on the original complaint (it didn't, and it would make no difference under Russian law if it had). The shareholder settled rather than fight a years-long battle in the upper appellate courts.

Berezovski's behavior hasn't improved since. After consolidating Noyabrskneftegaz, Sibneft announced its intent to behave properly towards minority shareholders in the future, adopting a nonbinding "Corporate Governance Charter," and appointed a high-profile Corporate

Governance Advisory Board. But anyone who believed that one should have remembered the old lyric—"Fool me once, shame on you. Fool me twice, shame on me." In early 2000, a Sibneft affiliate stiffed the European Bank for Reconstruction and Development on a $58 million loan, by persuading a persuadable Russian court that it had paid the loan.

Like Khodorkovski, Berezovski isn't a safe guy to sue, compete with, or write unflattering stories about. Those who try have a distressing tendency to end up beaten, jailed, or dead.

Potanin/Sidanko. Sidanko is another major Russian oil holding company, which in 1998 was 96% controlled by Vladimir Potanin through Oneksimbank and its affiliates, especially MFK (Mezhdunarodnaya Finansovaya Kompaniya). Since MFK was trying to establish itself as the first major Russian-owned investment bank, one might think that Potanin wouldn't tarnish his reputation by diluting the already small minority interest in Sidanko. That expectation, like many Western expectations about how Russian businessmen concerned about reputation ought to behave, turned out to be unjustified.

In early 1998, Potanin decided to kill two birds with one stone— simplify the share ownership structure within the Oneksimbank financial-industrial group and dilute the 4% minority in Sidanko. The chosen means: Sidanko issued convertible bonds to Oneksimbank affiliates in exchange for their shares in other group companies. The conversion price was around 0.1% of Sidanko's current market price (this isn't a typo either). The effect was to more than triple Sidanko's outstanding shares, once the bonds were converted, and to dilute the 4% minority down to 1.3%.

This story had a temporarily not-too-unhappy ending for Sidanko's minority shareholders. The shareholders screamed, the Securities Commission launched an investigation into company law violations, and Sidanko agreed to issue enough shares to minority shareholders at the same low price to compensate for the dilution caused by the convertible bond offering. But investor satisfaction didn't last long. After the ruble crash in mid-1998, Potanin found himself in financial trouble (not counting his offshore assets, anyway). He stripped Oneksimbank of most of its remaining assets and looted Sidanko and its subsidiaries as well. Sidanko's minority shareholders, including BP Amoco, which paid $571 million for 10% of Sidanko (after the shenanigans described above), found their shares nearly worthless.

Zarubezhtsvetmet/Erdenet. We described above Russia's illegal sale of its $250 million stake in Erdenet for $150,000 by privatizing Zarubezhtsvetmet. Now that Zarubezhtsvetmet's (unknown) owners held 49% of Erdenet, how would they behave? Would they improve Erdenet's operations or invest in the new refining capacity that Erdenet wanted?

The answer was not long in coming. In early 1998, it was discovered that Erdenet was bankrupt, unable to pay either its taxes or its overdue bills for electric power. Some $30 million had disappeared, surely with the connivance of Erdenet's general director, Mr. Elbegdorj. The unpaid electric bills meant the utilities couldn't pay Russia for fuel, leaving Mongolia's capital city, Ulaanbaatar, mostly without heat for several months of a bitterly cold Mongolian winter. The Mongolian government sought to fire Elbegdorj and trace the funds; the Russian members of Erdenet's board of directors refused to cooperate. Their resistance deadlocked the company (which has three Mongolian and three Russian board members) for the better part of a year. Mongolia finally used emergency legislation to wrest control of Erdenet away from Elbegdorj and his Russian accomplices.

Gazprom. Gazprom's wealth is fabulous. Even a conservative $600 billion estimate of its market value implies that privatizing this one company, on the basis of one citizen, one share, could have delivered $4,000 in value to each citizen. That, plus honest management that delivered this value to shareholders, would without more have redeemed the promise of mass privatization—that the state was returning ownership of its property to the people. Continued state ownership would have let the government finance its payments to pensioners and employees, while permitting future privatization.

This was not to be. Who owns how much of Gazprom is a secret, but its managers received a huge cut. In early 2000, the government still owned 38%, while the managers' official stake was around 35%, most of it held by a small group of people who reportedly received stakes of 1% to 5% each—with each percentage point worth multibillions at Western valuations. That left another 25% in other hands. Some of that ownership can be traced, but much is hidden. Some of the hidden shares are likely also held by Gazprom insiders. Former Gazprom chairman and former Russian Prime Minister Viktor Chernomyrdin is rumored to be a major owner. Meanwhile, Gazprom pays little in taxes, despite its wealth and despite IMF complaints that Gazprom is seriously undertaxed.

How (dis)honestly Gazprom has been run is impossible to know from the outside. Its reported revenues are around $30 billion per year. Its true revenues are hard to determine, because it faces political constraints on cutting off important nonpaying customers (including Ukraine and Belarus). Still, billions of dollars per year could easily be getting skimmed instead of appearing in Gazprom's financial accounts; Gazprom has also transferred reserves worth $30 billion or so to an unknown company that its managers presumably control. Gazprom also spends money lavishly—including building a glitzy new Moscow headquarters complex and buying top-of-the-line corporate jets.

NOTES

1. Why did the self-enforcing provisions of the Joint Stock Company Law not work in practice? What features of the Russian legal system did the drafters overlook? What are the limits of legislation as a tool for improving corporate governance?

2. Black and Kraakman, two distinguished American law professors, not only played a central role in the drafting of the joint stock company law, but gave legal advice to some of the minority shareholders in the transactions they describe in their article. Their role as advocates in the transactions described is worth keeping in mind. Some of these events led to litigation in the United States, although none led to recovery for the claimants. *E.g.*, Norex Petroleum Ltd. v. Access Industries, Inc., 416 F.3d 146 (2d Cir. 2005).

3. Not all of their case histories involve foreign investors, but some do. Could better lawyering at the outset have provided greater protection to these investors? What steps might they have taken?

4. The article mentions the use of bankruptcy procedures as a means of ousting incumbent owners of a firm. The following case describes in greater detail how this mechanism was thought to work.

Base Metal Trading SA v. Russian Aluminum

United States District Court for the Southern District of New York
253 F. Supp. 2d 681 (2003)

■ JOHN G. KOELTL, DISTRICT JUDGE:

This is a case about two Russian companies, Novokuznetsk Aluminum Zavod ("NKAZ") and Kochkanarsky GOK ("GOK"), Russia's largest producers of aluminum and vanadium, respectively. The plaintiffs' claims arise from the defendants' alleged illegal takeovers of these companies by means including bribery of local Russian political officials, judicial corruption in Russia, and armed force. The plaintiffs argue that the defendants drove NKAZ and GOK into bankruptcy and then gained control of the companies through sham bankruptcy proceedings overseen by allegedly corrupt local Russian judges. The plaintiffs seek over $3 billion for alleged damages. The defendants have now moved to dismiss the current Complaint on many bases, including *forum non conveniens*.

The plaintiffs, Base Metal Trading, SA ("BMT SA"), Base Metal Trading, Ltd. ("BMT Ltd."), Alucoal Holdings, Ltd. ("Alucoal") (collectively the "BMT Plaintiffs"), MIKOM (collectively, with the BMT Plaintiffs the "NKAZ Plaintiffs" or the "Aluminum Plaintiffs"); Davis International, LLC ("Davis"), Holdex, LLC ("Holdex"), Foston Management, Ltd. ("Foston"), Omni Trusthouse, Ltd. ("Omni") (collectively the "Davis Plaintiffs"); Nexis Products, LLC ("Nexis") and Polyprom (collectively the "GOK Plaintiffs") bring this action for violations of the Racketeer Influenced and Corrupt Organizations Act ("RICO"), 18 U.S.C. § 1961 *et seq.,* intentional interference with contract, and conversion. The defendants are Sibirsky Aluminum Group ("Sibirsky Russia"), Sibirsky Aluminum Products USA Corp. ("Sibirsky USA"), Bauxal Management, S.A. ("Bauxal"), Metcare Management, S.A. ("Metcare"), Unimetal Limited, S.A. ("Unimetal"), Mr. Oleg Deripaska ("Deripaska") ("collectively the "Sibirsky Defendants"), Russian Aluminum, RUAL Trade, Ltd. ("RUAL"), Mikhail Chernoi ("Chernoi"), Blonde Management, Inc.("Blonde Management"), Blonde Investments, Corporation ("Blonde Investments"), Pan-American Corporation ("Pan-American"), Arnold Kislin ("Kislin"), Iskander Makhmudov ("Makhmudov"), Moskovskiy Delovoi Mir Bank ("MDM Bank"), NKAZ, New Start Group Corporation ("New Start"), Venitom Corporation ("Venitom"), Unidale LLC ("Unidale") and Investland, LLC ("Investland") (New Start, Venitom, Unidale and Investland hereinafter the "GOK Defendants").

. . .

(A)

The Amended Complaint first tells the story of the defendants' alleged illegal takeover of the Russian aluminum industry, particularly with respect to NKAZ. The first steps in this scheme allegedly included takeovers of three other Russian aluminum companies: Krasnoyarsk Aluminum Zavod ("KRAZ"), Sayansk Aluminum Zavod ("SAZ"), and Bratsk Aluminum Zavod ("BRAZ"). The Conspirators allegedly effected the takeovers through various illegal means, including redirecting the shipment of finished aluminum from the factories, the murder of numerous rivals in association with the Izmailovo Mafia, the filing of false criminal charges against an official of KRAZ, rigged Russian court proceedings and economic extortion.

Beginning in late 1994 or early 1995, plaintiff MIKOM, under its president Mikhail Zhivilo ("Zhivilo"), entered into a contract to manage NKAZ. MIKOM then solicited Western trading partners such as BMT Ltd. to extend loans to NKAZ and to trade with the company. At that time, NKAZ purchased approximately 70% of its alumina, a raw material necessary to produce aluminum, from the Pavlodarsky Aluminum Zavod ("PAZ"). At about the same time, the plaintiffs allege, Chernoi and his allies gained control of PAZ and threatened to stop shipments of alumina to NKAZ unless NKAZ gave them 50% of its aluminum sales profits and 50% of the shares in NKAZ. Chernoi later manipulated NKAZ into buying all of its alumina from PAZ at a premium.

In August 1995, Zhivilo informed Chernoi that NKAZ and BMT Ltd. would no longer trade with PAZ. The plaintiffs allege that shortly thereafter, Deripaska and Chernoi made direct and indirect threats on Zhivilo's life that were followed by an unsuccessful attempt to assassinate him. One of the threats was allegedly made to Yuri Zhivilo, Mikhail Zhivilo's brother, in Chicago, Illinois in 1995. Other threats were allegedly made directly to Mikhail Zhivilo in Tel Aviv, Israel and in Paris, France. In response to the threats, BMT Ltd., NKAZ, and Alucoal allegedly paid millions of dollars in protection money to the Conspirators between April, 1996 and October, 1999. The payments were allegedly made through several New York banks and the funds were eventually laundered through various entities including defendants Pan-American and Blonde Management.

In or about 1997, Russian President Boris Yeltsin appointed Aman Tuleyev ("Tuleyev") as Kemerovo Regional Governor. The next year Tuleyev allegedly began demanding that Zhivilo pay bribes from NKAZ, MIKOM, BMT Ltd. and BMT SA. Tuleyev threatened that failure to pay would result in the transfer of NKAZ to the Conspirators.

In 1999, the Conspirators and Tuleyev allegedly joined together to take over NKAZ illegally with the assistance of the local energy provider, Kuzbass. The essence of the takeover scheme was for Kuzbass to "assert false tariff claims NKAZ], file suit upon them, and obtain a sham judgment against NKAZ, with the active assistance of Tuleyev, using the corrupt Russian regional court system." This would allow the Conspirators to force NKAZ into an involuntary bankruptcy after which the Conspirators could place their own agents in control of the company. The Conspirators would then cancel NKAZ's trading contracts with the BMT Plaintiffs as well as the management contract with MIKOM and replace those companies with affiliates of the Conspirators. The

Conspirators would profit from the scheme by supplying raw materials to NKAZ and then trading in the finished aluminum, while Kuzbass would receive higher energy payments for its participation in the takeover. For his role in the takeover, Tuleyev allegedly received $3 million between 1999 and 2000 paid at least in part with funds wired by Pan-American, Blonde Management, and Blonde Investments through American banks at Kislin's instruction.

The plaintiffs allege that the illegal scheme unfolded as follows. Beginning in late 1994, NKAZ contracted with Kuzbass to supply energy at agreed upon rates. In an action filed on November 12, 1997 in the Kemerovo Arbitrazh Court, Kuzbass repudiated its agreements with NKAZ in response to which NKAZ filed a counter suit. As a result of the dispute, the Kemerovo Arbitrazh court ultimately awarded Kuzbass a judgment of approximately $26.3 million on October 21, 1999. The plaintiffs contend that Tuleyev influenced the arbitrazh court to obtain this result. NKAZ unsuccessfully appealed the award to the appellate branch of the Kemerovo Arbitrazh Court which was "also apparently under the influence of Tuleyev" and which entered a final judgment upholding the award on December 24, 1999. NKAZ then appealed the award to the West Siberian Circuit Federal Arbitrazh Court in Tyumen. The court stayed the execution of the award on or about January 19, 2000 pending consideration of the appeal.

Despite the stay, Kuzbass prevailed on an *ex parte* petition to the Kemerovo Arbitrazh Court for an order declaring NKAZ bankrupt, appointing Sergey A. Chernyshev ("Chernyshev") as Provisional Manager, and imposing allegedly unnecessary conservatory measures on the company. The plaintiffs claim that the bankruptcy order constituted a clear violation of Russian law which requires an executable judgment of a creditor in order to place a business into involuntary bankruptcy. Moreover, the plaintiffs claim that NKAZ was never bankrupt.

The plaintiffs contend that Chernyshev proceeded to issue a series of unreasonable information requests on MIKOM and used MIKOM's failure to satisfy the requests promptly as a basis for his petition to remove the company as NKAZ's manager.[5] Kuzbass also petitioned the arbitrazh court to remove MIKOM using information supplied by Chernyshev from his investigation. The gist of the information was that MIKOM was hiding money that should have been used to pay current debts. In an allegedly unusual step, the local Kemerovo procurator filed a separate petition for bankruptcy against NKAZ at the behest of Tuleyev. The plaintiffs claim that the procurator did so "to signal to the Kemerovo court that the local political authorities supported Chernyshev's position and Kuzbass' petition." At an alleged sham hearing on February 16 and 17, 2000 the arbitrazh court summarily granted the motions for MIKOM's removal and Chernyshev's appointment. The plaintiffs claim that the BMT Plaintiffs, NKAZ, and MIKOM were denied important procedural rights at the hearing, including the full opportunity to present evidence and to properly cross-examine witnesses, as well as timely access to an interpreter.

---

[5]   As provisional manager in the early stages of a bankruptcy, Chernyshev's role was to gather information about the bankrupt company on behalf of the arbitrazh court.

Once installed as Acting Manager, Chernyshev instructed NKAZ's attorneys to cease to pursue the actions preceding the award and to withdraw prosecution of NKAZ's claims against Kuzbass. Chernyshev proceeded to recognize a series of allegedly fictitious claims against NKAZ by companies controlled by the Conspirators totaling approximately $70 million. Recognition of the false creditors provided the Conspirators with voting power at subsequent creditor meetings where control of the agenda was proportional to the sums due to each creditor. At the same time, Chernyshev allegedly refused to recognize valid claims asserted by BMT Ltd. and Alucoal worth approximately $60 million. These maneuvers altered the balance of power at future creditor meetings because prior to the allegedly illegal takeover the BMT Plaintiffs allegedly held the majority of NKAZ's debt.

At the first creditors' meeting, the new creditors voted to place NKAZ under external management and to appoint Chernyshev to the position of External Manager. The Kemerovo Arbitrazh Court confirmed the appointment on March 20, 2000, enabling Chernyshev to cancel NKAZ's contracts with the BMT Plaintiffs for the supply of raw materials and subsequent purchase of finished aluminum. Chernyshev then entered into substitute purchase and supply contracts with companies controlled by the Conspirators.

While not referred to in the Amended Complaint, BMT SA, supported by MIKOM, sought review of the Arbitrazh Court's March 20, 2000 decision in the West Siberian Circuit Federal Arbitrazh Court. The Circuit Court rejected all of the grounds for appeal finding, among other things, that NKAZ was insolvent.

The Conspirators allegedly reached a subsequent agreement with an unnamed powerful Russian oligarch to form Russian Aluminum, thus establishing a monopoly over the Russian aluminum industry. This partnership freed the Conspirators from their need to partner with Kuzbass, and Chernyshev subsequently attempted to remove Kuzbass from NKAZ's list of outstanding creditors. Tying up further loose ends, Tuleyev accused Zhivilo of conspiring to have him murdered. As a result, allegedly false charges were filed against Zhivilo before he sought asylum in France in February 2001.

In or about August 2000, the Conspirators secured total control of NKAZ by allegedly forcing its shareholders to sell their stock at distressed prices to four unspecified companies controlled by the Conspirators. At a final creditors' meeting on March 6, 2001, through the votes of the allegedly false creditors recognized by Chernyshev, the Conspirators won approval of a bankruptcy settlement. The settlement was allegedly highly prejudicial to NKAZ's legitimate creditors, including the BMT Plaintiffs. The Kemerovo Arbitrazh Court approved the allegedly sham settlement on April 3, 2001. Again, while not referred to in the Amended Complaint, BMT SA and others appealed the April 3, 2001 decision of the Kemerovo Arbitrazh Court to the West Siberian Circuit Federal Arbitrazh Court. On September 6, 2001, a panel of three judges, different from those who heard the previous appeal, approved the settlement agreement terminating the bankruptcy.

The Conspirators allegedly remain in control of NKAZ today and use the sales and purchasing power of the company to benefit their affiliates, including defendants Metcare, RUAL, Bauxal and Unimetal. The plaintiffs claim that the Conspirators also siphon profits from the company while failing to pay the legitimate debts owed to the NKAZ Plaintiffs.

(B)

The Amended Complaint contains a new series of claims not present in the Original Complaint and in which the BMT Plaintiffs play no part. The claims involve a conspiracy to take over GOK, "Russia's largest vanadium ore mining factory." GOK is located in the Sverdlosk Oblast which is situated on the east side of the Ural Mountains north of central Kazakhstan. Six new plaintiffs bring these allegations: Davis, Holdex, Foston and Omni (collectively the "Davis Plaintiffs"), as well as Nexis and Polyprom (collectively the "GOK Plaintiffs"). These allegations can be divided into two parts. First, the Davis Plaintiffs allege the fraudulent transfer of their shares in GOK which collectively totaled over 70% of the company. Second, the GOK Plaintiffs allegedly maintained contracts and loan agreements with GOK that GOK then breached.

The plaintiffs' narrative of the events involving GOK similarly begins with claims of extortion and threats of violence. In December 1998, Jalol Khaidarov ("Khaidarov") became general director of GOK after having worked as a financial advisor for Chernoi and Makhmudov. In April 1999, Khaidarov allegedly met twice with his former employers in Paris to discuss GOK. At the second meeting, Chernoi allegedly instructed Khaidarov to convince GOK's shareholders to transfer their shares to Chernoi and Makhmudov and reminded Khaidarov that, "Some people refuse my offers. But for the rest of their lives, they wear bullet proof jackets."

In response to ongoing threats, GOK's controlling shareholders agreed preliminarily to sell 20% of their shares to a company controlled by the Conspirators. Makhmudov and Chernoi made a $5 million down payment on the shares with money allegedly wired through an unnamed United States bank. However, Makhmudov and Chernoi were soon unsatisfied and demanded that Khaidarov arrange for the transfer of additional shares. Believing that the two men would never be satisfied, the shareholders returned the $5 million and cancelled the transfer.

Similar to the allegations concerning the NKAZ takeover, the plaintiffs allege that the Conspirators bribed the local Governor to aid in their scheme. Eduard Roussel ("Roussel"), Governor of the Sverdlovsk Oblast as of 1999, was allegedly paid for "protection" and "help" in support of the Conspirators' efforts to do business in the region. Makhmudov and Chernoi allegedly paid Roussel "more than $850,000 in bribes . . . so that Roussel would allow them to use the police to take over GOK and would exercise his influence over the corrupt Sverdlovsk judiciary." These "payments were made by Pan-American and Blonde Management through banks in the United States to MDM Bank for conversions into cash for payment at the direction of Roussel."

On or about January 28, 2000, with the support of regional authorities, Makhmudov and Chernoi allegedly sent a group of armed thugs to take over GOK physically. The Conspirators then used bribes and threats of physical force to convince four members of GOK's Board of Directors to vote to remove Khaidarov as general director and to replace him with Andrey Kozitsin ("Kozitsin"), an alleged agent of the

Conspirators. This vote allegedly violated GOK's charter which required five votes in order to remove the general director. The Complaint alleges that the three remaining board members asked prosecutors in the Kachkanar and Sverdlovsk areas to initiate criminal proceedings in connection with the GOK takeover. However, the Kachkanar City Court upheld the Board's vote in a decision dated February 1, 2000.

To thwart any further efforts by GOK shareholders to reacquire control of the company, the Conspirators and MDM Bank allegedly arranged for GOK to incur massive false debts in February 2000. By the end of this brief period, a series of sham transactions left a small company named Leybout in possession of approximately $39 million in demand promissory notes issued by GOK. The Conspirators then caused Krasnouralskmezhraigaz ("Kras Gas"), a local natural gas company in the Sverdlovsk Region, to file an involuntary bankruptcy petition against GOK on March 24, 2000. Although the plaintiffs claim that the petition should not have been granted under Russian law because Kras Gas' receivables were not overdue, the Sverdlovsk Arbitrazh Court did just that and appointed Oleg Kozyrev ("Kozyrev") Provisional Manager of GOK on March 30, 2000. After he was appointed Provisional Manager, Kozyrev refused to recognize what the plaintiffs contend was a $7 million valid claim by Nexis arising from a "certain" loan agreement with GOK.

At the time of the GOK creditors' initial meeting, Leybout's allegedly fraudulent claims left that company with 94% of the creditor votes. At the meeting the creditors nominated Kozyrev as External Manager. On March 30, 2000, the Sverdlovsk Arbitrazh Court approved Kozyrev's appointment, having been signaled allegedly to do so by Roussel's Sverdlovsk Oblast government.

What came next, according to the Davis Plaintiffs, was a series of fraudulent transfers of their shares in GOK, often through defendant New Start, and ultimately to defendants Venitom, Unidale, and Investland. The plaintiffs claim that these four companies are owned and controlled by the Conspirators. Defendant Kislin allegedly arranged for the incorporation of the companies, a process paid for with funds from Blonde Management or Pan-American.

The first step in the fraudulent transfers was allegedly to install VRK Company, a company "friendly" to the Conspirators, as GOK's registrar of shares. VRK Company then improperly "registered a transfer of about 35 million shares of GOK from Davis to New Start . . . " while disguising the transfer as a legitimate sale. The Amended Complaint alleges that the "Davis shares, in whole or in part, are currently registered in the name of Investland, Unidale, and/or Venitom, having been transferred to them by New Start."

Omni's shares in GOK, allegedly purchased from "various entities who had acquired the shares as a result of a judicial sale that occurred in September 1998," were transferred as the result of a lawsuit filed in the Chelyabinsk Arbitrazh Court in the spring of 2000 to set aside the judicial sale. The Chelyabinsk Oblast, in which the Chelyabinsk Arbitrazh Court is located, is situated south of the Sverdlosk Oblast and just north of Kazakhstan. In October 2000, the Appellate Instance for the Arbitrazh Court for the Chelyabinsk Region affirmed the lower court's decision setting aside the judgment and ordered that the stock be re-registered to Omni's detriment. The plaintiffs contend that "contrary to

thorough and dedicatedreview of the Parties' lengthy submissions and the exhibits attached thereto, the record as a whole, applicable case law and statutory authority, the Court finds that it cannot reach the merits of Plaintiffs' claims based on the doctrines of sovereign immunity and personal jurisdiction. Accordingly, the Court shall GRANT Defendants' Motions to Dismiss for the reasons that follow.

. . .

B. Overview of Yukos

Following the collapse of the Soviet Union in the early 1990s, the Russian Federation's oil and gas industry consisted of hundreds of separate state-owned entities that survived through state support. In 1993, the Russian Federation sought to restructure the nation's oil-and-gas sector, primarily through privatization. As part of that effort, the Russian government founded Yukos as a separate legal entity on April 15, 1993, and consolidated certain state-owned producing, refining, and distribution entities into its structure. Yukos became a very successful company, in part by implementing policies designed to attract foreign investment, and also by implementing various other internal reforms. By 2003, Yukos's combined production of natural gas and oil rivaled both ChevronTexaco and Total, and the company began to compete with the Russian company Gazprom.

Yukos sought to expand its operations and become an energy supplier to the United States, completing its first of eight crude oil shipments from Russia to the United States on July 3, 2002. Yukos announced that the initial shipment "signaled Company's intention to supply the U.S. market," and later announced that the eight shipments were part of its plans to create "a stable source of non-OPEC crude oil for the U.S." Yukos also had plans to increase its production of oil to the United States by constructing a pipeline that would link Yukos production to an Adriatic Sea terminal. In 2003, Yukos executives met with United States oil companies to discuss their potential acquisition of large stakes in Yukos. ExxonMobil apparently considered purchasing a large stake in Yukos following a potential merger with OAO Sibneft, a Russian oil company. According to Plaintiffs, the Sibneft merger did not occur because of Defendants' conduct detailed below.

By October 2003, Yukos's market capitalization was estimated to exceed $30 billion and it was outperforming its Russian competitors, including Gazprom and Rosneft. Yukos also was paying significant dividends to its shareholders at this time, including its ADR holders. Yukos's biggest asset, Yuganshoftegaz ("YNG"), had grown to account for more than one percent of the world's annual oil production. Yukos's success provides the background to what Plaintiffs allege happened next—Defendants, individually and collectively, engaged in actions that effectively expropriated Yukos without compensating Plaintiffs who held ADRs in Yukos.

C. Specific Allegations

The Court shall review Plaintiffs' specific allegations with respect to each of the three Defendant Groups.

1. *Russian Federation and Rosneftegaz*

Plaintiffs allege that beginning in 2003, the Russian Federation launched an assault on Yukos and the individuals responsible for owning or running Yukos. Utilizing the significant resources at its disposal, Plaintiffs allege that the Russian government expropriated Yukos through the following five means.

First, Plaintiffs allege that the Russian Federation arrested several of Yukos's owners, directors, and counsel. For example, on June 21, 2003, the Russian Federation arrested Alexei Pichugin, Yukos security manager, on charges of committing, or directing the commission of, murders or attempted murders. Plaintiffs allege that Pichugin's arrest was an attempt to coerce him into implicating one or more of the founders of GML Limited, a company that owns 51% of Yukos's stock. Pichugin was later convicted of the charges. On July 2, 2003, the Russian Federation arrested Platon Lebedev, Director of GML Limited, on charges of theft of state property, tax evasion, and fraud. Lebedev was found guilty of the latter two charges and, after an eleven-month trial, sentenced to a nine-year prison term. October 25, 2003, the Russian Federation arrested Mikhail B. Khodorkovsky, the founder of GML Limited, who was also a member of the Yukos Board of Directors and Chairman of the Board of Directors of OOO Yukos-Moscow, the company responsible for managing Yukos.[*] Khodorkovsky was charged with theft of state property, tax evasion, and fraud, and was found guilty of the latter two charges. Khodorkovsky received a nine-year prison sentence. Both Lebedev and Khodorkovsky appealed their sentences, and in September 2005, their sentences were reduced from nine to eight years, respectively.

The Russian Federation also filed charges against Leonid Nevzlin (former First Deputy Chairman of Yukos), Mikhail Brudno (former First Vice President of Yukos Refining and Marketing), and Vladimir Dubov (Yukos shareholder and associate of Khodorkovsky), and several of Yukos's in-house or outside counsel. One of Yukos's in-house counsel, Sveltana Bakhmina, was sentenced to seven years in prison for tax evasion and embezzlement. Plaintiffs allege that these charges, arrests, and convictions ultimately forced Yukos's management team, including Yukos CEO Steven Theede, to relocate to London. In 2006, "two Moscow-based Yukos executives refused to take future direction from Theede."

Second, Plaintiffs allege that various departments of the Russian Federation Government, "under the color of official right," began investigating Yukos and its affiliates, particularly in the fall and summer of 2003. Officials from the Tax Ministry, together with "FSB officers and armed militia," searched Yukos's offices, "intimidating personnel and seizing documents and electronic files." The Ministry of Natural Resources also reviewed Yukos's production licenses for compliance violations, and "threatened several important licenses," but did not interfere with them. On October 3, 2003, investigators and police searched a Yukos business center, the home of Platon Lebedev, the offices of Vladimir Dubov, and a Yukos-funded orphanage outside of Moscow.

---

*   "OOO" is the Russian acronym for a limited liability company. "OAO" is the acronym for an open joint stock company.

The Russian Federation also sought assistance from other countries in the course of its investigation. In 2003, the Russian Federation asked the Attorney General of Liechtenstein "to seize records allegedly located in Liechtenstein and relatingto illegal activity on the part of Khodorkovsky and GML Limited." Liechtenstein's highest court denied the request after finding insufficient supporting evidence. The Russian Federation also submitted "requests for mutual legal assistance to the Attorney General of Switzerland requesting the seizure of business documents related to, *inter alia*, GML Limited, it subsidiaries and counsel, Khodorkovsky, Lebedev, Yukos, and Yukos-related trading companies." In March 2004, the Russian Federation sought to freeze bank accounts located in Switzerland held in the names of the same entities and individuals. The Swiss Attorney General froze accounts which held approximately $4.9 billion, but some of those accounts were subsequently released by order of the Swiss Federal Supreme Court.

Third, on October 30, 2003, the Russian Federation seized all of the shares of Yukos common stock owned by Yukos Universal Limited ("YUL") and Hulley Enterprises Limited ("Hulley"), two subsidiaries of GML Limited which own a combined 51% interest in Yukos. A spokeswoman for the Russian Federation indicated that the stock was seized in connection with the criminal case against Khodorkovsky (a founder of GML Limited and member of the Yukos Board of Directors) to satisfy his liabilities to the Russian Federation, a reason Plaintiffs characterize as pretextual. According to Plaintiffs, this stock seizure expropriated Yukos in two ways. First, it transferred control of Yukos to the Russian Federation. Second, it prevented Yukos's principal shareholders from using their shares to facilitate a resolution of the tax claims (described below) against Yukos.

Fourth, Plaintiffs allege that the Russian Tax Ministry violated the Tax Code of the Russian Federation by assessing illegal and confiscatory taxes on Yukos. In December 2003, the Russian Federation conducted a "special" tax audit of Yukos. Whereas previous audits in 2003 revealed that Yukos had complied with its tax obligations, the December 2003 audit resulted in an additional $3.4 billion in taxes, interest, and penalties for the year 2000. Although Yukos representatives "identified numerous errors in the tax calculations that resulted in an overstatement of the amount owed rather than reducing the tax assessment by these amounts,[the Russian Federation] created new 'violations' that were equivalent to the originally assessed amounts." The $3.4 billion tax assessment apparently stemmed from Yukos's "use of trading companies in tax havens," which Plaintiffs characterize as a "tax-minimization program" that Yukos "voluntarily disclosed in its public financial statements." Yukos objected to the tax assessment. On April 14, 2004, the Tax Ministry issued a Resolution that adopted the findings of the "field tax audit" and required Yukos to pay the $3.4 billion. In May 2004, Yukos filed an "Application Seeking to Declare Unlawful the Resolution of the Ministry of Taxes of the Russian Federation and Levies with the Moscow Arbitration Court." On May 26, 2004, the Court of Arbitration upheld 99 percent of the government's tax claims.

Additional tax assessments and freezing of bank accounts followed. On April 15, 2004, and June 30, 2004, the Russian Federation obtained *ex parte* injunctions to freeze Yukos assets including, among other assets,

Yukos's majority interest in YNG. On July 1, 2004, the Russian Federation "directed Court officers to freeze all of Yukos's accounts in Russian banks" and "directed the Tax Ministry to file an entirely new $3.4 billion tax claim against Yukos, this time ostensibly for 2001 liabilities." On August 31, 2004, YNG's bank accounts were frozen. On September 9, 2004, 13 additional freezing orders were imposed on Yukos's other subsidiary operating accounts. On September 3, 2004, the Ministry of Tax levied a $4.1 billion tax levy on Yukos for the 2002 tax year. On November 1, 2004, the Russian Federation announced additional tax liabilities for FY 2001 and 2002 adding another $10 billion in claims. The Russian Federation announced $8 billion in additional levies for 2003, and in December 2005 announced another tax levy of $3.5 billion for 2004. The total amount of taxes levied against Yukos reached approximately $30 billion.

Fifth, on July 20, 2004, the Russian Federation announced that it would auction off YNG, Yukos's biggest asset, to satisfy Yukos's tax assessments. The auction was scheduled for December 19, 2004, with three entities indicating an interest in bidding: (1) OOO Gazpromneft ("Gazpromneft"), a limited liability company created by resolution of Gazprom, (2) OAO First Venture Company ("First Venture"), and (3) ZAO Intercom ("Intercom"). To stave off the auction, Yukos filed for bankruptcy protection in the United States District Court for the Southern District of Texas. *In re Yukos Oil Co.*, 320 B.R. 130 (S.D. Tex. 2004). Although the Court issued a temporary restraining order, Plaintiffs allege that Defendants evaded the order by replacing First Venture and Intercom in the auction and with BaikalFinansGroup ("BFG"), a sham company. BFG and Gazpromneft were the only two bidders on YNG, and BFG entered the winning bid at $9.3 billion. Plaintiffs allege that BFG bid against itself "to achieve what appeared to be a predetermined auction price." Several days after the YNG auction, Rosneft (an indirect subsidiary of the Russian Federation) purchased BFG. The Russian government "has admitted that BFG received its financing for the purchase of YNG from banks controlled by Defendant Russian Federation."

The allegations concerning the role of Rosneftegaz (a direct subsidiary of the Russian Federation) related to the foregoing conduct are relatively limited. Plaintiffs allege that the Russian Federation created Rosneftegaz as a special purpose vehicle in 2005, and that Rosneftegaz owns all but one share of Rosneft. In June 2005, Rosneftegaz entered into a $7.1 billion agreement to purchase a 10.74 percent interest in Gazprom. Therefore, Plaintiffs allege that the Russian Federation essentially has a controlling stake in both Gazprom and Rosneft, and that Rosneft was the ultimate recipient of YNG, Yukos's biggest asset.

While the Russian Federation was carrying out the five types of activities described above, Plaintiffs also allege that Russia's President, Vladimir Putin, "made several misstatements and omissions of material fact directed at U.S. and global securities markets." Although President Putin is not named as a Defendant in the instant action, Plaintiffs allege that these statements were made on behalf of the Russian Federation, Rosnefegaz, and Rosneft (a company described in the third Defendant Group below).

According to Plaintiffs, the cumulative effect of the foregoing conduct reduced Russian crude shipments to the United States. By November 2004, such shipments, including those from Yukos, fell to zero. Plaintiffs allege that the Russian Federation has re-nationalized Yukos by seizing control of a majority of Yukos shares, transferring Yukos's most valuable assets to commercial entities controlled by the Russian Federation, and diverting to state-controlled entities all remaining benefits of owning an interest in Yukos. Plaintiffs allege their ADRs are "now effectively worthless."

2. *Government Defendants*

In connection with the events described above, Plaintiffs allege that the Government Defendants used, and "direct[ed] the use of, color of official right to take Yukos from its owners and to obtain control of key Yukos assets, all for the private and commercial benefit of Defendants." In addition, Plaintiffs allege that four of the Government Defendants made misstatements that were directed at the United States and global securities markets that were designed to "deceive investors." The Court shall identify these statements below.

Minister Khristenko:

- *Platt's Oilgram News* (Nov. 22, 2004): "When the auction of is finally held, little competition is expected. Energy Minister Viktor Khristenko sidestepped the issue of the starting price Nov. 19, saying the auction would decide the firm's value."

- *Interfax Energy Daily* (Dec. 30, 2004): "The assets of the core production unit of Yukos sold at a December 19 auction, will be transferred to a separate, wholly state-owned company, the Russian Industry and Energy Ministry's Public Relations Center said in a statement, quoting Viktor Khristenko, the ministry's head. Khristenko was quoted as saying that up to 20% of the new company may be offered to China National Petroleum Corporation (CNPC)." Plaintiffs allege, based on these statements, that Minister "Khristenko stated that Rosneft did not intend to control YNG."

Minister Kudrin:

- *Kommersant* (Nov. 3, 2003): "I have heard [President Putin] saying myself that this was no redistribution of property." The article identifies Minister Kudrin as the Russian Federation Deputy Prime Minister and Minister of Finance.

- *New York Times* (Jun. 21, 2004): " 'As far as I know, Yukos has offered to cooperate with the tax ministry on settling the claims that have been made,' the finance minister, Aleksei L. Kudrin, told news agencies Monday. 'Cooperation on the possible settlement of the claims is under way. I think Yukos has enough funds to pay its liabilities.' "

- *Platt's Energy Economist* (July 1, 2004): "[Minister] Kudrin in fact appeared in a relaxed mood, suggesting that the government would be happy for Yukos to sell assets on the open market, rather than to the state or to 'state-approved' companies, to pay off its debts." Plaintiffs' allege that Minister "Kudrin also maintained that the tax claims against Yukos were not political but were part of a 'routine' investigation."

- *Financial Times* (Sept. 13, 2004): "The state will do everything possible to ensure a deal takes place in accordance with the law and in an absolutely transparent and market-oriented way,' Kudrin] said, implicitly confirming that asset sales through [the YNG] auction were likely to be part of a resolution to the company's stand-off with authorities." The article identifies Minister Kudrin as "Russia's finance minister."

Minister Yusufov:

- *Moscow Times*(Oct. 13, 2003): "Energy Minister Igor Yusufov said Friday that Russia would welcome [a deal between YukosSibneft and ExxonMobil] as a 'positive step.' 'Of course, it fills us with pride that discussions are under way with the first company in the world, ExxonMobil,' Minister Yusufov said at a news conference for foreign reporters, AP reported."

Minister Medvedev:

- *Financial Times* (Jan. 20, 2004): Minister Medvedev submitted an editorial wherein he stated that "[a]n independent and competent judiciary, protecting the rights of everyone, is an essential part of a prosperous society. The importance that people attach to the judiciary helps explain why the Yukos case became such a talking point for Russian and foreign media just before the polls. Mikhail Khodorkovsky, head of the oil company, was accused of tax evasion and taken into custody. But whatever the outcome, one point should be noted: this is not a story about prosecutors 'hounding businessmen,' but about equality before the law for everyone, however wealthy." Minister Medvedev is identified as "head of the Russian president's administration."

- *Deutsche Presse-Agentur* (Nov. 2, 2004): "We are proceeding on the assumption that these matters will be exhaustively examined and that a verdict on the guilt of the person in question will only be reached in accordance with Russian law."

- *BBC Monitoring Service* (Nov. 2, 2004): "At the same time, it is very important that the law, including laws about responsibilities, is applied not selectively but across the board to all Russian citizens I believe that the state must help law-enforcement bodies and ensure their independence in everyday work, not allowing various forces to intervene in their activities." Plaintiffs allege that Minister Medvedev made these statements as "Head of the Presidential Administration."

Although Plaintiffs do not allege that Minister Sechin made any misstatements, they allege that he "personally inspected the building where the sale of Yukos's assets took place," and that an unnamed senior Russian official close to Minister Sechin "was shorting Yukos shares on Monday morning before the arrest of the [YNG] shareswas announced."

3. *Non-Government Defendants*

In connection with the events described above, Plaintiffs also allege that the Non-Government Defendants participated in the conspiracy to expropriate Yukos.

i. Gazprom and Alexei Miller

Plaintiffs allege that Gazprom took part in the fraudulent auction of YNG by authorizing its subsidiary, Gazpromneft, to participate in the auction. According to Plaintiffs, Gazprom benefitted from its participation in the conspiracy to expropriate Yukos because Gazprom engaged in a short sale of Yukos stock having received information regarding the outcome of Yukos's pending challenge to the Russian Federation's tax demands.

As with the Government Defendants, Plaintiffs allege that Miller (Chairman of the Management Committee of Gazprom and Deputy Chairman of the Board of Directors of Gazprom) made misstatements on behalf of himself and Gazprom that were directed at theUnited States and global securities markets. These statements included the following: (1) Gazprom did not seek to destabilize Yukos, but, "on the contrary, it wants to develop joint projects with the company"; (2) "Gazprom is not considering acquiring Yukos assets"; (3) "Gazprom does not have any plans to buy Yukos assets. We are interested in this company being stable"; (4) "We are not considering the possibility of taking part in an auction" of Yukos assets; and (5) Miller has not "heard anything about this," referring to plans by Gazprom to take part in the auction of YNG.

ii. Rosneft, Sergey Bogdanchikov, and Nikolai Borisenko

Plaintiffs allege that Rosneft participated in the fraudulent transfer of Yukos' auctioned asset, YNG. The winning bidder, BFG, was acquired by Rosneft days after the auction took place. Although the amount Rosneft paid for BFG was not revealed, Plaintiffs cite several press accounts suggesting that the price was "laughable" and a "monumental bargain."

In April 2006, Rosneft allegedly warned banks not to pursuelegal action against Rosneft to recover for YNG's liabilities "if the banks wanted to maintain good relations with the Kremlin." With respect to Yukos, Rosneft agreed to pay $455 million to buy Yukos's outstanding $482 million debt from a consortium of international banks "on the condition that those banks launch involuntary bankruptcy proceedings against Yukos in Moscow." The banks accepted Rosneft's offer, "leaving Rosneft at the helm of the involuntary bankruptcy proceedings."

Plaintiffs allege that Rosneft's President, Bogdanchikov, was involved in the conspiracy to expropriate Yukos, and cite to a *Financial Times* article from December 20, 2004, reporting that he was a "key player in the redistribution of Yukos assets." Similarly, Plaintiffs allege Rosneft's Vice President, Borisenko, was involved in the conspiracy, as he represented Gazpromneft at the YNG auction. Plaintiffs also allege that Borisenko was awarded the "Order for Services to the Fatherland,

Second Class, under a Presidential Decree" in September 2005, presumably based on his conduct related to Yukos.

Finally, Plaintiffs allege that Rosneft made misstatements directed at the United States and global securities markets. Rosneft's press spokesman, Alexander Stepankenko, said that Rosneft was "not planning any asset acquisitions in the near future. None." On July 22, 2004, Rosneft "announced it not interested in bidding for [YNG]."

D. *Claims*

Plaintiffs allege 25 causes of action based on the foregoing facts, including: Common law conversion under District of Columbia law, Conversion under the law of the Russian Federation, Conspiracy to commit common law conversion under District of Columbia law, Expropriation in violation of International law, Violations under RICO, 18 U.S.C. §§ 1962(b), (c), and (d), Common law fraud and deceit under District of Columbia law, Fraud and deceit under the law of the Russian Federation, Conspiracy to commit common law fraud and deceit under District of Columbia law, Aiding and abetting common law fraud and deceit under District of Columbia law, Securities fraud under 15 U.S.C. § 78(b), Violation of Section 20A of the Exchange Act, 15 U.S.C. § 78t–1(a), Restitution based on unjust enrichment under District of Columbia law, and Restitution based on unjust enrichment under the law of the Russian Federation.

. . .

NOTES

1. The court dismissed the complaint because of sovereign immunity and lack of personal jurisdiction over the nonsovereign defendants. Yukos shareholders have invoked various international treaties to bring claims for compensation against the Russian government, and those matters remain pending.

2. The dispute over the Yukos expropriation has generated several arbitral decisions in favor of foreign investors as well as a decision of the European Court of Human Rights that condemned the manner in which the Russian government enforced its tax claim against the company. For a detailed discussion of the controversy, which remains ongoing even though the Russian government released Khodorkovsky from prison shortly before the 2014 Sochi Olympics, see Paul B. Stephan, *Taxation and Expropriation— The Destruction of the Yukos Oil Empire*, 35 Houston J. Int'l L. 1 (2013).

3. As the court indicates, months before the prosecution of Khodorkovsky and the launching of the tax investigation into Yukos, Yukos had consummated a merger with another private energy firm, Sibneft. The Sibneft assets would have fully satisfied all of the tax claims, if the authorities had permitted Yukos to dispose of them. Instead, the owners of Sibneft decided to unwind the merger over the objections of Yukos's management. One aspect of this strategy was a lawsuit initiated in a remote region of the country where Sibneft's owners held sway. Consider the court's application of the "interested party" provisions of the Federal Law on Joint Stock Companies.

Arbitration Court of the Chukotka
Autonomous District Anadyr

July 13, 2005
Case No. A 80–170/2005

■ JUDGE D.L. YAKIMIDI, . . .

Nimegan (the "Plaintiff") filed with the Chukotka Arbitration Court a lawsuit against Marthacello, Heflinham, White Pearl, Kindselia, Kravin, Gemini and Yukos for the invalidation of the Deed of Share Exchange, dated April 30, 2003 (the "DOSE") and the application of consequences of the invalidity of such transaction pursuant to Article 167 of the Civil Code of the Russian Federation (the "Civil Code").

. . .

Having considered the papers of the case, having heard the statements and explanations of the persons involved in the case, the court believes the arguments of the Plaintiff to be justified and its claims to be subject to satisfaction on the following grounds.

On April 30, 2003, Marthacello, Heflinham, White Pearl, Kindselia, Kravin and Gemini (the "Foreign Companies") and Yukos entered into the DOSE pursuant to which the Foreign Companies acquired from the latter, in the aggregate, 702,397,159 registered common shares in Yukos (Issues No. 1–02–00198–A and No.1–02–00198–A–002D), in exchange for 3,413,735,740 common shares in Sibneft (Issue No. 1–01–00146–A).

In accordance with the terms of the DOSE, Yukos transferred: (a) to Heflinham 101,170,652 Yukos shares and obtained in exchange 474,129,963 Sibneft shares; (b) to White Pearl 202, 341,302 Yukos shares and obtained in exchange 948,259,927 Sibneft shares; (c) to Kindselia 101,170,652 Yukos shares and obtained in exchange 474,129,963 Sibneft shares; (d) to Marthacello 102,418,721 Yukos shares and obtained in exchange 601,974,119 Sibneft shares; and (e) to Gemini 195,295,832 Yukos shares and obtained in exchange 915,241,768 Sibneft shares.

Kravin was a party to the DOSE but neither purchased any shares in Yukos nor transferred in exchange any shares in Sibneft.

The transactions with respect to the transfer of shares between Yukos and the Foreign Companies were carried out in accounts maintained by the Foreign Companies and by Yukos with OOO Deutsche Bank (the "Depositary") and in accordance with depositary agreements between the Depositary and each Foreign Company and a depositary agreement between the Depositary and Yukos. The performance of the DOSE between the Foreign Companies and Yukos is confirmed by statements of account issued by OOO Deutsche Bank with respect to the depo account of Yukos and depo accounts of Foreign Companies, respectively.

. . .

As of the date of the DOSE (April 30, 2003), Hulley held more than 20% of Yukos voting shares which is confirmed by Statement No. 1773 of DEPO account No. 90072 of Hulley issued by Investment Bank Trust (OAO) as of April 30, 2003 that has been filed with the papers of the case.

. . .

On April 8, 2003, the Memorandum was executed which, as follows from its contents, specified the objective of concerted actions of the parties thereto: the establishment, on the framework of Yukos, of a consolidated company using 92% of Sibneft shares, and the principal provisions of the share exchange procedure and the management of Yukos and Sibneft in the course of such exchange that subsequently underlay the DOSE.

As follows from the preamble of the Memorandum, the Parties that executed the Memorandum were the Sibneft Principal Shareholders that controlled at least 91.5%, and the Yukos Principal Shareholders that controlled at least 62% of Yukos charter capital.

Having analyzed the papers of the case and the evidence that has been submitted to the court, the court comes to a conclusion that the Sibneft Principal Shareholders that were involved in the execution of such Memorandum are the Foreign Companies that are the defendants under this case, and the Yukos Principal Shareholders that were involved in the execution of such Memorandum are Hulley and YUL that have been joined in on this case as third parties having no claims of their own.

. . .

On the basis of the combination of all submitted evidence, taken as a whole, the court came to a conclusion that the Memorandum was executed on behalf of and for the benefit of the Yukos Principal Shareholders, including on behalf of and for the benefit of Hulley, which as of April 8, 2003, the date of execution of the Memorandum, held more than 60% of Yukos shares. The Yukos principal shareholders and Yukos, the Defendant, followed such Memorandum and in accordance therewith took steps to establish a consolidated company on the framework of Yukos and Sibneft, including entered into the DOSE in accordance with the Memorandum.

As of the execution of the Memorandum, the Yukos Principal Shareholders and the Foreign Sibneft Shareholders that are the defendants hereunder established a group of persons and became affiliates pursuant to Article 4 of the Competition Law.

Pursuant to Article 4 of the Competition Law, a "group of persons" means a group of entities and (or) individuals that meet, inter alia, the following condition: one or more persons have power, in accordance with a contract or in any other way, to determine resolutions adopted by another person or other persons, including to determine the terms of business carried out by such other person or persons (Paragraph 16, Article 4 of the Law). Pursuant to such Article, the provisions with respect to a group of persons apply to each person that is a member of such group.

As a result of the Memorandum, the Yukos Principal Shareholders and the Sibneft Principal Shareholders gained power to determine resolutions with respect to Yukos and Sibneft, including determining the terms of business carried out by such companies. The provisions of the Memorandum evidence that the Memorandum was a document that in fact fixed the understandings on the terms of affairs of its Parties and that enabled them to determine resolutions adopted by each other.

. . .

Such influence does not provide that members of such group assume any civil obligations or that such obligations can be enforced in court. The Competition Law (Paragraph 16, Article 4) does not condition the existence of a group of persons on the existence of a formal civil agreement and the enforceability of a resolution determined by another person; instead, it provides for performance of such resolution on a fairly voluntary basis.

The Memorandum fixes in writing the result of understanding between the Yukos Principal Shareholders and the Sibneft Principal Shareholders that enable the persons on behalf of which the Memorandum was executed to determine resolutions taken by each other for the purposes of the achievement of the common objective: the establishment of a consolidated company on the framework of Yukos. Such understandings enabled such persons to determine resolutions adopted by each other which made them a group of persons pursuant to Article 4 of the Competition Law.

The court comes to a conclusion that in the event with the execution of the Memorandum, a group of persons was established in accordance with the criterion of the power to determine resolutions and the terms of business.

In addition to the foregoing, Article 4 of the Competition Law provides that even concerted actions between the parties would be sufficient for the establishment of a group of persons. On the basis of the circumstances under which the Memorandum was executed as evidenced by the papers of the case and of the analysis of the understandings contained in the Memorandum, the court comes to a conclusion that the actions of the parties were concerted. In the course of the preparation for the establishment of a consolidated company on the framework of Yukos and Sibneft, the principal shareholders of each of the companies that held in the aggregate the controlling interests agreed to influence the resolutions of such company through concerted actions.

On the basis of the foregoing, the court comes to a conclusion that by virtue of the execution of the Memorandum, the Yukos Principal Shareholders, including Hulley, gained power to determine in another way (pursuant to agreements fixed in the Memorandum and through concerted actions) resolutions adopted by the Sibneft Principal Shareholders and by Sibneft, i.e., they formed a group of persons and were affiliated with each other.

By virtue of the provisions of Article 81 of the JSC Law, the DOSE constitutes an interested party transaction of Yukos in which the Yukos Principal Shareholders were interested.

Pursuant to terms of the DOSE, Yukos disposed of more than 2% of its outstanding common shares, and the value of acquired property exceeded 2% of the book value of Yukos assets; therefore, by virtue of Article 83.4 of the JSC Law, the DOSE required the approval, prior to the execution thereof, at a general meeting of shareholders of Yukos by a majority of votes of all disinterested shareholders, i.e. solely by votes of Yukos minority shareholders.

The DOSE was executed in conflict with the procedure established in Article 83.4 of the JSC Law, i.e., without approval of a general meeting of shareholders.

Yukos was in breach of Articles 81 through 83 of the JSC Law and infringed the rights of shareholders provided for in Article 67.1 of the Civil Code, Article 6.1 of the Federal Law "On the Protection of Rights and Lawful Interests of Investors in the Stock Market," Articles 31, 51 and 83 of the JSC Law and Sections 9 and 32 of the Charter of Yukos.

. . .

The JSC Law (Article 84) provides that an interested party transaction may be invalidated in accordance with an action filed by the company or a shareholder. The objective of such rule was to ensure the compliance with the procedure provided for the approval of such transactions, and the protection of shareholders of the company.

Such rules reflect public interest in the compliance with statutory corporate procedures provided for in mandatory rules of Russian laws (Articles 81 through 83 of the JSC Law). The establishment of a special procedure of approval of interested party transactions constitutes an important part of the mechanism of protection of rights of minority shareholders of joint stock companies.

Refusal to apply Article 167 of the Civil Code to the consequences of invalidity of such interested party transactions would deprive of any sense the structure of protection by a shareholder of its rights through the invalidation of a transaction carried out by a company in conflict with the procedure provided for the approval of interested party transactions. The application of foreign law to the consequences of the invalidity of a transaction does not ensure the protection of infringed rights and lawful interests of shareholders.

With respect to Yukos shareholders, the relations with respect to the interested party transaction concluded by Yukos are governed by Russian laws. Such laws are of special importance as they protect and ensure the rights and lawful interests of shareholders of the company which is a Russian legal entity.

Articles 81 through 84 of the JSC Law specifically govern the relations between a company and its shareholders. The ground for the invalidation of the DOSE is the breach by Yukos of the procedure provided for the approval of the transaction which is of mandatory nature and cannot be changed by the parties to the transaction, because the transaction is carried out by a Russian legal entity.

. . .

Chapter XI of the JSC Law established the procedure of approval of interested party transactions that is aimed at the protection of rights and interests of shareholders when a company carries out interested party transactions, as such transactions can give rise to a conflict of interests between the persons interested in such transaction and those not interested.

Pursuant to Article 83 of the JSC Law, the procedure of approval of an interested party transaction includes its approval at a general meeting of shareholders at which those shareholders that are not interested in such transaction shall be present. An interested party transaction requires approval prior to the execution thereof (Article 83.1). After the transaction has been carried out, the right of a shareholder with respect to such transaction cannot be exercised due to the consummation of the transaction.

The right of a shareholder to participate in the resolution of the matter of the approval of an interested party transaction arises prior to the time of such transaction. Article 83 of the JSC Law provides that each shareholder of a company may participate in the management of the company by voting on an interested party transaction.

The participation of a shareholder in voting constitutes the exercise of such shareholder's right to participate in the management of the company and ensures such shareholder's lawful interest in the protection of its property and other rights (Article 31.2, Article 49.1, Article 51, Article 57.1, Article 83 of the JSC Law). Each shareholder has such right pursuant to Article 149 of the Civil Code, Article 31.2 of the JSC Law and Article 2 of the Securities Markets Law as a result of ownership of shares.

The failure to comply with the procedure provided for the approval of an interested party transaction infringes such right of the Plaintiff.

The ability to exercise the rights attached to shares in a company constitutes a lawful interest of each shareholder. A breach of the procedure provided for the approval of an interested party transaction also infringes the interest of the owner in the ownership of securities.

. . .

On the basis of the foregoing, the court comes to a conclusion that a breach of Article 83 of the JSC Law has occurred, in particular, the DOSE was entered into out of the procedure provided for in Article 83 of the JSC Law. Yukos has infringed the Plaintiffs right to participate in the management of the company and its lawful interest, as the holder of shares, to protect its property and other rights of a shareholder with respect to the company in connection with an interested party transaction.

NOTES

1. The principal shareholders of Yukos, led by Mikhail Khodorkovsky, and Sibneft, led by Roman Abramovich, agreed to a merger of the two companies in April 2003. The agreement provided that Yukos would transfer its stock to Sibneft shareholders, which in turn would transfer Sibneft stock to the Yukos. Sibneft thus became a subsidiary of Yukos and the former Sibneft shareholders became Yukos shareholders. The initial exchange of stock was carried out in the fall of 2003, shortly before the arrest of Khodorkovsky. The government's attack on Khodorkovsky and Yukos immediately diminished the value of Yukos and its stock, but did not affect the value of Sibneft. Why would a minority owner in Yukos seek to reverse this transaction, thereby giving back valuable Sibneft stock in return for near worthless Yukos stock? Might it be relevant that the minority shareholder brought suit in a court that was located in an area of Russia where Abramovich had great political and economic power? Why couldn't the Sibneft shareholders sue to reverse the transaction?

2. In an emerging market with weak legal institutions, how does an outside business partner protect itself from bad corporate governance? If the domestic courts do not offer much hope, can investors litigate elsewhere? Are there alternatives to litigation? What are they? (Hint: reread the section at the beginning of this chapter on selecting the right business partner.)

C. Tax Aspects of Organizational Form

Note that the event that triggered the bankruptcy proceeding in the Yukos controversy was an unexpected tax assessment. We will consider briefly the tax problems that a foreign investor is likely to confront when operating in an emerging market. Most tax systems attach significance to choices of organizational form. The fundamental issues include whether to treat some legal entities as separate taxpayers, if so which entities, and whether and how to permit owners to account for the tax treatment of entities. Choice of form also has an impact on the administration of taxes.

1. General Patterns of Taxation

Tax planning is a fundamental part of any business project. Money paid over as taxes reduces the investors' return. A business ultimately succeeds or fails based on its after-tax return, not its before-tax profits. A host country typically will impose a variety of taxes.

Income or Profits Taxes

Many emerging market countries distinguish between business profits and other kinds of income. What they call a profits tax might be called a corporate income tax in other systems. Whatever the name, such a tax measures, and claims a fraction of, the profits of a business enterprise.

Although measuring profit may sound simple, a number of controversies typically arise:

- *Sourcing.* How much of activity can be attributed to the territory of the host country, and how much should be regarded as extraterritorial? This problem can involve deductions as well as receipts. Tax treaties go a long way to sort out sourcing issues.

- *Timing.* When must a taxpayer tax a receipt or outlay into account, at the time it transfers payment or the time it assumes a legal obligation to pay (or be paid)? If the latter, when does that legal obligation arise?

- *Deductions.* What is a deductible expense? In particular, when can outlays that may be related to a long-term investment (such as drilling costs) be deducted, all at once or over the life of the investment? If the latter, how should the life of the investment be measured? We say that an outlay is "depreciated" if it generates deductions over the life of an investment, rather than producing a one-off deduction for the full amount of the outlay. The period for recovering depreciation deductions is called the "useful life" of the investment.

- *Related-party transactions.* Many investments take place through corporate subsidiaries of the foreign parent. The subsidiary will buy some inputs from its parent or other corporate affiliates and sell some or all of its product to these companies. When a transaction takes place within a single corporate family, the normal incentives to maximize the price (for the seller) and to minimize that price (for the buyer) do not exist. In such case, we have what is called a "transfer pricing" problem. Reviewing and revising transfer prices is one of the greatest challenges for an income tax.

Other income tax issues that go beyond the scope of this text include the proper treatment of host country taxes in the home country. U.S. taxpayers, for example, must include foreign-source income in their income but are entitled to a credit against their income taxes for foreign income taxes paid. How big a credit and what counts as a foreign income tax sometimes present difficulties. Other countries tend to exempt foreign income from taxation altogether.

VALUE ADDED TAX (VAT)

The United States is one of the few advanced economies that does not have a VAT. This tax in essence is a consumption tax, but collection occurs through transactions throughout the production process. Businesses that sell goods and services typically are VAT taxpayers. VAT taxpayers pay a flat tax (typically at a rate of ten to twenty percent) on their gross receipts. They pass these taxes on to their customers by including them in the bill. The customer pays the seller, who in turn pays the government.

A necessary refinement in a VAT involves transactions where one VAT taxpayer sells goods or services to another VAT taxpayer. The second VAT taxpayer will incorporate the goods and services it buys from its sellers into the products that it sells. If the second taxpayer cannot get a credit for the taxes it pays on these inputs, the system will distort production by driving producers into single, vertically integrated enterprises. All VAT systems thus gives a VAT taxpayer a full credit for the VAT taxes its pays when it buys goods or services from other VAT taxpayers.

A simple example may illustrate how this works. Assume taxpayer A makes steel, taxpayer B makes cars, and that the VAT rate is ten percent. If A sells B steel worth 100, A will charge B 110 and pay a tax of 10 to the government. A transferred the money to the government, but B effectively paid the tax through its payment to A. When B later sells a car containing this steel for 200, it will collect a VAT of 20 from its customer. B will pay the government only 10, however, because it already has paid 10 when it bought the steel. B, in other words, gets a credit against the tax due on the sale of the car for the taxes paid through its suppliers on the goods and services that went into the car.

A complication arises when goods or services are imported or exported. The easier case involves an imported good that subject to customs. In addition to any duty due on the good at the time of import, the importer also must pay a VAT equal to the value of the good at the border. Inputs of services are harder: Imagine a lawyer that provides advice in New York related to a transaction in Russia. Most VAT systems regard imports of capital as not a taxable service, although on occasion importing countries have sought to impose a VAT on loans or infusions of equity to domestic firms from foreign sources. Such a VAT typically results in a freeze on incoming investments and typically does not last.

Exports, however, tend to produce the most controversies. Because the VAT is a consumption tax, it applies only to domestic consumers. If a good or service is produced in one country for consumption elsewhere, no VAT should apply. Mechanically, the tax achieves this result by imposing a zero rate on exports. If taxable inputs went into the production of the good or service, however, the producer should get a full refund for the taxes it paid on these inputs. The earlier taxes were paid on the assumption that the products sold would go into a good or a service that would be consumed domestically. When exportation occurs, that assumption is proven wrong.

To go back to our previous example, assume B sells the car to a foreign purchaser for 200. This sale is zero-rated, meaning it generates no additional tax liability for B. At the same time, B remains entitled to a credit for the VAT of 10 paid on the steel. As a result, the export sale generates a refund of 10 to B.

Although a refund-on-export rule is simple in principle, it can prove tricky in practice. Dishonest taxpayers can game the system at least two ways. First, they can claim credit for taxes that they never paid. They might present forged documents claiming to prove past VAT payments, for example. Second, they can claim they have exported a good when they really have not. To fight both kinds of fraud, the tax system imposes stringent formal requirements on VAT refunds. These requirements by no means eliminate the prospect of fraud, and can be abused to deny valid claims for a refund.

EXCISE TAXES

Another common form of taxation is a levy on the production of certain commodities. Sometimes these are "sin" taxes applying to items such as alcohol or tobacco. Sometimes they target luxury items such as yachts or jewelry. On occasion they apply to the production of resources such as oil or minerals and thus function as a kind of royalty on the state's interest in natural deposits.

Domestically, an excise tax is assessed either on physical units or value, with the former being the more common. Normally excise taxes are not refunded on export. When an excisable good is imported, an excise tax still applies even though production occurs overseas. The customs service typically will collect duties, VAT and excise taxes simultaneously when goods pass through the border.

PROPERTY TAXES

Many states impose a tax on real and personal property owned by taxpayers. The form of the tax is an annual payment reflecting the stipulated tax rate multiplied by the assessed value of the property. Controversies arise around both the assessment of value and the actual ownership of the property. In some countries, for example, a tax exempt organization (perhaps a church or a veterans' group) will assume ownership so as to avoid property taxes and then rent the property to the real beneficial owner.

SOCIAL INSURANCE TAXES

In most countries employees are entitled to state-provided benefits such as payments during unemployment, pensions upon retirement, and health care. Typically states fund some or all of these benefits by levying a charge on employee salaries. The employer will pay the taxes due. Sometimes employers will seek to circumvent this obligation by paying employees through overseas mechanisms, such as a trust account. Tax authorities are not likely to accept such schemes as valid. When an employee splits her time between domestic and foreign work, difficult allocation issues may arise.

2. LEGAL EFFECT OF STABILIZATION AGREEMENTS

A foreign investor typically expects to realize profits over an extended period, rather than recovering the cost of the investment over a year or two. The more that the success of a project depends on a prolonged period of business activity, the greater the investor's concern that the rules governing its business remain stable. Taxation is not the only area where this concern holds, but it is one of the most important. An investment that may make sense if the investor surrenders forty percent of its profits as taxes may not make sense if the tax burden approaches eighty percent.

Most of all investors fear a bait-and-switch strategy on the part of the host government. Once the investment has been made, the investors may have few options if the host government surprises them with a tax hike. Fearing this possibility, some otherwise desirable investments will not be made. And to overcome this fear so as to induce desired investments, some host governments enter into agreements to stabilize the applicable law, taxation in particular. Typically this occurs by insertion of a specific clause into the general agreement.

Investors have used several categories of stabilization clauses in various types of international petroleum agreements in emerging market countries. They first employed the classic "freezing" clause designed to ensure that all laws applicable to a petroleum contract would not be changed by the host country government during the term of the petroleum contract. Subsequently, investors developed the so-called "intangible" clause to prohibit any modifications in the contract except by the mutual written consent of the contracting parties.

Contemporary practice involves the economic stabilization clause, also known as the economic equilibrium clause. This clause is designed to maintain the economic equilibrium of the IOC's investment in the event of any adverse effect caused by new or amended laws or regulations. All investors in the international oil and gas industry insist on the inclusion of such a comprehensive stabilization clause in the relevant petroleum agreement. It normally includes the following elements:

1. It requires the parties to negotiate in good faith to restore the IOC's economic equilibrium if the IOC suffers an adverse economic effect due to a change in laws or regulations or the interpretation thereof;

2. It establishes a detailed procedure for the negotiations and a deadline for their completion;

3. In the event of no agreement, it establishes a process and timeline for submitting the dispute to arbitration; and

4. It takes a comprehensive approach to the scope and types of changes in laws and regulations covered.

Some emerging market countries that use the PSA form of investment tend to take a minimalist approach to the inclusion of a stabilization clause. For example, in Angola, Sonangol's stabilization clause, as expressed in its form PSA template, is virtually hidden in a provision on "Double taxation and change of circumstances." It does not provide for a timeframe or good faith negotiations and requires the approval of "competent authorities" before it becomes effective.[13]

Kenya is another example of a country that offers a model PSA containing a very simple and ambiguous outline of an economic equilibrium clause placed in a separate paragraph within the provision on Governing Law. It states:

> If after the effective date of this Contract the economic benefits of a Party are substantially affected by the promulgation of new laws and regulations, or of any amendments to the applicable laws and regulations of Kenya, the Parties shall agree to make the necessary adjustments to the relevant provisions of this Contract, observing the principle of the mutual economic benefits of the Parties.[14]

While such a modest formulation of stability can be helpful, it is quite incomplete. It fails to define a process that the parties could follow if they failed to reach agreement on a resolution of such an adverse economic impact on the IOC. In a recent negotiation with the Kenyan government, the IOCs requested additions to the clause. They argued that legal and fiscal stability was essential to them, given their prospective exposure to the risks associated with petroleum operations. They also pointed out that such stability would benefit the government as well by providing an incentive to current and future investment. The IOCs maintained that the inclusion of a process for the renegotiation and possible submission of a dispute to arbitration would expedite any possible dispute resolution procedure and prevent protracted delays of petroleum operations that could arise in the event such a process was not included in the clause. They requested the following additional sentences:

> The Parties shall renegotiate and amend this Contract in good faith, so as to achieve the same economic benefits for the Contractor as would have been anticipated had there not been any adverse economic affects. The Parties shall meet within thirty (30) days after the Government's receipt of the notice from the Contractor regarding the adverse economic affects. If the Parties are unable to agree upon the modifications that are required to this Contract in order to resolve the adverse

---

[13] Sonangol Form PSA template, http://www.resourcegovernance.org/sites/default/files/Angola%20PSA%20Template.pdf

[14] 2013 Model Production Sharing Contract, National Oil Corporation of Kenya, http://www.eisourcebook.org/cms/Kenya%20Model%20Production%20Sharing%20Contract.pdf

economic impact on the Contractor within ninety (90) days after the expiration of the preceding thirty (30) day period, or within another time frame as may be agreed by the Parties, the matter may be referred to arbitration by either the Contractor or the Government in accordance with Clause 41.[15]

In response to these negotiations, the government accepted the proposed additions to the stabilization clause. The parties inserted the additional sentences into the text of their agreement below the original sentence provided by the model PSA. As written, this provision constitutes an economic equilibrium clause with the requirement of good faith negotiation and a specific timeframe for negotiations and referral to arbitration.

What is the legal effect of a commitment by a host government to stabilize the taxation of a project financed with foreign investment? Can a government surrender its discretion to respond to new circumstances, especially in an area as important as taxation? What are the remedies available to an investor if a host government violates a stabilization agreement? Consider how the following case addresses these concerns.

Duke Energy International Peru Investments No. 1 v. Peru

ICSID CASE NO. ARB/03/28
I.C.C. 334 (2008)
July 28, 2009

. . .

35. The current scheme for the promotion and protection of foreign investment in Peru originated in the early 1990s. At that time, Peru began efforts to attract and promote investment in the country, reversing the policies pursued by previous administrations.

36. It was in this context that Law No. 25327 was adopted, authorizing the Executive Branch to legislate on matters of investment and investment protection. Pursuant to it, Legislative Decree No. 662 (Foreign Investment Law), Legislative Decree No. 674 (Privatization Law) and Legislative Decree No. 757 (Private Investment Law) were promulgated, as were the Regulations of the Regime to Guarantee Private Investment, approved by Supreme Decree No. 1 62–92–EF ("Investment Regulations").

. . .

39. These instruments provide various guarantees to foreign investors in Peru. In connection with a specific investment, the guarantees may be implemented through binding contracts referred to as "legal stability agreements" ("LSAs"), entered into by Peru and the foreign investor. The authorization to enter into LSAs is contained in the Foreign Investment Law and the Private Investment Law. Relevant provisions of both laws are typically incorporated by reference into such agreements.

---

[15] Article 40 on Governing Law, Block L5 Kenya Production Sharing Contract, dated March 30, 2009.

40. The standard text for all LSAs is incorporated as an annex to the Investment Regulations. The text refers in general terms to the stabilization of legal regimes applicable to various fundamental rights of foreign investors, including: (i) the right to equal treatment and non-discrimination; (ii) the right to free convertibility of foreign currency; (iii) the right to free repatriation of invested capital, profits and royalties; (iv) the right to income tax stabilization; and (v) the right to resolve disputes arising out of or in connection with the agreement by arbitration or other agreed method.

41. Under Peruvian law, the *Civil Code* provisions governing private contracts in general are also applicable to LSAs and, as such, these agreements are subject to the principle of *Contrato-Ley,* as set forth in Article 1357 of the 1984 *Civil Code.* That Article states as follows:

> [By law, supported by reasons of social, national or public interest, the State may establish guarantees and assurances by means of a contract.]

42. Article 39 of the Private Investment Law confirms the foregoing:

> [Legal stability investment agreements shall be concluded subject to Article 1357 of the Civil Code and shall have the [legal] effect of contracts enforceable as law, such that they may not be modified or terminated unilaterally by the State. Such contracts shall have a private rather than administrative character, and shall only be modified or terminated by agreement between the parties.]

43. Furthermore, as set forth in the last paragraph of Article 62 of the Constitution of Peru, the investment protections provided for by LSAs are guaranteed by the Constitution:

> [Liberty to contract guarantees that parties may validly agree according to the legal norms in force at the time of the contract. Contract terms may not be modified by law or other dispositions of any type. Conflicts that arise from contractual relations may only be resolved by arbitration or judicial decree, according to the mechanisms of protection set forth in the contract or contemplated by law.
>
> Through contracts-law [special investment-related private contracts of an obligatory character], the State may establish guarantees and grant securities. These may not be modified by legislation, without prejudice to the protection referred to in the preceding paragraph.]

44. Thus, pursuant to the investment laws of Peru, the main features of LSAs are that (i) the stabilized legal regimes cannot be changed unilaterally by the State, and (ii) the agreements are subject to private or civil law and not administrative law. As private-law contracts, the negotiation, execution, interpretation and enforcement of the provisions set forth in LSAs are subject to the general principles applicable to contracts between private parties under the Peruvian *Civil Code.* As such, the rights granted by Peru pursuant to an LSA are private contractual rights that are enforceable against the State as if it were a private party.

45. In 1991, Peru began to pursue a far-reaching privatization program designed to attract the participation, in particular, of international investors. For this purpose, the Privatization Law established the *Comisión para la Promoción de la Inversion Privada* ("COPRI"), a Peruvian inter-ministerial body charged with overall supervision of the privatization process.

46. In implementing its privatization mandate, COPRI selected the largest state-owned electricity generation company in the country, Electricidad del Peru S.A. or Electroperú S.A. ("Electroperú"), to be restructured into distinct, smaller electricity companies for privatization. In September 1994, as part of the privatization process, COPRI authorized the creation of a company named Empresa de Generación Eléctrica Nor Perú S.A. ("Egenor"), as a wholly-owned subsidiary of Electroperú. Thereafter, assets were transferred to Egenor from three state-owned companies, including Electroperú. Electroperú contributed fixed assets (in addition to cash and inventory) to Egenor consisting of six thermoelectric plants (Chiclayo, Piura, Paita, Sullana, Chimbote and Trujillo) and two hydroelectric plants (Carhuaquero and Canon del Pato).

47. COPRI adopted the following privatization model for Egenor: a controlling 60 percent of the shares of Egenor, representing the company's Class "A" shares, would be sold to a private investor through an international tender process (the "60 Percent Tranche"); 30 percent of the shares, these being Class "B" shares, would be retained by Electroperú for a subsequent public offering or share auction (the "30 Percent Tranche"); and the remaining 10 percent of the shares (also Class "B" shares) would be held for sale to Electroperú's employees.

. . .

49. The winning bidder for the 60 Percent Tranche was Dominion Energy, Inc. ("Dominion") of the United States of America, which presented its bid through a locally incorporated wholly-owned subsidiary, Inversiones Dominion Perú S.A. ("IDP"). Between June 25 and August 9, 1996, a privatization agreement (itself dated June 20, 1996), governing the purchase of the 60 Percent Tranche, was executed between Electroperú and IDP, with Dominion and Egenor as intervening parties (the "Privatization Agreement"). Under the Privatization Agreement, Dominion (as "Operator" and "Holder of the Committed Interest") was required to maintain control of Egenor with a minimum stake totalling 51 percent of IDP.

. . .

53. Duke Energy acquired Egenor through a series of transactions in late 1999. . . .

54. As of the end of 1999, Duke Energy had become (through DEI Holdings USA) the 90 percent owner of Egenor S.A.A. for which it had paid approximately US$288 million.

55. Dominion's sale of DHP (*i.e.*, of its 51 percent interest in IDP) to DEI Holdings USA was subject to the approval of COPRI pursuant to the terms of the Privatization Agreement. Under the Privatization Agreement, Dominion (as Operator and Holder of the Committed Interest) was obligated to maintain its 51 percent interest in IDP for five years from the date of the Agreement (*i.e.*, until August 2001), unless another entity (to which the interest was being transferred) could meet

the requirements specified in the Bidding Rules for the Operator and Holder of the Committed Interest. COPRI approved the sale of DHP, and thus Dominion's ownership interest in Egenor, to Duke Energy (through DEI Holdings USA) on September 22, 1999. On October 5, 1999, Dominion obtained and provided Duke Energy with a Guarantee Agreement between IDP and Peru ("Guarantee Agreement") pursuant to which Peru guaranteed, in connection with the 60 Percent Tranche, that all of the original obligations assumed, representations and warranties made, and liabilities of Electroperú remained effective and enforceable against Peru.

56. Duke Energy's acquisition of Dominion's Latin American assets had a number of international tax implications which Duke Energy intended to account for in a corporate reorganization. At the same time, Duke Energy needed to implement an ownership structure for Egenor S.A.A. generally mirroring the structure reflected in the Privatization Agreement. It was against this backdrop that DEI Bermuda was incorporated in August 1999. Subsequently, in May 2000, Duke Energy International Peru Holdings SRL ("DEI Peru Holdings") was established as a holding company wholly-owned by DEI Bermuda.

57. On July 26, 2000, Egenor S.A.A. changed its name to Duke Energy International Egenor S.A.A. ("DEI Egenor"). This entity changed its name to Duke Energy International Egenor S.A. in February 2001 and on June 26, 2003, to Duke Energy International Egenor S en C por A, evidencing a change in its corporate form.

58. On October 29, 2002, DEI Bermuda acquired 99 percent of DHP from DEI Holdings USA (and hence 51 percent of IDP), and the remaining 49 percent of IDP from DEI Holdings USA. On December 1, 2002, DHP and IDP merged to form Duke Energy International Peru Inversiones No. 1 SRL ("DEI Investments SRL"), as a result of which DEI Bermuda became the 99 percent owner of DEI Investments SRL, through which it owned 60 percent of DEI Egenor. The remaining 30 percent of DEI Egenor continued to be held by DEI Holdings USA.

59. On December 18, 2002, Duke Energy made a capital contribution of US$200 million to DEI Peru Holdings, through DEI Bermuda. DEI Peru Holdings used these funds to acquire 90 percent of the capital stock of DEI Egenor from DEI Investments SRL and DEI Holdings USA.

. . .

116. In July 2000, President Fujimori began a controversial third term in office, following allegations that the third term was unconstitutional and the result of electoral rigging. His third term came to an end on November 18, 2000, amidst allegations of corruption.

117. An interim Government under Mr. Valentín Paniagua, acting as interim President of the country, was established immediately thereafter. Congress and the new interim Government launched investigations into Mr. Fujimori's policies, including foreign investments, privatization and LSAs.

118. It was in this context that, on November 24, 2000, SUNAT [the Peruvian national tax administration] initiated a tax audit of DEI Egenor for tax year 1999 (*i.e.,* the tax compliance of Egenor S.A.A.). Upon

being notified, DEI Egenor requested an extension of the term to initiate the audit, which was granted.

. . .

128. On November 26, 2001, SUNAT assessed a tax liability of approximately US$12.4 million against DEI Egenor for what SUNAT determined were tax underpayments in 1996, 1997, 1998 and 1999, plus just over US$35.9 million in interest and penalties (the "Tax Assessment").

129. The Tax Assessment had two main components. The first component was based on SUNAT's view, under its interpretation of Rule VIII of the Peruvian Tax Code, that the 1996 merger between Egenor and Power North, resulting in the creation of Egenor S.A., was a sham transaction concluded solely to take improper advantage of tax benefits provided for under the Merger Revaluation Law (the "Merger Revaluation Assessment"). Under its interpretation of Rule VIII, SUNAT determined that it had the authority to disregard the merger on the grounds that it was concluded to circumvent the payment of taxes.

130. The second component was based on SUNAT's view that Egenor should have depreciated the assets that Electroperú had transferred to it during the privatization process using the special decelerated rate that had been provided to Electroperú by SUNAT in December 1995, rather than the general statutory rate set forth in the income tax regulations (the "Depreciation Assessment").

. . .

135. The Tax Court issued its decision on DEI Egenor's appeal of SUNAT's decision on April 23, 2004. The Court found mainly in favour of SUNAT and against DEI Egenor. On July 27, 2004, SUNAT issued a revised tax assessment against DEI Egenor, in accordance with the Tax Court's decision, for approximately US$27.6 million.

. . .

C. Scope of Protection Provided by DEI Bermuda LSA

. . .

1. Tax Stabilization

a) Relevant Provisions of the DEI Bermuda LSA

186. Tax Stabilization is guaranteed in Clause Three, Section 1 of the DEI Bermuda LSA, which reads as follows:

THREE—By virtue of this Agreement, the STATE, and as long as it remains in effect, in connection with the investment referred in CLAUSE TWO, the STATE guarantees legal stability for DUKE ENERGY INTERNATIONAL, according to the following terms:

1.   Stability of the tax regime with respect to the Income Tax, as stipulated in subsection a) of Article 10° of Legislative Decree No. 662, in effect at the time this Agreement was executed, according to which dividends and any other form of distribution of profits, are not taxed, in accordance with the stipulations of subsection a) of article 25 of the Amendment Text of the Income Tax Law, approved by the Supreme Decree No. 054–99–EF in effect at the time this Agreement was executed. Neither the remittances sent abroad of amounts corresponding

to DUKE ENERGY INTERNATIONAL for any of the items contemplated in this subsection are taxed pursuant to the aforementioned law.

187. Clause Five of the DEI Bermuda LSA provides as follows:

This Legal Stability Agreement shall have an effective term of ten (10) years as from the date of its execution. As a consequence, it may not be amended unilaterally by any of the parties during this period, even in the event that Peruvian law is amended, or if the amendments are more beneficial or detrimental to any of the parties than those set forth in this Agreement.

. . .

211. Article 23, on which Claimant has relied in order to demonstrate the linkage between the Egenor LSA and the DEI Bermuda LSA, says, in terms, that the income tax may not be "amended" nor "modified" while the LSA is effective.

212. Similarly, the Preamble to the Investment Regulations provides that LSAs "only guarantee the investors and enterprises in which they participate, that the laws in force at the time of their subscription will not be modified, for a certain period . . . "

213. In the same vein, Article 24 of the Investment Regulations provides as follows:

Article 24.

Pursuant to the provisions of the regulations referred to in Article 1° of this Supreme Decree, legal stability agreements exceptionally granted stability to the legal system in force at the time of execution of the agreement, and as long as such is in effect, on matters to which the stability is granted.

The stability referred to in the foregoing paragraph implies that will continue to be applied the same legislation in force at the time of the agreement's execution, without being affected by the amendments thereto on the matters and during the term foreseen in such agreements, including the derogation of legal rules, even in the case of more or less favourable provisions.

214. Claimant argues that a guarantee of tax stability that protects the investor strictly only against amendments or modifications to legislation and regulations would weaken the ambit of the guarantee which, as the evidence demonstrated, the parties intended to include in the LSA. The Tribunal will inquire as to what additional changes to the tax regime, if any, are covered by the guarantee of stabilization in addition to amendment or modification of Peruvian laws or regulations.

215. The Tribunal begins its analysis of this difficult question with the principle that its jurisdiction does not include the power to review the correctness of SUNAT's decisions and assessments or of the Tax Court's decisions as a matter of Peruvian tax law. As the Tribunal ruled in its Decision on Jurisdiction, it does not sit as the appellate division of the Tax Court.

216. The Tribunal's jurisdiction, under this particular guarantee, is limited to determining whether the relevant decisions or interpretations of SUNAT and/or the Tax Court, be they right or wrong, are consistent

with the tax regime stabilized for Claimant in the DEI Bermuda LSA. The Tribunal's standard is therefore comparative in nature, rather than absolute. In other words, the Tribunal does not opine on the correctness of the relevant decision or interpretation, but only determines whether such decision of SUNAT or of the Tax Court in the present case represents a change from their respective decisions prior to the entry into force of the DEI Bermuda LSA.

217. This comparative exercise is reasonably straightforward for legislation and regulations, where a change is objectively demonstrable. Claimant establishes an actionable change by proving (i) the existence of a pre-existing law or regulation (or absence thereof) at the time the tax stability guarantee was granted, and (ii) a law or regulation passed or issued after the LSA that changed the pre-existing regime.

218. The exercise is considerably more difficult where the Tribunal must analyze changes in the interpretation or application of a law or regulatory instrument, which could give rise to a finding of breach of the stability guaranteed by the Respondent. The Tribunal is satisfied that Claimant in this instance must prove (i) a *stable* interpretation or application at the time the tax stability guarantee was granted, and (ii) a decision or assessment after the LSA that modified that stable interpretation or application.

219. Thus, if, at the time when the guarantee was granted, the application of the existing rules resulted in a consistent interpretation, such interpretation must be deemed to be incorporated into the guaranteed stability. In a broad sense, stability is the standard by which the legal order prevailing on the date on which the guarantee is granted is perpetuated, including the consistent and stable interpretation in force at the time the LSA is concluded. The Tribunal is convinced that the maintenance of such stable interpretations of the law, existing at the time the LSA was executed, is part of "the continuity of the existing rules."

. . .

225. The Peruvian courts are the appropriate forum in which to make a claim in relation to incorrect application of the law by SUNAT or the Tax Court. As explained earlier, as a consequence of DEI Egenor's use of the tax amnesty system, this Tribunal cannot substitute its own jurisdiction for the jurisdiction of the Peruvian courts in matters concerning the interpretation of tax law.

226. Therefore, since this Tribunal is not a Peruvian court of appeal, more is required than a mere demonstration of an erroneous interpretation of the law. It is not for the Tribunal to simply determine if Peruvian law was properly applied, to formulate its own theory on Peruvian law, or to determine what it would consider to be the appropriate interpretation from the variety of interpretations that one might reasonably formulate. By their very nature, laws often invite different interpretations based on fairly reasonable principles. For this reason, and in order to preserve the proper balance of fairness between the parties in this arbitration, it must be demonstrated, absent a demonstrable change of law or a change to a stable prior interpretation or application, that the application of the law to DEI Egenor was patently unreasonable or arbitrary.

227. The Tribunal therefore decides that tax stabilization guarantees that: (a) laws or regulations that form part of the tax regime at the time the LSA is executed will not be amended or modified to the detriment of the investor, (b) a stable interpretation or application that is in place at the time the LSA is executed will not be changed to the detriment of the investor, and (c) even in the absence of (a) and (b), stabilized laws will not be interpreted or applied in a patently unreasonable or arbitrary manner.

228. However, tax stabilization does not mean that the laws shall only be interpreted or applied based on the meaning that most favours the beneficiary, or the meaning that its legal advisors suggest would be the most appropriate. Tax stabilization does not provide a guarantee against the risk that the Government or the courts will interpret the law in a manner that is unfavourable to the investor, or that differs from the opinion of the investor's legal advisors. An interpretation adverse to the investor cannot *per se* be considered a modification or violation of legal stability unless it is so unreasonable that, in practice, it violates the very stability that was guaranteed.

V. Liability

A. The Depreciation Assessment

. . .

299. The Tribunal begins by observing that both the general statutory rate and the special decelerated rate were part of the tax regime in place at the time the Egenor LSA was executed. The real question for the Tribunal is to determine which particular rate should have been applied by Egenor to the assets that Electroperú transferred to it, as a matter of Peruvian tax law.

300. The Tribunal has already decided that it does not have the jurisdiction to rule on the correctness of particular interpretations of Peruvian tax law. This is therefore an instance in which the Tribunal must simply determine whether the Depreciation Assessment was based on a patently unreasonable or arbitrary interpretation of the tax rules. For the reasons explained below, the Tribunal concludes that it was not.

301. The Tribunal turns first to the issue of continuity. While it is true that the Tax Court decision of April 23, 2004 (Resolution No. 02538–1–2004) questioned the validity of Chapter XIII of the Tax Law prior to 1998, it nevertheless confirmed that the principle of continuity was part of the tax regime (as legal doctrine) at the time that Electroperú transferred assets to Egenor, and on the date of the Egenor LSA.

302. The Tribunal does not consider the Tax Court's decision unreasonable. It is reasonable that depreciation over the useful life of assets should not be changed by the mere fact that ownership thereof has been transferred, if the assets are used in the same way. Depreciation is linked to the depreciating asset and its economic use rather than to the identity of its owner. It is not illogical or arbitrary that the rate should be determined *intuitu rei* and not *intuitu personae*.

303. Nor does the Tribunal consider that the Tax Court's decision violates the principle of legality, given the particular circumstances in which it applied legal doctrine to fill the gap left by the assumed inapplicability of Chapter XIII of the Tax Law. Notably, it appears to the Tribunal that had the Tax Court not relied on legal doctrine in order to

ground the existence of the continuity rule, it could have done so on the basis of other sources of Peruvian tax law. For example, the Tax Court cited in its decision, among other arguments supporting the validity of Chapter XIII, a decision of the Constitutional-Social Division of the Supreme Court which had upheld the validity of a law (Law Decree No. 25764) even though its implementing regulations had not been adopted.

304. Indeed, having carefully read Articles 105 and 106 of Chapter XIII, the Tribunal is not convinced that the conclusion that Chapter XIII was not in force or inapplicable due to the absence of "implementing regulations" is sound. Articles 105 and 106 read as follows:

Article 105.—

The depreciable value and useful life of assets transferred in a company reorganization will be those that would have applied when they were in the possession of the transferor.

Article 106.—

The reorganization of companies or corporations occurs only in cases of merger and division, with limitations, and in accordance with the stipulations stated in the regulations.

Arguably, Article 106 affords the executive branch the opportunity to define limitations applicable to the concept of merger or division through regulation, but does not require such regulations for the general concepts to apply. In this respect, the Tribunal notes that the wording of Article 106 of Chapter XIII can be distinguished from more explicit language in other Peruvian legislation that makes it clear that a tax measure is necessarily contingent on the promulgation of regulations. For example, Article 2 of Decree Law No. 26009 provided that the applicability of a benefit in relation to the Consumption Selective Tax would be exclusively contingent upon its regulations. In contrast, the text of Article 106 does not expressly condition the entry into force of that provision, or any other article of Chapter XIII, on the promulgation of regulations.

. . .

305. The Tribunal now turns to the issue of "corporate reorganization". Prior to the Egenor case, in its Decision No. 594–2–2001 dated May 25, 2001, the Tax Court had held that the concept of corporate reorganization in tax law is a matter of substance and not of form. In that case, the Tax Court found that the term "division" or "spin-off" under Supreme Decree No. 003–85–JUS of 1985, the predecessor to the General Corporations Law, was understood as including the act of dividing the activity of a corporation, in the context of a corporate reorganization, even if a formal spin-off was not carried out. The Tax Court found that the assets transferred by a state-owned company to an acquiring company in the context of a privatization, pursuant to Legislative Decree No. 674, amounted to a "division" in the context of a corporate reorganization. Consequently, the acquiring company had to continue depreciating those assets in accordance with the useful life and cost basis that the state-owned company had applied to the assets prior to their transfer. . . .

306. Of course, it is possible to interpret these provisions in a different way, concluding that the concept of corporate reorganization should be applied identically for tax purposes and for corporate purposes.

That does not mean, however, that the decision of the Tax Court or the Depreciation Assessment itself were so unreasonable that they constitute a violation of the guarantee of tax stabilization. It is not unreasonable, in the Tribunal's view, that depreciation over the useful life of assets should not be modified by the mere change of ownership, provided that the economic use and nature of the assets remain the same. That was the case with the assets transferred by Electroperú to Egenor.

. . .

B.   The Merger Revaluation Assessment

324.   In the Merger Revaluation Assessment, SUNAT determined that it was permitted, under Rule VIII, to assess companies it concluded had undertaken "simulated" (or "sham") mergers in order to avail themselves of the Merger Revaluation Benefits. SUNAT concluded that the merger between Egenor and Power North did not constitute a "real economic transaction" and declared this transaction a "simulation".

. . .

344.   To determine whether the Merger Revaluation Assessment violated the guarantee of tax stabilization in the DEI Bermuda LSA, the Tribunal must determine the following issues: (1) was Rule VIII part of the tax regime stabilized for Egenor on July 24, 1996; and (2) if so, was SUNAT's assessment under Rule VIII consistent with any stabilized interpretation and application of the Merger Revaluation Law in 1996?

345.   For the reasons explained below, the Tribunal concludes that while Rule VIII could properly be invoked by SUNAT to evaluate the legitimacy of transactions for tax purposes, SUNAT violated the guarantee of tax stabilization by using Rule VIII to change the stable interpretation of the [Merger Revaluation Law (MRL)] that generally prevailed in 1996 and was thus part of the tax regime stabilized for Egenor.

346.   The Tribunal notes that Rule VIII was introduced in April 1996, several months before the date of the Egenor LSA. Arguably then, the tax regime that was stabilized for Egenor, and thus later for DEI Bermuda in respect of Egenor, included the original version of Rule VIII. This original version, by Claimant's own admission, permitted SUNAT to scrutinize the underlying purpose of a transaction, such as a merger, and to disregard it for tax purposes if it concluded that the transaction was fraudulent.

347.   In light of this observation, a claim for breach of the guarantee of tax stabilization based on a misuse of the new version of Rule VIII would not be upheld since the new version of Rule VIII was not the one that was stabilized. It seems to the Tribunal that Claimant could only complain that SUNAT had misinterpreted the new version of Rule VIII, but not bring a claim based on such complaint under the tax stabilization guarantee of the DEI Bermuda LSA.

348.   In any event, the Tribunal accepts that both versions of Rule VIII provided SUNAT with the authority to set aside for tax purposes transactions which it concluded were "simulated".

349.   The Tribunal therefore concludes that SUNAT did not violate the DEI Bermuda LSA's guarantee of tax stabilization merely by invoking Rule VIII.

350. Part of the stabilized tax regime for Egenor was the MRL, which was passed by Congress in 1994 and extended for annual periods until the end of 1998. The fact that the MRL was stabilized under Peru's LSA Regime was confirmed, as a general matter, by the Edelnor and Luz del Sur arbitral decisions. As for Egenor's specific situation, it was agreed by all advisors who considered the matter that the MRL was stabilized under the Egenor LSA. The Tribunal refers here to the due diligence report prepared for the privatization of the 30 Percent Tranche by Estudio Grau, the legal opinion prepared for Egenor by the same law firm on January 5, 1999, and the legal opinion prepared by Miranda & Amado for Duke Energy on September 20, 1999. Indeed, in the case of Egenor, SUNAT did not challenge this conclusion.

351. Claimant argues that the MRL imposed no prerequisites on the type of companies that could take advantage of the tax benefits of the law. Respondent, on the other hand, contends that it was implicit in the structure, framework and purpose of the MRL that only "real" companies, which would be genuinely strengthened by a merger, could avail themselves of the Merger Revaluation Law.

352. The Tribunal finds that Claimant has discharged its burden of demonstrating that SUNAT's use of Rule VIII to invalidate the tax consequences of the Egenor merger with Power North violated the stable interpretation or application of the MRL at the time the Egenor LSA was executed.

. . .

360. The Tribunal is satisfied that it is not unusual, following a period of hyperinflation of the kind that plagued Peru between 1985 and 1991, that companies should be allowed to revalue their assets tax-free. The book value of the assets, expressed in nominal terms, no longer reflects their actual value in the new currency adopted in the post-hyperinflation era. The re-valued figures are, of course, nominally higher than the old book values, but they do not reflect either any actual increase of value of the assets or any actual income or increase of wealth of the owner of such assets, *i.e.,* the taxpayer. Therefore, in such circumstances, it is reasonable that such revaluations should be tax free.

361. The Tribunal is also satisfied that, as a matter of legal or economic policy, the Peruvian Government did not implement a general legal regime that would have permitted revaluations with no tax consequences. Instead, the Peruvian Government allowed such revaluations in the context of corporate reorganizations under the MRL. The Tribunal is convinced that this restricted legal framework of beneficial revaluations clearly gave rise to a general practice in the country of using mergers and spin-offs mainly to revalue assets rather than to actually reorganize companies or corporations.

362. The general practice of allowing the MRL to be used in this way was based on a very broad interpretation of the literal terms of Article 1 of the MRL, which required a "merger or division agreement of any type of legal entity, whether mercantile, civil or cooperative . . . " (emphasis added). What was essential was the existence of a merger of "any type of legal entity", irrespective of whether the sole purpose of the merger was the revaluation of assets in order to claim the tax benefits associated with it. According to the normal and widespread practice at the time, "merger" meant a formal legal act through which two or more

companies joined together to form a new one, without regard to the underlying economic reality of the transaction.

363. In other words, at the time of the Egenor LSA, the prevailing interpretation of the MRL was that a formal merger was sufficient to invoke the tax benefits offered by this law. It was this interpretation that was stabilized by the LSA.

364. When SUNAT concluded in November 2001 that the Egenor-PowerNorth merger lacked economic reality, and thus invalidated its tax benefits under the MRL, SUNAT implicitly gave the word "merger" a meaning that was different from the meaning that prevailed in 1996, and which was thus the stabilized meaning under the Egenor LSA.

365. Therefore, based on the totality of evidence, the Tribunal concludes that SUNAT's use of Rule VIII in 2001 to disallow the tax benefits of the Egenor-PowerNorth merger constituted a change in the stable pre-existing interpretation of the MRL.

366. The Tribunal therefore concludes that the Merger Revaluation Assessment constitutes a violation of the guarantee of tax stabilization.

. . .

NOTES

1. Duke also claimed that Peru violated its duty under international law not to discriminate against a foreign investor, relative to the treatment of domestic investors, and to provide fair and equitable treatment to the foreign investor. Almost all investment treaties require a state to honor these obligations. What does a stabilization clause add from the perspective of a foreign investor?

2. Note that Duke brought its claim against Peru directly, rather than relying on the U.S. government to act on its behalf. Most modern investment treaties, including the one between Peru and the United States at issue in this case, refer to the Convention on the Settlement of Investment Disputes Between States and Nationals of Other States. The International Center for the Settlement of Investment Disputes (ICSID), a component of the World Bank, administers the arbitrations that fall within this Convention. For an investor to have the right to obtain arbitration against a foreign state, it must have rights under an investment treaty. ICSID then provides a forum for determining those rights.

3. One of Peru's arguments for increasing the tax burden on this investment was a claim that the merger was a sham, and thus DEI Egnor was not entitled to the tax benefits that it was otherwise legally entitled to receive. The authority of tax officials to disregard formal attributes of a transaction in order to reassess and raise taxes presents especially difficult problems. Tax officials argue that they need some degree of discretion to prevent well-funded and expensively advised taxpayers from exploiting tax rules in a manner that neither the legislature nor the administrative officials intended. Taxpayers argue that this discretion can be abused to punish disfavored taxpayers for reasons that have nothing to do with tax policy.

Perhaps the most notorious recent instance of the use of the sham transaction doctrine for suspicious purposes to the injury of foreign investors is the Yukos transaction, discussed earlier in this chapter. Simplifying greatly, Yukos, a production company, sold oil to affiliates at a price close to its cost. The affiliated companies were established in various regions of the Russian Federation that enjoyed tax privileges, including an exemption from the profits tax. The affiliates then would sell the oil to consumers, largely for the export market, at market prices. The effect of this arrangement was to reduce profits taxes by characterizing almost all the profits generated by the production and sale of oil as earned by the tax-exempt affiliates.

Russian tax authorities argued, and the Russian courts ruled, that the affiliates were "sham" companies and thus should be disregarded. They did this even though the Russian tax code had a special provision governing sham companies that seemed clearly to bar this claim. One effect of this determination was to significantly increase the profits tax owed by Yukos. An even greater, and legally more dubious, move was to claim that Yukos could not receive the VAT refund normally due on exported products. The government maintained, and the courts agreed, that the law required Yukos to apply on its own behalf to receive this refund, and by allowing the (supposedly sham) affiliated companies to apply instead Yukos had forfeited the refund (for which the affiliates were not eligible because they were shams). The lion's share of the tax assessment that drove Yukos into bankruptcy and then resulted in the nationalization of its assets involved the VAT assessment. Foreign investors in Yukos have attacked these transactions in several arbitral forums.

D. NEGOTIATIONS

Many different types of negotiating styles have been promoted over the years, but principled negotiation, or negotiation on the merits, is the type that should be considered by all negotiators. It is the primary alternative to positional bargaining, and contains four basic elements, which focus on people, interests, options and criteria, as set out below.

PROBLEM   SOLUTION

Positional Bargaining: Change the Game—
Which Game Should You Play?   Negotiate on the Merits

SOFT	HARD	PRINCIPLED
Participants are friends.	Participants are adversaries.	Participants are problem-solvers.
The goal is agreement.	The goal is victory.	The goal is a wise outcome reached efficiently and amicably.
Make concessions to cultivate the relationship.	Demand concessions as a condition of the relationship.	Separate the people from the problem.
Be soft on the people and the problem.	Be hard on the problem and the people.	Be soft on the people, hard on the problem.

Trust others.	Distrust others.	Proceed independent of trust.
Change your position easily.	Dig in to your position.	Focus on interests, not positions.
Make offers.	Make threats.	Explore interests.
Disclose your bottom line.	Mislead as to your bottom line.	Avoid having a bottom line.
Accept one-sided losses to reach agreement.	Demand one-sided gains as the price of agreement.	Invent options for mutual gain.
Search for the single answer: the one *they* will accept.	Search for the single answer: the one *you* will accept.	Develop multiple options to choose from; decide later.
Insist on agreement.	Insist on your position.	Insist on objective criteria.
Try to avoid a contest of will.	Try to win a contest of will.	Try to reach a result based on standards independent of will.
Yield to pressure.	Apply pressure.	Reason and be open to reasons; yield to principle, not pressure.

To summarize, the four basic elements of principled negotiation are as follows:

1. People—separate the people from the problem.

2. Interests—focus on interests, not positions.

3. Options—prepare a variety of possible solutions before deciding what to do.

4. Criteria—insist that the result be based on some objective standard.

See Roger Fisher & William Ury, Getting to YES—Negotiating Agreement Without Giving In (3d ed. 2011).

E. NEGOTIATION EXERCISE—ORGANIZING A PROJECT ENTITY

Global Petroleum Company ("Global"), which established a representative office in Moscow in June 2012, has decided it wants to acquire the rights to develop three large oil fields in the Balolsk Republic in northwestern Russia. After conducting a considerable amount of due diligence, Global has chosen Balolskneftegas ("BNG") as its potential partner in this upstream development project. Global and BNG have agreed to establish a new oil company ("Newoilco") in which each party would own an equity interest, and which could serve as their single purpose entity for the project.

Each company has specific plans for its negotiating teams with respect to its (i) ownership interest in Newoilco, (ii) representation on the Board of Directors, and (iii) membership on the management team. BNG and Global have already agreed that they should establish Newoilco as a closed Russian joint stock company. Global is willing to invest an unspecified amount of cash for its equity interest in Newoilco.

Unfortunately, BNG is having some financial difficulties and is having problems (i) meeting some of its payroll obligations to its employees, (ii) paying its income tax and VAT obligations on time, and (iii) paying its utility bills on time. Therefore, BNG would like to make contributions in kind to Newoilco, rather than investing with cash. The property that BNG wants to contribute includes such things as (i) two floors of its office space, (ii) the rights to a producing oil field located in the Balolsk Republic, and (iii) two of its drilling rigs and associated oil field equipment.

Assume that the transfer of BNG's rights to the producing oil field is not an issue in this exercise. The parties are only interested in forming Newoilco in order to develop other oil fields, so concentrate on the issues related to forming a project entity.

The issues that are to be negotiated by Global and BNG are set forth below.

1. Determine the percentage amount of equity interest that each of Global and BNG will own in Newoilco.

2. Decide whether BNG is able to contribute its assets to pay for its equity interest in Newoilco under the Russian Joint Stock Company Law.

3. If BNG's contribution in kind is permitted, decide whether there is any special procedure they should include in the Newoilco structure to protect those assets from the claims of creditors.

4. Decide how many members each party will have on Newoilco's Board of Directors, if a total of six members are to be appointed.

5. Decide which members of the management team each party will have the right to appoint (the management team will include the General Director, Deputy General Director, Operations Manager, Finance Manager, General Counsel, HS & E Manager, Production Manager, and Accounting Manager).

6. Decide whether any special liquidation rights would be appropriate to include under these circumstances?

7. What remedies should Global have if BNG is unable to meet its obligations to Newoilco, including a failure to contribute its assets to Newoilco?

8. Should any other issues under the Joint Stock Company Law or other matters we have discussed be addressed at this stage of the business relationship?

The negotiating teams representing Global and the negotiating teams representing BNG will be given separate, confidential instructions for this negotiation exercise. Each team will prepare and present the results of your negotiations in a 1–2 page memorandum. The memorandum should describe either the basis of your team's agreement on the issues or the reasons an agreement was not reached, as well as a brief statement about the negotiating styles utilized by each team.

CHAPTER 4

FINANCING EMERGING MARKET INVESTMENTS

Raising finance for a large scale infrastructure project in an emerging market presents special challenges. Because such projects are common in these markets, however, understanding how to address financial challenges is critical. Consider the range of alternatives. Debt finance requires borrowing from a source of funds, such as a private commercial bank or other financial intermediary, an international financial institution owned or controlled by one or more governmental organizations, or some combination of sources. The borrower must enter into a series of agreements that provide for the repayment of the debt plus interest, as well as for various mechanisms granting the lenders rights to collateral, which provide security in the event of a default under the agreements.

Equity finance involves the sale of a portion of the ownership of, and possibly control over, a company in exchange for funding based on an agreed valuation of the company's business. An equity investor may seek to negotiate certain influence through a seat on the Board of Directors or the appointment of members of management of the company. Further controls may be negotiated in the form of a shareholders agreement or its equivalent. The investor will also seek to negotiate an "exit" from the project, in the form of a right to have its interest purchased by other project participants after a certain period of time or upon the occurrence of certain events, or the right to participate in a sale of its interest as part of a public offering of shares in the company.

Many debt and equity combinations exist to provide the right mix of financing for the company. A finance arrangement may have the appearance of equity but have terms and conditions that resemble more closely debt, such as preferred stock with specific dividend rights and liquidation preferences.

In considering the possibilities, all investors, whether purchasing debt, equity or some combination, at bottom seek a return on their investments. The straight debt financing transaction involves a rate of return determined by reference to interest rates. While the actual rates may vary during the term of the loan, the return is fixed within the interest rate variation. The traditional equity investor has no such pre-determined, fixed return. This investor may reap huge returns if the project is profitable, far in excess of what a debt investor would earn. However, the equity investor may receive no return, or even lose its investment, if the project falters or fails entirely. These risks—the foregoing of upside gain by the debt investor for downside protection or the possibility of greater upside gain for the equity investor but without downside protection—can be hedged through some combination of debt and equity.

A. SOURCES OF FINANCE

Consider the following excerpts from the website of the International Finance Corporation, the private sector investment arm of the World Bank. The IFC is very active in emerging markets. How does its "Vision, Value & Purpose" statement affect its investment decisions? A review of its Investment Proposal requirements reveals the factors an investor will consider in judging the viability of a project. What features of an emerging market complicate this analysis? Consider, for example, problems of corruption and lack of transparency as well as legal systems where questions of ownership are not easily resolved and contracts not adequately enforced.

How do the objectives of commercial banks differ from those of the IFC? What factors make the former hesitant about lending in emerging markets and why is the IFC in a better position to invest in projects in these markets?

IFC'S Vision, Values, & Purpose[1]

Our vision is that people should have the opportunity to escape poverty and improve their lives.

Our values are excellence, commitment, integrity, and teamwork.

Our purpose is to:

- Promote open and competitive markets in developing countries.

- Support companies and other private sector partners.

- Generate productive jobs and deliver basic services.

- Create opportunity for people to escape poverty and improve their lives.

Our Shared Mission

IFC, as the private sector arm of the World Bank Group, shares its mission:

To fight poverty with passion and professionalism for lasting results. To help people help themselves and their environment by providing resources, sharing knowledge, building capacity, and forging partnerships in the public and private sectors.

An [IFC] investment proposal should include the following preliminary information[2]

1. **Brief description of project**

2. **Sponsorship, management & technical assistance:**

   - History and business of sponsors, including financial information.

   - Proposed management arrangements and names and curricula vitae of managers.

---

[1]   IFC, Frontier Focus—IFC in the World's Poorest Countries (2008).

[2]   http://www.ifc.org/wps/wcm/connect/corp_ext_content/ifc_external_corporate_site/what +we+do/about+ifc+financing_investment+proposals

- Description of technical arrangements and other external assistance (management, production, marketing, finance, etc.).

3. **Market & sales:**

- Basic market orientation: local, national, regional, or export.
- Projected production volumes, unit prices, sales objectives, and market share of proposed venture.
- Potential users of products and distribution channels to be used.
- Present sources of supply for products.
- Future competition and possibility that market may be satisfied by substitute products.
- Tariff protection or import restrictions affecting products.
- Critical factors that determine market potential.

4. **Technical feasibility, manpower, raw material resources & environment:**

- Brief description of manufacturing process.
- Comments on special technical complexities and need for know-how and special skills.
- Possible suppliers of equipment.
- Availability of manpower and of infrastructure facilities (transport and communications, power, water, etc.).
- Breakdown of projected operating costs by major categories of expenditures.
- Source, cost, and quality of raw material supply and relations with support industries.
- Import restrictions on required raw materials.
- Proposed plant location in relation to suppliers, markets, infrastructure, and manpower.
- Proposed plant size in comparison with other known plants.
- Potential environmental issues and how these issues are addressed.

5. **Investment requirements, project financing & returns:**

- Estimate of total project cost, broken down into land, construction, installed equipment, and working capital, indicating foreign exchange component.
- Proposed financial structure of venture, indicating expected sources and terms of equity and debt financing.
- Type of IFC financing (loan, equity, quasi-equity, a combination of financial products, etc.) and amount.
- Projected financial statement, information on profitability, and return on investment.
- Critical factors determining profitability.

6.   **Government support & regulations:**

- Project in context of government economic development and investment program.

- Specific government incentives and support available to project.

- Expected contribution of project to economic development.

- Outline of government regulations on exchange controls and conditions of capital entry and repatriation.

7.   **Timetable envisaged for project preparation & completion.**

Compare the information provided publicly by the U.S. Eximbank and the Overseas Private Investment Corporation, both U.S. government supported sources of finance for U.S. investors operating in emerging markets. Information on OPIC financing can be found at www.opic.gov. The European Bank for Reconstruction and development focuses its efforts on Eastern Europe and the former Soviet Union. See www.ebrd.com.

NOTES

1.   To what extent does the IFC's list of information required for an investment proposal reflect specific concerns that might arise in emerging markets? The requirements do contemplate that information will be provided on import restrictions for raw materials and on exchange controls and the repatriation of capital, but are there other items that should be included? For example, would the IFC be prudent to require information about corruption risk in a particular country, such as the Transparency International corruption rating? Even further, should the IFC require that the proposal include information on how the sponsor intends to manage such risk through, for example, the implementation of a compliance policy with particular focus on due diligence, training and monitoring of intermediaries.

2.   There seems to be a requirement that the project contribute to the economic development of the country in which the project is planned (See Item 6). Why is the IFC concerned about such information? What form would such contributions take and how are they likely to affect returns on the project?

B. MANAGING EMERGING MARKET RISK

For investors, whether using debt or equity, the key to success is proper risk management. Investors pursue this objective by insisting on, prior to providing funds, a careful review of the quality of both the project and the borrower or owner, obtaining appropriate contractual protections in the funding documentation, monitoring performance of the project and having appropriate recourse in the event of the failure of the project. The additional challenge posed by an emerging market requires that the investor also know the particular characteristics of that market—its political, economic, social and legal features—to manage risk properly.

Contractual undertakings from the borrower are an important aspect of a lender's security package. Consider the IFC Loan Agreement printed in the Documents Supplement. Under this Loan Agreement the lender, the IFC, has provided financing for a geothermal power generating facility in Nicaragua to PENSA, a Nicaraguan company, and SJPIC, a Panamanian corporation.

Note that the borrowers in the Loan Agreement make a series of representations and warranties in Clause 3.01 (through the companion Common Terms Agreement), which provide a wide range of assurances to the lender about its organization, financial performance, and compliance with law and organizational documents. How confident would a lender be in accepting these representations directly from these entities?

Why do lenders seek such protection, and why do borrowers give them? Once the borrower has received the loan proceeds, who has the upper hand? If the borrower were to fail to satisfy a term of the loan agreement, would a lender necessarily declare a default? What incentives does a lender have to cooperate with the borrower to negotiate a way around difficulties? Knowing that a lender might be reluctant to invoke its various remedies, is it surprising that the loan agreement contains so many protections?

The Limits of Legal and Contractual Remedies

The weaknesses of emerging market legal systems compel a broad-based, proactive strategy to minimize legal risks. Contractual documentation in financing and related investment transactions can deal with only a portion of this challenge. Specific problems arise because laws are poorly formulated, and regulators have broad discretion, without adequate accountability, to interpret and apply those laws. Judicial bodies often lack the competence to handle complex commercial matters, are corrupt or are subject to political influence. Indeed, corruption often pervades all levels of the legal system, tainting legislators, regulators and judges. These factors come into focus when a company's contractual partner—be it a joint venture partner, a distributor, sales representative or agent—defaults on its obligation.

Of course, it is very important to have the financing document specify that the laws of a jurisdiction with well developed and tested rules on financial transactions and contract interpretation will govern the contract. In addition, designating an acceptable foreign jurisdiction with adequate dispute resolution facilities, either courts or arbitral bodies, provides a lender or investor with the best opportunity to enforce its rights in a competent, disinterested forum free from narrow national or corrupt influences. Arbitration is typically the favored form of dispute resolution because of the New York Convention on the Enforcement of Arbitral Awards, to which many countries, including most key emerging market countries, are parties. The Convention obligates its signatories to enforce international arbitral awards in their respective courts, with very limited exceptions.

Lenders in financing transactions, however, prefer to enforce their rights in reliable courts rather than through arbitration. There are two reasons for this preference. First, lenders are typically attempting to enforce their right to be paid, which, if the financing documentation is well drafted, involves simple legal and factual issues. Courts are well-suited to such proceedings. Second, many lenders believe that arbitrators are more willing to consider broader issues than the simple legal and factual issue of failure to pay. They worry that arbitrators will approach the case with a desire to be even-handed even in the face of cut-and-dried legal and factual issues. However, the decision to submit disputes involving a financing in an emerging market such as Indonesia to a court in the United States also carries significant risks. For starters, enforcement of a judgment issued by a U.S. court in Indonesia is not governed by a treaty, such as the New York Convention, but rather by principles of international comity. Comity provides a shaky basis for obtaining satisfaction not only in Indonesia but in the courts of most other emerging markets as well.

Even elaborate precautions regarding the governing law and forum for dispute resolution often are insufficient to protect a lender's or investor's interests in difficult emerging markets. Two problems typically occur. First, when a dispute arises the local party may take its case to a local court that may refuse to honor the agreement for international arbitration under foreign law and instead apply local law. In such circumstances, all the reasons that the lender or investor sought arbitration outside of the emerging market return with a vengeance. Second, even if the lender or investor succeeds in obtaining a foreign arbitral award, there may be great difficulties in enforcing the award. The local court may refuse to enforce the award or, even if it issues the enforcement order, the local bailiff or similar service may fail to execute the order. These consequences can be mitigated if the judgment debtor has assets in jurisdictions outside of the emerging market that have reliable legal systems. But such situations are uncommon.

These difficult enforcement problems require lenders and investors to broaden their conception of protecting their legal rights. Companies need to use extreme care in providing funds to entities in emerging markets. A basic approach includes thorough due diligence and extensive periods building and "testing" the relationship before making formal legal commitments. Attention to the relationship itself must be a priority, because in so many emerging markets the weakness of the legal system is directly related to the strength of personal, familial and even clan or tribal relationships. The goal of all of this activity is to avoid disputes that may give rise to formal claims for legal remedies under contractual documents. Once a dispute reaches that stage, the relationship is likely over and, to make matters worse, the likelihood of the foreign party receiving an adequate remedy, or even making an easy exit from the market, is substantially diminished.

Another approach is to enter into contracts with solvent intermediaries to insure against the risk of default. At least until the recent financial crisis, a substantial industry existed to provide such contracts. But a lack of experience has given rise to controversies over the scope of coverage. Consider the following case, which grew out of the Argentine financial crisis in the early years of the present century.

Eternity Global Master Fund Limited v. Morgan Guaranty Trust Company of New York

United States Court of Appeals for the Second Circuit
375 F.3rd 168 (2004)

■ DENNIS JACOBS, CIRCUIT JUDGE:

Plaintiff-Appellant Eternity Global Master Fund Limited ("Eternity" or "the Fund") purchased credit default swaps ("CDSs" or "the CDS contracts") from Defendants-Appellees Morgan Guaranty Trust Company of New York and JPMorgan Chase Bank (collectively, "Morgan") in October 2001. Eternity appeals from a final judgment entered in the United States District Court for the Southern District of New York, dismissing with prejudice its complaint alleging breach of contract, fraud, and negligent misrepresentation by Morgan in connection with the CDSs. The CDS contracts were written on the sovereign bonds of Argentina and would be "triggered" upon the occurrence of a "credit event," such that if Argentina restructured or defaulted on that debt, Eternity would have the right to put to Morgan a stipulated amount of the bonds for purchase at par value.

In late November 2001, the government of the Republic of Argentina, in the grip of economic crisis, initiated a "voluntary debt exchange" in which bondholders had the option of turning in their bonds for secured loans on terms less favorable except that the loans were secured by certain Argentine federal tax revenues. Eternity informed Morgan that the voluntary debt exchange was a credit event that triggered Morgan's obligations under the CDS contracts. Morgan disagreed.

In February 2002, Eternity filed suit alleging breach of contract and fraudulent and negligent misrepresentation. Morgan moved to dismiss for failure to state a claim pursuant to Federal Rule of Civil Procedure ("Rule") 12(b)(6). In an unreported decision, the district court preserved Eternity's contract claim but dismissed the misrepresentation claims for want of the particularity required by Rule 9(b). Eternity amended its complaint in an effort to redress the deficiencies noted by the district court; and Morgan again moved to dismiss. The district court again held that Eternity's misrepresentation claims were insufficiently pled and went on to reconsider its ruling on the breach of contract claim. Upon reconsideration, the court held that the claim failed as a matter of law.

On appeal, Eternity challenges the dismissal of its claims. For the reasons set forth below, we affirm the dismissal of the fraudulent and negligent misrepresentation claims but reverse the dismissal of the contract claim and remand for further proceedings.

BACKGROUND

On behalf of its investors, Eternity trades in global bonds, equities and currencies, including emerging-market debt. During the relevant period, Eternity's investment portfolio included short-term Argentine sovereign and corporate bonds. In emerging markets such as Argentina, a significant credit risk is "country risk," *i.e.*, "the risk that economic, social, and political conditions and events in a foreign country will adversely affect an institution's financial interests," including "the possibility of nationalization or expropriation of assets, government repudiation of external indebtedness, . . . and currency depreciation or devaluation." Credit risk can be managed, however. Banks, investment funds and other institutions increasingly use financial contracts known as "credit derivatives" to mitigate credit risk. In October 2001, in light of Argentina's rapidly deteriorating political and economic prospects, Eternity purchased CDSs to hedge the credit risk on its in-country investments.

I

By way of introduction, we briefly review the terminology, documentation, and structure of Eternity's credit default swaps.

A. *Terminology*

A credit default swap is the most common form of credit derivative, *i.e.*, "[a] contract which transfers credit risk from a protection buyer to a credit protection seller." Protection buyers (here, Eternity) can use credit derivatives to manage particular market exposures and return-on-investment; and protection sellers (here, Morgan) generally use credit derivatives to earn income and diversify their own investment portfolios. Simply put, a credit default swap is a bilateral financial contract in which "[a] protection buyer makes[ ] periodic payments to . . . the protection seller, in return for a contingent payment if a predefined credit event occurs in the reference credit," *i.e.*, the obligation on which the contract is written.

Often, the reference asset that the protection buyer delivers to the protection seller following a credit event is the instrument that is being hedged. But in emerging markets, an investor may calculate that a particular credit risk "is reasonably correlated with the performance of [the sovereign] itself," so that (as here) the investor may seek to isolate and hedge country risk with credit default swaps written on some portion of the sovereign's outstanding debt.

In many contexts a "default" is a simple failure to pay; in a credit default swap, it references a stipulated bundle of "credit events" (such as bankruptcy, debt moratoria, and debt restructurings) that will trigger the protection seller's obligation to "settle" the contract via the swap mechanism agreed to between the parties. The entire bundle is typically made subject to a materiality threshold. The occurrence of a credit event triggers the "swap," *i.e.*, the protection seller's obligation to pay on the contract according to the settlement mechanism. "The contingent payment can be based on cash settlement . . . or physical delivery of the reference asset, in exchange for a cash payment equal to the initial notional [*i.e.*, face] amount [of the CDS contract]." A CDS buyer holding a sufficient amount of the reference credit can simply tender it to the CDS seller for payment; but ownership of the reference credit prior to default is unnecessary. If a credit event occurs with respect to the obligation(s) named in a CDS, and notice thereof has been given (and the CDS buyer has otherwise performed), the CDS seller must settle. Liquidity in a secondary market increases the usefulness of a CDS as a hedging tool, though the limited depth of that market "can make it difficult to offset . . . positions prior to contract maturity."

B. *Documentation*

The principal issue dividing the parties is whether the CDS contracts at issue are ambiguous in any material respect. "An ambiguity exists where the terms of a contract could suggest 'more than one meaning when viewed objectively by a reasonably intelligent person who has examined the context of the entire integrated agreement and who is cognizant of the customs, practices, usages and terminology as generally understood in the particular trade or business.' "

In this case, we assess ambiguity in the disputed CDS contracts by looking to (i) the terms of the three credit default swaps; (ii) the terms of the International Swaps and Derivatives Association's ("ISDA" or "the Association") "Master Swap Agreement," on which those swaps are predicated, (iii) ISDA's 1999 Credit Derivatives Definitions—which are incorporated into the disputed contracts; and (iv) the background "customs, practices, [and] usages" of the credit derivatives trade. Because customs and usages matter, and because documentation promulgated by the ISDA was used by the parties to this dispute, we briefly review some relevant background.

The term "derivatives" references "a vast array of privately negotiated over-the counter . . . and exchange traded transactions," including interest-rate swaps, currency swaps, commodity price swaps and credit derivatives—which include credit default swaps. A derivative is a bilateral contract that is typically negotiated by phone and followed by an exchange of confirmatory faxes that constitute the contract but do not specify such terms as events of default, representations and warranties, covenants, liquidated damages, and choice of law. These (and other) terms are typically found in a "Master Swap Agreement," which, prior to standardization efforts that began in the mid-1980s, "took the form of separate 15- to 25-page agreements for each transaction."

Documentation of derivatives transactions has become streamlined, chiefly through industry adherence to "Master Agreements" promulgated by the ISDA. In 1999, Eternity and Morgan entered the ISDA Multicurrency-Cross Border Master Agreement, which governs, inter alia, the CDS transactions disputed on appeal. Each disputed CDS also incorporates the 1999 ISDA Credit Derivatives Definitions, the Association's first attempt at a comprehensive lexicon governing credit derivatives transactions. Last year, due to the rapid evolution of "ISDA documentation for credit default swaps," the Association began market implementation of the 2003 Credit Derivatives Definitions, which evidently constitutes a work in progress.

C. *Eternity's Credit Default Swaps*

Eternity's Global Master Fund is managed by HFW Capital, L.P., including its Chief Investment Officer, Alberto Franco. In 2001, Franco engaged Morgan to facilitate Eternity's participation in the Argentine corporate debt market. Fearing that a government debt crisis would impair the value of Eternity's Argentine investments, Franco sought to hedge using credit default swaps written on Argentine sovereign bonds. In October 2001, the Fund entered into three such contracts. Each CDS incorporated (i) the ISDA Master Swap Agreement, and (ii) the 1999 ISDA Definitions. The total value of the contracts was $14 million, as follows:

CDS Entry Date	Termination Date	Value
October 17, 2001	October 22, 2006	$2 million
October 19, 2001	December 17, 2001	$3 million
October 24, 2001	March 31, 2002	$9 million
Total Value		$14 million

Except as to value and duration, the terms were virtually identical, as follows:

(i) Eternity would pay Morgan a fixed periodic fee tied to the notional value of each respective credit default swap.

(ii) The swaps would be triggered upon occurrence of any one of four credit events—as defined by the 1999 ISDA Credit Derivative Definitions—with respect to the Argentine sovereign bonds: Failure to pay, Obligation Acceleration, Repudiation/Moratorium, and Restructuring.

(iii) Each CDS called for physical settlement following a credit event, specifically:

(a) Upon notification (by either party to the other) of a credit event, and confirmation via two publicly available sources of information (*e.g.*, the Wall Street Journal), and

(b) delivery to Morgan of the requisite amount of Argentine sovereign bonds,

(c) Morgan would pay Eternity par value for the obligations tendered.

It is alleged (and we therefore assume) that Eternity entered the swaps in reliance on Morgan's representations that it would provide access to a liquid secondary market that would enable the Fund to divest the contracts prior to termination.

The parties dispute whether any of certain actions taken by Argentina with respect to its debt obligations in November and December 2001 constituted a credit event. The district court thought not, and dismissed Eternity's contract claim at the pleading stage. With the background and structure of the disputed CDS contracts in mind, we turn to Eternity's principal allegations.

II

. . .

The contracts at issue were signed in October 2001. By then, international financial markets had been speculating for months that Argentina might default on its $132 billion in government and other public debt. At an August 2001 meeting of bondholders in New York, Morgan acknowledged the possibility of a sovereign-debt default and advised that it was working with the Argentine government on restructuring scenarios. On October 31, 2001—after the effective date of the swap contracts at issue on this appeal—Morgan sent Eternity a research report noting that there was a "high implied probability of [a] restructuring" in which bondholders would likely receive replacement securities with a less-favorable rate of return. One day later, Argentine President Fernando de la Rua asked sovereign-bond holders to accept lower interest rates and longer maturities on approximately $95 billion of government debt.

On November 19, 2001, the Argentine government announced that a "voluntary debt exchange" would be offered to sovereign-bond holders. According to various public decrees, willing bondholders could exchange their obligations for secured loans that would pay a lower rate of return over a longer term, but that would be secured by certain federal tax revenues. So long as the government made timely payments on the loans, the original obligations would be held in trust for the benefit of Argentina. If the government defaulted, however, bondholders would have recourse to the original obligations, which were to "remain effective" for the duration of their life-in-trust. From late November through early December 2001, billions of dollars in sovereign bonds were exchanged for the lower-interest loans.

The complaint alleges that the debt exchange amounted to a default because local creditors had no choice but to participate, and that the financial press adopted that characterization. On November 8, 2001 Eternity served the first of three notices on Morgan asserting that the planned debt exchange was a restructuring credit event as to all three CDS contracts; but Morgan demurred.

On December 24, newly-installed interim President Adolfo Rodriguez Saa—appointed by the Argentine Congress on December 23 to replace President de la Rua—announced a public-debt moratorium. On December 27, Morgan notified Eternity that the moratorium constituted a credit event and subsequently settled the outstanding $2 million and $9 million credit default swaps (otherwise set to terminate on October 22, 2006 and March 31, 2002, respectively). According to Morgan, the third swap (valued at $3 million) had expired without being triggered, on December 17, 2001.

It is undisputed that the December 24 public-debt moratorium was a trigger of Eternity's outstanding swaps; in Eternity's view, however, the voluntary debt exchange had triggered Morgan's settlement obligations as early as November 8, 2001, as the Fund had been insisting throughout November and December of that year. In that same period, Eternity asked Morgan to liquidate the swaps on a secondary market. Notwithstanding Morgan's representations in February 2001 regarding the existence of a secondary market for the CDSs, it refused to quote Eternity any secondary-market pricing, though it did offer to "unwind" the contracts by returning the premiums Eternity had paid from October through November 2001.

III

. . .

To make out a viable claim for breach of contract a "complaint need only allege (1) the existence of an agreement, (2) adequate performance of the contract by the plaintiff, (3) breach of contract by the defendant, and (4) damages." Eternity alleges: (1) that the CDS contracts are valid agreements; (2) that the Fund satisfied its contractual obligations to

Morgan, *i.e.*, (a) paid its premiums; (b) supplied the requisite notification and public information following the announcement of the voluntary debt exchange; and (c) signaled its willingness to tender the necessary sovereign bonds; (3) that Morgan's refusal to settle the swaps was a breach of contract; and (4) that the Fund was damaged as a result of Morgan's breach—by the loss of the $3 million owed under the CDS that expired prior to the public-debt moratorium announced December 24, 2001, and by consequential damages arising from Morgan's refusal to settle the other swaps in November 2001.

The district court concluded that these pleadings were insufficient on the ground that the plain meaning of the CDS contracts conveyed the parties' unambiguous intention to exclude the voluntary debt exchange from the bundle of government actions that could qualify as a restructuring credit event. We disagree.

The question is whether at this stage it can be decided as a matter of law that the voluntary debt exchange was not a "restructuring credit event" covered by the Fund's CDS contracts with Morgan. Resolution of that issue turns on what the CDS contracts say. Under New York law, "the fundamental, neutral precept of contract interpretation is that agreements are construed in accord with the parties' intent." Typically, the best evidence of intent is the contract itself; if an agreement is "complete, clear and unambiguous on its face[, it] must be enforced according to the plain meaning of its terms." If the contract is ambiguous, extrinsic evidence may be considered "to ascertain the correct and intended meaning of a term" or terms. "Ambiguity exists where a contract term could suggest more than one meaning when viewed objectively by a reasonably intelligent person who has examined the context of the entire integrated agreement and who is cognizant of the customs, practices, usages and terminology as generally understood in the particular trade or business." Unless for some reason an ambiguity must be construed against the plaintiff, a claim predicated on a materially ambiguous contract term is not dismissible on the pleadings.

. . .

In support of its motion to dismiss, Morgan submitted, inter alia, the 1999 ISDA Credit Derivatives Definitions and English translations of portions of certain Argentine decrees purporting to explain the mechanics of the government's debt exchange program.

A. *The 1999 ISDA Definition of "Restructuring" and the Terms of Argentina's Voluntary Debt Exchange*

By their terms, Eternity's credit default swaps could be triggered by any of four credit events: Failure to Pay, Obligation Acceleration, Repudiation/Moratorium, and Restructuring. To flesh out these terms, Eternity and Morgan incorporated by reference the 1999 ISDA Credit Derivatives Definitions. Eternity concedes that Argentina's voluntary debt exchange is a credit event only if it qualifies as a restructuring under § 4.7 of the 1999 Definitions:

> "Restructuring" means that, with respect to one or more Obligations, including as a result of an Obligation Exchange, . . . any one or more of the following events occurs, is agreed between the Reference Entity or a Governmental Authority and the holder or holders of such Obligation or is announced (or

otherwise decreed) by a Reference Entity or a Governmental Authority in a form that is binding upon a Reference Entity, and such event is not provided for under the terms of such Obligation in effect as of the later of the Trade Date and the date as of which such obligation is issued or incurred:

> (i) a reduction in the rate or amount of interest payable or the amount of scheduled interest accruals;

> (ii) a reduction in the amount of principal or premium payable at maturity or at scheduled redemption dates;

> (iii) a postponement or other deferral of a date or dates for either (A) the payment or accrual of interest or (B) the payment of principal or premium;

> (iv) a change in the ranking in priority of payment of any Obligation, causing the subordination of such Obligation; or

> (v) any change in the currency or composition of any payment of interest or principal.

ISDA, 1999 Credit Derivatives Definitions § 4.7(a) (1999) ("1999 Definitions"). The "obligations" relevant to Eternity's credit default swaps are Argentine sovereign bonds.

The basic terms of the voluntary debt exchange are undisputed. Presidential Decree 1387, released November 1, 2001, declares at Title II ("Reduction of the Cost of Argentine Government Debt"), Article 17:

> The MINISTRY OF ECONOMY is instructed to offer on voluntary terms the possibility of exchanging Argentine government debt for Secured Loans or Secured Argentine Government Bonds, provided that the collateral offered or the change in debtor allows the Argentine Government to obtain lower interest rates for the Argentine or Provincial Government Sector.

The class of "government debt" referred to in Article 17 includes the sovereign bonds on which the disputed CDS contracts are written. Thus holders of those bonds were eligible to participate in the government's exchange program.

> Under Article 20 of Decree 1387, any exchange would be carried out

> at par value at a ratio of ONE (1) to ONE (1) in the same currency as the exchanged[, *i.e.*, originally held] obligation was denominated, provided that the interest rate on the Secured Loan for which each government debt transaction is exchanged is at least THIRTY PERCENT (30%) less than that established in the instrument submitted for exchange, per the terms of issue.

Under Article 22, the Ministry of the Economy was "authorized to appropriate funds belonging to the Nation," *i.e.*, certain federal tax revenues, "for up to the sum required to honor" the loans or other secured instruments for which any "original" sovereign-debt obligations would be exchanged.

On November 28, 2001, the Ministry of Economy issued Resolution 767 ("Government Debt"), which delineated the "exchange mechanism" contemplated in Decree 1387. Under Resolution 767, sovereign-debt holders would have until 3 p.m. on November 30, 2001 to submit "Offers of Exchange" to certain designated financial institutions. Between that date and December 3, the government would decide which offers it would accept, after which the bondholders so selected would have until December 7 to tender eligible securities. The exchanges would be "settled" on December 12, when former bondholders would receive the secured loans.

On December 12, the government approved (i) a "Secured Loan Agreement" to govern the new obligations, and (ii) a "Trust Agreement" governing the disposition of the original bonds. The Trust Agreement provides that any bonds exchanged for secured loans would be placed in trust for the benefit of the Republic of Argentina. The complaint alleges that as of December 6–7, 2001, holders of approximately $50 billion in Argentine sovereign debt had tendered their bonds.

B. *The Voluntary Debt Exchange as a Restructuring Credit Event*

Eternity contends that Argentina's voluntary debt exchange qualifies as a restructuring credit event in four ways: (i) as an obligation exchange under § 4.9 of the 1999 Definitions that constituted a "restructuring" under § 4.7; and even if not an obligation exchange, as an (ii) extension, and/or (iii) deferral, and/or (iv) subordination of the original obligations such that those obligations were restructured within the meaning of § 4.7. Morgan counters, and the district court agreed, that the voluntary debt exchange was not a restructuring within the meaning of the CDS contracts because it was not an obligation exchange, nor did it affect the payment, value, or priority of the original obligations.

(i) The voluntary debt exchange as an "Obligation Exchange"

Under the 1999 Definitions, an "Obligation Exchange" is "the mandatory transfer . . . of any securities, obligations or assets to holders of Obligations in exchange for such Obligations. When so transferred, such securities, obligations or assets will be deemed to be Obligations." 1999 Definitions, supra, § 4.9 (emphasis added). Section 4.7 states that an "Obligation Exchange" can qualify as a restructuring, id. § 4.7(a), and further provides:

> If an Obligation Exchange has occurred, the determination as to whether one of the events described under Section 4.7(a)(i) to (v) has occurred will be based on a comparison of the terms of the Obligation immediately before such Obligation Exchange and the terms of the resulting Obligation immediately following such Obligation Exchange.

Id. § 4.7(c). Thus if the voluntary debt exchange is an "Obligation Exchange," then it is a restructuring if the terms of the Secured Loans— as compared with the terms of the exchanged sovereign bonds—indicate that "one of the events [that constitutes a restructuring under § 4.7] has occurred." Id. Morgan concedes that such a comparison would show that the voluntary debt exchange was a restructuring credit event: The secured loans undeniably provide a lower return over a longer maturity than the original bonds, two features that qualify as restructuring occurrences under § 4.7. See id. § 4.7(a)(i), (iii).

Morgan argues, however, that because § 4.9 of the 1999 Definitions states that an "Obligation Exchange" is a "mandatory transfer" of one set of obligations for another, and because participation in the government's debt exchange program was "voluntary," a comparison of the two instruments is irrelevant.

The term "mandatory transfer" as it appears in § 4.9 of the ISDA definitions is not self-reading, and is therefore ambiguous if it could suggest more than one meaning when viewed objectively, in the context of each CDS agreement and the "customs, practices, [and] usages . . . as generally understood" in the credit derivatives trade. Morgan makes the intuitively appealing argument that a "mandatory transfer" cannot be an exchange offered on "voluntary terms." The district court was persuaded by this argument, citing Black's Law Dictionary:

> Argentina's [voluntary debt] exchange program cannot qualify as "mandatory." Eternity made a choice. Along with "a substantial portion" of holders of those Argentine obligations, Eternity chose to exchange the obligations for lower-interest secured loans. . . . Despite Eternity's attempt to argue that "mandatory" should be read to encompass situations that are "economically coercive," the plain meaning of the term "mandatory" does not permit such a finding. The term "mandatory" is defined by Black's Law Dictionary (7th Ed. 1999) as "of, relating to, or constituting a command" or "required." The choice made by Eternity may have been unpalatable, but that does not make it mandatory.

A dictionary definition, however, does not take into account what "mandatory transfer" means in the context of a particular industry.

Eternity makes the less obvious but plausible argument that to credit-risk protection buyers such as itself, a "mandatory transfer" includes any obligation exchange achieved by "economic coercion," regardless of its classification as "voluntary" or "mandatory" by the initiating party. According to Black's, "economic coercion" is "conduct that constitutes improper use of economic power to compel another to submit to the wishes of one who wields it." Black's Law Dictionary 252 (7th ed. 1999). Assuming that the government's debt exchange was economically coercive, "voluntary" participation by the "coerced" bondholders appears to resemble "mandatory" action. At the same time, from Argentina's perspective, the exchange may have been voluntary in fact, *i.e.*, the government may have had the intention to honor its debt obligations to nonparticipants without delay or reduction. But Argentina's characterization—which is self-serving—does not control, particularly when one considers Eternity's allegation that Morgan was an architect of the debt exchange. A proper interpretation of the CDS contracts must be drawn from the contract language and, where necessary, from other indicia of the parties' intent. Section 4.9 is silent as to whose perspective dictates whether an obligation exchange has occurred (*e.g.*, the issuer or the holder, or the investment press or community), and the parties' competing interpretations are plausible. We cannot resolve that ambiguity at this stage, as the district court took no submissions on the customs and usages of the credit derivatives industry, and the parties point us to no definitive source that resolves the difficulty.

Although the CDS contracts are silent on the precise meaning of "mandatory transfer," the ISDA has not ignored the issue. In its complaint, Eternity refers to a draft "User's Guide" to the 1999 Definitions, publication of which appears to have been tabled indefinitely. The draft guide explained that the "reference to 'mandatory transfer' in [the] definition of ['Obligation Exchange'] . . . should be read as clarifying rather than restricting the Restructuring definition and should not be read to mean that the optional exchange of Obligations for other assets cannot constitute a Restructuring." The User's Guide to the 1999 Definitions was never formally promulgated, but it does indicate that, (at least) as of the time Eternity purchased the credit default swaps, the meaning of "mandatory transfer" was perhaps more open-ended than Morgan contends.

Finally, in drawing its conclusion that the voluntary debt exchange was not an obligation exchange, the district court appears to have relied on its observation that Eternity "made a choice" to participate in the voluntary debt exchange. Any such reliance was misplaced. Whether Eternity actually owned Argentina's sovereign bonds (and whether it chose to participate in the government's debt swap if it did) is irrelevant to whether the exchange was a restructuring credit event under the disputed CDS contracts. The swaps were triggered if the government defaulted on its own debt obligations, *i.e.*, upon the occurrence of a "credit event" with respect to those obligations as a class. The CDS contracts did not require or contemplate that the credit protection buyer (here, Eternity) would hold the reference bonds except as may become necessary to exercise the put. Thus, if the Argentine government's voluntary debt exchange was a restructuring within the meaning of the 1999 Definitions, the CDS contracts were triggered; any election Eternity might have made with respect to its own bond holdings does not matter.

We go on to consider Eternity's arguments that the government's debt exchange was a restructuring even if it was not an obligation exchange.

(ii) The effect of the voluntary debt exchange on Argentina's original debt obligations

Under the 1999 Definitions, a restructuring credit event occurs when any one of five enumerated events "occurs, is agreed [to] . . . or is announced" with respect to an "obligation" upon which a credit default swap is written. 1999 Definitions, supra, § 4.7(a). These include:

(i) a reduction in the rate of payable interest or principal on the obligation, id. § 4.7(a)(i)–(ii);

(ii) a postponement of payment on interest or principal, id. § 4.7(a)(iii); and

(iii) a subordination of the obligation that did not exist prior to the occurrence of the restructuring credit event, id. § 4.7(a)(iv).

Eternity contends that each of these three events "occurred" with respect to certain classes of Argentine sovereign bonds as a consequence of the government's voluntary debt exchange.

The district court held that "under the terms of the 'voluntary debt exchange,' the obligations submitted into the Trust . . . themselves remained unchanged." That observation may be sound as far as it goes. But § 4.7 provides that a restructuring results if any event defined in the section "occurs" with respect to "one or more obligations." Thus, the proper inquiry is whether the debt exchange caused a restructuring to occur with respect to any of the Argentine sovereign bonds. For the purpose of this analysis, it is useful to consider separately the impact of the debt exchange on obligations that were exchanged pursuant to the government's "voluntary" offer (participating obligations), and on those retained by sovereign-bond holders who elected to forgo the government's program (nonparticipating obligations). To negative the possibility that there was a restructuring credit event, it must be clear that none of the "events" described in §§ 4.7(a)(i)–(v) occurred with respect either to the participating obligations or to the nonparticipating obligations.

(a) Participating Obligations

Participating obligations were ultimately deposited with the Central Bank of the Republic of Argentina pursuant to Article 23 of Presidential Decree 1387, issued November 1, 2001. Six weeks later, Presidential Decree 1646 approved both a Secured Loan Agreement to govern the terms of the loans that would replace the bonds tendered in the exchange, and a Trust Agreement that governed the status of obligations so tendered. Eternity contends that a restructuring credit event occurred with respect to tendered obligations because their terms were extended and/or payment was suspended for the duration of their life-in-trust.

Maturity Extension. On November 28, 2001 the Ministry of Economy promulgated Resolution 767 which, inter alia, defined the sovereign bonds eligible to participate in the voluntary exchange and, at Annex II, delineated the "exchange mechanism" for those securities, including the provision that "eligible Securities whose total or partial original maturity is prior to December 31, 2010 shall receive secured loans that will extend the average life of the Eligible Security by 3 years." (emphasis added). Morgan does not directly respond to Eternity's contention that this wording extends the maturity of certain debt obligations within the class referenced in the disputed CDS contracts. This provision creates a question of fact as to whether the three-year extension constitutes a restructuring credit event under § 4.7(iii) of the 1999 Definitions.

Suspension of Payment. Under the terms of the voluntary debt exchange (primarily laid down in Decree 1646), participating obligations were placed in trust. The Trust Agreement named Caja de Valores as trustee and provided that the government of Argentina would "acquire Participation Certificates in the . . . Trust, the underlying assets of which are the Argentine government debt securities" that participated in the exchange. By virtue of its participation, the Republic of Argentina was the "Original Beneficiary" of the trust. Decree 1646 further provided that "for purposes of determining the outstanding amount of Argentine government debt or of determining the national debt ceiling, . . . [tendered obligations] shall not be included in such calculations for so long as the Argentine Federal Government is the Beneficiary of any payments made in this regard." This provision implements Decree 1506, promulgated November 22, 2001, which amended Decree 1387 to provide that any obligations placed in trust pursuant to the voluntary debt exchange would be excluded from the calculation of Argentina's national debt. According to Decree 1506:

Such an arrangement [was] called for because, even when securities subject to exchange are held [in the manner contemplated] . . . it is the Argentine Federal Government that is the beneficiary of the economic rights thereby granted, with the liabilities thus becoming confused with the credits and offsetting same, inasmuch as the creditors of the ARGENTINE REPUBLIC can under no circumstances make simultaneous claims to credit rights that are granted by government securities in addition to those granted by Secured Loans substituting same.

Eternity contends that these provisions suspended Argentina's liability on the bonds held in trust because (i) former bondholders could not enforce the original instruments while they were held in trust; and (ii) Argentina's role as both beneficiary and obligor on the trust assets suspended, at least temporarily, any enforceable legal obligation created by those debt instruments. We think that there is a question, at least on the present record, as to whether this trust mechanism constituted "postponement or other deferral of a date or dates for payment of those obligations," within the meaning of § 4.7(a)(iii).

Morgan identifies three provisions of the Trust Agreement as support for its contention that the voluntary debt exchange did not affect Argentina's sovereign-debt obligations in any of the ways contemplated in § 4.7. Two of the three provisions refer directly or indirectly to a Secured Loan Agreement, a copy of which has been furnished to us, apparently from a website; but Morgan's otherwise voluminous submissions do not include a translation into English. That omission frustrates a complete analysis because we are left to guess whether, given the Trust Agreement's repeated references to particular provisions of the Loan Agreement, the latter has any bearing on the debt obligations placed in trust.

Moreover, the language cited to establish the continued effectiveness of Argentine bonds placed in trust is indefinite. Under Section C of the Trust Agreement's "Whereas" clause:

In accordance with the provisions of Article Ten of the Loan Agreement, an essential condition of same is that the Securities remain effective, with respect to both the economic and political rights of same, in such a manner that, under certain circumstances, their owners can recover fee simple thereof, all until such time as the Secured Loans have been settled. . . .

The economic and political rights of tendered obligations remain effective "in such a manner that, under certain circumstances" they can be recovered in fee simple. But it is wholly unclear what "such a manner" might mean on this record, or in what "circumstances" recovery would be allowed, or what it means for the bonds to "remain effective" when (under Decree 1506) they cannot be enforced by the former bondholders. In any case, it appears that tendered obligations "remain effective" only insofar as may be necessary to fulfill the contingency that former bondholders may one day have a right to reclaim their original obligations. Whether this qualified and contingent effectiveness constitutes a restructuring credit event is a question that cannot be resolved on the pleadings.

Morgan also invokes Section 2.1.3 of the Trust agreement, which provided that the transfer of sovereign bonds to the trust "shall include assignment of all present and future economic rights" of those obligations. This seemingly unqualified transfer may bear on the "effectiveness" of the obligations once they are part of the trust corpus, but that conclusion cannot be drawn from the text. Indeed, the "Whereas" clause relied on by Morgan explicitly contemplates that the effectiveness of the assets in trust will be less than their effectiveness in the hands of the original creditors—regardless of the mechanics of the transfer itself.

Finally, Morgan points to section 3.1 of the Trust Agreement, which directs the trustee to

> collect principal and interest payments due with respect to the Trust Assets and pari passu shall pay with such amounts payments due under the Participation Certificates [held by the Republic of Argentina], until such time as the Participation Certificates are fully amortized, except upon the occurrence [of a default as defined in the Secured Loan Agreement].

The force of Morgan's argument is blunted by the absence of the Secured Loan Agreement; nonetheless, the quoted language begs the question: If, as Eternity contends, the government's legal obligation to make bond payments was suspended or postponed when Argentina became the trust beneficiary of assets on which it was obligated to pay, were any interest payments actually "due" on the original obligations?

(b) Nonparticipating obligations

Eternity alleges that at some point during the voluntary debt exchange process, Argentina's Economy Minister announced that the "restructured loans held domestically will have the highest priority for payment." According to Eternity, this announcement "effectively" subordinated the original obligations to the secured loans, and was thus a credit event under § 4.7, which includes "a change in the ranking in priority of payment of any Obligation, causing the subordination of such Obligation." 1999 Definitions § 4.7(a)(iv). Morgan disagrees, primarily on the ground that there is "no language in the Domestic Exchange that changes the rank in priority of payment on the existing Obligations."

At the pleading stage, Eternity was required to furnish a "short and plain" statement of its claim for breach of contract. *Fed. R. Civ. P. 8(a)(2)*. The allegations concerning subordination, which recite the ISDA definition as well as the official statement referenced above, are both short and plain. Section 4.7(a)(iv) of the 1999 Definitions, which says that "subordination" is a reduction "in the ranking in priority of payment of any Obligation," does not in terms exclude policy declarations such as the one allegedly announced by Argentina's Economy Minister. True, "subordination" may denote more limited circumstances, such as a formal, contractual subordination of a particular debt. But that reading is not compelled by the wording of § 4.7(a)(iv).

The ISDA promulgated a "Restructuring Supplement" to the 1999 Definitions in April 2001 which included § 2.30(b) ("Pari Passu Ranking; Section 4.7(a)(iv)"), a provision that speaks directly to the definition of "subordination" under § 4.7(a)(iv):

> For purposes of Sections [sic] 4.7(a)(iv), "a change in the ranking in priority of payment of any Obligation, causing the

subordination of such Obligation," means only the following: an amendment to the terms of such Obligation or other contractual arrangement pursuant to which the requisite percentage of holders of such Obligations ("Subordinated Holders") agree that, upon the liquidation, dissolution, reorganization or winding up of the Reference Entity, claims of holders of any other Obligations will be satisfied prior to the claims of Subordinated Holders. For the avoidance of doubt, the provision of collateral, credit support or credit enhancement with respect to any obligation will not, of itself, constitute a change in the ranking in priority of payment of any Obligation causing the subordination of such Obligation.

The Eternity/Morgan CDS contracts incorporate the 1999 Definitions, but do not appear to incorporate the Restructuring Supplement, which must be invoked specifically. If the Supplement had been included, the subordination issue would likely be settled (in Morgan's favor); but the version of § 4.7(a)(iv) in use here is insufficiently clear as to whether subordination can be effected by policy statements such as the one cited by Eternity. Eternity and Morgan will have to resolve the issue in discovery or, if necessary, before a trier of fact.

[The remainder of the opinion, which ruled that Eternity had failed sufficiently to plead fraud or negligent representation by Morgan, is omitted.]

NOTES

1. The contracts sold by the Morgan entities used standard industry definitions, which in turn were updated in light of ongoing experience. What more could Eternity have done to ensure coverage under these facts? How can one draft language that attaches legal consequences to government statements that have political, but not legal, significance? Is that what happened here?

2. Insurance comes at a cost. Why did Eternity enter into these credit default swaps? Why are these instruments not more common in emerging markets financing, given the inherent instability of this environment?

3. During the financial crisis that started in the United States in 2007, credit default instruments played a significant role in destabilizing the global financial system. Ironically, it is unanticipated (or to be more precise, insufficiently covered) defaults in the U.S. market, especially residential mortgages, rather than the failure of emerging markets investments, that brought on the crisis. What do these problems suggest about the utility of insurance contracts as a means of laying off the risk from emerging market investments?

Planning Beyond Legal and Contractual Protections

The most critical lesson taught by the experience of major international financial institutions and strategic investors in emerging markets is that nothing can be taken for granted. Every important detail must be carefully managed. Significant managerial, financial, legal and other oversight responsibilities should be delegated to local partners only after an extensive period of testing their capabilities, character and experience. Rushing to advance local management to oversee a substantial loan or other investment either because it seems politically expedient or because a company's senior managers are unwilling to relocate to the emerging market creates a significant likelihood of inadequate oversight.

Often success becomes an excuse for withdrawing a foreign managerial presence from the emerging market. This phenomenon is particularly common where a local company in which the foreign partner has made an investment has enjoyed success. Paradoxically, this success promotes the atrophy of the lender or strategic investor's knowledge and experience regarding the emerging market. Such atrophy creates a significant risk that, if for any reason defaults arise, the foreign party may lose its investment.

This point suggests the extent to which a lender or strategic investor must go to maintain its position in the market. As a practical matter, a broader strategy to protect inherently weak legal rights means at least three key activities: learning, monitoring and maintaining a presence. "Learning" means developing and maintaining a knowledge base regarding the emerging market—its political, economic and social systems and its history, as well as its commercial culture and business practices. What particular challenges confront foreign financial institutions or strategic investors? Where are such entities vulnerable? Is there opposition to foreign investment activity? How can it be overcome, neutralized, or transformed?

"Monitoring" involves spending consistent and effective time with the local entity in which the investment has been made, particularly its management and ownership, to anticipate problems and to address them before they develop into serious disputes. Monitoring also involves effective oversight; for example, regular audits of the performance of the companies in which investments have been made. More broadly, monitoring involves determining what changes are occurring in the market and how political, economic, social and cultural developments affect the investments which have been made.

However, monitoring itself is not sufficient. Creating and maintaining a "presence" in the emerging market means building and reinforcing relationships with regulators, government officials and other leaders on local, regional and national levels. Such officials and leaders can be critical to resolving disputes with local companies or to providing assistance to the lender or investor when the relationship with the local company goes bad, whether because the local company has engaged in misconduct, illegal behavior or other activities harmful to the interests of the lender or investor. When difficult problems arise—criminal attacks, inappropriate demands from lower level bureaucrats, or employee misconduct, to name just a few examples—officials at higher levels can intercede to resolve these problems.

* * *

The key risk for financing and strategic investment transactions in emerging markets is instability, a problem which arises in two fundamental ways. First, an emerging market may be chaotic, characterized by convulsive, often rapid political, economic, social and legal changes. Russia had these features in the 1990s. Uncertain political authority, fluctuations in exchange rates, high inflation, multiple and ever changing taxes may wreak havoc with rates of return and even the opportunity to enforce rights as a lender or investor.

The second form of instability is less obvious. Where a regime appears to be firmly in the control of an autocratic figure, political, economic and social conditions may appear stable. Yet the lack of accountability resulting from no rule of law or separation of powers means that the project into which the lender or investor has committed capital may last only so long as the autocrat deems appropriate. The risk of confiscation or expropriation is always present.

Consider the following report on the consequences of the second form of instability on the capitalization of a major Russian company:

Russian Stock Markets Plunge
(Associated Press)
Friday, July 25, 2008; 6:54 AM

MOSCOW—Investors piled out of Russian stocks Friday after the abrupt departure from the country of a foreign oil boss and the prime minister's unexpected severe criticism of a large steel firm.

MICEX, the exchange where the bulk of trading in Russian stocks takes place, plunged by 4.8 percent as of 12:20 p.m. Russian time, while the RTS, a top stock index, lost 4.4 percent to drop beneath the critical 2000-point barrier for the first time since March.

After Prime Minister Vladimir Putin's scathing attack on Mechel late Thursday, heavy trading in New York sent the steel and coal maker's stock down by nearly 40 percent, losses mirrored Friday morning in Russian trading.

The premier criticized the company, which is the largest supplier of coal for steelmakers in Russia, for charging much higher prices for raw materials domestically than it does for its exports, and called for an antitrust investigation into its activities.

Earlier Thursday, Robert Dudley, CEO of the embattled Anglo-Russian oil producer TNK-BP, left the country three days before his visa was due to expire. Russia has not renewed the visa on the ground that he allegedly does not have a valid work contract.

The developments rattled investors, leading to a heavy sell-off in Russian stocks. The RTS is now down more than 20 percent from its mid-May high, pushing it into technical bear territory.

* * *

C. EQUITY SECURITIES AND THE DISCLOSURE OF RISKS

Companies based in emerging markets often succeed in accessing U.S. private and public securities markets, thereby attracting non-strategic, portfolio capital. Returns can be high but, as demonstrated in the prior materials in this chapter, so are the risks. How do companies disclose these risks to investors and what role does such disclosure play? Excerpts from a document issued by a prominent Russian consumer products company as part of a public offering of its shares in the United States are set forth in the Documents Supplement.

We will first consider the terms of the offering itself and then evaluate the specifically identified risk factors as to determine the nature and extent of the risks involved in these types of financings. The specific content of these disclosures may surprise you, but keep in mind that U.S. securities laws are based on the assumption that investors are best able to evaluate risk and that the role of regulation is largely to ensure that disclosure is made accurately and completely. That such disclosure may reveal serious problems with the offering is a matter for the investor to evaluate.

Wimm-Bill-Dann Private Placement Document

Review the Risk Factors disclosed in the Wimm-Bill-Dann document. Several raise particular problems of Russian law and practice. Note, for example, the Risk Factors relating to "Our Business and Industry". According to the disclosure, the Moscow City Government purchases 75% of Wimm-Bill-Dann's baby food products. Under normal circumstances, such a disclosure would alert the investor to the business problem of a single large customer and the potential for disruption if Wimm-Bill-Dann were to lose the City's business to a competitor. However, because the City of Moscow is notorious for corruption, the Risk Factor actually hints at a very serious potential legal problem, which should lead an informed investor to examine the extent to which Wimm-Bill-Dann has enacted an anti-corruption compliance program and taken steps to implement it effectively.

Consider, in the same section, the Risk factor that identifies the business's reliance on certain retailers and wholesalers. Reflect on the effect on a business of behavior by potential customers that might be an unlawful restraint of trade in a country with a well-established legal system and market economy. Consider also the Risk Factor focusing on the potential challenge to Wimm-Bill-Dann's privatization—a common hostile takeover tactic in the Russian business community, frequently coupled with payments to corrupt judges to overturn privatizations, many of which were accomplished without strict compliance with Russian law. How about the disclosure that one of Wimm-Bill-Dann's primary suppliers may be associated with organized crime and that its largest shareholder was convicted of a violent crime? Finally, why doesn't Wimm-Bill-Dann have proper insurance against standard business risks?

Note how the Risk Factors provide a picture of the Russian legal, economic and political systems, as well as a primer on Russian commercial practices. The challenge for an investor is to distinguish between risks that are passing phenomena, characteristics of a system in transition, and those that reflect deeply-ingrained dysfunctions in the emerging market that raise serious questions about the viability of the investment.

➤ 1.   How do these disclosures from the Wimm-Bill-Dann Prospectus assist an investor in managing the risks associated with this investment? What are the limits to this approach?

2.   What do these risk factors reveal about the specific characteristics of the Russian securities market at the time?

3.   What characteristics must be present in a capital market in order for a system based on the disclosure of information, including risks, to work? Consider the factors that determine the accuracy, quality and reliability of information disclosed to investors.

D. DEBT: PROJECT FINANCE AND THE MANAGEMENT OF RISK

For many years, investors in emerging markets have used innovative and complex project finance transactional structures to raise the substantial sums necessary to finance large scale oil and gas, infrastructure, mining and other projects. In its purest form, project finance is a simple concept. Theoretically, lenders in project finance transactions rely solely upon the revenues generated from the project for repayment of the debt rather than depending on traditional commercial lending techniques such as stock pledges, corporate guarantees, and security interests in assets, to secure repayment. No pure project finance transactions are done, however, because lenders always seek some appropriate blend of security to bolster their reliance on project revenues and provide a hedge against the perceived level of political risk.

These mixed or hybrid structures are accepted practice in emerging markets. "Pure" project finance is perceived as too risky, and traditional commercial lenders cannot rely on the security measures to which they are accustomed. Local laws are undeveloped, ambiguous, unevenly enforced, and unduly burdensome. As a result, lenders have no confidence in their ability to perfect security interests or to secure priority against other creditors.

In 1999, the IFC published a report on project financing in emerging markets, which included the description of the basic elements of project finance, the two types of project finance and compared them with corporate finance, as follows:

> Repayment of the financing relies on the cash flow and the assets of the project itself. The risks (and returns) are borne not by the sponsor alone, but by different classes of investors (equity holders, debt providers, quasi-equity investors). Because risks are shared, one criterion of a project's suitability for financing is whether it is able to stand alone as a distinct legal and economic entity. Project assets, project-related contracts, and project cash flows need to be separated from those of the sponsor. There are two basic types of project finance: nonrecourse project finance and limited-recourse project finance.
>
> *Nonrecourse project finance* is an arrangement under which investors and creditors financing the project do not have any direct recourse to the sponsors, as might traditionally be expected (for example, through loan guarantees). Although creditors' security will include the assets being financed, lenders rely on the operating cash flow generated from those assets for repayment. Before it can attract financing, then, the project must be carefully structured and provide comfort to its financiers that it is economically, technically, and environmentally feasible, and that it is capable of servicing debt

and generating financial returns commensurate with its risk profile.

Limited-recourse project finance permits creditors and investors some recourse to the sponsors. This frequently takes the form of a pre-completion guarantee during a project's construction period, or other assurances of some form of support for the project. Creditors and investors, however, still look to the success of the project as their primary source of repayment. In most developing market projects and in other projects with significant construction risk, project finance is generally of the limited-recourse type.

Traditional finance is corporate finance, where the primary source of repayment for investors and creditors is the sponsoring company, backed by its entire balance sheet, not the project alone. Although creditors will usually still seek to assure themselves of the economic viability of the project being financed, so that it is not a drain on the corporate sponsor's existing pool of assets, an important influence on their credit decision is the overall strength of the sponsor's balance sheet, as well as their business reputation. Depending on this strength, creditors will still retain a significant level of comfort in being repaid even if the individual project fails. In corporate finance, if a project fails its lenders do not necessarily suffer, as long as the company owning the project remains financially viable. In project finance, if the project fails investors and creditors can expect significant losses.

Traditionally, in developing countries at least, project finance techniques have shown up mainly in the mining and oil and gas sectors. Projects there depend on large-scale foreign currency financing and are particularly suited to project finance because their output has a global market and is priced in hard currency. Since market risk greatly affects the potential outcome of most projects, project finance tends to be more applicable in industries where the revenue streams can be defined and fairly easily secured.

Lessons of Experience No. 7: Project Finance in Developing Countries, IFC1999, http://www.ifc.org/wps/wcm/connect/publications_ext_content/ifc_external_publication_site/by+title/lessonsofexperienceno7

An example of limited-recourse project finance occurred in 1993 in connection with the Russian/American joint venture between Conoco Timan-Pechora Ltd. ("CTPL"), a subsidiary of Conoco Inc., and GP Arkhangelskgeologia, a Russian geological association whose name was later changed to OAO Arkhangelskgeoldobycha ("AGD") when it was privatized as a joint stock company. CTPL and AGD joined forces to form Polar Lights Company ("PLC"), a Russian limited liability company, to develop the Ardalin Field, which was located in the Nenets Autonomous Okrug in the Northern Timan-Pechora region of the Russian Federation 1,000 miles northeast of Moscow. The field was discovered by AGD in 1988, and had proven reserves of 130 million barrels of crude oil.

The fundamental problems that emerged in the period following the fall of the Soviet Union created an atmosphere that led both commercial and institutional lenders to conclude that an extremely high level of political risk existed in Russia. Also, financing for an oil project of this magnitude had not been attempted in Russia previously. As a consequence, CTPL and AGD, as the sponsors, were subject to considerable pressure to agree to a host of additional security mechanisms that are normally required only by commercial lenders.

International commercial banks were not interested in participating because they did not want to be exposed to the political risk associated with an oil field development project in Russia. In addition, Russian commercial banks did not have sufficient experience to act as a viable source for such funding. Therefore, the parties targeted the international financing institutions ("IFIs") and governmental export credit agencies ("ECAs") as the main sources for the loans. Ultimately, the European Bank for Reconstruction and Development ("EBRD"), the Overseas Private Investment Corporation ("OPIC") and the International Finance Corporation ("IFC") agreed to provide a total of $200 million in loans to PLC. The EBRD took the lead among the lenders, agreeing to provide $90 million, while the IFC and OPIC agreed to provide $60 million and $50 million, respectively.

The lenders undertook both a qualitative and quantitative analysis of the Ardalin Project. The quantitative portion used a financial model constructed with a computer spreadsheet package. This financial model showed the project's estimated cash flow under various circumstances. The most important variables contained in the economic model were the price of oil, the level of taxation, the production rate, estimated transportation costs, as well as the amount of debt service itself.

Due to the plethora of problems associated with the level of political risk and the perfection of security interests, PLC was forced to address demands from the lenders for other types of security, a completion guarantee and a detailed completion test, as depicted in the following excerpt from an article regarding those issues.

James W. Skelton, Jr., Arranging Project Financing for Polar Lights Company in Russia
VI Currents Int'l Trade L. J. 3 (Winter 1997)

VII. Addressing Security and Related Issues in Russia

The basic principle behind non-recourse or limited recourse financing is that lenders are only entitled to acquire security interests in certain assets of the borrower to secure the repayment of the loans.

A.   Security Interests in Russia

Under the Russian Law on Pledge, a borrower may pledge its assets under a loan agreement even if the agreement is entered into outside the Russian Federation. In addition, the law provides for the pledge of an enterprise, but requires registration of such a pledge agreement. This mortgage of an enterprise is not effective until it has been registered, and, to date, a state registry has not yet been established. Therefore, this has not proven to be an effective method of obtaining security interests, and it will continue to be ineffective until the registration regulations are clarified and an independent register is created.

B.   The Security Package

Since there were many problems associated with the perfection of security interests in Russia, Polar Lights was faced with a host of demands from the lenders for other types of security.

[i]   Offshore Bank Account

The establishment of an offshore bank account in London for the deposit of proceeds from the export sales of Polar Lights' crude oil was the first and foremost requirement of the lenders. In connection with the establishment of such an account at the Bank of America, the Security and Trust Deed and Designated Accounts Agreement were negotiated in order to govern the terms of the administration of the bank account. In addition, Polar Lights assigned all of its rights in the designated accounts to the lenders through the cash collateral trustee, which is Moscow Narodny Bank Limited, an affiliate of the Central Bank of Russia.

[ii]   Central Bank Licenses

The Central Bank of Russia issued both a borrowing license and designated accounts license to Polar Lights in order to facilitate the granting of the loans and the establishment of the offshore bank account. The bank regulations in Russia do not normally permit a Russian entity to establish a foreign bank account without express approval granted through a license that spells out the limits of the use of such an account. It is a prerequisite of the Central Bank that one of its affiliated banks be involved in the transaction and fill the role of a cash collateral trustee, such as Moscow Narodny Bank did for the Polar Lights transaction. By its very nature however, a Central Bank license is very limited, and any changes in the structure of the loans will require an amendment and reissuance of the licenses. The amendment process takes months to complete regardless of whether the change is simple or complicated.

[iii] The Security Agreements

Polar Lights entered into security agreements with the security agent for the lenders, which provided security interests in contract rights, goods in circulation, moveable goods, accounts, general intangibles, certain additional property and the Russian bank accounts. Each of the owners of Polar Lights also entered into security agreements pledging their ownership interest in Polar Lights, which involved the endorsement of ownership certificates that are being held in escrow by the security agent. Therefore, if an event of default occurred and was not cured within the required time frame, the lenders would have the discretion to take the place of the owners of Polar Lights and run the project themselves or through a contractor.

VIII.   Conversion to Non-recourse and the Completion Test

A.   The Completion Guarantee

The structure of the loans obtained by Polar Lights was such that the lenders were willing to accept certain political risks in return for a completion guarantee that was signed by Conoco. The guarantee included a list of "Specified Events" that were designed to provide political risk protection to the guarantor. AGD was not requested to provide a completion guarantee due to its weak financial standing. Therefore, Conoco provided a guarantee related to the entire amount of the Senior Debt. This guarantee is no longer applicable since the loans have been converted to a non-recourse basis.

The Specified Events were designed to encompass expropriatory events that were caused by the government. The lenders made it clear that they would not accept commercial risks, such as the ability to negotiate acceptable transportation agreements, but they were willing to provide limited protection against political risk. Conoco's guarantee would not have been exposed if a true confiscation or expropriation of the assets had occurred.

B.   The Completion Test

The completion test was designed to determine whether Polar Lights had satisfied all of the requirements for completing the development project. The satisfaction of the completion test was tied directly to the completion guarantee inasmuch as Polar Lights was permitted to convert the status of the loans from a limited recourse to a non-recourse basis if all of the conditions of the completion test were fully satisfied. Since the conditions were satisfied, the completion guarantee "fell away" and the outstanding balance of the loans became the risk of the lenders from that point forward.

The conditions that Polar Lights was required to fulfill in order to satisfy what was called the "First Project Completion Test" were related to both operational and legal matters, as follows:

[i]   delivery of a completion certificate issued by the facilities engineer relating to the construction, installation, testing and commissioning of project facilities; that a certain number of wells had been drilled in accordance with good international oil industry practices; and certain average daily production rates had been maintained over a 90-day period;

[ii]   that Polar Lights had exported an agreed number of barrels of oil within a 90-day period, including documentary evidence of such exports and sales;

[iii]   that no event of default had occurred;

[iv]   that all representations and warranties were true and accurate;

[v]   that all transportation and marketing agreements providing for the export of production and direct payment of sales proceeds to the designated accounts had been concluded; and

[vi]   the submission of legal opinions stating that Polar Lights had complied with applicable laws, that approvals had been obtained and that the project agreements were in full force and effect.

After submission of such documents, the lenders had 90 days to review them and give notice stating whether Polar Lights had satisfied such conditions. There was a certain amount of discretion involved in the calculation procedures that were undertaken by the lenders in making such a determination. This complication was caused by the involvement of the petroleum engineer who was required to submit calculations of oil reserves and revenues based on certain cost, tax and production rate assumptions. The petroleum engineer made conservative assumptions about production rates and amounts of reserves that conflicted with Polar Lights' calculations. Nevertheless, all of the limited recourse financing was converted to a non-recourse basis by the end of 1996.

* * *

Due to the strict nature of the requirements of the security package, completion guarantee and completion test, PLC lost some of the administrative and operational flexibility that it would have otherwise enjoyed. Nevertheless, due to the incessant nature of the transitional phase of the Russian economy, the Ardalin Project turned out to have been well suited to this type of financing and security structure.

In recent years, the volume of emerging market project finance (EMPF) transactions has shown a marked increase. For example, in 2010 over 200 financings were arranged for an aggregate amount in excess of $130 billion, which made the EMPF market almost two times as large as the market for IPOs in emerging markets.[3]

The magnitude of project finance resources made available in Russia increased significantly in the early 2000s. For example, in 2008, Sakhalin Energy Investment Company Ltd. obtained project financing for Phase 2 of the Sakhalin II project from Japan Bank for International Cooperation (JBIC), an ECA, and a consortium of international commercial banks in the amount of $5.3 billion, of which $3.7 billion was provided by JBIC. This financing set a new record for Russia in terms of the amount raised and has been reported to establish new standards for Russian and international oil and gas developments.[4]

Even when all these issues are properly addressed, emerging market risks can still thwart the project. Consider the following:

Kenneth Hansen, Robert C. O'Sullivan & W. Geoffrey Anderson, The Dabhol Power Project Settlement: What Happened? And How?

The Infrastructure Journal (Spring 2006)
http://www.chadbourne.com/files/Publication/a5aa1e52-4285-4bb5-87e6-
7201123895a0/Presentation/PublicationAttachment/352f8f09-ae96-40fc-a293-
720d0b8f0ca8/Dabhol_InfrastructureJournal12_2005.pdf

By late 2001, the $2.9 billion Dabhol power project had become, for the second time, a leading international investment disaster.

Six months earlier, cash flow from the Maharashtra State Electricity Board (MSEDB), the sole offtaker, had stopped. After a year or so of smooth operations followed by months of slow and defaulted payments, Dabhol Power Company (DPC) sent MSEB a notice of arbitration in May 2001. MSEB responded by, among other things, seeking an injunction to block that arbitration and by repudiating the power purchase agreement (PPA). Lacking income, the 740 MW Phase I power station was shut in June 2001, with all employees terminated.

---

[3]   Ernst & Young, 2011, Global IPO Trends 2011.

[4]   Sakhalin Locks in $5.3B in Largest Russian Project Finance Deal, Oil and Gas Financial Journal, June 17, 2008—http://www.ogfj.com/articles/2008/06/bsakhalin-locks-in-53b-in-largest -russian-project-finance-deal-b.html

Phase II, which would have trebled the plant's capacity to 2184 MW, was then roughly 5 percent shy of completion. With the shutdown of Phase I, refusals of state agencies to approve permits to test the Phase II turbines, and the purported repudiation of the PPA, lenders suspended funding for completion of Phase II. Construction stopped, and the contractors left the site.

In 1992 the government of India announced an invitation to private, including foreign, project developers and lenders to participate in the expansion of the Indian power sector through a "fast track" program. New laws were passed to assure protection of those investments. Enron responded by quickly signing a memorandum of understanding with the government of the state of Maharashtra for a project that would have included not only the largest independent power generation facility in the world but also its own LNG regasification plant, a related gas pipeline, an LNG tanker to access gas supplies in Qatar and a port at the site to accommodate it.

Execution of the PPA followed in December 1993. MSEB's payment obligations were guaranteed by both the government of Maharashtra (GOM) and, subject to a roughly $300 million cap, the Central Government.

Based largely on that PPA and those guaranties, Enron raised $1.9 billion in project debt. It was raised from a coalition of Indian government-owned banks, export credit agencies, a syndicate of offshore, commercial lenders and the Overseas Private Investment Corporation (OPIC), the US government's development-though-foreign-investment-promotion agency. OPIC supplied, at $160 million, the single largest offshore loan commitment. It also provided $200 million in political risk insurance for the investments by Enron, GE and Bechtel as well as roughly $32 million in coverage of one of the commercial banks.

Not everyone was clamoring to get involved, however. The World Bank was approached by India for support. In April 1993, however, the bank's manager for India concluded that the Dabhol plant was "not economically viable."

Within India, the project was the target of political and policy attacks. Critics noted that there had been no competitive bidding. Project costs and power tariffs were higher than other power projects in India, and the concern arose that the cost of Dabhol power could inflate power prices elsewhere. The cost of fulfilling its take-or-pay purchase promise would constitute half of the MSEB's entire budget. Concerns were raised that commitments were made to the project before an environmental impact assessment had been undertaken. Finally, it became known that Enron had allocated a $20 million "education fund" to prepare the way for the project in India. Critics assumed that these payments consisted of little more than bribes to procure official support for the project.

The controversies blew up shortly after ground was broken, when, in 1995, a change in political control led state of Maharashtra authorities to cancel the project. That dispute was resolved with a renegotiation of the tariff, a reduction of project costs and by the sale by Enron to an MSEB affiliate of a 30 percent equity interest in the project for $137 million, reducing Enron's interest in DPC to 50 percent. MSEB's 30 percent interest was subsequently diluted to roughly 15 percent upon its failure to contribute to further equity investments. Nonetheless, there was an expectation that creation of a shared interest in the success of the project would, going forward, reduce its vulnerability to political attack.

Construction recommenced. There was some cause to hope that the rough times were past. Indeed, Enron's 1998 annual report noted: "The Dabhol power project in the state of Maharashtra is the cornerstone of Enron's activities in India and is expected to be a strong contributor to Enron's earnings in 1999 and beyond."

In early 1999, Phase I achieved commercial operation and began supplying power to the Indian grid. It supplied power in a volume, and at a price, that might have been supportable given the demand projections taken seriously by both Enron and Indian officials in 1993. That demand did not, however, develop until after the subsidence of the Asian economic crisis and until roughly, ironically, the time that the project had collapsed.

The predictions that the project consisted of too much, too soon proved, however, to be prescient. It was clear by 2001 that MSEB neither needed, nor could afford, the energy it had committed to buy from the project. The October 2000 payment due from MSEB went unpaid until January 2001 when the state Government stepped in to bail out the cash-strapped MSEB. Months of slow payments, and non-payments followed. By June, the project had collapsed.

Though the allocation of responsibility for the allegedly expropriatory actions taken by Indian officialdom remains controversial and to some degree uncertain, it was clear that at the time Phase II was threatening to achieve commercial operation (which would treble MSEB's already taxing offtake obligations). Officialdom came to the rescue with: refusals to permit the testing, and thus the operation, of Phase II turbines; repudiation of Phase I and Phase II payment obligations; and injunctions blocking arbitration of the payment dispute and against taking the steps that would have triggered MSEB's obligation to buy-out the project. With no alternative customers, the project was brought to its knees.

Enron, at 65 percent the controlling project sponsor, might have been expected to have mounted an aggressive defense of the project. That is what had happened in 1995. Instead, Enron CEO Ken Lay led a delegation to India during the summer of 2001 to seek to close a sale of Enron's equity interest to Indian government interests. The price was rumored at $600 million to $1 billion. But India was not buying. By December 2001, Enron was no longer capable of maintaining its core operations, much less prepared to invest in the defense of a large, troubled project.

Thus, by late 2001, the fate of the world's largest independent power project and the largest foreign investment in India was put in the hands of creditors, minority investors, defaulting governmental stakeholders and lawyers.

The Workout

The initial months of attempts to restructure the project were characterized by stalemate. Lenders sought to subordinate the claims of the equity investors. Indeed, the offshore lenders were somewhat shocked when OPIC acted to block steps being considered to foreclose on the project assets and to expel the equity holders from further involvement. While the documents provided the lenders such rights, the technical expertise of, at least, GE and Bechtel appeared to be critical to restart the Phase 1 turbines and put the finishing touches on Phase II, much less to undertake the rehabilitation necessitated by the months of abandonment of the project site and facilities.

A key stakeholder whose interests and position were a source of constant guessing throughout meetings of the project lenders was the Government of India (GOI). The GOI was a party not only because of its defaulted counter-guaranty of the PPA and its inherent interest in seeing the power needs of the country satisfied, but also because of its risk of being held responsible under various international agreements to the extent arguments might be successfully advanced that Indian agencies had engaged in behavior that was, as least in effect, expropriatory. In fact, responsibility for Dabhol was passed rapidly through a series of officials, none of whom seemed charged with the issues long enough to take a position or, in the rare occasion when a position was taken long enough to follow through on it.

When the project was first conceived Enron's role was obviously key. By early 2002, Enron was variously termed "radioactive," "contaminated," and "obstructionist". Perhaps the only issue on which the offshore lenders, the Indian banks, GE and Bechtel, and the GOI could agree was that the continued presence of Enron made a difficult situation worse. It would be better for everyone if Enron were to go quietly, but at what price? No one was willing, or expected anyone else to be willing, to advance the sorts of funding that Lay had sought during his summer 2001 sales tour in India.

In an internal meeting at OPIC during the summer of 2002 the suggestion was raised that, notwithstanding the offer price of the previous summer, the continued deterioration of both the project and of the apparent prospects for early resolution of the various claims and disputes might well have led Enron's creditors' committee to ascribe a minimal value to Enron's investment. Perhaps Enron might be bought out for what previously would have been considered a small number. The further idea arose to propose that OPIC might return to Enron the roughly $16 million that had been paid over the years by Enron to OPIC for political risk insurance coverage of a portion of Enron investment. Rather than simply rescinding the contract and thereby resolving the pending claim, the proposal would be that Enron would turn over to OPIC, or its designee, its full interest in the project.

Enron countered with the request that it also receive interest on the returned premium and also be compensated for certain outstanding claims which it held against the project company. It was fairly quickly agreed, however, that, in exchange for the rough equivalent of a return by OPIC of the insurance premiums paid by Enron, Enron would walk away not only from its pending $142 million claim against OPIC but also from its full interest in the project, assigning the Enron-owned shares to OPIC or its designee.

A key issue was who would be that designee? DPC was an unlimited liability company embroiled in litigation and potential claims, so taking over a controlling interest in such an operation would carry risks. Two parties that were not interested in increasing their exposure were GE and Bechtel. So, for some weeks the search was on for someone who would accept the shares and control of DPC. In due course, however, GE and Bechtel decided that the liabilities could be managed and that control of DPC was the best way to assure that the claims and potential claims that DPC held against Indian authorities would be retained. So, the Enron-buyout was structured so that Enron's control of DPC passed to GE and Bechtel in exchange, in effect, for a return to Enron of insurance premiums previously paid to OPIC.

Though there was unanimous support for Enron's departure, an ironic impediment arose to closing the transaction—the GOI. One term of the GOI's counter-guaranty of the PPA was that Enron's ownership should not be less than 26 percent. While discussions with the finance ministry had led to concurrence that Enron should go, and that the GOI would waive the requirement of at least 26 percent Enron participation, as the transaction was being structured and approaching implementation, the GOI failed to provide consent. The GOI position was simply that they no longer cared whether Enron was in or out.

OPIC was not, however, willing to support a transaction that could have cost offshore lenders a $300 million asset. Thus evolved the transaction that came to be known as "Enron Lite." The decision was to structure the Enron buy-out in two phases. The first would reduce Enron's interest to just over the required 26 percent—enough to give GE and Bechtel control of DPC and to assure their ability to continue enforcement of DPC's claims against MSEB, the GOI, the GOM and other defendants. Enron would be fully compensated upon closure of the first phase, but would transfer the balance of its interest only when directed, which would occur after GOI had consented or the other parties had decided to go forward notwithstanding the absence of GOI consent.

Enron Lite was approved by the New York Bankruptcy Court on April 8, 2004, and closed by the end of that month.

Not much else that ultimately proved dispositive seemed to occur in workout efforts underway since 2001. There were a series of proposals regarding the buy-out of the project company and/or its assets. But lack of cooperation by one or another of the necessary participants stood in the way of progress. Efforts to clarify the completion and offtake support that a restarted and complete project would enjoy from Indian officialdom reached a dead end at the doors of the relevant ministries. Deposits proffered by prospective buyers were returned.

Indeed, a primary consequence of months of intermittent meetings and rebuffed proposals appeared to be deteriorating relationships and an ever-increasingly likelihood that the workout would ultimately consist of little more than pressing and settling lawsuits. That risk was enhanced when, in 2002, the Indian banks, in violation of their intercreditor agreement with the offshore lenders, appealed to the Bombay High Court for appointment of a receiver to assume control of DPC's assets. What from one perspective was merely the predictable action of lenders taking reasonable steps to preserve their collateral appeared from another to confirm that GOI-controlled interests were committed to expropriate this previously foreign-owned asset. It led to yet further litigation, as the offshore lenders collectively filed for arbitration against the Indian banks, claiming violation of their intercreditor agreement.

Workout discussions evolved from debates over the best way to sell the plant to third parties and allocate the proceeds—and losses—from that sale, into a focus on the offshore interests being bought out by the Indian banks already exposed to the project.

Most developments were litigious. In September 2003, an arbitral panel found against OPIC's position that certain protective provisions of the GE and Bechtel political risk insurance policies should be applied and ordered OPIC to pay their respective expropriation claims. In January 2004, at OPIC's instigation in order to recover these payments as well as payments made to an insured bank and, as described above, to Enron, the United States Government (USG) called for an arbitration against the GOI alleging expropriation of the Dabhol Power Project. This was the first time in OPIC's history that an arbitration was initiated against a host government under the bilateral agreements pursuant to which OPIC conducts its political risk insurance program. GE and Bechtel each initiated arbitrations under the India-Mauritius bilateral investment treaty, taking advantage of the structuring of their respective investments in DPC though Mauritian subsidiaries. Several offshore commercial lenders were exploring their options at following suit by filing bilateral investment treaty arbitrations.

Things were looking quite bleak when, in March 2005, the situation changed dramatically. In meetings in Washington among the Indian banks, the offshore commercial lenders and OPIC, the Indian banks tabled terms that were significantly better and, as it turned out, well within the range of what most commercial lenders had already decided would be acceptable. Within 48 hours, a deal had been initialed that included settlement of OPIC's pending claims against the GOI for reimbursement of what it had paid in claims to insured investors.

Separately, if not independently, talks were underway between the same Indian banks and GE and Bechtel seeking both an assignment of their equity interests in the project and their commitment to cooperate with the restart and completion of the project. There too, the prospect for progress appeared better.

While the precise terms evolved, and additional time was required to come to terms with the equity investors, by late June, the settlements were falling into place. On July 8, the GE settlement closed. On July 12, the offshore lender position was acquired by a special purpose vehicle acting for the Indian banks. On July 16, OPIC and Bechtel settled, leaving the project, for the first time, fully owned and controlled by Government of India interests. Part of the settlement is the expectation that Phase I will, within the coming year, be restarted and Phase II will be completed.

OPIC's Role Helped

OPIC played a pre-eminent role in both the creation of the Dabhol power project and the workout. On the creation side, OPIC's participation was crucial, as it agreed to provide $160 million in investment guaranties, in addition to providing roughly $225 million in political risk insurance on both the debt and equity sides. Wearing its governmental hat in the deal, OPIC brought the full faith and credit of the USG to the table, if ever needed. This nascent role proved pivotal at various stages of the workout.

From the time of the shutdown of the plant in 2001, OPIC's vision was unwavering: to conclude a comprehensive commercial settlement, with fair treatment of all stakeholders' claims. OPIC's strong opposition surprised the other lenders but kept alive the prospect of salvaging the project.

In pursuit of OPIC's vision, and to simplify the complex array of stakeholders, OPIC devised and executed a plan to buy out Enron's interest in the project, increase the equity shares of GE and Bechtel, and settle Enron's $142 million claim against OPIC under its insurance policy. By negotiating an acceptable price for Enron to relinquish its interests in Dabhol, and funding the cost of the transaction whereby Enron's equity shifted to GE and Bechtel, OPIC removed an onerous presence from the workout and settled a large claim on extremely favorable terms. It also advanced OPIC's goal of a fair settlement.

OPIC's position eventually prevailed, for many reasons. The change in the GOI's political leadership, the authority and resolve demonstrated by the new Indian negotiators, the looming $6 billion Bechtel and GE arbitrations, the USG arbitration, the offshore banks' threatened arbitrations under bilateral investment treaties, the shortage of power in Maharashtra, and even general frustration and the size of mounting expenses may all have contributed to the sudden change in the Indians' negotiating position in March 2005, and all therefore contributed to the comprehensive commercial settlement that was achieved.

. . .

Dabhol—Past or Prologue?

Disputes that share many characteristics of Dabhol, though smaller, are likely. The root causes of Dabhol's downfall are not grounded in any particular corporate culture, the politics of one nation or the economics of one business sector. Rather, a Dabhol-like controversy could arise in any privatization anywhere, and even if the investor were a model corporation. Such a dispute might be especially likely to arise in connection with a new private "greenfield" project in a sector that was previously the exclusive domain of state-owned enterprises.

Fifteen years ago, infrastructure firms saw enormous business opportunities in developing countries and the newly emerging market economies of Central and Eastern Europe and the former Soviet republics. Their expectation was that the combination of pent-up demand, projected economic growth, the need to modernize and upgrade existing infrastructure, and the realization that bilateral and multilateral assistance would not be provided on anything like the scale required to accomplish all of this, would create unprecedented new private investment opportunities.

Whether enthusiastic about rejoining the Western world or resigned to the passing of a statist world order of one sort or another, host governments entered into investment agreements for privatizations or new projects to modernize and expand their infrastructure: power, water, telecommunications, highways, sea ports, airports, etc. Some policymakers in the West took pride in the newly dominant role that private capital was playing in the economic development process, viewing this as yet another triumph over Marxism.

It did not take long for the contradictions between the assumptions of foreign private investors and the mentality of public officials and the general population of host countries to assert themselves.

Suddenly, running water is available that is safe to drink, it is possible to have a telephone installed within days instead of years, calls and faxes reliably go through, electric power functions 24/7, and better transportation infrastructure supports the growth of tourism, manufacturing, etc. But, utility rates rise, there are tolls to pay, privatized utility companies trim payrolls and expect the remaining workers to show up for work, and the profits from these impositions go to foreigners. What more does an opposition party need for a domestic campaign issue, to be followed by an international investment dispute, no matter which party wins the election? Indian politicians were criticized for making Dabhol a political issue at the state and national level, but few politicians anywhere could have resisted such a temptation.

Recent potential expropriation cases are unlike the Latin American claims of the 1970's, where host governments overtly asserted control over natural resources, or the fairly obvious claims that arose in Vietnam and Iran. Recent expropriation claims arise from various sorts of public/private partnerships that have gone wrong, privatizations that have been reconsidered, economic crises that have been mishandled, and even economic reform efforts that have unintended consequences. They are difficult to resolve as "all or nothing" liability claims, but the very presence of valid competing interests that makes a finding of liability difficult should offer grounds for settlement.

NOTES

1. What are the lessons from the Dabhol failure? Note how the usual problems faced in emerging markets, including risks such as political instability, uncertainty regarding the application of laws and their enforcement, hostile actions by governmental authorities, and delays in project implementation, were exacerbated by poor assumptions regarding the viability of the project itself. Clearly the investor made mistakes in assessing such basic issues as the market for power in India—demand and the ability to pay.

2. Multiple parties—lenders, sponsors, contractors, government agencies—may have competing and even mutually exclusive objectives, which may not be evident until the project is underway. Lengthy and costly delays occur while these differences are resolved in negotiation or even litigation.

E. LOCAL LAW CONSIDERATIONS

In spite of problems of ambiguity and enforcement, the requirements of local law will have a substantial impact on the structuring of a project involved in a major financing, and particularly on the enforcement of an investor's rights. Consider excerpts from the Russian Civil Code contained in the Documents Supplement that govern the pledge of assets. How is a pledge created? How would a borrower describe and properly document the assets to be pledged? What mechanism exists to perfect a creditor's security interests? Do the steps to secure a priority right vary depending on the assets? Considering these questions reveals the uncertainties and ambiguities inherent in dealing with such legislation.

As an example, imagine that you are seeking to perfect a security interest in inventory and all you have to work with under local law are Articles 341 and 357. What can you do to ensure that the creation of a security interest is effective? You can assume that "commodities in circulation" is the equivalent of "inventory." Still, what problems arise from an apparently simple issue such as transferring a concept like inventory from our legal system to that of an emerging market? It is also important not to overlook the even more basic problem of the translation of Western legal and accounting terms to a foreign language. Solutions require creative lawyering. Notwithstanding such efforts, the lack of a well-developed system for perfecting security interests, including precise and easy to follow rules, complicates and raises the costs of financing. Article 357 seems to require a regular system of monitoring and updating inventory in the possession of the pledger. What practical challenges does this requirement pose?

* * *

It is critical that the parties evaluate local law issues effectively to ensure that financing transactions comply with law and are enforceable to protect the rights of the lenders and investors. Even if the parties choose foreign law to govern their contractual relationship, many emerging markets impose mandatory laws. Local courts, and even foreign courts and arbitration tribunals, may insist on enforcing local laws.

Other investors, such as private equity funds, look at local law issues with a different set of concerns than a creditor does, as is evident from the following discussion of Brazilian law:

Bertan Ribeiro & Cinthia Daniela, Financial
Contracting Choices in Brazil: Does the Brazilian
Legal Environment Allow Private Equity Groups
to Enter into Complex Contractual Arrangements
with Brazilian Companies?

13 LAW & BUS. REV. AM. 355 (2007)

I.   INTRODUCTION

The main objective of this paper is to determine whether investors can and do enter into complex contractual arrangements with privately-held Brazilian companies. The more sophisticated the contractual structures adopted in investment transactions in a given country, the more investors depend on the set of contractually established rules. Consequently, more parties rely on the country's regulatory framework and legal enforcement. Therefore, the systematic use of complex financial contracts could be a good indicator of the quality of a country's institutional environment. A second goal is to understand whether the recent changes in Brazil's regulatory environment have encouraged investment in privately-held companies.

A. Cash Flow Rights in Brazil

1. Brazilian Legislation

When it comes to investments in privately-held companies, there are no significant legal restrictions on the use of any type of security, or on the use of provisions related to contingencies and control rights. According to Law 6404/76, companies may issue common (article 15) or preferred (article 15 and 17) stocks, warrants (article 75), debentures (article 52), convertible preferred stocks (article 22) or convertible debentures (article 57). The Law also explicitly allows the creation of shares with different classes, where different rights can be conferred to each class.

Convertible preferred stocks of privately-held companies can also be structured in a variety of ways, making it possible to adopt the features ordinarily used by PE-VCs [private equity-venture capital] in the United States. The Law only states that preferred stocks must have some preferential right in relation to common stocks, be it in the distribution of dividends or a priority claim in the event of liquidation. Like those in the United States, owners of preferred stocks in Brazil can enjoy voting rights as well as fixed and cumulative dividends. But there is a statutory limit on the number of preferred stocks that can exist without voting rights, or with restrictions to voting rights, which cannot exceed 50 percent of the total number of a company's stocks.

In general, the Brazilian corporate legislation establishes only minimum standards for the parties and provides private contracting with a fairly large degree of flexibility, allowing the local replication of most of the structures used in the United States. Even in situations where there is no equivalent legal mechanism in the Brazilian law, which is the case with escrow accounts, private parties can adapt to existing structures and create figures similar to the ones available in the United States.

. . .

B. Control Rights in Brazil

A major concern of PE-VCs investing in developing countries is understanding the pitfalls of being a minority shareholder in a local company. In other words, investors want to know what the chances are of facing expropriation by managers and majority shareholders and not being able to enforce their rights. Lerner and Schoar have identified that in developing countries with French legal origin like Brazil, PEs tend to have less contractual protections and less efficient legal enforcement. Consequently, PEs try to protect their investment by guaranteeing their returns through the ownership of the majority of the company's equity and by requiring more board representation, instead of relying on rights related to the protection of minority shareholders such as anti-dilution and supermajority provisions. In these countries, ownership concentration becomes a substitute for weak legal protection.

Brazil is not known for providing quality enforcement. Indeed, most practitioners interviewed do not believe Brazilian courts can properly analyze and timely enforce complex contracts.

. . .

V. THE IMPACT OF LEGAL ENFORCEMENT ON FINANCIAL CONTRACTING

Legal protection of investors encompasses the content and enforceability of laws. First, local law has to allow the use of complex contractual structures. But the content alone is worthless if not accompanied by the assurance of enforcement. The quality of legal enforcement has been measured through various methods. La Porta et al. created a "rule of law index" based on investors' estimates of the law and order environment in the countries where they had operations.

Lerner and Schoar compared the time a contract dispute takes to be resolved in the courts of various countries. Lerner and Schoar found that the longer the period, the less likely a PE-VC group is to rely on preferred stock. Also, while in low legal enforcement countries, investors tend to seek control through the purchase of the majority of shares as a substitute to contractual protection, in effective enforcement countries, investors are likely to separate cash flow and control rights, and rely on contract contingencies. As a practical result, in low enforcement countries, more capital has to be committed to one single investment, which may be not desirable depending on the portfolio diversification strategy of the investor.

In Brazil, a central concern of investors relates to the enforcement of contractual structures in place. Practitioners point out the long and costly process of going to court, the lack of case law, and judges' lack of knowledge in the financial contracting area. Statistics confirm that a contract dispute in a Brazilian court takes considerable time to be resolved; the process of enforcement of a contract encompasses twenty-five procedures and takes an average of 566 days—but it often takes several years. Contrastingly, in high-income states of the Organisation for Economic Co-operation and Development the process averages eighteen procedures and 213 days.

Until recently, the fears of facing the Brazilian judicial system would often lead foreign investors to adopt the law of New York, Delaware, London, or another location perceived to have more efficient courts. But since 1996, with the enactment of the Arbitration Act (Law 9307/96), arbitration started to be seriously considered as an alternative to Brazilian courts. Even greater support was given to this method in 2001 when the Brazilian Supreme Court recognized the constitutionality of the Arbitration Act.

. . .

VI. RECENT DEVELOPMENTS IN THE BRAZILIAN LEGAL FRAMEWORK RELEVANT TO PE-VC INVESTMENT

The main body of rules related to investment in Brazilian privately-held companies are found in Law 6404/76 (the Corporation Act), Law 11101/05 (Corporate Reorganization and Bankruptcy Act), and in regulations from Comissao de Valores Mobiliarios (CVM), the Brazilian equivalent of the Securities Exchange Commission in the United States. Focus is given to recent developments of the Brazilian laws that are relevant to PE-VC funds, namely laws that may impact a fund's investment and exit strategies.

A.   Capital Markets Regulatory Framework

The size of a country's capital market is central for PE-VC activity. Because PE-VC investments are typically meant to last for a pre-determined period, it is essential to analyze exit options prior to investing, as well as the contractual design of detailed rules related to exit. Therefore, although PE-VC funds focus on privately-held companies, the possibility of exiting the business through an Initial Public Offering (IPO) may be determinant for taking the investment decision. Not coincidentally, the United States and the United Kingdom, which have the largest capital markets in the world, also have the most active PE-VC industry and house the largest PE-VC deals. Strong capital markets are characterized by a dispersed shareholder base, which in turn is fostered by sound legislation protecting minority investors. Therefore, a well-developed legal system is the base for creating a virtual cycle of liquidity, growth, and wealth.

But exiting the business is a traditional problem associated with investing in Brazilian companies. Until recently the only realistic exit alternative for a PE-VC would be a trade sale, i.e., sale to a strategic buyer. IPOs were rare and public companies' ownership structure was extremely concentrated. This picture was a reflection of the legal framework, which was insufficient to protect minority investors and ensure good corporate governance in public companies. In 2001 substantial changes were introduced. First, Law 10303 brought significant corporate governance improvements to the then twenty-five year-old Law 6404, providing minority shareholders with more protection, such as tag-along rights, and with minimum requirements for preferred shares negotiated in the securities markets. Second, also in 2001, BOVESPA—Brazil's largest stock exchange and the ninth largest in the world—launched Novo Mercado, internationally recognized for its high requirements of corporate governance and accounting standards. The effect of these regulation improvements can already be seen. Novo Mercado has been attracting a record amount of new issuers and investors since 2004 and now represents a real exit possibility for PE-VC funds. Out of forty-two IPOs from 2004 to 2006, nineteen involved PE funds exiting the investment. A latest effort by BOVESPA to increase the Brazilian capital markets' size is called BOVESPA MAIS, launched at the end of 2005 and aimed at midsized companies, which could be compared to London Stock Exchange's successful branch AIM.

Bankruptcy Law

Bankruptcy legislation has substantially changed, now providing both equity investors and financial debt creditors with more protection. Under previous law, both equity and debt investors faced serious drawbacks. Equity investors faced significant risk because liquidation was highly likely for companies under the old reorganization rules (concordata); companies did not have the necessary legal assistance or a sustainable reorganization plan put in place to enable recovery from distress. And the latter, debt investors, had very small chances of recovering their capital; secured creditors could not seize the company's assets for two years (under concordata) and were behind tax and labor credits in the liquidation line.

Law 11101 of 2005 introduced the new bankruptcy and corporate reorganization legislation, providing equity owners with real possibilities of reorganizing the firm, and placing secured creditors in a more favorable position in liquidation, now before tax credits and just behind a capped amount of labor credits. The reorganization plan can be judicial or out-of-court, and must be approved by the creditors.

Another innovation is the possibility to sell the bankrupt company without transferring the succession of liabilities to the new owner. All these changes are likely to give an impulse to funds focused on distressed companies.

NOTES

1. To what extent has Brazil changed its laws, and to what extent has it changed its general approach to foreign investment? Are the remaining issues due to a failure to adopt the most advanced legal structures available, or instead insecurity around the most basic questions of contract enforcement?

2. Is international finance part of the problem or part of the solution? That is to say, is the ability of capital (the pooled savings of both the rich and the middle class) to move across national borders a force for economic growth and human fulfillment, or instead does mobile capital destabilize and destroy, undermining national sovereignty and political development? Why do some countries seem to tolerate foreign investment better than others?

F. NEGOTIATION EXERCISE—FUNDING AN ENERGY PROJECT

Global Petroleum Russia, Inc., a Delaware corporation ("Global") and Balolskneftegas, a private Russian limited liability company ("BNG"), have established the Balolsk Oil Company ("BOC"), a closed joint stock company under Russian law. BOC will act as the project company that will develop the Kerikov Field, which is an oil field discovered in the Balolsk Republic, and which has 400 million barrels of proven reserves of crude oil. Global and BNG have entered into a joint venture agreement ("JVA"), which provides that the Kerikov Field will be developed during a 3-year development phase, after which commercial production will begin in accordance with the development and production license that has recently been reissued to BOC.

Global estimates that it will cost approximately $750 million to develop the Kerikov Field and bring it to the point of commercial production. Global has contributed $80 million in cash to BOC's capital account, whereas BNG has contributed $30 million in cash and $40 million in kind, including the rights to the Kerikov Field, oil field equipment and four oil rigs, to BOC's capital account. Each company holds a 50% ownership interest in BOC, and an equal number of positions on the board of directors and the management team. BNG has only recently recovered from some cash flow problems. Global has established a line of credit for start-up operations from a U.S. commercial bank in the amount of $200 million under a full recourse corporate guaranty (the "Subordinated Debt") provided by its parent company, Global Petroleum Company, Inc. Global and BNG, as the sponsors, are seeking to obtain an additional $400 million in project financing (the "Senior Debt") through international financing institutions ("IFIs"). BOC has begun negotiations with the International Finance Corporation ("IFC") to establish the basic terms and conditions of a term sheet for a project financing package.

The IFC has agreed to take the lead in providing project financing for BOC. The IFC has told BOC that it prefers to arrange a financing package that would include the acquisition of a small, cost-bearing equity interest in BOC, as well as providing either the entire amount of Senior Debt, or the majority of the Senior Debt if other IFIs agree to participate. The IFC has also mentioned that it is concerned about BOC's ability to bring the project to the point of commercial production within the 3-year period, as required by the license.

The IFC and BOC negotiating teams have received instructions from their respective management representatives. Set forth below are the issues to be negotiated by BOC and the IFC for the term sheet.

1. <u>Control</u>. Whether BOC (through Global and BNG) will allow the IFC to acquire a cost bearing equity interest in BOC, and, if so, on what terms, and what role would they play on the board of directors and within the management structure of BOC?

2. <u>Completion Guarantees</u>. Whether a pre-completion guarantee will be required by the IFC from either or both of the sponsors of BOC, and, if so, will the IFC have some exposure to political risk?

3. <u>Security Interests</u>. What types of security interests will be granted to the IFC in case the project fails or is delayed significantly?

4. <u>Special Requirements</u>. Will the loan agreements only include the typical elements of a completion test, or will special requirements, such as an escrow account or other mechanisms, be added?

5. <u>Representations and Warranties</u>. Will any representations and warranties be required beyond those that are directly related to the Kerikov Field development plan?

6. <u>Covenants</u>. Will there be any special covenants or other arrangements included to protect the IFC, such as cover ratios?

Supplemental Readings

Atif Ansar, *Project Finance in Emerging Markets* in THE PRINCIPLES OF PROJECT FINANCING 287 (Rod Morrison ed. 2012)

Stephen Mills, *Project Financing of Oil and Gas Field Developments: The Bankers' View*, 11/12 OIL & GAS L. & TAX REV. 359 (1993)

Hossein Razavi, *Financing Oil and Gas Projects in Developing Countries*, FINANCE & DEVELOPMENT 1 (Jun. 1996)

CHAPTER 5

HOST STATE AUTHORIZATIONS, DEAL STRUCTURES AND POLITICAL RISK

There are many kinds of transactions that might take place in an emerging market. A common theme, however, is the existence of a substantial initial investment by a foreign enterprise, often involving real estate or rights granted under petroleum contracts. The investment might involve, for example, a production facility, a retail outlet, or the extraction of natural resources. Depending on the nature of the business project, the investor may have to wait years before it recovers its initial costs, much less turn a profit. Yet, once it has made the investment, it faces a risk of "hold up," that is a demand by a foreign partner or the host government that the project be configured to reduce the investor's share. Hold up can come in the form of an outright demand, or instead take the form of increased and unanticipated regulatory burdens or taxes. Knowing that this risk exists, the investor might take a pass on potentially valuable projects.

A host government's initiation of a hold up usually reflects a phenomenon called resource nationalism. For various reasons, governments may attempt to gain greater benefit from their natural resources. Resource nationalism can take a host of forms, such as outright expropriation, the imposition of new types of taxes, and changes in regulations. Other motivations for these actions include energy security concerns coupled to a rising demand for energy in the host country, environmental awareness regarding climate change, "and an anti-Western sentiment of resource-rich developing countries against economic globalization and the Western IOCs."[1]

Resource nationalism usually arises cyclically. A new episode in the cycle emerged in the early 2000s. Host governments and NOCs became increasingly unwilling to negotiate certain economic issues contained in production sharing agreements ("PSAs"). Several factors caused this new phase of resource nationalism. First and foremost was a gradual but startling reversal of fortune regarding the control of resources. In the 1970s the IOCs held 85% of the world's known reserves of petroleum; by 2008 the NOCs controlled as much as 94% of this resource.[2] Emboldened by this development, the NOCs and host governments tended to take less flexible positions. Another factor was the host governments' enlightened view that their natural resources were "a tool for financing social reform,

---

[1]   A. Maniruzzaman, *The Issue of Resource nationalism: Risk Engineering and Dispute Management in the Oil and Gas Industry*, 5 TEXAS J. OIL, GAS, AND ENERGY. 79, 82 (2009).

[2]   Thora Qaddumi, International Companies Adapt to Rise of National Oil Companies, Houston Business Journal, week of November 14–20, 2008, at 11.

boosting economic development, improving infrastructure and creating jobs, along with addressing a number of other individualized needs."[3]

In some of the less experienced emerging market countries, the so-called anti-Western sentiment has generated a trust barrier that looms large due to the lack of qualified and knowledgeable negotiators and economists. When one side perceives the other as having superior resources and negotiating skills, it will be less willing to take any chances and will tend to stonewall rather than engaging in useful discussion. In addition to this wide discrepancy in comparative levels of knowledge of the respective negotiating teams, the government officials are constantly under scrutiny from NGOs and civil society groups, which makes them more defensive. This problem places the burden on the IOCs to find a way to break through the trust barrier by compromising readily with the NOCs on issues that are not crucial while being less confrontational and more patient when dealing with the most critical questions.

In contrast, the IOCs have had to deal with their own symmetrical reversal of fortune. Not only do they have fewer prospects to pursue, but they face more challengers because the NOCs now compete "directly against the IOCs for reserve access in foreign markets."[4] This sea change in what the IOCs had perceived as their superior competitive position forced an adjustment in their approach to the acquisition and negotiation of new PSAs. For instance, some redoubled their efforts to demonstrate their worth as both a valued technical and financial partner for the NOCs. IOCs also have accepted increases in the levels of local content in a PSA project as a means to win the confidence of host governments and NOCs. More often than not, they have tried to treat their new competitors as equals and provide more assistance in the training of the NOCs' employees.

Some commentators have argued that IOCs must address a government's demands even if they have no legal basis "either because host government consent is required for the transaction or because the buyer will need the cooperation of the host government in the future."[5] Such advice, however, would not have helped ward off the Kosmos Energy debacle in Ghana, where Kosmos expected "that it would be difficult for Ghana to withhold its consent because ExxonMobil undeniably had the technical and financial resources to develop the field."[6] GNPC, the national oil company of Ghana, refused to agree to the transfer of Kosmos' interest to Exxon Mobil, claiming it "was not in the public interest because although Kosmos was entitled to a 'fair' price from the host government it was not entitled to a windfall from an international oil company."[7] The government never gave consent and the $4 billion transaction was terminated. The Kosmos/Ghana story is an example of the exercise of resource nationalism as an overreaction by governments of emerging market countries to unexpectedly large

---

[3]   Id.

[4]   See Thora Qaddumi, International Companies Adapt to Rise of National Oil Companies, supra note 66.

[5]   Thomas Moore, *Accommodating Host Governments in International Oil and Gas Transactions*, Houston Lawyer, Dec.2012, at 17.

[6]   Id.

[7]   Id.

discoveries and the consequent attempts by IOCs to profit from their success.

To maximize the number of valuable transactions involving foreign investment, then, a host government and potential local partners have a common interest with the investor in reducing the risk of future hold ups. The law does not provide perfect protection against opportunistic behavior, but it does offer mechanisms that may ameliorate this problem. In this chapter, we consider both pitfalls and safeguards for foreign investors, as well as the types of agreements that foreign investors in the international oil and gas industry may use.

A. GOVERNMENT AUTHORIZATIONS AND LIMITS ON PRIVATE OR FOREIGN OWNERSHIP

At the outset, the foreign investor must ensure that it has all the necessary permissions for conducting its business. Countries in the midst of a transition from comprehensive state control of the economy to something less structured typically retain the habit of requiring approvals by multiple levels of government, and sometimes the parliament, as a condition of undertaking particular activity. The approval may be based on environmental or financial considerations, as well as general public interest standards. The possibility of corruption never lurks very far from the surface, as we considered in Chapter 2. But that problem aside, lining up the necessary approvals can be challenging, especially if the rules are unclear.

In some instances, local law either imposes an outright ban on foreign participation in designated industries or provides for strict licensing requirements. This is not unique to emerging markets: U.S. law bans foreign ownership of broadcasters, domestic airlines, and coastal shipping lines and requires executive branch approval of any foreign investment with a potential effect on national security. But countries that have only recently permitted large scale private economic activity often are particularly apprehensive about foreign ownership. In India, for example, foreign law firms are completely barred from operating. The Russian Law on Insurance originally forbade foreign-owned firms from writing liability insurance and other forms of insurance contracts, although a later law substituted this ban with a licensing regime. Article 9 of the Russian Law on the Subsurface, provided below, did not itself impose any restrictions on foreigners seeking access to extraction projects but left open the possibility that other legislation could impose limitations. In 2008 Russia adopted a law forbidding majority foreign ownership of companies of strategic importance, including prospecting and extraction of subsurface resources in designated federal areas.

With an outright ban, the legal question is one of scope, and in particular what kinds of organizations are considered foreign. Legislation might specify the range of permitted foreign investment in a domestic entity before it acquires the taint of foreignness, or may instead rely on general, and nonspecific, standards. With licenses, the question is ultimately what requirements exist and whether they have been satisfied. In practice these can be very hard to determine in advance.

The following case illustrates how incorrect guesses about the approval process can lead to failure of a project, as well as indicating one possible avenue for relief.

Metalclad Corporation, Claimant and the United Mexican States, Respondent

Case No. ARB(AF)/97/1
International Center for Settlement of Investment Disputes (Additional Facility)
September 2, 2000

. . .

VII. THE TRIBUNAL'S DECISION

. . .

77. Metalclad acquired COTERIN for the sole purpose of developing and operating a hazardous waste landfill in the valley of La Pedrera, in Guadalcazar, [San Luis Potosi].

78. The Government of Mexico issued federal construction and operating permits for the landfill prior to Metalclad's purchase of COTERIN, and the Government of [San Luis Potosi] likewise issued a state operating permit which implied its political support for the landfill project.

79. A central point in this case has been whether, in addition to the above mentioned permits, a municipal permit for the construction of a hazardous waste landfill was required.

80. When Metalclad inquired, prior to its purchase of COTERIN, as to the necessity for municipal permits, federal officials assured it that it had all that was needed to undertake the landfill project. Indeed, following Metalclad's acquisition of COTERIN, the federal government extended the federal construction permit for eighteen months.

81. As presented and confirmed by Metalclad's expert on Mexican law, the authority of the municipality extends only to the administration of the construction permit, " . . . To grant licenses and permits for constructions and to participate in the creation and administration of ecological reserve zones . . . " *(Mexican Const. Art.115, Fraction* V). *H*owever, Mexico's experts on constitutional law expressed a different view.

82. Mexico's General Ecology Law of 1988 (hereinafter "LGEEPA") expressly grants to the Federation the power to authorize construction and operation of hazardous waste landfills. Article 5 of the LGEEPA provides that the powers of the Federation extend to:

> V.[t]he regulation and control of activities considered to be highly hazardous, and of the generation, handling and final disposal of hazardous materials and wastes for the environments of ecosystems, as well as for the preservation of natural resources, in accordance with [the] Law, other applicable ordinances and their regulatory provisions.

83. LGEEPA also limits the environmental powers of the municipality to issues relating to nonhazardous waste. Specifically,

Article 8 of the LGEEPA grants municipalities the power in accordance with the provisions of the law and local laws to apply:

> [l]egal provisions in matters of prevention and control of the effects on the environment caused by generation, transportation, storage, handling treatment and final disposal of solid industrial wastes which are <u>not</u> considered to be hazardous in accordance with the provisions of Article 137 of [the 1988] law.

84. The same law also limits state environmental powers to those not expressly attributed to the federal government.

85. Metalclad was led to believe, and did believe, that the federal and state permits allowed for the construction and operation of the landfill. Metalclad argues that in all hazardous waste matters, the Municipality has no authority. However, Mexico argues that constitutionally and lawfully the Municipality has the authority to issue construction permits.

86. Even if Mexico is correct that a municipal construction permit was required, the evidence also shows that, as to hazardous waste evaluations and assessments, the federal authority's jurisdiction was controlling and the authority of the municipality only extended to appropriate construction considerations. Consequently, the denial of the permit by the Municipality by reference to environmental impact considerations in the case of what was basically a hazardous waste disposal landfill, was improper, as was the municipality's denial of the permit for any reason other than those related to the physical construction or defects in the site.

87. Relying on the representations of the federal government, Metalclad started constructing the landfill, and did this openly and continuously, and with the full knowledge of the federal, state, and municipal governments, until the municipal "Stop Work Order" on October 26, 1994. The basis of this order was said to have been Metalclad's failure to obtain a municipal construction permit.

88. In addition, Metalclad asserted that federal officials told it that if it submitted an application for a municipal construction permit, the Municipality would have no legal basis for denying the permit and that it would be issued as a matter of course. The absence of a clear rule as to the requirement or not of a municipal construction permit, as well as the absence of any established practice or procedure as to the manner of handling applications for a municipal construction permit, amounts to a failure on the part of Mexico to ensure the transparency required by NAFTA.

89. Metalclad was entitled to rely on the representations of federal officials and to believe that it was entitled to continue its construction of the landfill. In following the advice of these officials, and filing the municipal permit application on November 15, 1994, Metalclad was merely acting prudently and in the full expectation that the permit would be granted.

90. On December 5, 1995, thirteen months after the submission of Metalclad's application—during which time Metalclad continued its open and obvious investment activity—the Municipality denied Metalclad's application for a construction permit. The denial was issued well after

construction was virtually complete and immediately following the announcement of the *Convenio* providing for the operation of the landfill.

91. Moreover, the permit was denied at a meeting of the Municipal Town Council of which Metalclad received no notice, to which it received no invitation, and at which it was given no opportunity to appear.

92. The Town Council denied the permit for reasons which included, but may not have been limited to, the opposition of the local population, the fact that construction had already begun when the application was submitted, the denial of the permit to COTERIN in December 1991 and January 1992, and the ecological concerns regarding the environmental effect and impact on the site and surrounding communities. None of the reasons included a reference to any problems associated with the physical construction of the landfill or to any physical defects therein.

93. The Tribunal therefore finds that the construction permit was denied without any consideration of, or specific reference to, construction aspects or flaws of the physical facility.

94. Moreover, the Tribunal cannot disregard the fact that immediately after the Municipality's denial of the permit it filed an administrative complaint with SEMARNAP challenging the *Convenio*. The Tribunal infers from this that the Municipality lacked confidence in its right to deny permission for the landfill solely on the basis of the absence of a municipal construction permit.

95. SEMARNAP dismissed the challenge for lack of standing, which the Municipality promptly challenged by filing an *amparo* action. An injunction was issued, and the landfill was barred from operation through 1999.

96. In 1997 [San Luis Potosi] re-entered the scene and issued an Ecological Decree in 1997 which effectively and permanently prevented the use by Metalclad of its investment.

97. The actions of the Municipality following its denial of the municipal construction permit, coupled with the procedural and substantive deficiencies of the denial, support the Tribunal's finding, for the reasons stated above, that the Municipality's insistence upon and denial of the construction permit in this instance was improper.

98. This conclusion is not affected by NAFTA Article 1114, which permits a Party to ensure that investment activity is undertaken in a manner sensitive to environmental concerns. The conclusion of the *Convenio* and the issuance of the federal permits show clearly that Mexico was satisfied that this project was consistent with, and sensitive to, its environmental concerns.

99. Mexico failed to ensure a transparent and predictable framework for Metalclad's business planning and investment. The totality of these circumstances demonstrates a lack of orderly process and timely disposition in relation to an investor of a Party acting in the expectation that it would be treated fairly and justly in accordance with the NAFTA.

100.Moreover, the acts of the State and the Municipality—and therefore the acts of Mexico—fail to comply with or adhere to the requirements of NAFTA, Article 1105(1) that each Party accord to investments of investors of another Party treatment in accordance with international law, including fair and equitable treatment. This is so particularly in light of the governing principle that internal law (such as the Municipality's stated permit requirements) does not justify failure to perform a treaty.

101. The Tribunal therefore holds that Metalclad was not treated fairly or equitably under the NAFTA and succeeds on its claim under Article 1105.

[The portion of the tribunal decision dealing with the claim that Mexico was responsible for the expropriation of Metalclad's investment appears later in this chapter.]

NOTES

1. Did Metalclad suffer from a "bait-and-switch," with the federal government encouraging its investment and then local authorities imposing new regulatory requirements? Could Metalclad's lawyers have done more to prevent this problem? If so, what?

2. Metalclad had a claim to relief because of a treaty, the North American Free Trade Agreement (NAFTA). Chapter XI of NAFTA contains provisions that are common in investment protection treaties. Older treaties imposed an obligation on host states not to discriminate against foreign investors or to expropriate their investments, except for a public purpose and with payment of full compensation. Those treaties, however, left it to the foreign investor's government to seek relief. The more modern treaties, of which Chapter XI is an example, allow the investor to pursue its rights directly through arbitration. Another treaty, the Washington Convention on the Settlement of Disputes Between States and Nationals of Other States, establishes the International Center for the Settlement of Investment Disputes (ICSID) and commits its signatories to enforce awards resulting from such arbitration. In this case, Metalclad sued Mexico in Canada to enforce the arbitration award. Mexico, supported by the Canadian government as *amicus curiae*, argued that the panel had exceeded their jurisdiction under Article 11 and therefore had rendered an invalid award. The British Columbia Supreme Court ruled that the panel erred in finding that Article 1105 created transparency obligations but that the ecological decree issued by San Luis Potosi constituted an expropriation. United Mexican States v. Metalclad Corp., [2001] B. C. D. Civ.60 (B. C. Sup. Ct.). Subsequently, the Canadian, Mexican, and U.S. governments issued a statement asserting that the tribunal in *Metalclad* had read too much into the "fair and equitable treatment" standard.

3. Putting aside the issue of whether Mexico had accepted an international law obligation not to abuse Metalclad, is it appropriate to protect foreign investors from democratic decisions to safeguard against environmental dangers? Was this a case of environmental dumping, where a rich world investor sought to exploit local poverty to carry through a project it could not undertake in its home country? Or was this a classic case of hold up? Some critics attack NAFTA's Chapter XI as a surrender of sovereignty and a sell out to multinational corporations that impermissibly impairs a state's ability to safeguard the environment. Does the result in *Metalclad* mean that Mexico could not prevent an unwanted waste disposal facility from being built? Or does it mean only that a state that changes its mind about regulation should pay compensation?

4.   Metalclad in essence had two international law arguments. First, it maintained, the arbitrary administrative process resulted in a denial of "fair and equitable treatment," a somewhat amorphous concept found in most investment treaties. Second, the net effect of the governmental actions amounted to an "expropriation," which treaties forbid except for a public and nondiscriminatory purpose and then only upon payment of full compensation. We consider the expropriation argument later in this chapter.

Land Use Permits

Metalclad involves a dispute over the use, as distinguished from ownership, of land. In the case of resource extraction, such as an oil and gas project, the foundation of either a joint venture agreement or a PSA is the existence of a right to exploit a natural resource. In many legal systems, a sharp distinction exists between surface and subsurface rights. Private persons may have the right to occupy the surface, to exclude others and to transfer their rights to others. But often the state has exclusive and inalienable rights over what lies beneath. Private persons accordingly cannot own the subsurface, although they may acquire a license to extract. Such licenses are the creature of public, and particularly administrative, law, rather than private or civil law.

We will focus on Russia's administrative law regime here. Unusually for an emerging market, Russia initially tried to split the difference between state monopoly of natural resources and full privatization. The 1992 Law on the Subsurface, as noted above, creates a licensing mechanism under which a license holder has the right to explore for and exploit subsurface resources, including oil and gas. But as a license issued by the state, the holder's interest does not enjoy the status of a property right under the civil law. Instead it remains subject to administrative law, with particular restrictions on alienability. Consider these excerpts from the law:

ARTICLE 1.2. TITLE TO SUBSURFACE

Subsurface within the territory of the Russian Federation, including the subsurface domain and mineral resources contained therein, energy and other resources shall be state property. Issues of ownership, use and disposal of subsurface shall fall under the joint jurisdiction of the Russian Federation and the subjects of the Russian Federation.

Subsurface areas shall not be subject to purchase, sale, gift, inheritance, deposit, pledge or any other form of alienation. Rights for the use of subsurface may be subject to alienation or assignment by one person to another insofar as such transfer right is permitted by federal laws.

Mineral and other subsurface produced under license terms may have the status of federal property, the property of the Russian Federation sub-divisions, municipal, private or any other property status.

ARTICLE 9.   SUBSURFACE USERS

The users of subsurface resources shall be persons engaging in entrepreneurial activities, including members of simple partnerships, foreign citizens and legal entities if federal laws carry no restrictions on the granting of the right to use the subsurface resources.

Under the terms of production sharing agreements users of subsurface resources can be legal entities as well as associations of legal entities' which are set up on the basis of joint operations agreements (contracts of simple partnership), such associations not having the status of an association of legal entities, provided that the participants in such an association have joint and several liability on obligations arising from the production sharing agreements.

If federal laws establish that a permit (license) is required to perform certain kinds of activities involved in the use of subsurface, subsurface users must hold permits (licenses) required to perform the relevant kinds of activities or conclude contracts with organizations that hold the right to perform the activities involving the use of subsurface resources.

The users of subsurface resources who carry out the extraction of radioactive raw materials and burial of radioactive wastes and toxic substances shall only be legal entities registered in the territory of the Russian Federation and holding a permit (license) issued by a duly authorized federal executive body to carry out the extraction and use of radioactive materials, toxic and other hazardous waste.

Rights and obligations of subsurface users shall arise from the state registration date of the license to use subsurface plots, and from the time the production sharing agreement enters into force, if the right to use subsurface is granted under the terms of a production sharing agreement.

ARTICLE 10. TERMS OF USE OF SUBSURFACE PLOTS

The right to use subsurface plots shall be granted either for a fixed or unlimited period of time. The right to use subsurface plots shall be granted for a fixed period of time in the following cases: for the purpose of geological exploration—up to 5 years;

in order to extract mineral resources—for the period of extraction of the mineral deposit, which is calculated on the basis of the feasibility study for the extraction of the mineral deposit ensuring the rational use and protection of subsurface;

in order to extract underground water—up to 25 years;

in order to extract mineral resources on the grounds of a short-term right granted to use subsurface in keeping with Article 21.1. Of this Law—up to one year.

The right to use subsurface areas shall be granted for an unlimited time in order to construct and operate underground facilities unrelated to mining production, to construct and operate underground facilities involved in the burial of waste generated by the construction and operation of crude oil and natural gas storage facilities and in order to establish specially protected geological facilities and for other purposes.

The period of use of a subsurface plot shall be extended at the initiative of the user of the subsurface, if there is a need to complete exploration and assessment or development of a mineral deposit or to carry out liquidation works, provided there are no breaches of the license's terms and conditions by this subsurface user.

A production sharing agreement shall stipulate the terms for extending the period of use of a subsurface plot.

The starting date of a period of use of subsurface plots shall be the date of state registration of licenses to use such subsurface plots.

ARTICLE 10–1.   GROUNDS FOR AWARDING THE RIGHT TO USE SUBSURFACE PLOTS

The following shall be the basis for granting the right to use subsurface plots:

1) a decision of the Government of the Russian Federation based:

on the results of an auction or tender for the purposes of exploration and extraction of mineral resources on subsurface plots in internal sea waters, the territorial sea and on the continental shelf of the Russian Federation;

in the event of establishing the fact of discovery of a mineral deposit by a subsurface user that has carried out works aimed at the geological survey of subsurface plots in internal sea waters, the territorial sea and on the continental shelf of the Russian Federation at the expense of its own funds (including raised fund) for the purpose of exploration and extraction of the mineral resources of such deposit and have reimbursed the outlays of the State on the exploration and assessment of mineral resources on this subsurface plot in the procedure established by the Government of the Russian Federation (if any);

for the purpose of burying radioactive, toxic and other dangerous waste at deep levels ensuring the localization of such waste;

2) a decision of the federal body in charge of managing the state mineral reserve for the purpose of geological survey of subsurface plots in internal sea waters, the territorial sea and on the continental shelf of the Russian Federation;

3) a decision of the federal body in charge of managing the state mineral reserve or of a territorial body thereof on granting the right of short-term (up to one year) use of a land plot for the exercise by a legal entity (operator) of activities on the land plot whose right of use is terminated ahead of schedule;

4) a decision of the commission established by the federal body in charge of managing the state mineral reserve and including likewise representatives of the executive body of the appropriate subject of the Russian Federation for consideration of applications for granting the right to use subsurface plots;

for the purpose of geological survey of subsurface plots, except for subsurface plots of inland sea waters, the territorial sea and the continental shelf of the Russian Federation;

in the event of establishing the fact of discovery of a mineral deposit by a subsurface user that has carried out works aimed at the geological survey of subsurface plots at his own expense (including raised funds) for the purpose of exploration and extraction of mineral resources of such deposit and has reimbursed the outlays of the State, if any, on the exploration and assessment of mineral resources on this subsurface plot in the procedure established by the Government of the Russian Federation, except for subsurface plots of internal sea waters, the territorial sea and the continental shelf of the Russian Federation;

for the purpose of extracting ground water used for water supply of the population or technological water supply of industrial objects;

for the purpose of construction and operation of underground structures not connected with the extraction of mineral resources;

for the purpose of constructing oil and gas storage facilities in rock beds and operating such oil and gas storage facilities, placing industrial and domestic waste;

for establishing specially guarded geological objects;

5) a decision of a tender or auction commission on granting the right to use a subsurface plot for the purpose of exploration and extraction of minerals or for the purpose of geological survey of subsurface plots, exploration and extraction of minerals (under a combined license), except for land plots of inland sea waters, the territorial sea and the continental shelf of the Russian Federation;

6) a decision of the executive body of a subject of the Russian Federation coordinated with the federal body in charge of managing the state mineral reserve or with a territorial body thereof for the purpose of collecting mineralogical, paleontological and other geological specimens;

7) a decision of the authorized state power bodies of the subjects of the Russian Federation in keeping with the laws of a subject of the Russian Federation on granting the right to use subsurface plots containing deposits of commonly occurring minerals or subsurface plots of local importance, as well as subsurface plots of local importance to be used for the purpose of construction and operation of underground structures that are not connected with the extraction of minerals;

8) instances of the lapse of right to use subsurface plots for the reasons established by the federal laws regulating subsurface use relations;

9) an effective agreement on production sharing made in compliance with the Federal Law

ARTICLE 11. LICENSE FOR THE USE OF SUBSURFACE

The right to use subsurface shall be granted by a specific government permit in the form of a license comprising a specific form with the Russian Federal state emblem, as well as text, graphic and other attachments constituting an inseparable part of the license and setting forth the basic terms and conditions for the use of subsurface.

Allocation of a plot (of plots) of subsurface for use under the terms of production sharing agreements shall be documented by drawing up a license to use the subsurface. The license shall confirm the right to use the aforementioned plot (plots) of subsurface under the terms of production sharing agreements where the latter sets out all necessary conditions for the use of subsurface in accordance with the Federal Law on Production Sharing Agreements and the legislation of the Russian Federation on subsurface.

The license is a document certifying the right of its holder to use a subsurface plot within specific boundaries in accordance with the purpose stated therein over an established period of time, provided its holder complies with the terms and conditions agreed in advance. A contract may be concluded between the duly authorized bodies of state power and the subsurface user to establish the terms for the use of such a plot as well as the obligations of the parties under the aforesaid contract.

The authorized government bodies and license holders may enter into an agreement establishing specific terms and conditions related to the use of subsurface.

The license shall certify the right of geological exploration, development of mineral fields, utilization of waste products of mining and related processing industries, use of subsurface for purposes other than mineral production, establishment of specially protected geological features, sampling mineral, paleontological, and other geological materials for collection purposes.

A license for the use of subsurface may be awarded for several types of concurrent activities.

A license for the use of subsurface shall be awarded subject to prior agreement by a land resources management body or a land owner for allotment of an appropriate land area for the use of subsurface. The allotment of a land area in its final boundaries and certification of the user's right for the use of subsurface shall be performed as provided for by the land code approval of the work program for the use of subsurface.

ARTICLE 17.1. ASSIGNMENT OF RIGHTS FOR THE USE OF SUBSURFACE AND RENEWAL OF THE EFFECTIVE LICENSE

The rights for the use of subsurface plots shall be assigned to another in the following cases: reorganization of the legal entity acting as the subsurface user by way of its transformation such as change of its organizational and legal status; transformation of the legal entity acting as the subsurface user by incorporating another enterprise or by merging with another legal entity in accordance with legislation of the Russian Federation;

termination of the activity of a legal entity that is a user of mineral resources due to its incorporation into another legal entity in accordance with the legislation of the Russian Federation on condition that the other legal entity meets the requirements placed on mineral resources users and also has qualified specialists and the necessary financial and technical facilities for the safe performance of the works; transformation of the legal entity acting as the subsurface user by way of dividing it or spinning-off from it another legal entity in accordance with the legislation of the Russian Federation, provided the newly-established legal entity plans to carry out operations under the license for the use of subsurface plots granted to the former subsurface user; a legal entity acting as the subsurface user is the founder of a new legal entity established in order to carry out operations on the allocated subsurface plot in accordance with the license to use the subsurface plot, provided the new legal entity has been established in keeping with the legislation of the Russian Federation and the equipment required to perform the activities specified in the license to use the subsurface plot has been transferred to it, including the plant located within the licensed plot, and provided permits (licenses) are available necessary to carry out the types of activities involved in the use of subsurface, and at the time of assignment of the right to use the subsurface plot the stake of the previous legal entity (the subsurface user) in the authorized capital of the new legal entity is at least fifty per cent of the authorized capital of the new legal entity; if a legal entity acquires in the manner established by the Federal Law property (a property complex) of an insolvent enterprise (the subsurface user), provided the property acquirer is a legal entity established in keeping with the legislation of the Russian Federation and it meets the qualification standards established by the legislation on subsurface matters of the Russian Federation for users of subsurface.

The assignment of the right to use subsurface plots shall require license renewal. In this case the terms and conditions for the use of the subsurface plot laid down by the previous license shall not be subject to revision.

The transfer of rights to use subsurface plots granted on the basis of production sharing agreements and the reissue of existing licenses to use subsurface plots shall be performed in accordance with the Federal Law Sharing Agreements.

The license shall also be subject to renewal in the case of the change of name of legal entities acting as users of subsurface plots.

The Procedure be set by the federal mineral reserve management body.

The subsurface user shall have the right to appeal in court against refusal to renew a license.

The right to use a subsurface plot or plots acquired by a legal entity in the established manner may not be transferred to any third parties, including under an assignment provided for by civil legislation, except as otherwise provided for by this Law or other federal laws.

A subsurface use license acquired by a legal entity in the established manner shall not be assigned to third persons, including, for use.

Is a subsurface license like a right or a power? Is it freely alienable? Is it transferable at all? With a few exceptions, each new holder of a license must go through a new application process to obtain government approval. How onerous is this likely to be? We will consider the interrelationship between these licenses and transactional structures below.

B. THE PRODUCTION SHARING AGREEMENT AND OTHER TYPES OF INTERNATIONAL PETROLEUM AGREEMENTS

Historically, the extraction of hydrocarbons in developing countries has taken a number of forms. The classic structure involved a concession agreement between an international oil company (IOC) and the host state. The host government would grant the IOC the mineral rights to the applicable contract area. This arrangement provided the IOC with ownership of the oil or gas that it discovered and produced. The IOC would pay a mixture of up-front fees, a royalty based on the amount and value of the hydrocarbons extracted, and taxes on its revenues or profits, as well as fees for various services provided by the government. The investor would accept the full residual risk and cost related to the project, in the sense that its gain or loss would rest on the value of the oil or gas extracted, minus the fees, royalties and taxes due the government. The IOC, in other words, owned the resource when it was produced, subject to the taxes and royalties imposed by the host government. During the first half of the twentieth century, for example, most energy projects in the Middle East and Latin America took the form of concession agreements between host governments and IOCs. The modern forms of these tax-royalty systems are called license agreements and are used primarily in developed countries.

During the second half of the century, national governments increasingly resisted the concept of foreign ownership of their natural resources. On the one hand, this resistance provided a convenient ground for renegotiating prior arrangements, many of which reflected political and economic relations that had substantially changed in the post-colonial world. On the other hand, the NOCs that host governments created often lacked the managerial and technical expertise to operate existing production projects or to carry out exploration operations on new ones. The challenge became one of drawing on the resources of the IOCs while maintaining ownership in the hands of the government or the NOCs.

One alternative was the no-risk service agreement, which required an IOC to provide services as needed to the government or the NOC. But IOCs, unlike multinational engineering companies such as Bechtel, KBR and Schlumberger, did not like the fee-for-services model. They preferred to have their return rest at least in part on the value of the hydrocarbons they discovered. The IOCs specialize in assuming exploration risk, and, if a discovery is made, the risk of fluctuation of international market prices. A simple no-risk service agreement does not do this. In response, some parties created risk service agreements, under which the IOC would receive payment only if it made a discovery. This arrangement subjected the service fee, paid in cash or in kind, to the inherent exploration risk. The structure made it easier for an IOC, if successful, to book the discovered reserves for accounting and financial purposes.

In response to these concerns, IOCs, host countries and NOCs developed two kinds of structures—joint venture agreements ("JVAs") and PSAs. Simplifying greatly, a JVA involves investment by an IOC and either the NOC or a private host-country company in a single joint venture company (JVC). The JVC, a jointly owned equity entity, takes on the responsibility of the exploration or development operations. The terms of the JVA and the law governing it will determine the extent of the IOC's role in its management, as well as its control over operations, marketing, and revenues. Under this structure, the IOC can obtain its share of any profits only if the JVC declares dividends payable to its joint owners because it does not have an individual right of ownership of production under the JVC framework.

The PSA, unlike a JVA, is based on specific rights of ownership of production, a low degree of governmental control and particular methods of compensation. The most basic PSA concept is a grant to the IOC/contractor of the exclusive right to conduct petroleum operations in the contract area, but not of any ownership rights with respect to the underlying minerals. Instead, the oil still belongs to the mineral rights owner, i.e., the host government, at the wellhead. The IOC obtains title to its share of the oil only at the lifting point, i.e., the point where the oil passes the flange of an oil tanker for shipping to potential customers. Lifting usually occurs somewhere near the border or outside the host country. Because the IOC's rights depend entirely on contracts and not ownership, logic would suggest that the PSA should not provide for the payment of royalties as an element of government take. Due to the overriding need to create sources of revenue, however, many governments/NOCs disregard this conceptual issue and include royalties as an element of PSAs.

Due to its similarities to a service agreement, the PSA does not undermine the host government's imperative of not compromising its "inherent and inalienable" rights over its natural resources. But because the amount of compensation depends on the extent and value of the petroleum produced, the IOC assumes the full cost and expense of the petroleum operations and gets a return based on the market value of the production. A PSA, in other words, uses the law of contract to mimic an outcome that otherwise would exist under the law of property.

PSAs in the international oil and gas industry have enabled host governments around the world to encourage and promote foreign investment. Under this structure, IOCs have paid large bonuses and committed to ambitious work programs in return for obtaining the exclusive rights to perform the petroleum operations in remote and offshore areas at their sole risk and expense. This type of activity creates an influx of capital into the economy of the emerging market country, and it creates jobs for its citizens and local contractors. The more PSA projects the emerging market country can generate, the greater potential for producing benefits that may extend to other segments of its economy.

The premise that underlies the PSA as a separate form of investment is that it will provide the host government with an ample opportunity to negotiate a sufficient share of the production to allow it to exempt the IOC from the taxes and other duties that a foreign investor otherwise would pay. For example, the government/NOC could lower the percentage of cost recovery oil allocated to the IOC and retain a larger share of the profit oil for itself. Such an arrangement should provide the government a sufficient amount of revenue, thus eliminating the temptation to participate as one of the contractor parties. If, however, the NOC does participate, it places itself in an ambiguous legal position. It must act in its supervisory role under the host country's law while simultaneously acting as a contractor unto itself. This inevitably leads to major conflicts of interest for the NOC and induces it not to share responsibility for proper petroleum operations. Accordingly, IOCs would prefer not to have NOC participation in a PSA. Most, however, would not consider such participation a deal breaker if the government/NOC were to insist on this outcome.

If a host state conditions an IOC's bid to conduct oil operations on compliance with a model PSA, the parties may negotiate a number of significant commercial issues. The most important are the percentage share applied to cost recovery oil, the allocation of profit oil among the parties, the minimum work and financial obligations for exploration, and the amount of the signature, commercial discovery and production bonuses. The outcome of these negotiations will have a major impact on the economics of any PSA project.

Other very important issues exist. The level of royalties and taxes will affect the project's viability, although the applicable laws and regulations of the host country typically dictate these terms. Negotiations usually are limited to the issue of whether these levies may be cost recoverable or tax deductible. Other items may be subject to negotiation, such as the payment for use of the NOC's technical data and ongoing training fees, but these matters usually do not have a significant impact on the project's overall economics.

One of the most distinctive elements of the PSA is its procedure for the sharing of production. The IOC will have the contractual right to recover its costs out of the portion of the production designated as cost recovery oil, while the balance of the production is devoted to profit oil shared by the IOC and the NOC/government. The applicable terms for cost recovery oil and the split of profit oil vary from country to country and depend on matters such as whether the operations will take place in uncomplicated onshore areas or in more challenging onshore or offshore areas:

> *(1) Cost recovery oil* typically constitutes 40% to 60% of total production. It is used to reimburse the IOC's exploration, development and production costs. The parties will set a higher rate for costly projects in onshore frontier areas or deepwater offshore areas.

(2) Profit oil represents the remaining balance of the total production. The IOC and the NOC/government share this amount of production. The PSA may use either a set or progressive percentage split to divide this amount. The progressive method bases the split on either the project's production rate or its internal rate of return.

IOCs traditionally have insisted on several principles regarding the PSA's legal regime, regardless of whether the host country possesses a free market economy. These include: (1) the unfettered right of the IOC to export its share of the production and to retain the proceeds from sales abroad; (2) the ability to exert some degree of control over operational and managerial matters; (3) the stabilization of contractual rights; (4) the settlement of disputes by third party international arbitration; (5) neutral governing law; and (6) the waiver of sovereign immunity. We discuss each of these principles briefly below.

Right to Export. IOCs regard the right to export petroleum freely and to retain proceeds from sales abroad in foreign bank accounts as a minimum requirement in a PSA. This right is fundamental to the economic feasibility of any investment project. By exporting petroleum, the IOC gains access to the international crude oil trading market and does not face the constraints caused by the peculiarities of the host country's domestic market.

Degree of Control. Because the IOC must procure all of the funds needed to undertake an exploration and development project under a PSA, the IOC expects to exert a high degree of control over the making of operational, managerial, and technical decisions. IOCs regard operational control as the natural corollary to accepting the project's risk and cost. Accordingly, the IOC will want to use its technical and managerial expertise in accordance with the international petroleum industry's sound and accepted business, commercial and technical principles, subject to the host country's environmental and operational regulations. In particular, it will regard its appointment as the project's operator an extremely critical requirement.

Stabilization. Because most projects require an IOC to make extremely long-term investments, it must depend on the stabilization of contractual rights and economic benefits. This principle is especially relevant when the project takes place in an unstable political environment that could lead to major changes in laws and regulations, as well as nationalization or expropriation. The principle objective is to ensure subsequent legislation will not have an adverse effect on the economic feasibility of the project. In Chapter 3 we discussed the reasons for including a stabilization clause in a PSA and what such a clause should contain.

International Arbitration. An IOC will regard a guarantee of third party international arbitration at a neutral foreign location for the resolution of disputes as an extremely important part of the negotiation of any PSA. It does not want to take the risk of resolving disputes in the courts of the host country, where, depending on the development of the legal system and the independence of the judiciary, arbitrary and capricious decisions may harm it.

Governing Law. To provide additional protection, IOCs also will seek a governing law clause that will specify a neutral foreign law to govern the resolution of disputes. Some governments/NOCs will agree to this as long as the PSA makes it absolutely clear that local laws will apply to the performance of the petroleum operations. Some, however, will insist on the host country's law as the governing law. In such cases, the PSA may contain an additional reference to the principles of international law or the principles and practices of the international petroleum industry to further internationalize the contract.

Waiver of Sovereign Immunity. The waiver of sovereign immunity is a critical element in the dispute resolution process. Without such a waiver, the IOC may not be able to obtain jurisdiction over the NOC or the host government if a dispute arises under the PSA. In a waiver clause, the NOC or host government agrees that (1) all of the transactions contemplated by the PSA shall constitute commercial activities, and (2) it expressly and irrevocably waives any immunity to which it otherwise would be entitled. This approach eliminates the possibility of the NOC/government trying to avoid making an appearance in the arbitration proceeding.

Many refinements and complications exist among the various types of international petroleum agreements. Even single countries vary over time the forms of investment they may accept, and international practice is remarkably diverse. The following article reflects nearly twenty years' work on energy transactions in the Soviet Union and Russia.

James W. Skelton, Jr.,
Status of Russian Petroleum Legislation

30 Houston J. Int'l L. 315 (2008)

The Author's first exposure to the laws of the Soviet Union and Russia took the form of an international contract conference presentation in Moscow in October 1989. The Ministry of Geology, the main point of contact in the Soviet Union for foreign investors, had invited the Author's employer to make a presentation about the three main types of international petroleum contracts (tax royalty/concession agreements, service contracts, and production sharing agreements), covering both the legal and economic aspects of each. Three specialists and an interpreter were sent to conduct the conference. There were many lawyers in attendance from various institutes around the country, as well as a few KGB agents and some Ministry personnel. Many insightful questions were asked, and it was apparent that there was a fairly high level of understanding of many issues.

Although the Author was convinced that the audience would view the tax/royalty system, which is basically the modern concession agreement, as the most suited to their own administrative law system, they were indifferent to the suggestion. Unfortunately, due to the bad experience with concession agreements during the 1920s, the Russians viewed these agreements as giveaways. So, concession agreements had a bad name, and the audience was not interested for that reason. The attendees said, in effect, it didn't work before, so what else can you tell us about?

It was made clear to the audience that international oil companies prefer to acquire equity interests in available properties and would usually not be interested in entering into a service contract unless it was the only option. As a consequence, not much time was devoted to discussing service contracts, which shifted the focus of the legal presentation to the production sharing agreement (PSA) form of investment. It became a theoretical discussion, however, because the existing legislation would not support such a system.

The only legislation that existed in the Soviet Union in connection with foreign investment from 1987 to early 1992 was the Joint Venture Law (JV Law). The JV Law permitted a foreign investor to own an interest in a Soviet limited liability joint venture company (JVC) that was formed with an existing domestic license holder to obtain the rights to develop an oil field under a reissued license. Due to the lack of alternatives and the desire to participate in the Russian oil industry, a few foreign investors entered into such joint venture agreements (JVAs). Most of these joint ventures were established through the execution of a JVA between a U.S. or European international oil or service company and a Russian exploration or production association, followed by the registration and formation of a JVC. All of these JVCs suffered through countless changes in the tax laws, increases in the rates of tariffs and taxes, battles for VAT refunds, and pipeline access complications throughout the 1990s. It was, therefore, no wonder that the foreign investors became convinced that the PSA approach must be a better way to make investments in Russia.

In general, JVCs were subject to the infamous current tax regime (CTR), there were no exemptions from any of the tax laws, and those that were granted on an ad hoc basis were short term in nature and subject to change without notice. Investors came face to face with the fact that once a foreign investor was captured within a JVC in Russia it was subject to all new and amended laws, the JVA lacked tax and fiscal stability, and neither the JVC nor the foreign investor was in privity of contract with either the federal government or the local government, both of which were the ones that granted the JVC the ultimate rights through the license. By contrast, upon entering into a PSA, the foreign investor would be in privity of contract with the host country government or its national oil company as the rights granting authority, meaning that there could be significant exemptions from various tax and customs laws, and there could be some predictability and stability under a separate legal and fiscal regime.

. . .

The first time the words "production sharing" were ever published officially in Russia was on February 21, 1992, when the Law on Subsurface Resources (Subsurface Law) was enacted. The next significant event occurred on Christmas Eve, 1993, when President Yeltsin signed the Presidential Decree on Production Sharing and its Implementation in the Russian Federation, which was quickly dubbed the "Christmas Present" because it paved the way for the executive branch to propose this new system of production sharing to the State Duma.

By July 1995, a draft Law on Production Sharing Agreements (PSA Law) had been passed by the State Duma. In the draft, there were a number of excellent provisions that would have provided the type of stability and predictability that foreign investors and financing institutions would need in a country that was in a volatile state of transition like Russia. Unfortunately, between June 1995 and December 1995, the opposition legislators, who viewed the PSA Law as some sort of wholesale giveaway of Mother Russia's natural resources, had the influence to modify the draft to the point at which it became only marginally viable.

Consequently, when the PSA Law came into effect on January 11, 1996, it was apparent to the reformist legislators and outside observers that many other laws needed to be amended, more laws needed to be passed, and normative acts had to be enacted. The conflicts that were created by this final version of the PSA Law were so striking that most foreign oil companies decided they were not going to invest under the PSA Law until these conflicts and contradictions were resolved. Many of those conflicts were resolved by the amendments to the PSA Law and the enabling legislation. Nevertheless, there were still a few significant shortcomings in the legislation that were never addressed by the Russian government or the State Duma. As a result, the international oil companies refused to invest under the PSA Law until the remaining conflicts and contradictions were eliminated.

Despite the fact that Russia was viewed as the last frontier in the oil industry, there was no good reason to commit to a major investment until the time when the legal and fiscal regime that was constructed for PSAs would provide such investments with adequate protection—especially a stable tax regime. That time never came. In fact, just the opposite occurred in June 2003, when an amendment to the PSA Law was passed, making it virtually impossible to obtain approval to utilize the PSA form of investment. The new amendment provided that: (1) projects are only eligible for PSA terms under exceptional circumstances, *e.g.*, huge investments for greenfield projects; (2) eligible projects must endure a dual auction process in order to become qualified; and (3) the applicable license holders must surrender their licenses in favor of such auctions. This type of legislative interference rendered the PSA Law useless for all practical purposes. Some have claimed that the Russian legislators confused the PSA concept with privileges for foreign investors. The Author believes, however, that the legislators knew exactly what they were doing and that they intended to strike a mortal blow against the PSA form of investment because they viewed it as being both incompatible with the administrative law system and inadequate in providing sufficient control mechanisms.

As stated in the section above, the Subsurface Law was passed in February 1992. The Subsurface Law served to perpetuate the only available rights-granting mechanism in the Russian petroleum industry and codified the application of the old Soviet command system of administrative law licensing. In so doing, the Subsurface Law essentially memorialized the old nationalist approach and made it more difficult for the reformist legislators to introduce alternative legislation.

Certain provisions of the new law made it clear that licenses could not be issued through direct negotiations and that competitive bidding would be required in all cases. The Russian legislators claimed this was necessary in order to minimize corruption in the licensing process, but that ignored the practical reality that enormous projects in remote locations that require complicated development operations are usually enhanced by the give and take of negotiations as a means of agreeing to a mutually beneficial set of terms and conditions.

The Committee on Geology then promulgated a new set of regulations on the licensing procedure (licensing regulations), which did not provide any details about the types of contracts (concession agreements, PSAs and service contracts) that were referred to in Article 12 of the Subsurface Law.

There have been various revisions over the years, including the recent amendments to the Subsurface Law that introduced important fundamental provisions such as the conditions required for renewing subsurface licenses, as well as the transfer of rights from a subsidiary to a parent company and between subsidiaries. Otherwise, the basic framework of the Subsurface Law supported by the licensing regulations has remained relatively unchanged in terms of there being no express restrictions on foreign ownership participation. As a practical matter, however, there had always been an unspoken fifty percent cap placed on foreign ownership in a JVC.

That all changed on February 10, 2005, when officials of the Ministry of Natural Resources (MNR) began openly discussing new rules for licensing terms. In particular, Yuri Trutnev, the Minister of the MNR, announced that only companies registered in Russia and at least fifty-one percent owned by Russian investors would be eligible to participate in "closed auctions" for development of Russia's most important strategic fields. This restriction on foreign participation was revealed as part of the overall plan to pass a new foreign investment law that would replace the current version of the Subsurface Law and was viewed as further evidence of the "growing government efforts to reassert control over the oil industry."

This unprecedented attempt to produce a substitute for the Subsurface Law has been in the works for more than two and a half years, but it has not been finalized. Just recently, however, it was reported that the State Duma has asked the government for clarification of what the term "strategic" means in connection with those strategic industries in which foreign investment would be limited to forty-nine percent. Thereafter, a spokesman for the Ministry of Natural Resources stated that, "the government has effectively abandoned its efforts to pass a new foreign investment law," and the Ministry would seek changes to the existing Subsurface Law instead. Such sudden changes in direction are not uncommon in the recent history of the Russian legislative process. Whether the restriction on foreign ownership takes the form of an amendment to an existing law or a new law is not the main issue, however. What matters is that the Russian government appears to be determined to place express restrictions on foreign participation in the oil industry.

This is significant because transactions like BP's purchase of fifty percent of TNK for $6.75 billion in February 2003 would not have been possible if the new rule had been in effect at that time. Some other joint ventures would have been possible since the foreign ownership share was less than fifty percent, but the effect of this new legislative effort is very negative in terms of its perception and its practical applicability to future transactions in Russia.

During the past five years, we have witnessed the demise of Yukos and the emergence of Rosneft as a significant and powerful national oil company, and Gazprom has gained more influence and power in the gas industry. These and other events have provided more than enough evidence to show that the Russian government is wielding a tremendous amount of influence in its effort to renationalize a portion of the oil industry. Both the political will and the practical need to reform are distant memories due to the onset of very high crude oil prices and the change in the political climate.

It appears that foreign investors expected too much too soon in terms of market and legislative reforms in the 1990s, and now the tide has turned against them. Contrary to the investment climate in the 1990s, not many officials in Russia are making an effort to encourage foreign investment. On the other hand, a limited number of examples have been recognized as being models for the new paradigm, such as ConocoPhillips' equity investment in OAO Lukoil.

The legislative landscape is cluttered with countless numbers of drafts of abandoned and forgotten proposals, some of which could have been beneficial to the Russian economy and foreign investors. While the prospects for any improvements in the legislation appear to be gone, there is still a possibility that further attempts to prohibit foreign investment will fail.

––––––––––––

In the Documents Supplement we provide a Model PSA promulgated by Kenya in 2013. Note Article 27, which deals with cost recovery oil and profit oil. These formulas are at the heart of the PSA structure. As noted above, they determine the division of the production between the IOCs, on the one hand, and the NOC and the host government, on the other hand. It is important not to confuse "profit" and "cost" as used in this PSA with actual profit and cost. Rather, these clauses specify what percentage of the first X barrels of oil goes to the IOCs, and not to the NOC and government. Note also how the percentage allocation changes as more oil is produced. How does this allocation reflect the risk of the size of the discovery?

Note the stabilization clause in Article 40(3) of the model PSA. Are there ways to hold a NOC party to a PSA accountable for its government's breach of a stabilization clause? Does this sample clause in the Kenya Model PSA address this problem effectively?

Property and Contract Rights Revisited

Consider the Russian Law on the Subsurface, excerpted above. It is not uncommon for a local entity to acquire a subsurface license and then seek foreign partners who will supply finance and technical expertise in return for a share in the venture. Under the Law on Subsurface, can the holder of a license contribute its interest to a common enterprise? One the one hand, Article 1.2 seems to indicate that, although the subsurface itself is inalienable, rights to use the subsurface may have some of the characteristics of a property interest. But other provisions of the Law seem to limit the right to transfer licenses. Consider how a Swedish arbitral tribunal analyzed the ownership issue in the following case.

Archangel Diamond Corporation v. OAO Arkhangelskoye Geologodobychnoye Predpriyatiye ("Arkhangelskgeoldobycha")

Stockholm Chamber of Commerce Arbitration Tribunal[8]
June 25, 2001

Gunnar Nordrum, chair

Jeffrey M. Hertzfeld

K. L. Razumov

CIRCUMSTANCES OF THE CASE. INTRODUCTION

1.   In view of the availability in the Arkhangelsk region of RF of promising diamond deposits, the territorial Northern Committee for geology and the use of the subsurface decided in 1993 to hold a tender for the development of seven such areas.

2.   In that tender (in respect of two areas) participated the State-owned Enterprise Arkhangelskgeologiya (hereinafter—GPA) together with the Canadian company Canmet Resources Limited. On 24 November 1993 these two legal entities made the Diamond Venture Agreement (hereinafter—the DVA) on co-operation in the tender, and in the event of a positive result, on co-operation in the exploration, prospecting. Evaluation and production of diamonds. From 5 August 1994 on Canmet Resources Limited changed its name to Archangel Diamond Corporation (hereinafter—ADC).

3.   GPA won the tender for an area which was called the Verkhotina area, of 440 km%g2%g, located 40 km to the North from the city of Arkhangelsk, and on 30 December 1993 it received licence No. APX 00026 6P, which during 25 years shall ensure the right for the geologic study of diamond deposits with further development thereof.

4.   Therefore, both partner parties concluded a number of agreements with the purpose of strengthening the basis for their further co-operation.

5.   So, in accordance with Memorandum of 25 February 1994 they agreed to create a joint stock company and *"in case of favourable changes in the current legislation to make reassignments (of the licence) to the new legal body"*. They also agreed to grant a shareholding in the charter fund of such joint stock company to International Business Management Enterprises, hereinafter IBME, the founder of which was Michael Krel who emigrated from the USSR in 1978. In 1993, while living in Australia, he acted as a mediator in the relations between the two above mentioned parties.

---

[8]   This award was introduced as part of the record in a subsequent lawsuit brought by Archangel Diamond Corporation in the United States against Arkhangelskgeoldobycha and its subsequent owner, Lukoil. A full copy of the opinion is available at the District Court for the City and County of Denver, Colorado, Case No.: 01–CV–6514.

6. These three partners concluded on March 2, 1994 the Founders agreement on the creation of a joint stock company, which was registered by them in Moscow on June 15, 1994 under the name International joint stock company of open type "Almazny Bereg" (hereinafter—AB):

7. On May 10, 1994 these three companies concluded agreement on joint activity No.1/1994 (hereinafter—the JAA). Subsequently they concluded additional agreements relevant to both JAA and the AB company.

8. Prospecting works were going on in the area. Under the DVA the financing was vested to Canmet and the performance [of works] was vested to GPA. After drilling of several resultless pipes in February 1998 they discovered promising pipe No.441, which was called the Grib pipe by the surname of a deputy general director of GPA.

9. The former state-owned enterprise GPA was privatised by resolution of the State Property Management Committee of the Arkhangelsk region of August 7, 1995 and its name became OAO "Arkhangelsk Geologic Enterprise" (hereinafter—AGD). Licence APX 00026 BP was re-registered on April 12, 1996 in the name of AGD under No. APX 00248 KP.

10. Upon the instruction by the law of March 3, 1995 of amendments into the Law of the Russian Federation On the Subsurface of June 26, 1992, and adoption by the Committee for geology and the use of the Subsurface of Order No 65, ADC and AB presumed that the legislation of Russia allowed a transfer of the licence in favour of AB. Starting from June 1995 they repeatedly applied to AGD and requested to conduct the re-registration of the licence. In fact, twice during the year 1996 AGD by the letters to the Northern Committee for geology and the use of the Subsurface dated 4 June and 11 November 1996 requested the licence to be re-registered in favour of AB. But following the submission AGD revoked such letters.

11. ADC and AB were insisting on the transfer of the licence and were seeking support in different instances of the regional and federal levels, presuming that such transfer was a contractual obligation of AGD, but without success.

12. In August 1998 ADC, represented by the law firm Norton Rose, applied with a statement of claim to the Arbitration Institute of the Stockholm Chamber of Commerce, guided by the DVA and the contained therein arbitration clause, which provided for the settlement of disputed in accordance with the UNCITRAL Rules. In the statement of claim ADC demanded to oblige AGD to transfer the licence to AB, to recognize a violation from the part of AGD of its contractual obligations, as well as made a number of other claims which were based on the factual situation as of the date of the submission of the claim.

13. The request for arbitration was filed against the Respondent (AGD), as well as against six more legal entities and individuals, *i.e.*, shareholders of AGD, who, in the opinion of ADC, were responsible for the non-performance by AGD of its contractual obligations.

. . .

MOTIVATION OF THE AWARD

107. This case covers a number of most complex matters a decision of which is not univocal.

108. The Tribunal and especially its Chairman, does not conceal, that concerning different issues had long felt hesitant and doubtful before it actually became convinced in the following.

109. The substance of the award is that the Tribunal does not have jurisdiction on this case. Nevertheless, the rendered Award is not unanimous, since the Arbitrator Jeffrey M. Hertzfeld has a dissenting opinion on the issue of competence, see appendix hereto.

110. The following award reflects the opinion of the majority: of the Chairman and of the Arbitrator Razumov K. L.

4.1 On competence of the Tribunal

111. In clause 16 of the DVA the parties agreed to resolve disputes by way of arbitration. Arbitration shall be held in accordance with the UNCITRAL Rules in Stockholm.

112. By its decision of 12 April 1999 the Tribunal acknowledged its competence of the Tribunal on issues that arise from the DVA, and denied its competence on issues that arise from other agreements and transactions with the participation of the parties in dispute, as well as on the claims filed by the Claimant against the other respondents, save for AGD.

113. Nevertheless, such decision does not prohibit (the fact) that the Tribunal has to renounce its competence for cogent reasons that were not set out in such decision.

114. In this connection, the Tribunal considers first of all the question whether this dispute can be the subject of arbitration, since in the Russian legislation there is a prohibition in this regard.

115. In order to answer the raised question. The Tribunal has investigated the following issues:

1. By what law—Swedish or Russian—shall this question be regulated?

2. If Russian law is applicable, then whether it contains or not a prohibition for arbitration of the dispute which arose between the parties.

116. First the Tribunal will consider the second issue.

Is there in the Russian law a prohibition on arbitration of the dispute that arose?

Article 50 of the Law "On the Subsurface" read as follows:

"Disputes regarding matters of the use of the subsurface shall be settled by bodies of state power, a court or a court of arbitration in accordance with their powers and in the procedure established by legislation".

The following disputes shall be subject to settlement by a court or a court of arbitration:

1) financial, property and other disputes connected with the use of the subsurface;

2)   appeals against decisions of government bodies counter to this Law, including denial of the request for a licence for the use of the subsurface or early termination of the right for the use of the subsurface.

3)   appeals against actions or decisions by government officials and bodies in violation of this law;

4)   appeals against the application of standards (norms, regulations) for technological operations related to the use of the subsurface, conservation of the subsurface and environmental protection counter to applicable legislation."

. . .

120. In considering this issue the Tribunal proceeds from the following: Article 50 establishes that *"financial property and other disputes"* shall be subject to *"settlement by a court or a court of arbitration."* It is quite obvious, "that a court of arbitration" here means the state court of arbitration. A consideration of disputes by arbitration in terms of an arbitration tribunal, is, consequently, excluded. This also relates to purely administrative disputes between individuals. While in this instance a resolution of the disputes also depends on the position of the state authorities, because it goes about a re-registration of the licence as a title document issued by a state authority.

121. Article 16 of the DVA providing for a settlement of disputes by arbitration in Stockholm is, therefore, null and void, what directly follows from article 49 of the Law On the Subsurface. Thereunder the nullity comes in virtue of law and cannot create any obligations in respect of a Submission of disputes to arbitration. Such conclusion must be made in virtue of the norms of the Russian law in relation to Art.16 of the DVA, notwithstanding whether it goes about an interpretation of such agreement or about the responsibility of the parties thereunder. Determining here is the fact that in both instances it goes about disputes related to the use of the subsurface.

122. Is this conclusion subject to an amendment due to the fact that by the law of 2 January 2000; "On amendments and additions to the Law of the Russian Federation 'On the Subsurface' " article 50 was extended with a new subsection three, which reads:

"Upon mutual agreement of the parties, property disputes connected with the use of the subsurface may be submitted for settlement to arbitration tribunal (third party court)"

123. This addition relates only to ' "property" disputes, while a re-registration of the licence is a requirement which is not of property nature. Besides, this Federal law came into force "from the date of an official publishing thereof" (art.2), what happened on 13 January 2000, when it was published in the Rossisskaya Gazeta newspaper, while the claim was filed in 1998.

124. This issue concerns the relation of the new legislation back to agreements concluded before the adoption thereof. The Russian law regulates this issue quite, univocally by excluding the retroactive force of a law, unless otherwise expressly provided for thereby.

125. Pursuant to article 4 of the Civil Code of RF "Operation of civil legislation in time" any acts of civil legislation do not have retroactive

force and shall apply to relations which arose after the introduction thereof into operation. The operation of a law shall extend to relation which arose before the introduction thereof into operation only in instances when this is expressly provided for by such law.

126.   For contractual relations the same Article 4, paragraph 2, of the Civil Code contains a special exception from this general rule:

> *"Relations of the parties under an agreement concluded prior to the introduction of an act of civil legislation shall be regulated in accordance with Article 422 of this Code"*

127.   In accordance with Article 422, paragraph 1, a contract must correspond to the rules established by a law and other legal acts (imperative norms) which are binding upon the parties and prevailing at the moment of its conclusion. Disobservance of such terms shall make the agreement null and void and not only invalid out legally but having emerged at all.

128.   Article 422. Paragraph 2, deals with such a case when following conclusion of a contract a law is adopted which establishes rules binding upon the parties other than rules that were prevailing when concluding the contract: in such case:

> *"the terms of the contract concluded shall retain force except for instances when it is established in a law that its operation extends to relations which arose from the contracts previously concluded".*

129.   As "Commentaries to the Civil Code", 1997 (edited by O. N. Sadikov) (p.877) point out:

> *"a consequent arbitration of imperative norms of contractual law shall not affect the terms of the agreement concluded earlier except in cases when the law (but not other normative acts) grants it a retroactive force. Such cases are rare in practice. Article 9 of the Introductory Law to the Civil Code can serve as an example".*

130.   The Law dated 2 January 2000 *"On introducing amendments and additions into the Law of the Russian Federation 'On the Subsurface' "* says nothing about a retroactive force of its provisions. Therefore a general principle shall apply: It is only after this law entered into force that private persons had the right to resolve their differences through arbitrage. If contracts concluded earlier contained such arbitration clauses, the parties should have reinforced their consent by entering into a new agreement after 13 January, 2000 (the date the new law entered into force). No such consent was reached between the parties relating to our case.

131.   Therefore the majority of the Tribunal sticks to the opinion that if Russian law is applicable for resolving this dispute, then a conclusion should be drawn that the Tribunal did not have competence to consider this case.

4.1.2   Which law is applicable to the arbitration clause: Swedish Law or Russian Law?

   . . .

Factors in favour of the appliance of Russian law

146.   The majority of the Tribunal studied the question of whether or not it is appropriate from the point of view of Swedish law to discuss arbitrability of the dispute on the basis of the norms of Russian law.

147.   In view of this the Tribunal deems it important to analyse the substance of the matter and define its relation to Sweden and Swedish legal order.

148.   The parties of the dispute, Russian and Canadian firms, have no relation to Sweden. The agreement was signed by them in Russia. Subject to the agreement is a long-term investment co-operation of the parties to be conducted in the Russian territory in respect of the realty located in Russia, exploration of natural resources in the subsurface of the Russian Federation which subsurface, according to, RF Constitution, Article 9, "*is used and protected in the Russian to Federation as the ground for the life and activity of the population living on the respective territory*". And the parties agree that their contractual relations are regulated by Russian law.

149.   Taking into account above-mentioned factors Russia is apparently the country with which the legal relations of the parties, all their elements taken together, have closest ties, Swedish interests are in no way whatsoever involved in this dispute. The one and only tie with Sweden is the place of arbitration proceedings Ties with the third party are absent either save for the fact that the Claimant is registered in Canada.

150.   All these factors determine in principle the application of Russian law not only to settling the dispute essentially but to the question of the validity of the arbitration agreement and in particular to the following question: can the dispute arisen be the subject of such agreement and consequently the subject of arbitration hearings based on such agreement.
    . . .

There are other elements as well:
    . . .

158.   There is a principle in the Swedish international private law on applying of the country with which there are closest legal ties in a whole complex of legal relationship. In our case it is Russian undoubtedly. It seems acceptable that this principle also applies to Swedish international procedural law in absence of imperative norms stating otherwise.
    . . .

162.   If Russian law denies jurisdiction of arbitration courts in considering disputes related to the use of subsurface, then the Canadian government should recognise this position. Both countries have laws on arbitration based on the Standard law on international commercial arbitration UNCITRAL, 1985, operating in Canada both on the federal level and in province. This is referred to by Prof. S. N. Lebedev in his conclusion on the case, and the same is noted in preparatory works for the new Swedish Law on Arbitration.
    . . .

167. The enforceability of an arbitration award is also of significance for the rendering thereof. In principle the competence of the Tribunal and the satisfaction of its awards constitute a separate legal matter. But if all elements related to the case are considered in total seems desirable to obtain such results which would lead to the possibility to satisfy the arbitration award. The New York Convention, Article 5(2)(a), provides that an arbitration award may not be recognised and its satisfaction denied if "the object of the dispute can not be the subject of the arbitration proceedings according to the law of this country" (the country where enforcement of the award is sought).

168. It is obvious to the Tribunal that the enforcement of the arbitration award made in favour of the Claimant shall be denied in Russia since this dispute, according to Article 50 of the Law on Subsurface, cannot be subject to settlement by way of arbitration.

. . .

178. When taking into account the conclusion on the lack of competence of the Tribunal to consider this dispute if (the Tribunal) does not consider it necessary to resolve the question of whether the JAA either fully or partially cancelled the DVA. In any case there is a close mutual connection, between the transactions and the circumstance is an additional argument in favour of conclusion about the expediency of the application of the same method in the settlement of disputes arising out of the above mentioned transactions.

179. As a conclusion to this issue one should emphasise that the majority of the Tribunal treats as convincing, on the one side, the exclusive connections of the legal relationships under dispute with the law and order of the Russian Federation and [, on the other side,] the lack of connection with Sweden or third countries.

. . .

184. Taking into account the foregoing, the majority of the Tribunal consents as grounded and proved the conclusion, that the arbitration clause contained in article 16 of the DVA from the viewpoint of the Russian law is null and void. Therefrom follows the conclusion, that the majority of the Tribunal acknowledges the lack of the competence thereof to consider this dispute.

. . .

199. In view of the foregoing, The Tribunal, guided by articles 21 and 31 of the Arbitration Rules UNCITRAL,

HAS AWARDED:

1. To disallow the claim of Archangel Diamond Corporation versus OAO Arkhangelsk geological enterprise in connection with the lack of jurisdiction of the Tribunal to consider the case.

2. To collect from OAO Arkhangelsk geological enterprise in favour of Archangel Diamond Corporation over half of the costs of arbitration in the size of SEK 2,952.494 (two million nine hundred fifty two thousand four hundred and ninety four) Sweden kronas.

3. This award shall be subject to satisfaction within thirty (30) days from the date of the receipt thereof.

DISSENTING OPINION OF
JEFFREY M. HERTZFELD

1.   It is with great regret that I find myself obliged to dissent vigorously from the decision rendered by my learned colleagues on the Arbitration Tribunal in the above-captioned case. In my view, their decision that the present dispute is not arbitrable in Sweden is manifestly erroneous and contrary to the overwhelming body of law, practice and legal commentary in Sweden. It also represents a striking departure from the prevailing trends in international arbitration around the world favoring the arbitrability of international business disputes. Finally, it improperly overrules the Tribunal's own previous Award on Jurisdiction rendered over two years ago in the same case and in so doing directly violates the principle of the finality of arbitration awards, as contained in the Swedish and UNCITRAL rules governing this arbitration.

Context of the Dispute

2.   The present dispute arises out of a Diamond Venture Agreement (the "DVA") entered into by and between the legal predecessors of Claimant, Archangel Diamond Corporation ("ADC"), a Canadian company, and Respondent, OAO Arkhangelskgeoldobycha ("AGD"), a Russian entity, on November 24, 1993. The original Russian signatory was a Russian State Enterprise known as AGE. Subsequently, that enterprise was corporatized under the name AGD and privatized. As a result of its privatization, it came under the direct and/or indirect control of the Russian oil company, Lukoil.

3.   Pursuant to the DVA, the parties assumed certain civil law rights and obligations vis-à-vis each other, the alleged breach of which by Respondent led to Claimant's commencement of the present arbitration according to the terms of the arbitration clause set forth in Article 16 of that Agreement and quoted in the Tribunal's original Award on Jurisdiction.

4.   The substantive claims have been fully presented in the majority opinion. Suffice it to say here, by way of summary, that Claimant had assisted Respondent in winning a tender for the license to explore and develop potential diamond fields in the Verkhotina Territory in Archangelsk, Russia, and thereafter had provided over $8 million of financing for the exploration and evaluation of those fields. Respondent had agreed in the DVA, among other things, that it would "not grant rights in relation to the License to any third party without the prior written consent of [Claimant]," (Article 6.1) that it would "at all times act in the utmost good faith with respect to the commercial interest of [Claimant]," (Article 6.4) and that it would "grant to the Stock Company to be formed [jointly by Claimant and Respondent] the sole and exclusive right . . . To carry out the Development and Mining as may be determined as a result of Feasibility." (Article 9.2)

5.   Claimant alleged *inter alia* in this arbitration that, notwithstanding the establishment of the joint company, Respondent in bad faith failed to respect its above-mentioned obligations by refusing to re-register its license to the joint company after it had been created and by taking steps instead to transfer the license rights to another entity that Respondent had created without Claimant's participation, and

which would have made future transfer to the joint company impossible. The evidence in the case established that the exploration work had led to the discovery in early 1996 of an extremely rich diamond field (known as the Grib Pipe) on the territory and that, in late 1996, Respondent did indeed establish another company without Claimant's participation or consent, to which it continuously attempted to transfer its rights to the field over Claimant's objections until the commencement of the present arbitration in 1998.

6.   The parties agreed in the DVA to arbitration under UNCITRAL rules before a Tribunal of three arbitrators sitting in Stockholm. They did not specify the procedural law governing the arbitration agreement. Neither party contests that Russian substantive law governs performance of the rest of the agreement.

7.   At the outset of the arbitration in 1998, Respondent challenged the jurisdiction of the Tribunal alleging that the arbitration clause in the DVA had been superseded by other dispute resolution clauses in subsequent contracts, namely the Charter of the Stock Company and a Joint Activity Agreement.

. . .

The Law Applicable to Determining Jurisdiction

16.   The law is very well settled in Sweden that, where the parties to an international contract have not directly specified the law applicable to the arbitration agreement contained in their contract, as in the present case, the law of the place of arbitration, Sweden, shall apply. This is so regardless of the substantive law that may be applicable to the rest of the contract. It is premised on the notion that the arbitration clause is a separate agreement and, in selecting a particular place of arbitration, the parties are deemed to have chosen that jurisdiction's law to determine questions of arbitrability.

17.   The majority opinion states that, since the parties are Canadian and Russian companies, since the dispute does not concern relations in Sweden, and since the contract was signed in Russia and concerns a long-term cooperation of the parties on Russian territory, there is no "Swedish interest" here or reason for applying Swedish law to determine arbitrability. I believe that this totally misses the point. If this view were correct, Swedish arbitration law would rarely if ever apply to an international commercial dispute in Sweden. Indeed, the very reason why two foreign companies choose to submit their disputes to arbitration in Sweden is because they believe Sweden provides a clear, equitable and modern set of principles favorable to arbitral resolution of international disputes. It has nothing to do with the parties or the contracts being somehow tied to Sweden.

18.   While it is true that not every dispute is necessarily open to arbitration in Sweden, the limitations are those established by Swedish law, and not by the national law of one of the parties. In the present case, there is nothing in Swedish law that would preclude the arbitrability of the contract between Claimant and Respondent, which concerns breach of civil law obligations under a long-term international contract. The Claimant submitted unrebutted testimony to this effect by its expert witness, Mr. Lundblad of the Mannheimer Swartling firm. . . .

19. The Tribunal, at its own initiative, sought confirmation or rebuttal of Mr. Lundblad's opinion from Professor Michael Bogdan, a highly regarded Swedish law professor, whose opinion is quoted in its entirety in the majority decision. His opinion fully confirms the views expressed by Mr. Lundblad. According to Professor Bogdan, "It is, in my opinion, quite clear that the question of arbitrability is to be classified as a matter of procedure, governed in casu by Swedish law." He goes on to conclude that "Due to the parties' choice of proceedings in Sweden, the arbitration clause is governed by Swedish law, unless the parties have themselves agreed on another legal system (see the Act (1929:147) on Foreign Arbitral Agreements and Awards, which applies in this case because the proceedings started before the entry into force of the new Swedish Arbitration Act of 1999 . . .)" He further states: " . . . It suffices to say that the risk that recognition and enforcement may be refused in Russia due to the above-mentioned Russian mandatory jurisdictional rule does not, as such, affect the arbitrability of the dispute in Sweden."

    . . .

22. Perhaps the main motivation for the Tribunal's refusal to accept jurisdiction over the current dispute despite what appears to be clear Swedish law to the contrary is its concern over the enforceability in Russia of an eventual award. Since the majority of the Tribunal has concluded that Russian law, in particular Article 50 of the 1992 Subsurface Law, prohibits arbitration of a dispute of this type, they reason that an award would serve no purpose because it could not be enforced in Russia.

23. This is an erroneous conclusion based on erroneous assumptions.

24. First, whether or not an award may be enforced in the country of the judgment debtor is not determinative of the jurisdiction in the country of the place of arbitration. This is a well-known and well-established principle both in Sweden and in international arbitration in general. It is borne out by the opinions of both Mr. Lundblad and Professor Bogdan, cited above and in the majority opinion itself. If it were not the case, then Sweden's jurisdiction over international arbitration disputes would be the lowest common denominator of the rules applicable in the countries of the parties to the dispute, which would dictate and unreasonably narrow the scope for international arbitration in Sweden.

25. Second, even though Russia would be perhaps the most obvious place for Claimant to seek to enforce an award, it is free to search for assets of Respondent in any NY convention country against which to enforce a monetary award, such as requested in its statement for relief. We know that Sweden would not oppose enforcement of such an award and there is no reason at this time to assume that any other treaty country would oppose such enforcement.

26. Third, in light of the amendment of the 1992 Subsurface Law in 2000, a Swedish award should be enforceable in Russia under the NY Convention in the present case, even if the dispute would have been non-arbitrable in Russia at the time when the action was brought in 1998. Since the role of the enforcing court is not to make a new determination on the merits but rather to determine whether the award compiles with NY Convention criteria for enforcement, it should look first to see whether, under Swedish law as the place of arbitration, the matter was

arbitrable (which it was) and then, under Russian law, whether there are any public policy reasons to refuse enforcement. Since the 2000 amendment to the 1992 Subsurface Law today permits arbitration of property disputes related to the use of subsurface resources, there is today no argument to reject recognition and enforcement of the award.

27. Fourth, the Tribunal has chosen to interpret Article 50 of the 1992 Subsurface Law in a way that would prohibit arbitration of the present contract. However, the Tribunal received no official interpretation of Article 50, no legislative history, no pertinent Russian court decisions, although it requested this information. In fact, Article 50 is not as clear as the majority seems to believe. Read in the context of the entire Law, it is equally possible to interpret Article 50 as applying solely to disputes relating to subsurface license agreements envisaged by the Law as the legal basis (together with the license) for the use of the subsurface. It is not obvious that the legislative intent was to reach agreements between two private parties wholly ancillary to the use rights themselves.

28. Let me give an example by analogy. While it may well be that real estate disputes under Russian law are also restricted to Russian court jurisdiction, this certainly would not be interpreted by a Russian arbitral tribunal to mean that a joint venture agreement pursuant to which the Russian partner undertakes the obligation to lease real estate to the venture is an agreement that cannot be subjected to the jurisdiction of a treteiski sud (ad hoc arbitral tribunal). A distinction would be drawn between the joint venture agreement and the lease itself. The same could and should have been done in the present case, since a similar distinction clearly exists as between the DVA, on the one hand, and the license agreement, on the other.

. . .

30. Finally, the majority addresses but dismisses the importance of the fact that the Russian signatory to the DVA was a Russian State Enterprise. There is indeed a highly pertinent line of published international arbitration cases holding that a State's internal law cannot, as a matter of international public order, be used to invalidate an arbitration agreement which one of its State enterprises has entered into with a foreign party.

* * *

38. For all of the above reasons, I consider that the majority decision is clearly incompatible with basic principles of Swedish law and hereby dissent from the present Award rendered by this Tribunal.

[ADC asked the Swedish courts to nullify the arbitral decision as inconsistent with Swedish law. The Stockholm District Court concluded that the majority opinion misapplied the law on the arbitrability of the dispute. AGD appealed to the Svea Court of Appeal, which affirmed the lower court decision.]

OAO Arkhangelskoe Geologodobychnoe Predpriyatie v. Archangel Diamond Corporation

Svea Court of Appeal
November 15, 2005

. . .

The Court of Appeal finds that it is generally held that foreign public law will not be treated in the same manner as foreign civil law in all respects. The main principle should instead be that public legal requirements of foreign states shall normally not be met by Swedish courts, except in cases where Sweden's international undertakings provide the opposite standpoint. . . . The legislative history of the present arbitral legislation states that when it comes to economical-political regulation in a foreign state, there is usually no reason to let the mandatory provisions affect the possibility of an amicable settlement in Sweden and thereby the arbitrability under Swedish law. This approach agrees with the international tendency to accept that an international dispute will be settled through arbitration also when a similar national dispute would fall outside the arbitrable scope. . . .

It is also accepted that the principal agreement may be governed by the law of one country, while the law of another country applies to the arbitration agreement. Bogdan stated in his opinion to the arbitrators that it was evident that the issue of arbitrability should be considered as a procedural issue that in casu will be governed by Swedish law. If, and under which circumstances, the applicable law, here Russian law, admitted arbitrability, was not decisive in any material aspects.

The District Court has found that it is most in accordance with the doctrine of separability and a general requirement of predictability to let the issue of arbitrability be settled by applicable law in connection with examination of other grounds for invalidity, i.e., the law that applies to the arbitration agreement. The Court of Appeal agrees to this and finds that the main rule should be that the issue whether the dispute is arbitrable should be examined under the same law that applies to the arbitration agreement. . . . Probably this issue should primarily be characterized as procedural and by this naturally linked to the issue in respect of the arbitration agreement.

The Court of Appeal finds that it is generally held that foreign public law will not be treated in the same manner as foreign civil law in all respects. The main principle should instead be that public legal requirements of foreign states shall normally not be met by Swedish courts, except in cases where Sweden's international undertakings provide the opposite standpoint. . . . The legislative history of the present arbitral legislation states that when it comes to economical-political regulation in a foreign state, there is usually no reason to let the mandatory provisions affect the possibility of an amicable settlement in Sweden and thereby the arbitrability under Swedish law. This approach agrees with the international tendency to accept that an international dispute will be settled through arbitration also when a similar national dispute would fall outside the arbitrable scope. . . .

It is also accepted that the principal agreement may be governed by the law of one country, while the law of another country applies to the arbitration agreement. Bogdan stated in his opinion to the arbitrators that it was evident that the issue of arbitrability should be considered as a procedural issue that in casu will be governed by Swedish law. If, and under which circumstances, the applicable law, here Russian law, admitted arbitrability, was not decisive in any material aspects.

The District Court has found that it is most in accordance with the doctrine of separability and a general requirement of predictability to let the issue of arbitrability be settled by applicable law in connection with examination of other grounds for invalidity, i.e., the law that applies to the arbitration agreement. The Court of Appeal agrees to this and finds that the main rule should be that the issue whether the dispute is arbitrable should be examined under the same law that applies to the arbitration agreement. . . . Probably this issue should primarily be characterized as procedural and by this naturally linked to the issue in respect of the arbitration agreement.

The Court of Appeal has already found that Swedish law will apply to the arbitration agreement and agrees with the opinion of the District Court that Swedish law will apply to the issue whether the dispute—as referred to in the decision of the arbitrators—is arbitrable.

[The Supreme Court of Sweden denied AGD's application to review this decision, and the arbitral proceedings resumed. After three years, however, ADC sought to terminate the proceedings without prejudice because of its financial difficulties. The arbitral body agreed.]

NOTES

1. Parallel to the arbitration, ADC sued AGD and Lukoil, which had purchased AGD after the dispute arose, in Colorado state court, alleging various commercial torts and breach of contract. The complaint initially was dismissed for lack of jurisdiction over the defendants, but the Colorado Supreme Court reversed on the ground that the trial court should have held an evidentiary hearing on contested facts regarding jurisdiction. Archangel Diamond Corp. v. Lukoil, 123 P.3d 1187 (Colo. Sup. Ct. 2005).

2. To what extent did Archangel's lawyers let them down in the initial arbitration? Could they have achieved the desired result by first forming a joint stock company in which AGD initially had full ownership, followed by a transfer of the license to the joint stock company? Could Archangel then have acquired an interest in the joint stock company as a condition of contributions to the project? Would transfer of AGD's license to a wholly owned joint stock company have been easier under the Law on Subsurface?

3. Suppose Archangel had ended up with a minority interest in a joint stock company in which AGD (and later Lukoil) had the majority stake. How secure would its investment be? Recall the materials on corporate governance in Chapter 3 of this text. What stakes might Archangel have taken to protect itself from exploitation by the majority owners of a Russian company?

4. Recall Skelton's observation that the present strategy of Western energy companies operating in Russia is to take a minority, but strategic, stake in preexisting Russian firms. This approach has not been free from problems, as demonstrated by ConocoPhillips' decision to sell its entire 20% ownership of shares in Lukoil back to Lukoil in 2011. Indeed, British Petroleum made a radical change in 2013 when it closed the sale of its 50% ownership interest in the TNK-BP joint venture to Rosneft in return for $12.5 billion and a 19.5% share interest in Rosneft.

The history of BP's alliance with the Alfa-Access-Renova (AAR) consortium, which represented four Russian oligarchs, illustrates the challenges and opportunities of petroleum investment in Russia. These investors formed TNK-BP, of which BP and AAR each owned half, to exploit valuable production opportunities in Russia as well as to acquire BP assets in Venezuela and Vietnam. During the decade of its existence, TNK-BP generated significant profits, including dividends of $19 billion to BP on an $8 billion investment, but also severe conflicts, including threats against the enterprises' British chief executive that forced him to flee Russia in 2008 and a lawsuit that nullified BP's 2011 attempt to form a strategic alliance with Rosneft, the majority government-owned petroleum company. These disputes frequently led to the blockage of payment of BP's dividends. At the end of 2012, BP and AAR negotiated the acquisition of BP-TNK by Rosneft. AAR received $27.7 billion and exited the venture, while BP obtained 19.5% of Rosneft's shares as well as $12.5 billion in cash. AAR and BP also settled all their claims against each other.

When the dust settled, BP had swapped a half share and a major voice in managing a valuable private petroleum enterprise in return for a minority stake in a much larger entity dominated by the Russian government. Russian obstacles on the ground had made BP's significant role in managing TNK-BP less desirable. Partnering with the Russian government, however, presents its own challenges. On April 28, 2014, the U.S. government imposed financial sanctions and a travel ban on Igor Sechin, the chair of Rosneft, in retaliation for Russia's involvement in Ukrainian political unrest. How these developments will affect BP remains to be seen.

5.   The stability of strategic investment as a form of joint venturing in Russia remains uncertain. In March 2009, the Norwegian cell phone company Telnor found its 29.9% stake in Vimpelcom, a valuable Russian cell phone company, seized by a Siberian court at the behest of Alfa Group, which also was BP's partner in the BP-TNK venture. Alfa had brought suit against Telnor for allegedly interfering with Vimpelcom's expansion into Ukraine, where Telnor had a stake in other telecommunications providers. At Alfa's behest, the Siberian court fined Telnor $1.7 billion and then seized Telnor's shares in Vimpelcom in payment. Andrew E. Kramer, Norwegian Stake in Russian Joint Venture Seized, New York Times, March 13, 2009.

6.   On reflection, what are the strengths and weaknesses of a joint venture in comparison with a PSA? Which more clearly specifies the rights and duties of the foreign investor? Is clarity necessarily good?

7.   We will revisit dispute resolution with respect to particular transactional structures in the next Chapter. One should not lose sight, however, of the central point that dispute resolution may neither constrain inappropriate behavior nor fully compensate the victim. Transactors enter in a relationship expecting to do well, not with the intention of buying a lawsuit. What kinds of transactional structures encourage parties to work out their disagreements without resort to formal mechanisms? Is this a strength or a weakness?

C. EXPROPRIATION

To one degree or another, all property rights exist at the pleasure of the state. In almost all legal systems, the question is not whether the state has the power to take private property from its owners, but rather the limits on such takings and the terms of compensation. The Takings Clause of the U.S. Constitution expresses two important limits: The taking must be for a public purpose and the state must provide just compensation. A secondary question is the effectiveness of the institutions that enforce these limits. U.S. courts have a mixed record in this respect, but they generally have manifested a greater willingness to challenge government decisions than have the courts of emerging market countries.

Dissatisfied with the level of security of property rights provided under local law, foreign investors over the last fifty years increasingly have turned to international treaties, particularly bilateral investment treaties, and international enforcement mechanisms to bolster the protection of their interests. The treaties vary, but in general they allow an investor to receive compensation (but not the return of the investment) if government action is not for a public purpose, is arbitrary or discriminatory, or if local law does not provide prompt and full compensation. In the Documents Supplement we provide the 2012 U.S. Model Bilateral Investment Treaty. Its Article 5 describes the Minimum Standard of Treatment for an investor, while Article 6 covers Expropriation and Compensation. Over the last thirty years, investors have had direct access to enforcement mechanisms in the form of arbitral tribunals, typically organized by the World Bank's International Center for the Settlement of Investment Disputes (ICSID).

The following case illustrates how the international law regulating government expropriation of property works.

AIG Capital Partners Inc. and CJSC Tema Real Estate Company v. Republic of Kazakhstan

(ICSID Case No. Arb/01/6)
11 ICSID Reports 3
7 October 2003

1. INTRODUCTION

1.1 On October 5, 2001, the International Centre for Settlement of Investment Disputes ("ICSID" or "the Centre") notified to the above mentioned parties that this Arbitral Tribunal in ICSID Case No. ARB/01/6 was deemed to be constituted—whether validly or otherwise is one of the preliminary questions, amongst others, that arise for determination in this case.

This case arises out of a Request for Arbitration filed on May 3, 2001 by AIG Capital Partners Inc.("AIG" or "the first Claimant") and CJSC Tema Real Estate Company ("Tema" or "the second Claimant")—(jointly referred to as "the Claimants")—with the Centre requesting for arbitration of an "investment dispute" with the Republic of Kazakhstan ("Kazakhstan" or "the Respondent"). The claim in the Request for Arbitration arises out of the alleged expropriation of the Claimants' investment in a Real Estate Development Project in Kazakhstan, before the construction of the Project had been completed. The Request for Arbitration was made by the Claimants pursuant to and relying upon:

i. Article 36 of the 1965 Washington Convention on the Settlement of Investment Disputes between States and Nationals of Other States ("the Convention").

ii. Rules 1–4 of the Rules of Procedure for the Institution of Conciliation and Arbitration Proceedings ("Institution Rules").

iii. Article VI of the Treaty dated May 19, 1992 between the United States of America and the Republic of Kazakhstan Concerning the Reciprocal Encouragement and Protection of Investment ("the BIT" or "the Treaty").

2. THE PARTIES

2.1 The first Claimant, AIG, is a corporation constituted under the laws of Delaware (USA) and is entirely owned and controlled by a holding company, American International Group Inc. Also incorporated in Delaware (USA). AIG, through American International Group Inc. And its subsidiaries (including AIG Silk Road Investors Inc.—a US Company), is engaged in a broad range of activities and services world-wide including financial services. The second Claimant, Tema, is a joint venture company ("the Joint Venture") incorporated in Kazakhstan comprising (34%) LLP Tema (a Kazakhstan Real Estate Development Company) and (66%) AIG Silk Road Investment I Ltd (a Bermuda Company), a wholly owned subsidiary of AIG Silk Road Fund Ltd (a Bermuda Company). The entire voting power and all voting rights of the AIG Silk Road Fund Ltd are vested solely and exclusively in the holders of Class A shares viz. AIG Silk Road Investors Inc. USA, and AIG (Claimant No.1) is entitled to exercise all voting rights in respect of these Class A shares of AIG Silk Road Fund Ltd owned by AIG Silk Road Investors Inc., USA.

The Respondent, the Republic of Kazakhstan, has been an independent sovereign State since 1991.

2.2 The BIT was signed by the parties on May 17, 1992 and on exchange of instruments of ratification it came into force on January 12, 1994.

The United States of America (hereinafter referred to as the "US" or "USA") and the Republic of Kazakhstan are parties to the Convention—the Convention was signed by the USA on August 27, 1965, ratified on June 10, 1966 and came into force on October 14, 1966; the Convention was signed by the Republic of Kazakhstan on July 23, 1992, ratified on September 21, 2000 and came into force on October 21, 2000. The Request for Arbitration—in respect of the Claimants' alleged investment dispute with the Respondent—was filed with the Centre on May 3, 2001 relying on the provisions both of the Convention, as well as the Bilateral Investment Treaty.

3. PROCEDURAL HISTORY OF THE CASE

3.2 The facts as stated in the Request for Arbitration—and later supported by documentary evidence filed by the Claimants (and indicated in footnotes)—are as follows:

A. AIG, the first Claimant, had established AIG Silk Road Fund Limited, a private equity fund organized under the laws of Bermuda ("the Fund") to make equity investments in projects throughout Central Asia and the Caucasus. AIG Silk Road Fund Ltd ("the Fund") was controlled by AIG through AIG Silk Road Investors Inc.(a US Company). The Fund established two wholly owned subsidiaries: AIG Silk Road Investment I Limited ("the Investment Company", a Bermuda Company) and Kazakhstan Housing Limited ("the Financing Company"—also a Bermuda Company) to invest in a real estate project in Kazakhstan ("the Project"). AIG directly controls AIG Silk Road Investors Inc.(a US Company), which directly controls the Fund and its two subsidiaries (viz. The Investment Company and the Financing Company). The Investment Company is the majority owner of (66%) and directly controls the Joint Venture (Claimant No.2). Accordingly, AIG indirectly controls the Fund, the Investment Company, the Finance Company and the Joint Venture . . . ;

B. that the investment was in a Project—a residential housing complex to be called "Crystal Air Village" in Almaty— expected to involve a total investment of approximately USD 16.3 million over a three-year period; to implement this investment the Fund, through its wholly owned subsidiary (the AIG Silk Road Investment I Limited—"the Investment Company"), entered into a joint venture with LLP Tema (a Kazakhstan Company owned and controlled by Kazakhstani principals); the majority ownership and control of this joint venture being vested in the Investment Company which was in turn controlled by the Fund (AIG Silk Road Fund Limited), and indirectly and ultimately controlled by AIG (Claimant No.1);

C. that with financial assistance from the Fund, LLP Tema purchased for the Joint Venture ten hectares of land on which it was intended to construct the "Crystal Air Village": the land (the Project Property) was located in one of the most exclusive residential areas of Almaty, adjacent to the private residence of the President of Kazakhstan; subsequent to its purchase by LLP Tema, the property was assigned in May 1999 to the Joint Venture for the purpose of the Project.

D. that as required by the municipal laws of Kazakhstan, the purchase of the Project Property and its intended use as the site for the Crystal Air Village was specifically approved by local governmental authorities namely the Karasai Raion Committee on Management of Land Resources and the Almaty Oblast. Administration and all necessary building permits were also obtained for the Project;

E. that the Project itself was approved by Kazakhstan's Agency on Investment with which the Joint Venture had entered into a written agreement on December 13, 1999 which constituted further tacit approval of the Project; the agreement dated December 13, 1999 obligated the Investment Agency to act as an advocate for the investor in the event of any dispute with other agencies or instrumentalities of the Government of Kazakhstan; the investment agreement was also registered by the Investment Agency of the Republic of Kazakhstan by means of a Certificate dated December 13, 1999, which recognized the purpose of the Project, viz. "Construction of residential complex Crystal Air in Almaty suburb";

F. that after the Project Property was purchased, AIG, through affiliated companies, began the design, engineering, procurement and the financing work required to implement the Project, and retained various consultants and contractors for that purpose; it also built engineering networks and implemented other improvements on the Project Property. The Joint Venture then entered into a USD 7.3 million contract with Tuna LLP, a Kazakhstan subsidiary of the Turkish Architectural and Design Company (Tuna Insaat Sanayi ve Ticaret) for the construction of the first phase of the Project; the Joint Venture also retained Scott Holland Estates, a Kazakhstan company owned by UK interests, to undertake a full scale marketing and advertising campaign, and (it is stated that) Scott Holland Estates launched a marketing programme geared towards the high-end market based on a combination of direct marketing contracts and various types of advertising and made presentations to prospective clients; "all told approximately a sum of USD 3.5 million was spent in designing and implementing the Project; before the Government (of Kazakhstan) ordered the Joint Venture to permanently halt construction";

G. that on February 26, 2000, the Government of Kazakhstan verbally notified the Joint Venture that it had decided to cancel the Project for the reason that the Project Property was needed for "a national arboretum";

H. that on March 1, 2000, the Joint Venture wrote to the Chairman of the Investment Agency, explaining what had happened, requesting the Agency's assistance pursuant to the investment agreement dated December 13, 1999. In response, the Chairman of the Agency wrote a letter to the Akim (Governor) of the Almaty Oblast stating that the rights of an Investor having been violated by the actions of the Government the Investment Agency should be informed (by the Akim) of the reasons for the decision to terminate the investment and the intentions of the Almaty Oblast management in this regard;

I. that on March 2, 2000, representatives of the Fund met with the Akim of the Almaty Oblast, who said that he had made "a mistake" in having the Oblast administration permit the sale of the Project Property to the Joint Venture and to issue the necessary approvals for the construction of the Crystal Air Compound on the Project Property. He (the

Akim) stated that notwithstanding the authorization to purchase the site, the Joint Venture would not be permitted to construct the residential compound on the Project Property; he said that it was a decision made at the highest levels of the Government and that the only recourse available to the Joint Venture and the Fund would be to construct their residential compound on an alternate site which was offered;

J. that on March 17, 2000, the Oblast issued a resolution (Resolution No.3–79) ordering the transfer of the Project Property, and also other areas, to the City of Almaty. This resolution provided for compensation to agricultural users in other areas for the taking of their property, but offered no compensation to the Joint Venture. On March 20, 2000, the Investment Agency received a letter from the Almaty Oblast declaring invalid the construction permits issued for the Project—permits that had been previously authorized by the Oblast;

K. that on April 6, 2000, the Almaty City State Architecture and Construction Inspection Agency issued an Ordinance ordering that all work on the Project Property be stopped;

L. that in late February 2001, the Respondent, through the City of Almaty, physically seized the Project Property and began earthworks on it;

M. that these acts of the political subdivisions of Kazakhstan effectively resulted in the expropriation of the investment of AIG and the joint venture, and AIG and the Joint Venture had no choice but to accept the fact that the Respondent had terminated the Project;

. . .

10. ON MERITS

10.1.1   *Applicable Law*

10.1.2   Article 42(1) of the Convention deals with the law applicable to an investment dispute. It provides that the Tribunal shall decide a dispute in accordance with such rules as may be agreed by the parties. In the absence of agreement it shall apply the law of the host State and "such rules of international law as may be applicable". Historically, treaties (whether bilateral or multilateral) are an acknowledged source of international law—such treaties are often referred to as "law-making treaties". In principle, all treaties are law-making in as much as they lay down rules of conduct which the parties are bound to observe as law. Bilateral treaties are law-making in the narrow sense that the rights and obligations to which they give rise are legally binding on the parties to them.

The function of international law under Article 42(1) is to close gaps in domestic law as well as to remedy any violation of international law which may arise through the application of the host State's law.

10.1.3   The BIT itself establishes a rule of law as between the parties thereto: Article VI(I) of the BIT provides that an investment dispute (for the purposes of that Article) is a dispute between a party and a national or company of the other party that arises out of or relates to inter alia "an investment agreement between that party and such national or company" as well as "an investment authorisation granted by that Party's foreign investment authority to such national or company". Contract No.0159–12–99 dated December 13, 1999 is the Investment contract or authorization with respect to which an investment dispute has been raised—by the Claimants in the instant case: [it] has been entered into by the Claimant No.2 (the Joint Venture) with the Agency of the Republic of Kazakhstan for investment—the only State body invested with authority to conduct negotiations, establish conditions and sign contracts with Investors making direct investments in the Republic of Kazakhstan. The object of Contract No.0159–12–99 is to establish a certain legal framework regulating relationships between the Agency and the Investor in accordance with the legislation of the Republic of Kazakhstan for the purpose of providing various incentives and State support of investment activity in the construction sector of commercial housing. The Investment Agreement/authorization specifically provides that the applicable law, "unless otherwise stipulated by International Treaties signed by the Republic of Kazakhstan", shall be the law of the Republic of Kazakhstan. The law of the Republic of Kazakhstan on Foreign Investments of December 27, 1994 and the law of Kazakhstan [on] State support of Direct Investments of February 28, 1997 are the relevant basic laws of the host State.

10.1.4   In the circumstances the Tribunal holds that the applicable law in this case is the law of the Republic of Kazakhstan (State party to the dispute)—in particular that which is contained in Claimants' Exhibit Nos.2 and 34—read with and controlled by the provisions contained in the BIT.

10.3 Expropriation

10.3.1   Legal Position

Article HI of the BIT reflects a balance between the legitimate interests of the Contracting State where the investment is made and the need to protect from arbitrary action by that State those who provide foreign capital—particularly since such capital is essential to the full development of natural resources of any State and would not be forthcoming unless assured of reasonable protection.

Article III incorporates into the BIT international law standards for "expropriation" and "nationalisation". Paragraph 1 describes the general rights of investors and the obligation of the parties with respect to expropriation and nationalization: they apply to direct and indirect measures (of the State) tantamount to expropriation or nationalization— i.e., to what are known as "creeping expropriations" which result in substantial deprivation of the benefit of an investment without taking away of the title to the investment. Expropriation (in relation to investments) conveys in a general sense the deprivation of an owner of his investment and its equivalent—i.e., to a "taking" of that investment. Expropriations ("or measures tantamount to expropriation") include not only open deliberate and acknowledged takings of property (such as outright seizure or formal or obligatory transfer of title in favour of the Host State) but also covert or incidental interference with the use of property which has the effect of depriving the owner in whole or in significant part of the use or reasonably to be expected benefit of property even if not necessarily to the obvious benefit of the Host State.

10.3.2   Factual Position: Expropriation of Claimants' Investment

The following factual position regarding "expropriation" or "measures tantamount to expropriation" emerges from the evidence oral and documentary produced by the parties:

(a) That on February 18, 2000, the Joint Venture received an oral request (telephone call) from the Chairman of the Oblast Land Committee, Mr Nauryzbay Taubaev, to the effect that a billboard which had been put up three months back advertising the Crystal Air Village Project be removed from the Project Property. Mr Taubaev said that the billboard was offensive to low-income residents of Almaty who could not afford the advertised project. Accordingly, the Joint Venture removed the billboard, "for fear of the billboard being taken down forcibly and damaged".

This part of the evidence was not contradicted by the Respondent; Mr N. Taubaev Chairman of the Oblast Land Committee did not attend the hearings or give any oral evidence on behalf of the Respondent. His absence is the more significant since Mr Nurkadilov (at the relevant time the Akim of Almaty Oblast) who did give evidence for the Respondent deposed that the Land Committee did not have information and was not aware of "the fact" that according to the general plan of the City the land which was given to Talap to build the residential compound was to be developed as a green area for Almaty and the Land Committee made a "mistake" when it gave its consent: "According to that same general plan, they were supposed to develop a Green Area for Almaty. The Land Committee did not have the information or it was not aware of this . . . ": there is no independent evidence to corroborate this assertion viz. That the Land Committee made a mistake and/or was unaware of building construction being not permitted on the Project Site Property, and the person who could have deposed to this as a fact was Mr N. Taubaev, Chairman of the Oblast Land Committee, whose non-availability to give evidence for the Respondent is neither explained nor accounted for.

(b) That on February 26, 2000, the Joint Venture received a telephone call from the Chairman of the Oblast Architectural Committee, Mr Sairan Fazylov, who said that the Joint Venture must stop construction of the Crystal Air Village project because the Project Property was to be taken for use "as an arboretum". After the Joint Venture was told to stop construction Mr Nurkadilov, Akim of Almaty Oblast, was contacted and he confirmed this.

. . .

(c) That in response to the telephone calls from Mr Taubaev and Mr Fazylov, the Claimants requested a meeting with Mr Nurkadilov, the Akim of the Almaty Oblast.

(d) That the Claimants' representatives met with Mr Nurkadilov on 2 March 2000. At this meeting, Mr Nurkadilov confirmed to the Claimants that their property was being taken for use as an arboretum and that they must therefore stop construction of the Crystal Air Village Project.

(e) That following the meeting with Mr Nurkadilov, the Claimants "strongly persuaded for nearly four months" (i.e., persuaded governmental authorities) to reverse the Government's decision to cancel the Crystal Air Village Project. The Claimants even sought and obtained the intervention of US Ambassador to Kazakhstan, Richard Jones. The Claimants and Ambassador Jones both wrote to President Nazarbayev's advisor, Mr Bolat Utemuratov, seeking to have Mr Nurkadilov's decision to cancel the Project overturned. The Claimants also met repeatedly with Mr Dulat Kuanyshev, the Chairman of the Agency for Investment, which represents the Republic of Kazakhstan in its dealing with foreign investors. At the Claimants' request Mr Kuanyshev wrote Mr Nurkadilov warning him of the legal implications of his decision to cancel the Project and asking for an explanation of that decision. The Claimants also met with the Mayor of the City of Almaty, Mr Victor Khrapunov, because they were told that their property was being transferred to the City and it was the City that would build the arboretum. By letter dated March 21, 2000, Mr Scott Foushee, a Managing Director of Claimant No. I and the Managing Director of Claimant No.2, wrote the Advisor to the President of Kazakhstan informing him of the Akim's intimation to confiscate the Project Property in order to construct a National Arboretum (a copy of this was forwarded to the Prime Minister of Kazakhstan): this document is also on record.

(f) That on April 6, 2000, the Architecture and Construction Department of the City of Almaty issued a Resolution ordering the Joint Venture to suspend all works of construction of the Project.

(g) That on May 15, 2000, when the Joint Venture attempted to resume construction on the Project Property, the City authorities, accompanied by police, expelled the Joint Venture's contractor from the site.

(h) That the Fund's Investment Committee decided not to proceed further with the Project, to mitigate their mounting losses, and to release the construction contractor. Accordingly, the Joint Venture invoked force majeure, and terminated the construction contract on June 16, 2000, paying $182,000 in furtherance of a mutual release of claims.

(i) The Claimants treated the date of expropriation as June 16, 2000 and on July 17, 2000 a Notice of Investment Dispute was submitted by AIG Silk Road Fund pursuant to Article VI of the BIT and Article 27 of the Law of Kazakhstan on Foreign Investments dated December 27, 1994.

(j) That on August 2, 2000, the Chairman of the Agency for Investment, Mr Dulat Kuanyshev, wrote to the First Deputy Prime Minister, Mr Alexander Pavlov, concerning the Notice of Investment Dispute filed by AIG Silk Road Fund, Ltd on July 17, 2000. In this letter, the Chairman stated:

> An analysis of the notice submitted and the preceding correspondence points to violation of a series of legal procedures concerning the seizure of the land plot owned by CJSC Tema Real Estate Company. Given all of the above, with the aim of preventing the dispute from going to international arbitration, which could prove very expensive for the government of the Republic of Kazakhstan, we think it acceptable to seek a path to constructively resolve this conflict in an out-of-court settlement.

(k) That to consider the notice of Investment Dispute on September 2000, an ad hoc Working Group (Protocol of Inter-Ministry Working Group) was set up consisting of representatives of the Foreign Ministry, the Ministry of Finance, the Ministry of Justice, the Agency for Investment, the Almaty Oblast and the City of Almaty: these representatives concluded that the cancellation of the Project was "in violation of [applicable] legislation". The Working Group recommended that the Akim's order to stop construction of the Project be invalidated and the Project Property be returned to the Joint Venture, or if this was not possible, that the Joint Venture be compensated for the taking of the Property.

(l) That, inexplicably, and despite what was stated in the letter of Mr Idrissov (March 13, 2001) to the Deputy Prime Minister—recommending that the prior decision of the Local Executive Body which was "in breach of certain procedures" be cancelled—on April 2, 2001, transfer of Project Property from Almaty Oblast to City of Almaty was decreed.

...

(o) The case suggested to the Claimants' witnesses on behalf of the Respondent, and also mentioned in the arguments of the Respondent, that the Akim Oblast had no authority at all to grant the construction permits on the Project Property or that there had been a mistake in granting them—because of some lack of authority—has not been established by reference to any law of Kazakhstan. On the contrary what is established on the evidence is that the cancellation of the construction permits and continuous course of impediments to the Project being proceeded with on the Project site, were contrary to procedures established by Kazakhstan law.

10.3.3   In the circumstances aforesaid the Tribunal holds:

(a) That it has been proved that the investment of the Claimants was expropriated, directly or indirectly through "measures tantamount to expropriation" (Article III(1) of the BIT); the date of taking was treated according to the Claimants as June 16, 2001 [*sic*], shortly after the date on which the Claimants were physically and forcibly dispossessed from the project site (May 15, 2000)—making their ownership rights to the plot allocated practically useless. By May–June 2000 the practical and economic use of the Project Property by the Claimants was irretrievably lost—and could not thereafter be used for development purposes.

(b) The later recommendation of the Working Group to revoke the "expropriation" (even though it was at a very belated stage) was never finally accepted by the Government: in any event the Claimants were never informed of the same, and

(c) The Tribunal also holds that the expropriation of the Project Property was not in accordance with "procedures established by current (Kazakhstan) legislation".

10.4   *Was the Expropriation for a Public Purpose? Was there any Direct Intervention by the President of Kazakhstan in the Taking as Suggested in the Evidence?*

10.4.1   Under Article 111(1) of the BIT investments shall not be expropriated or nationalized either directly or indirectly through measures tantamount to expropriation or nationalization "except for a public purpose . . . ". This is only a reiteration of one of the essential elements of State sovereignty viz. The right to take by compulsory acquisition private property for public purposes: the fact-situation in this case is that there is no dispute whatever between the parties that the "taking" was for an arboretum or public park, which is manifestly a "public purpose". The Tribunal holds that the taking was for a public purpose.

10.4.2   However, in the course of the evidence of Boris Evseev, it was alleged that the President of Kazakhstan was involved and implicated in the decision to cancel the project. This assertion must now be dealt with.

. . .

10.4.4   In the Request for Arbitration, the only mention of the President of Kazakhstan is in the context that the Project Property was located in one of the most exclusive residential areas of Almaty, "adjacent to the private residence of the President of the Republic of Kazakhstan" (page 3 of the Request for Arbitration).[The] verbal intimation to the Joint Venture that the Government had decided to cancel the project (February 26, 2000) was "for the purported reason that it was needed for a national arboretum"; this is further amplified by the statement (in the Request for Arbitration) that on March 2, 2000, the Representatives of the Fund and the Joint Venture met with the Akim of the Almaty Oblast, who said he had made a "mistake" [in] having the Oblast Administration permit the sale of the Project Property to the Joint Venture. There is no mention in the Request for Arbitration that it was at the express instance and request of the President of the Republic of Kazakhstan that the project was cancelled. In the Claimants' Memorial (page 22) it is once again mentioned that on February 26, the Chairman of the Oblast Architectural Committee (Mr Sairan Fazylov) stated that the Oblast Administration had decided to take the Project Property for use as an arboretum and that the construction on the property should cease. No mention of the President is made. It is however stated that the mistake of the Akim was that he had failed to obtain the permission of the President before authorizing commercial authorization of the project.

10.4.5   It is in the oral evidence (of the Claimants' witness Boris Evseev) that it is sought to directly implicate the President with regard to cancellation of the project . . .

10.4.6   In the Claimants' Post-hearing Memorial filed on October 18, 2002 there is no mention of the direct intervention of the President of Kazakhstan—and what is more significant, no reliance is placed on the oral evidence of [Mr] Boris Evseev given in that behalf. In fact when dealing with Respondent's liability under the BIT there is no reference to Mr Boris Evseev's evidence that the billboard advertising the Crystal Air Village be removed since it was offensive to the President.

And even with regard to the meeting of March 2, 2000 with Mr Nurkadilov, it is stated that Mr Nurkadilov confirmed that the property was being taken to build an arboretum and therefore construction must stop (no mention of the President). . . .

10.4.7   The Tribunal finds the invocation of the name of the President of the Republic of Kazakhstan and his alleged involvement with the cancellation of the project (mentioned in the oral evidence of Mr Boris Evseev) not proven.

. . .

10.5   Was the Expropriation Arbitrary?

10.5.1   Expropriation of alien property is not itself contrary to international law provided certain conditions are met, and perhaps the most clearly established condition is that expropriation must not be arbitrary (i.e., must not be contrary to "the due process of law") and must be based on the application of duly adopted laws. The requirement that expropriation should be in a non-discriminatory manner (i.e., as between alien and national) and in accordance with due process is also widely accepted, and is relevant to the assessment whether the expropriation was or was not arbitrary and in furtherance of the public interest. . . .

10.5.2   In the facts and circumstances of the case—particularly the events that occurred between February [and] May 2000—and in the light of the findings recorded in the Minutes of the high-powered Working Group (of September 5, 2000) to the effect that the decision of the local executive body impeding implementation of construction by the investor on the Project Property was adopted "in violation of the procedures established by the current legislation", this Tribunal records a finding that the taking (by measures tantamount to expropriation) was arbitrary, in wilful disregard of due process of law and the series of acts from February 26, 2000 and culminating in the events of May 15, 2000 were shocking to "all sense of juridical propriety".

Notes

1.   The Tribunal awarded AIG approximately $7 million on compensation. Typically states pay ICSID awards as a matter of course, absent some credible argument about misconduct on the part of the tribunal. Kazakhstan, however, refused to honor the award. AIG then brought suit in the United Kingdom, seeking to levy against funds held by the Kazakh Central Bank on behalf of the state energy fund. A British Court ruled that sovereign immunity barred attachment of this account. *AIG Capital Partners Inc. v. Kazakhstan*, E.W.H. C. 2239 (Comm.), I.I.C. 9 (2005). Kazakhstan later paid the award, reportedly after the U.S. government raised the issue in the context of negotiations over Kazakhstan's entry into the World Trade Organization.

2.   The conduct of the Kazakh government here was transparent. There was little question but that it had behaved illegally. The interesting question was one of making the legal remedy effective. More difficult are cases where the host government imposes new regulatory requirements that, in and of themselves, reflect legitimate government policies, but does so in a way that upsets the reasonable expectations of a foreign investor. Such behavior can give rise to a claim of indirect or "creeping" expropriation. Consider the analysis of this issue in the following case.

Metalclad Corporation, Claimant
and the United Mexican States,
Respondent

Case No. ARB(AF)/97/1
International Center for Settlement of Investment Disputes (Additional Facility)
September 2, 2000

[For the background of the dispute, see the excerpts earlier in this chapter.]

C.   *NAFTA, Article 1110: Expropriation*

102. NAFTA Article 1110 provides that "[n]o party shall directly or indirectly . . . Expropriate an investment . . . Or take a measure tantamount to . . . Expropriation . . . Except: (a) for a public purpose; (b) on a non discriminatory basis; (c) in accordance with due process of law and Article 1105(1); and (d) on payment of compensation. . . ." "A measure" is defined in Article 201(1) as including "any law, regulation, procedure, requirement or practice."

103. Thus, expropriation under NAFTA includes not only open, deliberate and acknowledged takings of property, such as outright seizure or formal or obligatory transfer of title in favor of the host State, but also covert or incidental interference with the use of property which has the effect of depriving the owner, in whole or in significant part, of the use or reasonably to be expected economic benefit of property even if not necessarily to the obvious benefit of the host State.

104. By permitting or tolerating the conduct of Guadalcazar in relation to Metalclad which the Tribunal has already held amounts to unfair and inequitable treatment breaching Article 1105 and by thus participating or acquiescing in the denial to Metalclad of the right to operate the landfill, notwithstanding the fact that the project was fully approved and endorsed by the federal government, Mexico must be held to have taken a measure tantamount to expropriation in violation of NAFTA Article 1110(1).

105. The Tribunal holds that the exclusive authority for siting and permitting a hazardous waste landfill resides with the Mexican federal government. This finding is consistent with the testimony of the Secretary of SEMARNAP and, as stated above, is consistent with the express language of the LGEEPA.

106. As determined earlier, the Municipality denied the local construction permit in part because of the Municipality's perception of the adverse environmental effects of the hazardous waste landfill and the geological unsuitability of the landfill site. In so doing, the Municipality acted outside its authority. As stated above, the Municipality's denial of the construction permit without any basis in the proposed physical construction or any defect in the site, and extended by its subsequent administrative and judicial actions regarding the *Convenio,* effectively and unlawfully prevented the Claimant's operation of the landfill.

107. These measures, taken together with the representations of the Mexican federal government, on which Metalclad relied, and the absence of a timely, orderly or substantive basis for the denial by the Municipality of the local construction permit, amount to an indirect expropriation.

NOTES

1. What does a finding of expropriation add to a determination that Mexico violated its obligation to provide fair and equitable treatment? What distinguishes expropriation issues?

2. Many investment treaties limit the applicability of the obligation to provide fair and equitable treatment, and some state categorically that this obligation is inapplicable to tax issues. Why do you think states exempt taxation from fair and equitable treatment? To what extent does this sharpen the issue of whether indirect expropriation has occurred?

3. The tribunal's determination that an expropriation occurred rested in part on its determination that, as a matter of Mexican law, the Municipality lacked the authority to regulate a hazardous waste facility. Why was it necessary to make this determination? Is it binding on Mexico in other cases? Does this illustrate why international arbitration is preferred by foreign investors?

D. NEGOTIATION EXERCISE—NEGOTIATING THE TERMS OF A PRODUCTION SHARING AGREEMENT

The teams will negotiate some of the basic terms and conditions of a production sharing agreement ("PSA") covering the exploration, development and production of crude oil in Block 21, located onshore in the northern region of Turkana in the Republic of Kenya. Global Oil Company, Inc. ("Global"), a corporation organized and existing under the laws of the State of Delaware, USA, submitted an application to the Government of Kenya (the "Government") for the right to negotiate the terms of the PSA for Block 21 and the Minister of Energy has granted the application.

Global intends to use its wholly owned subsidiary, Global Oil Company Kenya Limited ("Global Kenya"), a corporation organized and existing under the laws of Kenya, as the contracting entity under the PSA. The Government has given the authority to negotiate the PSA to the National Oil Corporation of Kenya ("NOCK"), a company that is wholly owned by the Government and incorporated under the laws of Kenya. Global has submitted enough background information to convince the Government that Global has all of the resources that may be required to conduct the exploration, development and production operations, and is able to provide the highest levels of support in connection with the resulting financial obligations.

The project involves the exploration of Block 21, a block close to other blocks in which other companies made commercial discoveries of crude oil reserves in 2011. It also entails the possible development, production, transportation and refining of any crude oil that Global may discover in Block 21. The parties assume that the exploration activities will include seismic data gathering and interpretation and exploration drilling. Assume that Kenya and the US have not entered into a BIT.

The Global and NOCK negotiating teams have each received separate special instructions from management setting out the goals of their initial negotiating session. These instructions are to be kept confidential. Your task will be to prepare a memorandum that describes the basic agreement between Global and NOCK with respect to the issues set forth below. Assume that NOCK has been given the authority by the Government to grant the exclusive rights under a PSA to Global Kenya in accordance with the Petroleum (Exploration and Production) Act of 1986.

1. Term and Relinquishment. Decide on the term of the Initial Exploration Period and the First and Second Additional Exploration Periods under Article 2 of the PSA, as well as the percentage amount of the contract area that will be relinquished at the end of the various Exploration Periods under Article 3.

2. Work Program and Expenditure Obligations. Decide on the Minimum Exploration Work and Expenditure Obligations under Article 4 of the PSA.

3. Production Sharing. Determine the share of the production that will be devoted to cost recovery oil and how the parties will divide the profit oil under Article 27 of the PSA.

4. Government Participation. Determine the percentage amount of the participating interest that will be applicable to the Government's option to participate under Article 28 of the PSA.

5. Domestic Market Requirements. Agree on the amount of the production, if any, that will be devoted to the domestic market requirements of Kenya under Article 29.

6. Local Content. Decide on the amount of local content that will be included in Article 31 of the PSA in terms of Kenyan materials, supplies, services and equipment to be provided by local contractors during the Exploration Period, as well as standard to be used for comparing them with non-Kenyan bidders. In addition, decide on the percentage of Kenyan nationals that will be employed during the Exploration Period of the PSA.

7. Oversight. Determine what role, if any, NOCK or the Government will have in overseeing the project and its implementation by Global Kenya.

8. Stabilization. Decide on the details of the stabilization clause that will be used in Article 40(3) of the PSA, including the coverage of the clause, the procedures and time limits to be used and other applicable elements.

9. Dispute Resolution. Decide on the details of the dispute resolution clause that will be used for Articles 40 and 41 of the PSA, including the governing law, number of arbitrators, the type of arbitration rules that will be used, the place of arbitration and the waiver of sovereign immunity.

CHAPTER 6

DISPUTE RESOLUTION

Problems arise in any business transaction. Emerging markets by definition comprise societies undertaking social, economic and political, as well as legal change. This makes it more difficult to anticipate problems and provides a rich environment for disputes to fester and grow. In theory, lawyers are supposed to anticipate these difficulties and help to resolve them. In reality, the barriers may be insurmountable.

Most disputes never make it to formal procedures for their resolution. Some transactions put an aggrieved party in the position of retaliating. Banks can cut off future loans, for example, punishing a state enterprise or a government that fails to meet its obligations or disappoints the legitimate expectations of investors. Moreover, misconduct can harm a party's reputation, denying it future business opportunities with persons who see it as untrustworthy. Alternatively, parties may reach some reciprocal adjustment, thereby both enhancing their reputations as trustworthy business partners and inducing greater confidence between themselves.

In a few cases, "lawfare" breaks out. The aggrieved person might sue in a national court or, where a contract or governing law so provides, seek to arbitrate a dispute. Even though such formal dispute resolution is the exception, it is important. Sometimes a court or an arbitral award can provide some satisfaction. Moreover, the possibility that one side might invoke these procedures may affect the willingness of all the parties to seek an amicable settlement of their disagreements.

We recognize that international litigation and arbitration constitute an entirely separate law-school course. In this chapter we will focus on disputes where the parties are a foreign investor, on the one side, and an emerging-market government or state-owned enterprise, on the other side. As the cases indicate, satisfaction is hard to obtain, but not impossible.

A. LITIGATION AND ITS LIMITATIONS

Absent a prior promise to commit disputes to arbitration, an aggrieved party can seek relief through litigation in a national court. Two problems immediately arise. First, a foreign government or its enterprises might not be subject to jurisdiction in another country's courts. Second, even if a court issues a judgment, enforcement may present its own challenges. Consider the following case, which arose not long after the resumption of diplomatic relations between the People's Republic of China and the United States.

Jackson v. The People's Republic of China

United States Court of Appeals for the Eleventh Circuit
794 F.2d 1490 (1986)

■ GODBOLD, CHIEF JUDGE:

We must decide whether in this case the courts of the United States have subject matter jurisdiction over the People's Republic of China. This requires us to examine whether the Foreign Sovereign Immunities Act of 1976 (FSIA), 28 U.S.C. § 1330, 1391 and 1602, *et seq.*, which confers subject matter jurisdiction over foreign sovereigns (with various exceptions), is to be applied retroactively with respect to actions by the governments of China relating to bonds issued by the government of China in 1911.

Before reaching the central issue, we must decide whether the district court erred in setting aside a default judgment entered against the PRC.

The People's Republic (PRC) also raises as a preliminary issue whether, under principles of international law, despite the domestic law of the United States, the courts of the United States have no jurisdiction over any claims against the PRC as a sovereign nation.

. . .

We hold that the district court did not err in setting aside the default judgment against the PRC. And, reaching the central issue, we hold that the district court was correct in holding that it lacked subject matter jurisdiction because the FSIA did not apply retroactively to confer subject matter jurisdiction in this case.

I. *The facts and the proceedings in the district court*

In 1911 the Imperial Government of China issued bearer bonds to assist in financing the building of a section of the Hukuang Railway that runs between Guangzhou (Canton) and Beijing (Peking). The loan was for 6,000,000 pounds sterling, negotiated and participated in by a consortium of British, German, French and American banks. The loan agreement authorized the issuance of bonds for sale in the United States and bonds were sold to purchasers in this country.

Soon after the bonds were issued the Revolution of 1911 ensued, and the Republic of China supplanted the Imperial Chinese government. The Republic of China made interest payments on the Hukuang bonds until the mid-1930s when it began to have financial and other difficulties.

Plaintiffs introduced expert testimony in the district court attempting to show that the bonds were renegotiated in 1937 by an agreement between the Chinese Nationalist government and an American bondholders' committee representing the lenders, providing for an interim interest rate reduction and for amortization to begin again in 1949 and to be completed in 39 years from 1937, which would be 1976. Statements filed by the PRC say that renegotiation was discussed but no agreement reached. Plaintiffs say that the obligations under the bonds were "reaffirmed" by the Nationalist government just before its departure for Taiwan in 1948. The district court found that the renegotiation was never agreed upon, and that the bonds matured in 1951, the original maturity date. Plaintiffs assert that these findings are plainly erroneous.

This class suit was filed November 13, 1979. Jurisdiction was alleged under the FSIA. Service of process was carried out under 28 U.S.C. § 1608(a)(4). PRC responded with a diplomatic note to the Department of State asserting that it enjoyed absolute sovereign immunity. In October 1981 the district court certified a class consisting of all persons who, as of October 22, 1981, were holders of the bonds. On October 28, 1981 the district court held that service of process was proper and, PRC not having appeared, ordered a default. PRC was served with a copy of the class certification order and the notice of default but returned them to the State Department, reasserting absolute immunity.

At plaintiffs' request an evidentiary hearing was conducted. On September 2, 1982, the court held that it had subject matter jurisdiction and that plaintiffs were entitled to all unpaid principal and interest on the bonds, and it entered a judgment of $41,000,000-plus. The PRC sent a diplomatic note to the district court in January, 1983, stating that the rulings of the district court violated "basic norms of international law," and should the court proceed with the default judgment against China and attach China's properties in the United States, the Chinese government reserved its right to take "corresponding measures."

In mid-1983 the plaintiffs began efforts to execute on their judgment. In July or August 1983 the PRC appeared in the case for the first time, filing motions to vacate the judgment under Rule 60(b)(1), (4) and (6) and to dismiss the case. The United States, through the Departments of State and Justice, filed two statements of interest, supported by numerous documents, backing the PRC's motions.

The district court granted the motion to vacate and conducted an evidentiary hearing on the motion to dismiss and determined it would be treated as a motion for summary judgment. Plaintiffs presented expert testimony. PRC did not appear; the United States was present but did not participate. The district court entered an order dismissing the case on the ground that the FSIA did not have retroactive effect so as to confer subject matter jurisdiction over transactions that predated 1952.

In this court the PRC filed a brief but instructed its counsel not to appear for oral argument. The United States filed a statement of interest and was permitted to argue.

II. *Changing concepts of sovereign immunity under U.S. law*

For more than a century and a half, since *The Schooner Exchange v. McFaddon*, 11 U.S. (7 Cranch) 116, 137 (1812), the United States usually granted foreign sovereigns complete immunity from suit in the courts of this country. Under our law foreign sovereign immunity is a matter of grace and comity on the part of the United States and is not a restriction imposed by the Constitution itself. *Verlinden B.V. v. Central Bank of Nigeria*, 461 U.S. 480 (1983). Accordingly, until 1952, our courts consistently deferred to the decisions of the executive branch on whether to take jurisdiction of actions against foreign sovereigns and their instrumentalities. Ordinarily the State Department would request immunity in all actions against friendly foreign sovereigns. However, in the decade before 1952 the Supreme Court's doctrinal foundation for sovereign immunity began to shift from formal principles of international law to avoiding embarrassment to those responsible for the conduct of our foreign affairs.

In 1952 the State Department issued the "Tate Letter," which announced formal adoption by it of the "restrictive" theory of foreign sovereign immunity. Under this theory immunity is confined to suits involving the public acts of a foreign sovereign and does not extend to cases arising out of strictly commercial acts of a foreign state. After the Tate Letter the executive, acting through the State Department, usually would make "suggestions" on whether sovereign immunity should be recognized by a court, and courts generally abided these suggestions. This proved troublesome, because foreign nations at times placed diplomatic pressure on the State Department, and political considerations led to suggestions of immunity where it was not available under the restrictive theory. Moreover, foreign nations did not always make requests to the State Department, and responsibility fell to the courts to determine whether sovereign immunity existed. With two different branches involved the governing standards were neither clear nor uniform.

In 1976 Congress passed the FSIA, effective in January 1977.

> By reason of its authority over foreign commerce and foreign relations, Congress has the undisputed power to decide, as a matter of federal law, whether and under what circumstances foreign nations should be amenable to suit in the United States.

It was adopted to free the government from case by case diplomatic pressures, to clarify the governing standards, and to assure that decisions are made on purely legal grounds and under procedures that insure due process. In 28 U.S.C. § 1330 the Act confers jurisdiction of any in personam nonjury civil action against a foreign state with respect to which the foreign state is not entitled to immunity under §§ 1605–1607. The latter sections codify into federal law the restrictive theory of sovereign immunity. Thus in many instances the substantive immunity law issues arising out of the sovereign immunity sections, §§ 1605–1607, must be resolved to determine if the court has jurisdiction.

Both subject matter jurisdiction and personal jurisdiction turn on application of the substantive provisions of the FSIA. If none of the exceptions to sovereign immunity set forth in the Act applies, the court lacks both statutory subject matter jurisdiction and personal jurisdiction. In determining whether the court has jurisdiction through application of one of the exceptions, the court must apply the detailed federal law standards set forth in the Act itself.

III. *Absence of jurisdiction because of international law*

At the threshold China stands on the principle of absolute sovereign immunity as a fundamental aspect of its sovereignty. Its position is that under principles of international law it is immune from any suit in a domestic court of any other nation unless it consents. According to the United States' statement of interest:

> China's adherence to this principle results, in part, from its adverse experience with extraterritorial laws and jurisdiction of western powers [within China] in the nineteenth and early twentieth centuries.

China asserts that restrictive sovereign immunity has not become a rule of international law, although in recent years some nations have begun to follow it, but these are, China says, only a small number of nations and by and large do not include developing countries, which find restrictive sovereign immunity not in their interest.

China contends that the United States cannot, by a change in its domestic law, abrogate the long accepted international law principle of absolute sovereign immunity. Even though restrictive sovereign immunity may be a developing customary rule of international law, China says that it is not binding upon sovereign states that do not agree to it. Thus, according to China, restrictive sovereign immunity is applicable only within the group of nations that have adopted it and is not applicable to China, which continues to adhere to the principle of absolute sovereign immunity. Finally, China contends that even if sovereign immunity can be changed by the United States, to apply the change retroactively would violate international law.

The district court did not rule on these international law questions, since it held that the suit was barred under United States domestic law. We follow the same course.

. . .

We hold that the district court did not abuse its discretion in granting the PRC's motion under subsection (6) of Rule 60(b), which authorizes the court to set aside a judgment for all reasons except those set forth in the five preceding clauses. This subsection gives the courts ample power to vacate judgments whenever appropriate to accomplish justice. Relief under this clause, however, is an extraordinary remedy, which may be invoked only upon a showing of exceptional circumstances. This case presents extraordinary circumstances justifying the district court's exercise of its equitable discretion.

Until January 1, 1979 the United States recognized the Republic of China, not the PRC, as the sole government for all of China. After recognition of the PRC, and beginning as early as 1980, representatives of the State Department attempted to explain to the PRC that the issue of sovereign immunity in this case must be decided by the courts of the United States and could not be determined by the executive branch and that PRC should retain counsel to appear in the district court and urge sovereign immunity and any other defenses.

In 1983 the United States sent a delegation to Beijing, and six days of meetings ensued concerning major international matters. The Chinese leader Deng Xiaoping brought up the default judgment and indicated to Secretary of State Schultz that the PRC regarded it as a serious matter and a major irritant in bilateral relations with the United States. During 1983 the foreign minister of China presented the Secretary of State with an *Aide Memoire* stating that the PRC recognized no obligation to pay external debts incurred by earlier Chinese governments and that the PRC enjoyed absolute sovereign immunity. In additional meetings in Washington and Beijing the United States sought to assure China that it could appear through counsel without conceding jurisdiction under the FSIA and without waiving its position that it enjoyed absolute immunity under international law. The PRC reluctantly agreed to retain counsel to present its views in court.

The United States explained in its statements that because of the long absence of relations between the United States and the PRC there were only limited communications between the two governments on legal matters, leaving PRC authorities generally unfamiliar with United States judicial practice and procedure; that the Chinese view the bonds as an improper part of the Western powers' domination of China at the beginning of this century and as a direct cause of the Revolution of 1911; and that the PRC maintains that under the principle of non-liability for "odious debts" China bears no responsibility for the bonds.

In its statements of interest the United States urged that the default be set aside. In support of this position, Secretary of State Shultz filed an affidavit, setting out *inter alia*:

> The United States has had extensive consultations with the PRC [Peoples Republic of China] about this case and is informed about its facts and history. The United States believes that the PRC's initial failure to appear in these proceedings was based on its belief that international law did not require it to do so. . . . The United States has expended considerable diplomatic efforts over the last two and one-half years to persuade the PRC that it is appropriate under international and United States law, and in the best interest of bilateral relations between the two nations, that the PRC appear and present its defenses to this Court. . . . Permitting the PRC to have its day in court will significantly further United States foreign policy interests; conversely denying it that day in court is likely to have a negative impact on United States interests.

> * * *

> The present proceedings, and the default judgment against the PRC in particular, have become a significant issue in bilateral United States/China relations, as evidenced by Chairman Deng's personal representations to me in February [1983], by China's representations to other Department officials throughout the duration of this lawsuit, and by the repeated diplomatic notes from the PRC that have been filed in these proceedings. The manner in which these proceedings are finally resolved can be expected, therefore, to have ramifications for other important United States interests with respect to China.

Also the district court had been notified by the PRC that if China's property in the United States was attached it reserved its right to take "corresponding measures."

We hold that the district court did not abuse its discretion in setting aside the judgment under Rule 60(b)(6). . . .

V. *Jurisdiction under the FSIA*

In the district court, after the default was set aside, and before this court, the United States has asserted that the FSIA was not intended to apply to transactions that predate 1952.

. . .

We agree with the district court's general approach to retroactivity. Courts normally presume that a legislative enactment is to apply prospectively, the presumption is a strong one. We agree with the court's analysis of the language of the statute itself and of the legislative history. Indeed, both Senate and House Reports state that FSIA was not intended to affect the "substantive law of liability." We agree that to give the Act retrospective application to pre-1952 events would interfere with antecedent rights of other sovereigns (and also with antecedent principles of law that the United States followed until 1952). It would be manifestly unfair for the United States to modify the immunity afforded a foreign state in 1911 by the enactment of a statute nearly three quarters of a century later.

. . .

We find no case, and plaintiffs refer us to none, where the FSIA has been applied to confer subject matter jurisdiction over pre-1952 transactions, activities and events. . . .

NOTES

1. Note the procedural posture of the case. The Foreign Sovereign Immunities Act by its terms provides for jurisdiction over, and service of process for, any lawsuit brought in the United States against a foreign sovereign. At that point the foreign sovereign defendant is in legal jeopardy, in the sense that the court has acquired the power to enter a judgment against it. Whether such a judgment would have any practical effect, of course, remains another matter. Some sovereigns, regarding a suit in a foreign court as an affront to their dignity, will not deign to respond. The People's Republic initially took this path. As a result, the court entered a default judgment, even though as a technical matter it has the obligation, as well as the authority, to determine whether a statutory bar to its jurisdiction existed. Ultimately the People's Republic retained counsel, who requested the United States government to enter an appearance to support an assertion of immunity from the suit. The Department of State has primary responsibility for determining how the Foreign Sovereign Immunities Act, as well as common-law immunities that foreign officials may invoke, should apply in any given case. The Department of Justice in turn represents the United States government in court. In this case lawyers for both the People's Republic and the United States filed briefs, but only a lawyer representing the United States actually appeared before the court and argued on behalf of immunity.

2. The legal theory of the *Jackson* decision, namely that a sovereign's immunity depends on the state of the law at the time that the claim arose rather than at the time of the filing of suit, later was rejected by the Supreme Court. *Republic of Austria v. Altmann*, 541 U.S. 677 (2004). In that case the United States government argued that *Jackson* had reached the right result, but the Court was unpersuaded. It noted that the issue involved construction of a statute, namely the Foreign Sovereign Immunities Act, and that this was a distinctly judicial function. "While the United States' views on such an issue are of considerable interest to the Court, they merit no special deference." *Id.* at 701.

Another Supreme Court case, also decided after *Jackson*, makes clear that the issuance of bonds by a foreign state normally will constitute a commercial function falling within one of the exceptions to immunity provided by the Foreign Sovereign Immunities Act. *Republic of Argentina v. Weltover, Inc.*, 504 U.S. 607 (1992). This case, when combined with the holding in *Altmann*, indicates that, whatever other defenses to the suit that the People's Republic might have had, sovereign immunity probably did not exist. One should note that in most modern loan agreements, whether a syndicated bank loan or a bond issue, the lenders will insist on an express written waiver of sovereign immunity, as well as choosing a particular judicial forum, such as the Southern District of New York or the High Court in London, if the parties do not opt for arbitration).

3. Aside from sovereign immunity, what other defenses might the People's Republic have raised in this suit? How is it possible to bring a lawsuit for a debt that has been in default for decades? Are there other defenses that the People's Republic might have raised? Note that other defenses normally would be made without the support of the United States, which typically does not intervene in commercial litigation once the question of sovereign immunity has dropped out.

4. Recall the *Chang* case in Chapter 3. The bonds at issue here originated in the same era of Chinese history. Could China have argued that the foreign lenders knew, or should have known, that the bond proceeds would be used to maintain an illegitimate and corrupt regime, rather than to benefit the Chinese people? If this were true, could the People's Republic have argued that it was not bound by an "odious debt" that its predecessor had wrongfully incurred? For more on this doctrine, see Paul B. Stephan, *The Institutionalist Implications of an Odious Debt Doctrine*, 70 LAW & CONTEMP. PROBS. 213 (Summer 2007).

5. Suppose the People's Republic ultimately had lost this case. What would have happened? Note that the Foreign Sovereign Immunities Act provides much wider immunity from the seizure of a state's property than it does from a suit itself. Study 28 U.S.C. §§ 1609–11. As you can see, many assets that a foreign state might own in the United States cannot be used to satisfy a judgment.

6. Suppose the bondholders had won this case in the United States but could not track down any assets of the People's Republic against which they could execute a judgment. What would be left to them? Would a U.S. judgment have any effect in the People's Republic? Anywhere else? There are some regional treaty regimes that make judgments issued in one country enforceable in another, much as a judgment of a state court in one part of the United States is entitled, under the U.S. Constitution, to "full faith and credit" in the courts of the remaining U.S. states. U.S. Constitution Art. IV § 1. The most significant of these regimes covers the members of the European Union, as well as a few other European states. But there is no generally applicable treaty governing mutual enforcement of money judgments in commercial disputes, and the United States is not a party to any such treaty.

Foreign Law in Domestic Jurisdiction

Even if a case can be brought in a domestic court, the underlying rights might rest on foreign law. Suppose that this law is murky, but that one side has access to the relevant lawmakers and can induce them to produce friendly decisions that bear on the domestic dispute. To what extent should a domestic court defer to such decisions? For an unusual situation where a U.S. court refused to follow Russian judicial decisions because the court believed them to be improper, see the following case.

Films by Jove, Inc. v. Joseph Berov

United States Court for the Eastern District of New York
250 F. Supp. 2d 156 (2003)

■ TRAGER, DISTRICT J.

This litigation began in December of 1998 when plaintiffs Films By Jove, Inc. ("FBJ") and Soyuzmultfilm Studio ("SMS") brought an action for copyright infringement, breach of contract, unfair competition, and RICO violations against Joseph Berov ("Berov"), Natasha Orlova, Rigma America Corporation, and the St. Petersburg Publishing House and Group. A state-owned Russian company, the Federal State Unitarian Enterprise Soyuzmultfilm Studio ("FSUESMS"), subsequently intervened as a third-party plaintiff. The central dispute between the parties concerns the ownership of copyrights in approximately 1500 animated films created by a state-owned Soviet film studio, Soyuzmultfilm Studio, between 1946 and 1991.

On August 27, 2001, this court granted summary judgment in favor of the plaintiffs, relying primarily on the submissions of the parties' Soviet law experts, and also, in part, on interpretations of Soviet law from a series of decisions by the commercial courts of the Russian Federation, known as arbitrazh courts. On December 18, 2001, the Presidium of the High Arbitrazh Court of the Russian Federation issued an opinion apparently overruling two of these lower court opinions. Following the High Arbitrazh Court's ruling, as well as an October 2, 2001 decision from the Paris Court of Appeals, which defendants claim supports some of their arguments, defendants filed a motion, pursuant to Rule 60(b)(2) of the Federal Rules of Civil Procedure, for reconsideration of this court's August 27, 2001 decision, and for a stay of any enforcement proceedings pursuant to Rule 62(b).

. . .

Background

. . .

(6)
This Court's Ruling in Favor of Plaintiffs:
August 27, 2001

On August 27, 2001, this court granted summary judgment in favor of the plaintiffs, concluding that: 1) the copyrights in Soyuzmultfilm Studio's animated films belonged ab initio to the studio itself, rather than to the Soviet state; 2) these rights were transferred to the lease enterprise by operation of law in 1989, when the state enterprise was transformed into the lease enterprise and ceased to exist; 3) Perestroika reforms solidified the lease enterprise's rights of commercial exploitation in its copyrights; 4) accordingly, in 1992, the lease enterprise entered into a valid licensing agreement with FBJ, granting FBJ exclusive international distribution rights in Soyuzmultfilm Studio's animated films; and 5) the underlying copyrights, subject to FBJ's license, passed in 1999 to SMS, when the lease enterprise was reorganized as a joint stock company, still bearing the Soyuzmultfilm Studio name.

(7)
Presidium of the High Arbitrazh Court for the Russian Federation: December 18, 2001

On December 18, 2001, some four months after this court's August 27, 2001 decision, the Presidium of the High Arbitrazh Court for the Russian Federation issued a ruling overturning the reasoning of the April 3, 2001 decision of the Moscow Region Arbitrazh Appeals Court, and the June 4, 2001 decision of the Federal Arbitrazh Court for the District of Moscow. Again, the High Court's opinion does not explicitly address the issue of copyright ownership. In fact, as plaintiffs correctly point out, the word copyright appears nowhere in the opinion. The central issue in that litigation was the validity of FSUESMS's corporate registration. However, the High Arbitrazh Court did reach relevant conclusions regarding legal succession under the Fundamental Principles on Leasing—the same law under which plaintiffs have previously persuaded this court that the execution of the Soyuzmultfilm lease agreement in 1989 effected the transformation of the state enterprise film studio into the lease enterprise, triggering the transfer of the disputed copyrights to the lease enterprise by operation of law.

The High Arbitrazh Court begins by noting that the First Deputy Prosecutor General of the Russian Federation officially protested the [lower court] rulings, requesting that the court "exclude" several conclusions from the "motivational part," i.e., the reasoning, of those decisions. Specifically, the state prosecutor asked the High Arbitrazh Court to reverse the lower courts' conclusions:

> [1] about the state enterprise [Soyuzmultfilm Studio] being converted into a lease enterprise; [2] [that] the succession of rights of the lease enterprise based on the lease agreement is not restricted by the term of the agreement [; and] [3] [that SMS] is a legal successor of the state enterprise [Soyuzmultfilm Studio].

The High Arbitrazh Court ruled that the disputed court acts would be "canceled," and that the January 25, 2001 decision of the Moscow Region Arbitrazh Court would be left in effect:

> The Appeals Court made the conclusion that the activity of the state enterprise [Soyuzmultfilm Studio] ceased through the conversion into a lease enterprise and that the succession of rights of the lease enterprise based on the lease agreement is not restricted by the term of such agreement.
>
> This conclusion is made as a result of the wrong interpretation of law by the court.

In explaining the "grounds" for its conclusions, the court offered an interpretation of Article 16 of the "Fundamental Principles of Legislation of the USSR and Union Republics on Lease," the Soviet legislation governing the formation of lease enterprises. Like the January 25 decision that it reinstated, the High Court concluded that the relevant provisions of the leasing statute did not provide for the conversion of a state enterprise into a lease entity, and furthermore that any succession of rights from a state enterprise to the lease entity would not survive the expiration of the lease term.

Pursuant to Item 1, Article 16 of the Fundamentals of USSR and Soviet republics law on Leasing, not a state enterprise but an independent legal entity—such as an organization of lessees created by a labor collective of a state enterprise—is converted into a lease enterprise. The organization of lessees obtains the status of a lease enterprise after signing a lease agreement.

Pursuant to Item 4, Article 16 of the Fundamentals, a lease enterprise becomes a successor of property rights and obligations of the state enterprise leased by it. Because a lease is a possession and use for a fixed period of a property complex (Article 1 of the Fundamentals), this succession of rights is restricted by the term of the lease agreement.

The court proceeded to rule that the Federal Arbitrazh Court for the District of Moscow erred in determining that the joint stock company is a successor to the original state enterprise Soyuzmultfilm Studio founded in 1936:

The property complex leased under the said agreement, was not privatized and after the formation of the joint stock company it remained state property. Pursuant to the Order of the Russian Federation Government of June 30, 1999 . . . , the property of [Soyuzmultfilm Studio] which is in state property, is used for the formation on its basis of an enterprise to which it is assigned to under the right of economic management by Order of the Ministry of State Property of October 8, 1999. . . . With the expiration of the lease agreement, the plaintiff had no further legal grounds for the use of rights and property obtained under this agreement.

Thus the Lower Court's conclusion that the company is not the successor of the state enterprise . . . is well-grounded and complies with the case materials.

Discussion

. . .

(4)

Defendants argue that the December 18, 2001 decision categorically rejects fundamental conclusions of Russian law underlying this court's August 27, 2001 decision granting summary judgment to the plaintiffs, and, therefore, warrants reconsideration of that opinion. FSUESMS's expert, Professor Maggs, points out that the High Arbitrazh Court is the "court of last resort" in the Russian legal system for commercial disputes. Because there is no higher court to which SMS can appeal, defendants view the December 18, 2001 decision as definitive proof that this court was "thoroughly misled by plaintiffs' arguments, premised on certain fundamental conclusions which the High Arbitrazh Court has now refuted." Defendants argue that the High Court's decision provides "dispositive and unappealable Russian legal authority" refuting plaintiffs' claim to the copyrights in Soyuzmultfilm Studio's Soviet-era films. As a result, defendants contend, plaintiffs lack standing to pursue their infringement action against Berov, and this court should, accordingly, vacate the previous order and issue a new order, dismissing plaintiffs' claims with prejudice.

Disputing defendants' contention that the December 18, 2001 decision of the High Arbitrazh Court warrants reconsideration, plaintiffs first argue that this court's August 27, 2001 decision "did not rely on any Russian decisions and found that all prior decisions were irrelevant because none of the decisions had ruled on issues relating to copyright." Because the December 18, 2001 decision was simply an appeal of earlier Russian decisions that this court previously considered, plaintiffs assert that it is likewise irrelevant and thus, whatever its holding, does not warrant reconsideration of the August 27, 2001 decision.

Although my ruling did not treat any Russian opinion as conclusive or dispositive, the characterization of the arbitrazh court decisions as "irrelevant" surely overstates the case. At the very least, the December 26, 2000 decision by the Moscow Region Arbitrazh Court expressly ruled on the issue of copyright ownership, by and large adopting plaintiffs' theory of the case. The decisions on remand in the SMS-initiated litigation did not expressly reach the question of copyright ownership, but they did address, in general terms, the succession of rights from the state enterprise Soyuzmultfilm Studio—an issue that is hardly irrelevant to the instant dispute, considering that plaintiffs' primary claim to ownership of the Soyuzmultfilm copyrights depends on the premise that the lease enterprise succeeded to the rights of the state enterprise by operation of law upon execution of the lease agreement in 1989.

. . .

There is no question that the High Arbitrazh Court rejects the conclusion that the lease agreement resulted in the transformation of the state enterprise. Among the findings of the April 3 and June 4 decisions that the High Arbitrazh Court "canceled" at the outset of the December 18 opinion, was the conclusion "about the state enterprise being converted into a lease enterprise." As its sole support for this determination, the High Arbitrazh Court adopts a facially plausible, though analytically problematic, reading of the Fundamental Principles on Leasing. . . .

In support of this result, the court engages in a form of statutory construction previously employed by FSUESMS's expert, Professor Maggs. The court cites Article 1 of the Fundamental Principles, the "General Provisions" of the statute, which establishes that a lease shall be for "fixed term possession and use." Professor Maggs had previously suggested that under normal Soviet civil law drafting style, the General Provisions section of a statute should be considered applicable to the subsequent provisions except where it is "clearly negated." The High Court appears to adopt a similar approach here, concluding that "because a lease is a possession and use for a fixed period of a property complex" under the General Provisions of the statute, the succession of rights provided for in a subsequent section is properly understood to be "restricted by the term of the lease agreement."

Proceeding from this interpretation of the Fundamental Principles on Leasing, the High Court goes on to observe that in the case of Soyuzmultfilm Studio, the "property complex" leased to the lease entity in 1989 was never privatized, and, thus, when the lease entity was converted into the joint stock company, SMS, the state retained its ownership interest in the leased property. Upon the expiration of the lease in December 1999, the property reverted to its owner and was properly transferred by the state to FSUESMS.

The High Court's conclusions concerning the disposition of the tangible leased property are not inconsistent with plaintiffs' theory of the case, or with this court's August 27, 2001 order. Neither, for that matter, does the observation that the studio's tangible property remained in state ownership necessarily contradict the conclusions of the April 3 and June 4 opinions, which the High Arbitrazh Court purports to overturn. In the present proceeding, SMS does not claim any interest in the equipment and facilities leased by the state to its predecessor, the lease enterprise, and, in any event, the ownership of that property is not relevant to the instant dispute over the copyrights in Soyuzmultfilm Studio's Soviet-era films. The High Arbitrazh Court goes on to conclude, however, in somewhat broader language, that "with the expiration of the lease agreement, [SMS] had no further legal grounds for the use of rights and property obtained under this agreement." On this basis, the court reinstates the January 25, 2001 ruling of the Moscow Region Arbitrazh Court that "[SMS] is not the successor of the state enterprise."

. . .

Plaintiffs' expert Professor Stephan contends that defendants read too much into the December 18, 2001 decision, which, he maintains, has no bearing on the disposition of Soyuzmultfilm Studio's copyrights. Professor Stephan reminds the court that Soviet law recognized three types of property that a lease enterprise could possess: 1) property acquired by lease; 2) property accumulated by the enterprise as the result of its economic activity; and 3) property acquired through legal succession. He argues that in ruling that SMS is not a "successor" to the original state enterprise Soyuzmultfilm Studio, the December 18, 2001 opinion was concerned solely with the tangible property that passed under the lease agreement, i.e., property of type 1. This argument picks up on the High Court's conclusion that, upon expiration of the lease, SMS "had no further legal grounds for the use of rights and property obtained under this agreement," referring to the 1989 lease agreement. Plaintiffs have argued that the lease agreement itself did not, indeed could not, have transferred the copyrights to the lease enterprise because the lessor, Goskino, lacked the authority to transfer them. Thus, according to Professor Stephan, the December 18 opinion, which, by its terms, reaches a conclusion about rights and property transferred "under [the lease] agreement," says nothing about non-leased property, including intellectual property, that the lease enterprise might have acquired through its own economic activity during the lease term or, more importantly, by operation of law under Article 498 of the Soviet copyright law.

As Professor Stephan would have it, the High Arbitrazh Court's ruling is, therefore, limited to the narrow proposition that "the ownership of balance sheet property rights transferred from [the state enterprise] to [the lease enterprise] pursuant to the lease [was] limited by the terms of the lease and that [the lease enterprise] did not receive any additional rights in this property as a result of legal succession." Thus, he concludes that "the December 18, 2001 decision . . . does not state that with the termination of the lease either [the lease enterprise] or ESMS] ceased to own any rights, but only that the property obtained by [the lease enterprise] had to be surrendered to the Russian state, which in turn had the right to transfer that property to [FSUESMS]."

In reaching a conclusion concerning the succession of rights acquired under the lease agreement, the High Arbitrazh Court does appear to pass over the lower courts' distinction between property transferred for a limited term under the lease, and other rights that passed independently through legal succession. The deficiency in Professor Stephan's argument, however, is that it is ultimately unresponsive to the unequivocal conclusion of the December 18, 2001 High Court decision that, pursuant to the Fundamental Principles on Leasing, the lease agreement did not effect the conversion of the state enterprise into the lease enterprise. Even if Professor Stephan were correct that the court only referred to tangible property when it concluded that "with the expiration of the lease agreement, the plaintiff had no further legal grounds for the use of rights and property obtained under this agreement," the fact that the state enterprise was not converted into the lease entity would still undermine plaintiffs' central theory of the case: that the transformation of the state enterprise into the lease enterprise triggered the transfer of the copyrights to the lease entity by operation of law. In other words, even if the High Court argument Professor Stephan addresses were focused on what he terms "type 1 property," the conclusion that the state enterprise was not transformed (a conclusion Professor Stephan sidesteps) would nevertheless mean that no category 3 property, i.e., no copyrights, passed by operation of law under Article 498 of the 1964 Soviet Civil Code.

. . .

In the final analysis, plaintiffs' efforts to dismiss the December 18, 2001 decision of the High Arbitrazh Court as irrelevant are unavailing. The opinion does not address the question of copyright ownership, but it does expressly, if somewhat unconvincingly, reject the premise upon which plaintiffs base their claim to the Soyuzmultfilm copyrights, viz, that the state enterprise was converted into the lease enterprise in 1989 and thereafter ceased to exist, triggering the transfer of the studio's copyrights to the lease enterprise by operation of law. Plaintiffs' narrower reading of the opinion as relating only to tangible property that passed under the lease fails to account for how the copyrights could have passed to the lease enterprise by operation of law, if, as the High Court explicitly held, the lease agreement did not effect the transformation of the state enterprise into the lease enterprise.

However, the analysis of defendants' motion for reconsideration does not end here. It is apparent that the High Arbitrazh Court's December 18, 2001 ruling undermines certain operative premises supporting my previous decision. However, it still remains to be seen whether I am required to defer to that court's interpretation, or whether my decision may stand in spite of what appears to be contrary authority from the Russian courts.

(5)

Under Rule 44.1 of the Federal Rules of Civil Procedure, the determination of a foreign country's law is an issue of law to be resolved by considering "any relevant material or source." To the extent it addresses issues relevant to the present dispute, the High Arbitrazh Court's December 18, 2001 decision clearly constitutes relevant (indeed, presumptively highly probative) evidence of the foreign law upon which this case turns.

. . .

Thus, this court is faced with a conflict of laws problem, viz, how much weight to afford the High Arbitrazh Court's conclusions, in assessing the parties' rights, under Russian law, to the Soyuzmultfilm Studio copyrights. This determination may likewise implicate comity concerns. However, deference to a foreign adjudication as a matter of comity is by no means automatic. In particular, such deference is appropriate only if it "does not prejudice the rights of United States citizens or violate domestic public policy."

Therefore, although we begin with a presumption that the High Arbitrazh Court's December 18, 2001 decision constitutes probative evidence of the matters of Soviet law addressed therein, this court is not under any absolute obligation to follow the lead of the Russian courts in construing Soviet law. Deference to the High Court's legal conclusions, without analysis of their persuasiveness or consideration of other factors that might counsel against following that court's interpretation of Russian law, is not required.

Plaintiffs point to several factors that weigh against deference to the High Arbitrazh Court's December 18, 2001 decision. First, Russia's civilian legal system does not follow the principle of stare decisis, and therefore, the precedential import of the December 18, 2001 decision as a generally applicable articulation of Soviet law is questionable. More importantly, plaintiffs have submitted a declaration from a Russian jurist casting doubt on the independence of the Russian judiciary in general, and, in particular, challenging the legal accuracy and ultimately the integrity of the High Arbitrazh Court's December 18, 2001 ruling.

. . .

In the ordinary case, this court would be inclined to adopt the High Arbitrazh Court's positions with respect to issues of Soviet law. However, this is no ordinary case. First, there are strong reasons to question the accuracy of the December 18, 2001 decision on its face. Furthermore, plaintiffs have presented specific evidence indicating that the decision was, in fact, animated by coordinated efforts on the part of the Russian government to re-nationalize studio copyrights, recapturing for the state property rights that were acquired nearly a decade earlier by an American investor.

(b) The Persuasiveness of the High Arbitrazh Court's Decision

This court has already expressed skepticism about various aspects of the High Arbitrazh Court's December 18, 2001 decision. The conclusion that the state enterprise Soyuzmultfilm Studio was not transformed into the lease enterprise would seem to run counter to the apparent purpose of the Fundamental Principles on Leasing, which was to effect the incremental privatization of the Soviet economy. At the very least, the High Court's suggestion that the "activity of the state enterprise" was not terminated by virtue of the lease agreement, is plainly contrary to the facts and the reality on the ground. Neither defendants nor the High Arbitrazh Court have offered any evidence to contradict this court's previous observation that "the state enterprise did not undertake a single act, either official or unofficial, to which anyone can point between 1989 and 1999." Defendants characterize FSUESMS's registration in 1999 as an "amendment" to the 1936 charter of the state enterprise Soyuzmultfilm Studio—an amendment that was supposedly necessitated by the adoption of the Civil Code of the Russian Federation, First Part, in 1994. The suggestion is that FSUESMS and the state enterprise Soyuzmultfilm Studio are one and the same, the latter having reemerged from hibernation as a continuation of the former. However, defendants do not explain why the 1999 "amendment" to the charter of the state enterprise—if it truly were an amendment—did not occur until five years after the enactment of the law that supposedly created the necessity for the change. Neither do they adequately reconcile the alleged existence of the state enterprise during (and after) the lease term with an admitted decade of complete inactivity.

> . . .

In sum, the High Arbitrazh Court is plainly incorrect in concluding that the establishment of the lease enterprise did not result in the transformation of the original state enterprise into the lease entity—a position that is inconsistent with the court's prior treatment of similar transactions. Accordingly, just as a court in a civil law jurisdiction is not strictly bound by prior judicial decisions, this court, in seeking to discern Russian law, is free to apply its best understanding of the relevant statutes—especially when this understanding is supported by the majority of the lower arbitrazh court decisions in the record, by the overwhelming scholarly consensus that motion picture copyrights belong to the studio and not the state, and by the undeniable fact that the state enterprise could not be found and did not exist in any practical sense after the execution of the lease agreement, in December 1989.

If the High Arbitrazh Court's clearly erroneous decision impacted only the rights of Russian parties, this court might, nevertheless, defer to the High Court's arbitrary departure from what appears to have been the consensus understanding of the leasing legislation. However, insofar as this ruling affects the rights of a non-Russian party, FBJ, which invested over three million dollars in acquiring a copyright license for Soyuzmultfilm Studio's films, and in developing the commercial value of these copyrights, the sudden shift in Russian law effected by the High Arbitrazh Court's decision, which operates to deprive an American corporation of its substantial investment, is simply unconscionable. For these reasons, this court will not defer to the conclusions articulated in High Arbitrazh Court's December 18, 2001 decision.

(c) Allegations of Judicial Misconduct

As an explanation for the High Arbitrazh Court's abrupt turnabout concerning the role of lease enterprises in the privatization of Russia's formerly socialist economic system, plaintiffs have advanced allegations of pervasive corruption in the Russian courts, and in particular of bias against private enterprises engaged in disputes with the state concerning property ownership. Beyond these general allegations, plaintiffs have submitted documents from the High Arbitrazh Court's case file, which they claim demonstrate improper governmental influence over the arbitrazh court proceedings in the FSUESMS-SMS litigations, in violation of various provisions of the Arbitrazh Procedure Code and the Constitution of the Russian Federation. According to plaintiffs, this alleged illicit conduct unfairly biased the High Arbitrazh Court against SMS.

The resulting decision, plaintiffs maintain, amounts to a thinly-veiled attempt to re-nationalize Soyuzmultfilm Studio's copyrights to the detriment of FBJ, a foreign investor that expended millions of dollars to develop the commercial value of the studio's library of animated films. FBJ acted in reliance on the copyright license it acquired from the lease enterprise Soyuzmultfilm Studio, without any remotely contemporaneous objection from the Russian government or from any other party. Plaintiffs assert that, under these circumstances, for this court to reverse the previous ruling in deference to the December 18, 2001 decision would "harm a United States corporation [FBJ] in violation of Constitutional safeguards such as due process, [and the prohibitions against] ex post facto laws and the unlawful taking of personal property."

Dr. Pashin, who has done considerable work in the area of judicial reform in the Russian Federation, provides some illuminating and troubling commentary on the present state of the Russian judiciary. According to Dr. Pashin, although Russian constitutional and statutory law provide that "in consideration of economic disputes, no priority should be given to the state and those in possession of its property," this principle is not widely adhered to in practice. For one thing, Dr. Pashin explains, the judges and staff of the current arbitrazh courts are for the most part former employees of the Soviet "State Arbitrazh," a system that was designed to resolve disputes between socialist enterprises administratively rather than judicially, "with an implied objective of [protecting] the Soviet state's interests." Until August 7, 2000, long after the fall of the communist regime, the civil procedure code under which the arbitrazh courts operated recognized "the protection 'of the Socialist economic system and Socialist property'" as a guiding principle in civil legal proceedings, and judges were instructed to resolve civil cases based on law "in accordance with the socialist sense of justice." Thus, Dr. Pashin contends, the current generation of Russian judges, having been "raised in the spirit of Soviet law," perpetuates a pro-state approach "simply by inertia."

. . .

Evidence undermining "the essential fairness of [a] judicial system" can, in a sufficiently extreme case, justify nonrecognition of a judgment or decision rendered by the courts of that system. In this regard, "evidence that the judiciary was dominated by the political branches of government . . . would support a conclusion that the legal system was one whose judgments are not entitled to recognition."

Although the alleged flaws in the Russian judicial system are troublesome, the present record does not support a sweeping condemnation of Russia's judiciary. However, in this case, it is unnecessary to reach any broad conclusions as to the impartiality and essential fairness of the arbitrazh system as a whole. Plaintiffs have produced specific evidence—in the form of documents obtained from the High Arbitrazh Court's file—of improprieties in the specific arbitrazh court proceedings leading up to the December 18, 2001 decision. The relevant documents were discovered by Larissa N. Riabchenko, an attorney who has represented SMS in the arbitrazh courts since 1999.

In an affidavit submitted in conjunction with Dr. Pashin's Declaration, Ms. Riabchenko explains that, contrary to Russian law, SMS never received a copy of the complaint that the Deputy Prosecutor General of the Russian Federation filed with the High Arbitrazh Court on October 15, 2001, initiating the appeal that led to the December 18, 2001 decision. Therefore, she went to the court to review the complaint. While Ms. Riabchenko was perusing the court file, two documents caught her attention, both of which have been presented to this court in English translation. The first of these documents appears to be the minutes of a "consultation meeting" of the Deputy Chairman of the Russian Federation, held on March 30, 2001. The agenda of the meeting concerned the "creation of necessary conditions for the activity of the Federal State Unitarian Enterprise [Soyuzmultfilm Studio]." In addition to the director of the third-party plaintiff here, FSUESMS, an array of officials from the executive branch of the Russian Federation government attended the meeting, including representatives of: 1) the Ministry of Culture; 2) the Ministry of Property; 3) the Prosecutor General's office; 4) the Russian agency for Patents and Trademarks; 5) the Department of the State Regulation and Development of Cinematography; 6) the Staff of the Russian Federation Government; and 7) the Administration of the President of the Russian Federation. Controversially, at least according to plaintiffs, a representative of the High Arbitrazh Court, E. A. Lyubichev, was also present at the meeting.

The attendees appear to have concluded that "as a result of the uncoordinated actions of the interested state organizations the measures necessary for the preservation of the state interests in the process of the settlement of the situation surrounding [Soyuzmultfilm Studio] have not been undertaken." To remedy this situation, the parties agreed to undertake various efforts on behalf of FSUESMS, with the stated purpose of protecting "state interests." The Ministry of Culture, for instance, was to develop a long-term plan for the development of FSUESMS, and, together with the Ministry of Property, to look into procuring additional premises for the activity of the Unitarian Enterprise. It was also decided that the Russian Agency for Patents would take steps to "secure" FSUESMS's control over the use of the Soyuzmultfilm Studio trademark within Russia and would assist in the protection of the trademark internationally. The Ministry of Culture was assigned the task of studying the lawfulness of the use of Soyuzmultfilm Studio films by Russian television stations.

In the context of these various strategies to aid FSUESMS, the participants at the consultation meeting also addressed the litigation between SMS and FSUESMS, which was at that time ongoing before the arbitrazh courts. To this end, the Ministry of Property was instructed to secure the participation of its representative in the legal proceedings "on a permanent basis." It was decided that the Prosecutor General would be asked "to take necessary measures to supervise over court acts which have become legally effective, which were made under the appeals by [FSUESMS] and the Moscow Region Prosecutor's Office, for the purpose of verifying their lawfulness and groundedness." Plaintiffs' allegations of misconduct focus primarily on item 7 on the agenda, which expressed the intent to "ask the High Arbitrazh Court of the Russian Federation (V. A.

Yakovlev)[49] to carry out, in procedural forms established by federal law, the court supervision over the cases re: the appeals of [FSUESMS], the Moscow Region Prosecutor's Office, and [SMS], which are being considered in the Arbitrazh courts of Moscow and the Moscow Region."

Plaintiffs' expert Dr. Pashin argues that the participation of a High Arbitrazh Court representative at the March 30, 2001 consultation meeting constituted an unlawful form of collaboration between the executive and judicial branches of the Russian government in violation of the principle of division of authorities set forth in Article 10 of the Russian Federation Constitution. As Dr. Pashin sees it, the minutes uncovered by Ms. Riabchenko demonstrate that "a representative of the highest level body of judicial power [participated] in a consultation meeting organized at the highest level body of executive power, in order to discuss, in particular, the specific issues being considered by arbitrazh courts in a specific case and to develop recommendations to the General Prosecutor's Office of the Russian Federation and the High Arbitrazh Court." For Dr. Pashin, this participation in itself "makes doubtful the impartiality of both the High Arbitrazh Court and the lower arbitrazh courts in their consideration of the cases in question."

The second document Ms. Riabchenko uncovered is an office memorandum from E.A. Lyubichev, the High Arbitrazh Court representative who attended the March 30 consultation meeting, to A. A. Arifullin, whom plaintiffs identity as a High Court judge. The letter's subject heading references the case number of the appeal that resulted in the December 18, 2001 decision; the text of the letter relays the substance of the consultation meeting and in particular conveys the request outlined in item 7 of the minutes:

> At the aforesaid consultation meeting at the Deputy Chairman of the Russian Federation Government a wish was expressed about the necessity by all state organs to provide the protection of interests of the Russian Federation (the Federal State Unitarian Enterprise [Soyuzmultfilm Studio]) and in particular the reinforcement of control on behalf of the General Prosecutor's Office and the High Arbitrazh Court of the Russian Federation over the decisions of the said courts.

Dr. Pashin contends that item 7 of the consultation meeting minutes, together with the follow-up office memorandum, provides convincing evidence that executive officials improperly pressured the High Arbitrazh Court to intervene in the Soyuzmultfilm Studio litigation on behalf of FSUESMS. More specifically, according to Dr. Pashin, the High Arbitrazh Court Chairman was assigned the task of conducting "court supervision" over pending litigation between FSUESMS and SMS. Thus, the High Arbitrazh Court was treated "not as the independent body of judicial power that it is supposed to be, but as if it was some mid-level department, one of, as it is said in the preamble to the [minutes], 'the interested state organizations.' " Moreover, because at the time of the consultation meeting, the lower arbitrazh courts were still considering appeals in the FSUESMS-SMS litigation, the request for High Arbitrazh Court "supervision" over these cases was inappropriate. Under Russian constitutional law, High Court intervention in matters pending before a

---

[49]   V.A. Yakovlev is the Chairman of the High Arbitrazh Court of the Russian Federation.

lower court constitutes "an unlawful interference [with] the court's activity." The Chairman of the High Arbitrazh Court is empowered to initiate review of lower court decisions only "upon the completion of court proceedings in the lower courts and only after the lower courts' decisions take effect."

Thus, Dr. Pashin infers that the "court supervision" contemplated at the consultation meeting was in fact a euphemism for the concept of "control." He does not explain precisely what this concept entails, but it appears to refer to various practices, common during the Soviet period but in principle illegal in the Russian Federation, through which court officials, under pressure from other branches of government, would take steps to ensure pro-state outcomes in court proceedings. Dr. Pashin supports his deduction by noting that the office memorandum to High Arbitrazh Court Judge A. A. Arifullin specifically refers to "the reinforcement of control" over the decisions of the courts presiding over the litigation between FSUESMS and SMS.

Defendants argue that, contrary to plaintiffs' allegations of improper, indeed illegal, conduct, the presence of a High Court representative at a consultation meeting of executive branch officials was entirely appropriate. Professor Maggs notes that the Arbitrazh Procedure Code and the Federal Constitutional Law, entitled "On Arbitrazh Courts in the Russian Federation," both of which Dr. Pashin helped draft according to his affidavit, expressly provide for ex parte contact between officials of the High Arbitrazh Court and litigants seeking High Court review of lower court decisions.

This is because under Articles 180–181 of the 1995 Arbitrazh Procedure Code, review of a lower court ruling by the High Arbitrazh Court is possible only if the Chairman or Deputy Chairman of the court or the Prosecutor General or Deputy Prosecutor General makes a formal "protest" of the lower court decision. Under Article 185, the parties to an arbitrazh court litigation can only petition these officials for review. According to Professor Maggs, in practice, parties seeking High Arbitrazh Court review make their petitions in writing and also request meetings to argue that the decisions should be reviewed. Under High Arbitrazh Court procedure, these petitions and meetings are ex parte, and the opposing party is only afforded notice and an opportunity to be heard if and when a formal protest is made and a hearing is scheduled. Professor Maggs notes that the Russian government, represented by the Ministry of State Property, was a party to the FSUESMS-SMS litigations. Therefore, Professor Maggs claims, it was proper for the various agencies representing the government's interests to meet with High Arbitrazh Court officials for the purpose of asking the High Court Chairman to exercise his discretion to "protest" the lower court rulings.

Even if Professor Maggs were correct that some sort of ex parte hearing would have been an appropriate means for the Russian government, as a party to the arbitrazh litigations, to petition the Chairman of the High Arbitrazh Court to initiate review of lower court decisions, the stated objective of the March 30 meeting was not to argue the merits of FSUESMS's case against SMS or to seek High Court review of the lower courts' rulings against FSUESMS. Rather the broader purpose of the meeting was to coordinate efforts of government officials to advance state interests by "securing [the] necessary conditions for the

activity of [FSUESMS]." Indeed, the memorandum sent to High
Arbitrazh Court Judge A.A. Arifullin does not simply relay a request for
High Court intervention in the FSUESMS-SMS litigations, but rather
specifically conveys the Russian government's view concerning "the
necessity by all state organs to provide the protection of interests of the
Russian Federation." Thus, the assertion that the Arbitrazh Procedure
Code provides for some ex parte communications between High Court
officials and would-be appellants of lower court rulings (including
representatives of the Russian government in those cases in which the
government happens to be a litigant) does not explain or justify what is
alleged to have happened here: improper ex parte collaboration between
representatives of the executive branch and the judiciary.

Viewed in the light most favorable to defendants, the consultation
meeting documents Dr. Pashin discusses demonstrate that the December
18, 2001 decision of the High Arbitrazh Court resulted from a concerted
attempt on the part of Russian government officials to assert state
property interests that certain of these officials may feel were
improvidently (or improperly) transferred to private ownership, and
ultimately conveyed to a foreign investor, perhaps without adequate
compensation to the state. In the first of his many submissions to this
court, Professor Maggs explained that the privatization of the Russian
economy in the late 1980s and 1990s was riddled with corruption. During
this period, Professor Maggs reports, it was distressingly common for
managers entrusted with state property to engage in systematic
plundering of former state enterprises, selling the state-owned property
abroad and often hiding the proceeds in off shore bank accounts.
According to Professor Maggs, in the case of Soyuzmultfilm Studio

> allegations that the Lessee Organization and the joint stock
> company have been engaged in "asset stripping" are at the heart
> of the ongoing litigation in Russia. This is why it was the Public
> Prosecutor of the Moscow Region who brought the case against
> the Joint Stock Company in the Arbitrazh Court of [the] Moscow
> Region and why the Ministry of State Property of the Russian
> Federation has been a party to all the litigation taking place in
> Russia related to this case.

Without gainsaying the prevalence of corruption among many
managers charged with administering state property during the
tumultuous transformation of the Russian economy to a system of private
ownership, it is difficult to see precisely what state-owned assets the
lease enterprise and SMS can be said to have "stripped" as a result of the
copyright license granted to FBJ in 1992. The tangible property
transferred to the lease enterprise was obviously not a subject of that
agreement, and, moreover, that property was by all accounts duly
returned to the state after the expiration of the lease. As far as the
studio's intangible property is concerned, it is clear that since at least
1928 (eight years before the establishment of Soyuzmultfilm Studio)
Soviet law vested ownership of film copyrights in the studio that
produced the film. What is more, by the time FBJ acquired the disputed
copyright license, in 1992, the Soviet government had already, some
three years earlier, deliberately abdicated its longstanding monopoly
over the foreign distribution of films produced by state enterprise film
studios. Under these circumstances, it appears that the Russian

government is now seeking to reacquire rights that were knowingly and voluntarily relinquished even before the December 1989 lease agreement initiated the privatization of Soyuzmultfilm Studio.

. . .

Instead, the current record establishes to the satisfaction of this court that at the time FBJ obtained the disputed copyright license in May 1992, there was only one entity that purported to exercise any ownership interest in the Soyuzmultfilm copyrights: the lease enterprise, which was subsequently transformed into the joint stock company, SMS. Moreover, from 1992 to 1999 no body of the Russian government—not Goskino, not the Property Ministry, not the Public Prosecutor, not the supposedly existing, though admittedly non-functioning, state enterprise—sought to challenge the legality of the copyright license FBJ obtained from the lease enterprise.

There is absolutely no evidence of any attempt on the part of the lease enterprise or SMS to conceal the licensing transaction with FBJ or to hide the proceeds acquired therefrom. On the contrary, as Professor Stephan notes, the 1992 licensing agreement specifies that payments to the lease enterprise are to be made in a Russian account controlled by a Russian government bank. Tax records submitted to the court by plaintiffs further demonstrate that the lease enterprise paid taxes to the state for revenue received from FBJ under the 1992 agreement. These uncontroverted facts cast significant doubt on any claims that the actions of the lease enterprise in granting a copyright license constituted illicit asset-stripping.

The Russian government may well have reasons to rethink the propriety of various privatization reforms enacted over the past decade. As far as its own citizens are concerned, the Russian government is free to embark on a course to reclaim ownership rights through legislation, or through re-distributive litigation in the arbitrazh courts of the sort that appears to have been attempted here. The propriety of such actions is not for this court to determine. However, vague and dilatory allegations of asset-stripping cannot now, at this late date, be used to impair the contractual rights of FBJ, an American corporation that acted in good faith, expending millions of dollars to develop the commercial value of Soyuzmultfilm Studio's animated films.

Aside from the faulty legal analysis underpinning the High Arbitrazh Court's December 18, 2001 decision, these considerations provide an independent basis to reject the High Court's rationale, but also reinforce the conclusion that Russian law provided for the transformation of the state enterprise Soyuzmultfilm Studio into the lease enterprise, resulting in the transfer of the studio's copyrights to the lease enterprise by operation of law. To the extent the High Arbitrazh Court's decision undermines this court's determination that FBJ acquired a valid copyright license from the lease enterprise in 1992, that decision is entitled to no deference and will not be followed.

NOTES

1.   The court here refused to pass judgment on the entire Russian legal system, but did characterize a particular foreign legal proceeding as the product of improper government pressure. Does a U.S. court have the

capacity to assess the propriety of particular proceedings, or does its lack of familiarity with foreign procedure and dependence on party-supplied experts make it vulnerable? Does a meeting between government officials and a judge, for which a written protocol exists, indicate undue influence? Couldn't such meetings substitute for a written brief? Was it necessary for the U.S. court to condemn the Russian decision as improper, given that the opinion did not bind the parties to the U.S. suit or even discuss the specific legal interests at issue in the U.S. litigation? For the court's initial decision in the case, see *Films by Jove, Inc. v. Berov*, 154 F. Supp. 2d 432 (E.D.N.Y. 2001). For a later decision refusing to follow a directive by the Russian government claiming ownership of the copyrights, see *Films by Jove, Inc. v. Berov*, 341 F. Supp. 2d 199 (E.D.N.Y. 2004).

2. Note that the rights in dispute here—the foreign, and particularly the U.S., copyright to a catalogue of cartoons—did not rest on Soviet or Russian law. The question rather was the validity of a transaction by a Russian legal entity. Should this make a difference? Should a U.S. court apply Russian law to determine who owns a U.S. asset? Does this choice of law invite interference in the foreign courts to retroactively invalidate transfers that one side ends up regretting? What does this approach do for legal stability?

3. By making the case turn on foreign law, the court opened up the proceeding to a duel between experts. Each side had senior U.S. law professors offering up their opinions on the details of Russian law. Should a court rely on the parties to identify and to compensate experts, or should it hire its own experts? How else might a court educate itself as to questions of foreign law? Consider these issues again in the *Noga* and *Karaha Bodas* cases below.

B. ARBITRATION

Many international disputes, especially when a state or one of its enterprises is involved, wind up in arbitration rather than litigation. Typically parties will agree in advance to submit any disagreements that may arise to arbitration. An international transactional lawyer always should insist on the inclusion of a dispute resolution clause that provides for international arbitration. This affords the following advantages:

(1) *Neutrality*. Arbitration is not associated with the institutions of any one country, and thus avoids the perception of "home court advantage" that litigation might create. Sovereign states in particular resist submitting to the jurisdiction of foreign courts.

(2) *Flexibility*. Arbiters generally allow parties to customize their dispute resolution procedures, including choice of applicable law, to a greater extent than do domestic courts. Moreover, the default rules in most arbitral mechanisms tend to be less formal and more party-driven than in litigation. In addition, although arbitral awards constitute evidence of an underlying consensus about the relevant law, they do not have the same precedential authority as does a judicial opinion in many national legal systems. Freedom not to worry about precedential consequences allows arbiters greater discretion. Finally, parties have greater control over the choice of individual arbiters than

they do over the choice of a judge. Arbiters know that if they behave in an idiosyncratic or surprising way, they are not likely to get much business as an arbiter in the future. Judges, by contrast, do not lose their jobs simply by producing surprising results.

(3) *Privacy.* Litigation typically is a public function and a party has to seek a special order from the judge to prevent disclosure of any portion of the record and filings. Arbitration is typically confidential, meaning that information can be released only with the consent of all parties.

(4) *Enforceability.* Unlike judicial judgments, arbitral awards benefit from a treaty, the New York Convention on the Recognition and Enforcement of Foreign Arbitral Awards. This international instrument, which almost every country in the world has joined, does two things. First, it obligates sovereign states to respect agreements to arbitrate, which means refusing to allow a party to litigate a matter covered by a valid agreement to arbitrate. Second, it obligates sovereigns to enforce any arbitral award covered by the Convention, with only narrow exceptions for awards that were procured improperly or that violate the public policy of the state in which enforcement is sought. The public policy exception in particular for the most part has been construed fairly narrowly.

(5) *Exclusivity.* Some bilateral investment treaties (BITs) provide for arbitration of disputes between private investors and host states in conformity with another multilateral treaty, the Convention on the Settlement of Investment Disputes between States and Nationals of Other States (the ICSID Convention). Some, although not all, of these disputes would not be litigable due to sovereign immunity and related doctrines. Where such treaties apply, they afford at least one formal dispute resolution mechanism involving neutral third parties. In the absence of such a treaty, an aggrieved investor may have no resort to any formal mechanism, although it might be able to persuade its government to espouse its claim in state-to-state negotiations. The BIT network is not nearly as comprehensive as the New York Convention, which means that many investors may not enjoy this protection at all. For example, there is no BIT in force between the United States and either the People's Republic of China or the Russian Federation. The 2012 US. Model Bilateral Investment Treaty is included in the Documents Supplement.

For all these reasons, arbitration clauses are very common in business transactions involving emerging markets.

The parties to an international arbitration agreement can choose between two types of arbitration, namely institutional arbitration and ad hoc arbitration. Institutional arbitration is carried out within an established, structured institutional framework of procedural rules, such as the following:

1. International Arbitration Rules of the International Centre for Dispute Resolution of the American Arbitration Association (AAA);

2. Rules of Arbitration of the International Chamber of Commerce (ICC);

3. Arbitration Rules of the London Court of International Arbitration (LCIA);

4. Arbitration Rules of the Singapore International Arbitration Centre (SIAC);

5. Rules of the Arbitration Institute of the Stockholm Chamber of Commerce (SCC Institute);

6. The Netherlands Arbitration Institute, Rotterdam (NAI); and

7. International Centre for Settlement of Investment Disputes (ICSID), which is the only institutional arbitration framework established by an international treaty (Convention on the Settlement of Investment Disputes between States and Nationals of Other States), and is designed to deal specifically with disputes to which a government is a party.

By contrast, ad hoc arbitration is conducted outside a structured institutional framework, using a set of established arbitration rules, such as the following:

1. CPR Institute for Dispute Resolution Rules for Non-Administered Arbitration of International Disputes; and

2. United Nations Commission on International Trade Law (UNCITRAL) Arbitration Rules.

Most emerging market countries tend to favor the use of ad hoc arbitration through the UNCITRAL Arbitration Rules. These countries played an important role in the United Nations Commission on International Trade Law at the time of the rules' adoption in 1976. Although foreign investors generally prefer institutional arbitration that is connected with the proposed place of arbitration, they regularly agree to the use of the UNCITRAL Arbitration Rules.

The UNCITRAL Arbitration Rules were revised in 2010 and again in 2013 to reflect changes in arbitral practice since 1976.[1] The 2013 version of the UNCITRAL Arbitration Rules includes a new clause in Article 1 that ensures the incorporation of the new UNCITRAL Rules on Transparency in Treaty-based Investor-State Arbitration, which became effective on April 1, 2014.[2]

In the Documents Supplement, Article 41 of the Kenya Model PSA sets out a fairly standard arbitration clause, which includes the following elements: (1) referral to arbitration in accordance with the UNCITRAL

---

[1] See UNCITRAL, http://www.uncitral.org/uncitral/en/uncitral_texts/arbitration/2010 Arbitration_rules.html

[2] UNCITRAL Arbitration Rules and Rules on Transparency. http://www.uncitral.org/pdf/english/texts/arbitration/arb-rules–2013/UNCITRAL–Arbitration–Rules–2013–e.pdf

Arbitration Rules if a dispute cannot be settled amicably within 30 days; (2) requiring three arbitrators to be appointed using a detailed procedure; (3) naming the place of arbitration (here Nairobi, Kenya); (4) stating that the award of the arbitrators shall be final and binding; and (5) stating that any judgment on the award shall be enforceable in any court of competent jurisdiction. Each component of the clause would be acceptable to most IOCs, except the fourth part that provides for the place of arbitration to be in Nairobi, Kenya. Since international arbitration in a neutral venue is viewed as a requirement, IOCs would most likely suggest the substitution of London, England as the venue.

An agreement to arbitrate does not absolutely foreclose litigation. First, the parties may disagree as to whether an arbitration agreement covers their dispute Consider the interpretation of the relevant clauses in the following case.

JSC Surgutneftegaz v. President and Fellows of Harvard College

United States District Court for the Southern District of New York
2005 U.S. Dist. WL 1863676 (2005)

■ CASEY, J.

[Surgutneftegaz, a Russian oil and gas company, issued preferred stock pursuant to its corporate charter and the Russian Federal Law on Joint Stock Companies. The preference right of this stock included an annual fixed dividend states as a percentage of the company's profits. Neither the charter nor the Federal Law defined the term "profits," however. Surgutneftegaz then sold some of this stock in the United States in the form of American Depositary Shares (ADRs). ADRs are designed to be legally distinct from the underlying stock, even though each ADR share represents ownership of one share of stock. The mechanism allows the investor to own an interest that rests on U.S., rather than foreign, law, and gives the investor rights against the trustee, a U.S. bank, in addition to rights against the company that issued the stock.

Surgutneftegaz earned profits for tax and accounting purposes, but its managing board determined that, with respect to the preferred stock, "profit" had a distinct meaning and that, for purposes of calculating the dividend due on this stock, no profits had occurred. Shareholders who owned this stock outright, rather than through an ADR, challenged this decision in the Russian courts but lost. A Russian court ruled that Russian law reserved to the managing board the power to determine what constitutes profit for purposes of the preferred stock dividend, and that they were not obliged to use the same definition of profit that the tax law and their financial accounting rules employed.

Holders of ADRs then brought the same claim that had been presented to the Russian court, but demanded arbitration in accordance with the ADR agreement. Surgutneftegaz then brought suit in the New York courts to enjoin this arbitration.]

. . .

I.   BACKGROUND

Petitioner is an oil and gas company organized under the laws of the Russian Federation. Petitioner's common and preferred stock is publicly traded in Russia, and since 1996 its stock has been available for purchase by investors in the United States under an arrangement between Petitioner and The Bank of New York. Under this arrangement, ING Eurasia holds shares of Petitioner's stock in Moscow as custodian for The Bank of New York, which issues what are called American Depositary Shares ("ADRs") to investors in the United States. Respondent is one of those investors, owning over three million ADRs that represent preferred shares in Petitioner.

Respondent claims that as an owner of ADRs, it is entitled to an annual fixed dividend guaranteed in Petitioner's company charter and prospectus. Respondent maintains that Petitioner has been paying insufficient dividends. The sale of ADRs representing preferred shares is governed by a deposit agreement of March 19, 1998 among Respondent, The Bank of New York, and owners of ADRs.[1] Section 7.06 of that agreement is an arbitration clause that states:

> (a) Any controversy, claim or cause of action brought by any party hereto against the Company arising out of or relating to the Shares or other Deposited Securities, the American Depositary Shares, the Receipts or this Agreement, or the breach hereof or thereof, shall be finally settled by arbitration in accordance with the rules of the American Arbitration Association, which rules are deemed to be incorporated by reference into this Section 7.06, . . . and provided further that any such controversy, claim or cause of action relating to or based upon the provisions of the Federal securities laws of the United States or the rules and regulations promulgated thereunder may, but need not, be submitted to arbitration as provided in this Section 7.06.

> The place of arbitration shall be New York, New York, and the language of the arbitration shall be English.

> . . .

> (b) Any controversy, claim or cause of action arising out of or relating to the Shares or other Deposited Securities, the American Depositary Shares, the Receipts or this Deposit Agreement not subject to arbitration shall be litigated in the Federal and state courts in the Borough of Manhattan.

(JSC Surgutneftegaz and The Bank of New York as Depositary and Owners and Beneficial Owners of American Depositary Receipts Deposit Agreement, Mar. 19, 1998 ("Deposit Agreement") § 7.06.)

Pursuant to the arbitration clause in the Deposit Agreement, Respondent sought to compel arbitration against Petitioner before the American Arbitration Association ("AAA") in New York by filing a notice of arbitration. Respondent asserts three substantive claims: (1) breach of

---

[1]   The Deposit Agreement provides that "Owners and Beneficial Owners of [ADRs] from time to time shall be parties to this Deposit Agreement and shall be bound by all of the terms and conditions hereof and of the [ADRs] by acceptance thereof." (JSC Surgutneftegaz and The Bank of New York as Depositary and Owners and Beneficial Owners of American Depositary Receipts Deposit Agreement, Mar. 19, 1998 § 7.04.)

the Deposit Agreement, (2) violation of Petitioner's company charter by failing to declare and pay the required dividends, and (3) securities fraud under the U.S. securities laws. Petitioner, in response, filed a motion to stay arbitration in New York State Supreme Court. Respondent removed the petition to this Court pursuant to 9 U.S.C. § 205, which provides for removal of cases relating to arbitration agreements that fall under the United Nations Convention on the Recognition and Enforcement of Foreign Arbitral Awards ("New York Convention").

II. DISCUSSION

A. Federal Not State Law of Arbitrability Applies

As an initial matter, Petitioner argues that the Court must decide whether arbitration should be stayed as a matter of New York State law. But the question is governed by federal, not state, law. Chapter 2 of the Federal Arbitration Act ("FAA") incorporates the New York Convention. *See* 9 U.S.C. § 201. Section 202 of the FAA explains:

> An arbitration agreement . . . arising out of a legal relationship, whether contractual or not, which is considered as commercial, including a transaction, contract, or agreement described in section 2 of this title, falls under the [New York] Convention. An agreement . . . arising out of such a relationship which is entirely between citizens of the United States shall be deemed not to fall under the [New York] Convention unless that relationship involves property located abroad, envisages performance or enforcement abroad, or has some other reasonable relation with one or more foreign states.

Id. § 202. For the New York Convention to apply to this dispute, there must be a written arbitration agreement that provides for arbitration in the territory of a signatory to the Convention, the subject matter of the relationship between the parties must be commercial, and the dispute cannot be entirely domestic in scope. These requirements are all undisputedly met here: The Deposit Agreement contains a written arbitration clause providing for arbitration in the United States regarding the purchase and sale of securities in a foreign corporation. As such, it is governed by the New York Convention through the FAA.

The Court must apply the "federal substantive law of arbitrability" in determining whether the disputes are arbitrable under the FAA. That substantive law includes a presumption in favor of arbitration, which requires that "any doubts concerning the scope of arbitrable issues" shall be resolved in favor of arbitration, but a presumption that the Court, rather than the arbitrator, is to decide whether matters are subject to arbitration.

In deciding whether the matters raised in Respondent's notice of arbitration are properly arbitrable under the FAA, the Court's role is limited to determining whether a valid and enforceable arbitration agreement exists between the parties and whether one party has improperly failed, neglected, or refused to arbitrate. Petitioner's arguments as to the first question (that the arbitration agreement is unenforceable on grounds of public policy) are without merit. As to the second question, the Court finds that the parties have committed the decision on whether their disputes are arbitrable to arbitration.

B. The Arbitration Agreement Is Not Unenforceable on Public-Policy Grounds

Petitioner maintains that the arbitration agreement should not be enforced on the public-policy grounds of international comity, the internal-affairs doctrine for corporations, and *forum non conveniens*. None of these is a valid reason for refusing to enforce the arbitration agreement. Article II(1) of the New York Convention provides:

> Each Contracting State shall recognize an agreement in writing under which the parties undertake to submit to arbitration all or any differences which have arisen or which may arise between them in respect of a defined legal relationship, whether contractual or not, concerning a subject matter *capable of settlement by arbitration.*

The Convention also permits refusal to enforce arbitration agreements on the grounds that they are "null and void, inoperative or incapable of being performed." The Court need not wade very far into the murky waters of Article II to reject Petitioner's arguments.[5] It has been suggested that the public policy of the enforcing jurisdiction may provide a means to refuse enforcement of an arbitration agreement under Article II. *See Mitsubishi Motors Corp. v. Soler Chrysler-Plymouth, Inc.,* 473 U.S. 614, 639 n.21 (1985) ("We do not quarrel with the Court of Appeals' conclusion that Art. II(1) of the Convention . . . contemplates exceptions to arbitrability grounded in domestic law."). If that is so, then it must be public policy as a matter of federal, not state, law. Even if the public policy of the United States is a valid reason for declaring an arbitration agreement unenforceable under Article II, that public policy does not embrace the grounds that Petitioner urges.

Petitioner's first argument—that international comity requires rejection of the arbitration agreement—is unavailing. "International comity is the recognition which one nation allows within its territory to the legislative, executive or judicial acts of another nation." The basis for its purported application here is that other holders of preferred shares litigated and lost similar claims before the Russian courts. According to Petitioner, enforcing the arbitration agreement would signal a disrespect for the judgments of those courts. But as the Supreme Court has held, "concerns of international comity, respect for the capacities of foreign and transnational tribunals, and sensitivity to the need of the international commercial system for predictability in the resolution of disputes" counsel *in favor of* enforcing international arbitration agreements, "even assuming that a contrary result would be forthcoming in a domestic context." *Mitsubishi Motors Corp.,* 473 U.S. at 629. The Supreme Court has therefore rejected the claim that enforcing arbitration agreements is inconsistent with concerns of international comity.

Notwithstanding the general principle that international comity favors enforcement of international arbitration agreements, Petitioner's argument fails for two other reasons. First, the Russian Federation is a party to the New York Convention, and therefore has agreed that other

---

[5] It is not clear under Article II whether the enforcing jurisdiction's law applies to questions of enforceability or whether some other law controls such as the law of the place of arbitration, the substantive law to be applied to the dispute, or general principles of law. The scope of the exceptions in Article II is also not entirely clear.

nations should enforce arbitration agreements to which its nationals are parties. Second, it is undisputed that Respondent was not a party to the litigation before the Russian courts or in privity with those who were parties to the litigation such as to make the Russian courts' decisions binding on Respondent. There is therefore little chance that enforcing the arbitration agreement in the manner in which the Russian Federation agreed when it acceded to the New York Convention would circumvent or undermine the decisions of the Russian courts. Thus, even if international comity were a valid ground for refusing enforcement of an arbitration agreement under Article II of the New York Convention, it is of no aid to Petitioner here.[6]

Petitioner's second ground for refusing to enforce the agreement—the internal-affairs doctrine—is equally meritless. Not surprisingly, Petitioner has failed to cite a single case in which a court has refused enforcement of an arbitration agreement under the New York Convention because the subject matter of the dispute went to a foreign corporation's internal affairs. The FAA does not carve out disputes relating to the internal affairs of corporations as an exception to the general enforceability of arbitration agreements. The Supreme Court has rejected the claim that particular areas of law are not arbitrable under the FAA without express congressional direction. To the extent that New York law would exempt matters going to the internal affairs of corporations from arbitration, it is preempted by the FAA.

The doctrine of *forum non conveniens* is also no bar to arbitration here. In *Mitsubishi Motors Corp.,* the Supreme Court held that an arbitration agreement is a particular type of forum-selection clause. The parties here agreed to arbitrate their disputes in New York and even to litigate such disputes that were not arbitrable in "the Federal and state courts in the Borough of Manhattan." (Deposit Agreement § 7.06.) The forum-selection clause is enforceable unless the Court finds that it is unjust or the product of fraud or overreaching. Given the importance of such clauses in international transactions, the parties' agreement is presumptively valid.

It is Petitioner's burden to show that litigating in the selected forum "will be so gravely difficult and inconvenient that [it] will for all practical purposes be deprived of [its] day in court." Petitioner has not met that burden. Instead, Petitioner merely relies on the standard *forum non conveniens* analysis to argue that it would be more convenient to decide the parties' disputes in a Russian court than before an arbitral tribunal. But that standard analysis is inapplicable when the parties have included a mandatory forum-selection clause. The arbitration agreement states that arbitrable disputes "shall be" decided before arbitrators in New York and that nonarbitrable disputes "shall be" litigated in New York courts, making the choice of forum mandatory rather than permissive. Given this mandatory language and the failure of Petitioner to demonstrate any ground under *M/S Bremen* for refusing to enforce the forum-selection clause, Petitioner must be held to its bargain.

---

[6]   To the extent that Petitioner raises comity as an affirmative defense to the merits of the arbitration, rather than as a ground for refusing to enforce the arbitration agreement, that argument must be addressed to the arbitrators and not to the Court.

Petitioner's claims that the Deposit Agreement's arbitration clause is unenforceable all fail. Public-policy considerations of the United States, whether or not a valid ground for refusing to enforce an arbitration agreement under Article II of the New York Convention, do not impose an obstacle to arbitration here. And the FAA preempts any principles of New York State public policy that are less favorable to arbitration. Having thus concluded that the agreement is enforceable, the Court must address whether the particular disputes between the parties are arbitrable. But the arbitration agreement clearly and unmistakably refers the question of arbitrability to arbitration.

C. The Parties Have Committed the Issue of Arbitrability to Arbitration

As explained above, it is presumed that parties to an arbitration agreement that falls under the FAA have not agreed to arbitrate whether their disputes are subject to arbitration. "Unless the parties clearly and unmistakably provide otherwise, the question of whether the parties agreed to arbitrate is to be decided by the court, not the arbitrator." The Second Circuit has held, however, that "when . . . parties explicitly incorporate rules [in an arbitration clause] that empower an arbitrator to decide issues of arbitrability, the incorporation serves as clear and unmistakable evidence of the parties' intent to delegate such issues to an arbitrator." The arbitration clause in the Deposit Agreement provides that disputes arising out of or relating to the ADRs, "shall be finally settled by arbitration in accordance with the rules of the American Arbitration Association, which rules are deemed to be incorporated by reference into this Section 7.06." (Deposit Agreement § 7.06.) The incorporation of the AAA rules serves as clear and unmistakable evidence of the parties' submission of arbitrability to the arbitrator.

. . .

D. The Arbitration Shall Be Conducted Under the Auspices of the AAA

Finally, Petitioner's argument that the rules of the London Court of International Arbitration rather than those of the AAA control must be rejected. The ADRs state that "[t]he Deposit Agreement provides" for the settlement of disputes "by arbitration in London, England, in accordance with the Rules of the London Court of International Arbitration." (The Bank of New York American Depositary Receipt for Preferred Shares of the Nominal Value of 1,000 Rubles Each of JSC Surgutneftegaz art. 22.) This is plainly incorrect because the Deposit Agreement provides for AAA arbitration in New York. The ADRs include a caveat explaining that "[t]he statements made on the face and reverse of this receipt are summaries of certain provisions of the Deposit Agreement and *are qualified by and subject to the detailed provisions of the Deposit Agreement,* to which reference is hereby made." Therefore, any inconsistency between the Deposit Agreement and the ADRs must be resolved by reference to the Deposit Agreement. The arbitration clause in the ADRs, by its own terms, does not constitute a separate agreement to arbitrate, but was merely meant to summarize the obligations included in the Deposit Agreement. Petitioner does not argue to the contrary.

Petitioner may also raise the issue of the place of arbitration before the arbitral tribunal. The situs of the arbitration is of critical importance because the law of the jurisdiction in which the arbitration is conducted ordinarily provides the procedural law of the arbitration. The courts of the jurisdiction in which an award is rendered have greater authority to decline confirmation of an arbitral award under the New York Convention than do the courts of other jurisdictions. The AAA recognizes this importance in its rules. Article 13.1 of the AAA International Rules states, "If the parties disagree as to the place of arbitration, the administrator may initially determine the place of arbitration, subject to the power of the tribunal to determine finally the place of arbitration within 60 days after its constitution." Similarly, the Commercial Rules provide, "If a party objects to the locale requested by the other party, the AAA shall have the power to determine the locale, and its decision shall be final and binding." AAA Commercial Arb. R. 10 (2003). Accordingly, Petitioner retains the opportunity to argue to the arbitrators that London and not New York is the proper venue for the arbitration.

NOTES

1. On appeal the Second Circuit affirmed this decision in an unpublished opinion. *JSC Surgutneftegaz v. President & Fellows of Harvard College*, 167 Fed. Appx. 266 (2d Cir. 2006). Subsequently the arbitral panel authorized the matter to proceed on a class basis, and the district court refused to vacate that award.

2. The internal affairs doctrine—the idea that an outsider, whether court or arbitral tribunal, will not review decisions reached in accordance with a firm's prescribed decisionmaking process as regard those matters committed to those processes—is a fundamental principle of corporate law. *See* James Y. Stern, *Property, Exclusivity, and Jurisdiction*, 100 Va. L. Rev. 111, 177–79 (2014). Is allowing arbitration of such a matter inconsistent with that doctrine? Or is it enough to expect the arbiter to respect the doctrine? Similarly, if the Russian court decision regarding the propriety of the Surgutneftegaz board's decision merits comity, can't the arbitral tribunal honor that principle by agreeing to respect the court's decision?

3. Recall the ADC v. AGD dispute, excerpted in Chapter 5 above. That case also involved the question of arbitrability of a particular issue, namely ownership of rights in land. To what extent did that question resemble the application of the internal affairs doctrine in this case? What does the internal affairs doctrine have in common with matters of land ownership? Can an issue be both local and arbitral?

4. Does ownership of a foreign company's shares through an ADR enlarge the owner's rights or simply alter them? Could the ADR owners sue in the Russian courts, or would they have to rely on The Bank of New York, the nominal owner of the shares, to enforce their rights? Note that shareholders do not have a general and comprehensive right to second guess the decisions of officers or directors of a company. Instead, they must demonstrate a violation of a specific legal duty owed to them. What legal duty did the preferred shareholders claim was violated in this case?

5. Over the last several decades the Supreme Court has taken a consistently pro-arbitration approach in its decisions, showing considerable deference to the decision of parties to submit a dispute to arbitration and limiting the power of courts to refuse to enforce an arbitral award. *BG Group, PLC v. Republic of Argentina*, 134 S. Ct. 1198 (2014) (deference to arbitral discretion to determine which issues committed to arbitral determination); *American Express Co. v. Italian Colors Restaurant*, 133 S. Ct. 2304 (2013) (enforcing contractual arbitration clause waiving class arbitration); *AT & T Mobility LLC v. Concepcion*, 131 S. Ct. 1740 (2011) (invalidating state law banning waivers of class arbitration); *Hall Street Associates, L.L.C. v. Mattel, Inc.*, 552 U.S. 576 (2008) (parties cannot contract to broaden grounds for judicial review of an arbitral award); *Vimar Seguros y Reaseguros, S.A. v. M/V Sky Reefer*, 515 U.S. 528 (1995) (arbitration clause does not violate statutory provision forbidding diminution of a carrier's liability under Carriage of Goods at Sea Act); *Mitsubishi Motors Corp. v. Soler Chrysler-Plymouth, Inc.*, 473 U.S. 614 (1985) (claim that termination of automobile dealership violated antitrust law subject to arbitration). *Mitsubishi Motors* is especially instructive, because the terminated dealer argued that the claim rested on public law (the Sherman Act) and thus was not a simple commercial dispute. The Supreme Court ruled that the dealer nonetheless had to comply with its contractual commitment to submit all disputes to arbitration. If the arbitral body failed to take into account the dealer's public law claims, the Court noted, the courts then could vacate the award as against public policy. But the Court refused to assume that the arbitral body would not do an adequate job of considering the antitrust claim.

C. ENFORCEMENT OF FOREIGN JUDGMENTS AND ARBITRAL AWARDS

Once a person prevails in arbitral proceeding, it has an award that, under the terms of the New York Convention, any domestic court must enforce on essentially the same terms as a domestic judicial judgment. But enforcement still requires the presence of assets belonging to the losing party that are subject to attachment and sale. A common problem is relating the ownership of assets to the person against who an award has been made.

In the case of a sovereign state, it may act in different capacities and have various legal identities. Different departments of the government, including state-owned legal entities, may have a separate legal identity from the state as a whole. When will assets owned by one aspect of a sovereign be used to satisfy a legal obligation of a distinct aspect of the same sovereign? Consider the following case.

Compagnie Noga D'Importation et D'Exportation S.A. v. The Russian Federation

United States Court of Appeals for the Second Circuit
361 F.3d 676 (2004)

■ MINER, CIRCUIT JUDGE:

In these consolidated appeals, we are confronted with the issue of whether a foreign arbitration award can be confirmed and enforced against a sovereign nation where the arbitration agreement was signed by an organ of that nation's central government and where that organ—and not the nation itself—participated in the underlying arbitration proceedings. Specifically, plaintiff-appellant Compagnie Noga

D'Importation et D'Exportation S.A. ("Noga") sought to confirm and enforce a Swedish arbitration award against defendant-appellee Russian Federation. The Russian Federation opposed confirmation principally on the ground that it was a party to neither the arbitration agreement nor the Swedish arbitration proceedings. Instead, it argued that the proper party to these proceedings should be the Government of Russia (the "Government"), a political organ of the Russian central government. The United States District Court for the Southern District of New York (Pauley, J.), accepted the Russian Federation's argument and denied Noga's motion to confirm. For the reasons set forth below, we conclude that, for the purposes of these proceedings, the Russian Federation and the Government are the same party, and accordingly, we vacate the judgment of the District Court. Furthermore, we remand for further proceedings with respect to, among other things, (i) whether Noga's assignments of its arbitration proceeds to certain of its creditors deprived it of standing to seek confirmation of the arbitral award; and (ii) whether the creditors to whom Noga assigned the arbitration proceeds must be joined as necessary and indispensable parties under Fed. R. Civ. P. 19.

BACKGROUND

I.   *Loans That Were the Subject of the Underlying Arbitration*

In December 1990, Noga entered into supply contracts to provide $550 million worth of food and consumer goods to foreign trade agencies of both the Union of Soviet Socialist Republics ("USSR"), the predecessor to the Russian Federation, and the Federative Socialist Soviet Republic of Russia ("RSFSR"), a constituent republic of the USSR. When anticipated third-party financing for these supply contracts did not materialize, Noga agreed to finance them in part

In April 1991, Noga entered into a $422.5 million loan agreement ("1991 Loan Agreement") with the Government of the RSFSR, which was represented by its Council of Ministers and defined in the agreement as the "Borrower." The stated purpose of the 1991 Loan Agreement was to finance Noga's existing supply contracts with the state-owned agencies and enterprises of the RSFSR. As consideration for the 1991 Loan Agreement, the Borrower agreed to cause the RSFSR-owned oil company to deliver crude oil products to Noga pursuant to a schedule extending into September 1993. Moreover, the Borrower represented that it had obtained all the "required licenses, approvals and consents from the appropriate Authorities of the U.S.S.R." to provide this consideration. As contemplated in the 1991 Loan Agreement, Noga and the RSFSR state oil company entered into a separate agreement for the delivery of crude oil products. In anticipation of receiving the crude oil products on schedule, Noga advanced cash and credit to finance RSFSR imports of food and consumer goods and the development of a baby food factory and a television station in the RSFSR.

In January 1992, Noga and the Government of the Russian Federation[2] entered into a $400 million loan agreement ("1992 Loan

---

[2] The Soviet Union collapsed between the execution of the 1991 and 1992 Loan Agreements. By the time the 1992 Loan Agreement was executed, the Russian Federation had succeeded the RSFSR. Moreover, during the period 1992–1993, the Russian Federation assumed both the debts and the assets of the former Soviet Union and its constituent republics. *See* Paul Williams & Jennifer Harris, *State Succession to Debts and Assets: The Modern Law and Policy*, 42 HARV. INT'L L.J. 355, 366–83 (2001).

Agreement"), which defined the term "Borrower" as "the Government of the Russian Federation, acting for and on its own behalf and responsibility [sic]." The 1992 Loan Agreement provided that half of the $400 million loan would be used to finance supply contracts executed between Noga and another agency of the Russian Federation for the import of agro-chemical products and that the other half would be used to discharge state debt to foreign suppliers for deliveries of similar products to the RSFSR during the period 1990–1991. The promised consideration for the 1992 Loan Agreement was the delivery of crude oil from an agency of the Russian Federation under a separate contract with that agency and pursuant to a delivery schedule extending through the end of 1994. In anticipation of these deliveries and pursuant to the 1992 Loan Agreement, Noga financed imports of agro-chemical products into the Russian Federation.

Both the 1991 Loan Agreement and the 1992 Loan Agreement provided for: (i) binding arbitration of any disputes between the parties and their successors in the Chamber of Commerce of Stockholm, Sweden; (ii) the choice of Swiss law to resolve those disputes; (iii) the waiver of immunity with respect to the enforcement of any arbitration award; and (iv) consent to suit in the state and federal courts of, inter alia, New York.

II. *Swedish Arbitration Proceedings*

Disputes eventually arose between Noga and the Government regarding performance of the Loan Agreements. In December 1992, Noga declared the Government to be in default, claiming that it owed Noga $300 million in principal and interest. In April 1993, Noga terminated the agreements and accelerated payment on the loans. In June 1993, Noga filed a Request for Arbitration with the Stockholm Chamber of Commerce, seeking over $275 million for unpaid balances, plus consequential damages. Noga's Arbitration Request identified the Russian Federation as the respondent and explained that its decision to do so was based on the facts that (i) "both the 'buying' and the 'selling' Agencies '[were]' the Russian Federation, i.e. under the [Russian Federation's] control"; (ii) "all contracts between [Noga] and the Agencies [made] express reference to the contracts entered into by Noga and the Russian Federation, since such contracts represented the performance of the Loan Agreements"; and (iii) "the Russian Federation guaranteed performance by the 'selling' Agencies for repayment of the Loans."

The Russian Federation made no response to the Arbitration Request. Instead, attorneys representing the Government objected to Noga naming the Russian Federation as the respondent and requested that the arbitrators require Noga to amend its Arbitration Request to name the Government and the state agencies that had signed the contracts as the proper respondents. In response, Noga argued that the arbitrators should "overrule" the Government's objection on the ground that the Russian Federation and the Government were the same legal person and thus the Government's acts were directly attributable to the Russian Federation. The arbitrators never ruled on the Government's objection, and Noga never sought judicial intervention to compel the Russian Federation to participate in the arbitration.

Eight years of arbitration proceedings followed. The arbitration was conducted in two phases. Phase I related to liability and damages, except for consequential damages; Phase II related to consequential damages.

Throughout the arbitration proceedings, the Government—and not the Russian Federation—appeared and arbitrated with Noga.

A. *Phase I*

At the conclusion of Phase I, the arbitrators issued two awards, both of which are the subject of this appeal. In the first award, dated February 1, 1997, the tribunal determined that Noga had been justified in both declaring a default and in accelerating the remaining oil deliveries. The arbitrators awarded Noga approximately $23 million in damages, plus accrued interest from April 1993 until the date of payment. On May 15, 1997, the tribunal issued a supplemental award, which increased the amount of the earlier award by approximately $4 million for management fees that Noga had alleged were omitted from the first award. Together, the two awards (collectively, the "Phase I Award") totaled approximately $50 million, including interest through May 1997. The caption of the arbitration awards refers to the respondent as the "Government of the Russian Federation (Russia)" Throughout the awards, however, the arbitrators refer interchangeably to the "Government of the Russian Federation," the "Russian Federation," and "Russia."

The Government appealed the supplemental award to the District Court of Stockholm, which dismissed the appeal and awarded attorneys' fees and costs to Noga. The caption contained in the Swedish court's decision identified the "Russian Federation, the Ministry of Finance" as the plaintiff. The court's decision repeatedly refers to the plaintiff as the "Russian Federation," although the issue of which entity was the proper party was not before it, and it was not being asked to confirm the Phase I Award. The Stockholm District Court's decision was affirmed by the Svea Court of Appeal, which also referred to the "Russian Federation" in both the caption and text of its decision and awarded Noga additional attorneys' fees and costs. Neither the Russian Federation nor the Government has paid the Phase I Award.

B. *Phase II*

On March 13, 2001 (while the actions giving rise to this appeal were pending), the arbitrators issued an award finding that Noga was entitled to approximately $25.3 million in consequential damages, plus interest that had accrued during the eight years since the Arbitration Request had been filed. As of the date the briefs in this appeal were filed, an appeal of the Phase II Award was still pending in the Swedish courts, and Noga had not yet sought to confirm or enforce this award.

[The court's discussion of Noga's assignment of its claims to creditors and the question of whether Noga had retained an interest in the awards is omitted. The district court dismissed Noga's suit to recognize and enforce the awards on the ground that the Russian Federation was legally distinction from the Russian government and thus not liable under the awards.]

. . .

DISCUSSION

I. *Can the Phase I Award Be Confirmed Against the Russian Federation?*

A. *Framework for Confirming International Arbitration Awards*

Because Noga is seeking to enforce an arbitration award rendered in a foreign state, the confirmation of the Phase I Award is governed by the framework set forth in the Convention on the Recognition and Enforcement of Foreign Arbitral Awards ("Convention"), as implemented by, and reprinted in, the Federal Arbitration Act ("FAA"). "Under the Convention, [a] district court's role in reviewing a foreign arbitral award is strictly limited" and "the showing required to avoid summary confirmance is high." Specifically, the FAA provides that, upon the application of a party to an arbitration award made pursuant to the Convention, a district court shall enter "an order confirming the award as against any other party to the arbitration," unless the court "finds one of the grounds for refusal or deferral of recognition or enforcement of the award specified in the . . . Convention." As the party opposing confirmation, the Russian Federation bore the burden of establishing that the Phase I Award should not have been honored. This burden is imposed because "the public policy in favor of international arbitration is strong."

The District Court declined to confirm the Phase I Award on the grounds that (i) the Russian Federation was not a party to the Swedish arbitration proceedings and (ii) this case did not fall under one of the limited exceptions in which we have held that an arbitration award can be enforced against a nonparty. Consequently, the District Court concluded that it lacked jurisdiction to confirm the award against the Russian Federation. For the reasons that follow, we disagree with the District Court's conclusion that it lacked jurisdiction to confirm the Phase I Award against the Russian Federation.

B. *Choice of Law*

On appeal, Noga principally challenges the District Court's legal conclusion that the Russian Federation and the Government are not the same entities for the purpose of confirming the Phase I Award, and urges that we apply principles of federal common law or public international law to reach this conclusion. The Russian Federation counters that: (i) this case should be decided under principles of private international law, which dictate that Russian law be applied in determining whether the Russian Federation and the Government are the same entities; and (ii) under Russian law, the Russian Federation and the Government are separate entities.

In making their respective choice-of-law arguments, both parties rely on the Supreme Court's decision in *First National City Bank v. Banco Para El Comercio Exterior de Cuba*, 462 U.S. 611 (1983) ("Bancec"). There, the Republic of Cuba established a state-owned trade bank "with full juridical capacity . . . of its own." This trade bank sued to collect on a letter of credit issued by an American bank. The American bank counterclaimed, asserting a right to set off the value of its assets in Cuba that had been nationalized by the Cuban government. The Cuban trade bank claimed immunity from this counterclaim under the Foreign Sovereign Immunities Act ("FSIA"), 28 U.S.C. § 1602 *et seq.*

The Supreme Court concluded that the FSIA did not control the determination of whether the seized Cuban assets could be set off against the claim of the Cuban trade bank. Instead, the Court held that principles of public international law and federal common law—rather than Cuban domestic law—should be applied to determine the "effect to be given to [the Cuban trade bank's] separate juridical status." According to the Court, "to give conclusive effect to the law of the chartering state in determining whether the separate juridical status of its instrumentality should be respected would permit the state to violate with impunity the rights of third parties under international law while effectively insulating itself from liability in foreign courts." On the other hand, the Court cautioned that "freely ignoring the separate status of government instrumentalities would result in substantial uncertainty over whether an instrumentality's assets would be diverted to satisfy a claim against the sovereign, and might thereby cause third parties to hesitate before extending credit to a government instrumentality without the government's guarantee." Consequently, "the efforts of sovereign nations to structure their governmental activities in a manner deemed necessary to promote economic development and efficient administration would surely be frustrated." Thus, "due respect for the actions taken by foreign sovereigns and for principles of comity between nations" led the Court "to conclude . . . that government instrumentalities established as juridical entities distinct and independent from their sovereign should normally be treated as such."

As the principal issue in this appeal is whether the Government is an instrumentality established as a juridical entity distinct and independent from the Russian Federation, the *Bancec* decision is of little help to us here. In any event, because we conclude that the answer to this question is the same regardless which of the bodies of law advocated by the parties is applied here, we need not cut the Gordian choice-of-law knot presented to us by the parties.

C.   *Russian Law*

We turn first to the Constitution of the Russian Federation in determining whether the Government and the Russian Federation should be treated as separate parties for the purposes of this confirmation proceeding. That charter provides a detailed discussion of the relationship between these two entities. The Russian Constitution provides for a bicameral federal executive consisting of the President of the Russian Federation, who is described as being "the head of State," Konst. RF art. 80(1), and the Government, which shall exercise "executive power in the Russian Federation," id. art. 110(1). The Government consists of the Chairman of the Government (who is appointed by the president, subject to consent of the State Duma, the federal legislature), and the Deputy Chairman of the Government and the federal ministers (who are appointed by the president in consultation with the Chairman of the Government). Id. arts. 83(a), (e), 110(2), 111(1).

The Russian Constitution also enumerates the responsibilities of the Government, which include, among other things: (i) submitting a federal budget to the State Duma; (ii) "ensuring the implementation . . . of a uniform financial, credit, and monetary policy"; and (iii) "exercising any other powers vested in [the Government] by the Constitution of the Russian Federation, [Russian] federal laws, and decrees of the President of the Russian Federation." Id. art. 114(a), (b), (g). To carry out these responsibilities, the Government is empowered to "issue decrees and orders," which "shall be binding throughout the Russian Federation." Id. art. 115(1), (2). Finally, the members of the Government serve at the pleasure of the President: they must resign upon the election of a new President, id. art. 116; they may resign only with the consent of the President, id. art 117(1); and the President also can require them to resign at any time, id. art. 117(2).

Plainly, in light of the description of the Government in the Russian charter, that entity is not a sovereign, corporation, or instrumentality separate from the Russian Federation. Rather, the Government is a political organ of the Russian Federation, analogous to the cabinet of the American president. Most significantly, in the words of one scholar, the Government "is not a juridical person and enjoys no autonomous legal capacity." Indeed, given the Supreme Court's *Bancec* decision, had either the Government or the Russian Federation wanted to shield the latter entity from being the subject of these confirmation proceedings, either could have designated a publicly-owned state corporation or instrumentality as the entity to contract with Noga. At bottom, the Government was performing a quintessential "governmental" function: financing the purchase of massive quantities of basic necessities and infrastructure improvements to provide for the Russian people and paying for those necessities and improvements with the country's natural resources.

Finally, the Russian Federation has not satisfied its burden of proving that the Government is a separate juridical entity that can sue and be sued in Russian courts for obligations that are analogous to the ones set forth in the Loan Agreements or, indeed, for any legal obligations. For example, the Russian Federation could have presented docket entries or court filings from Russian courts indicating that the Government had sued or been sued in this capacity. No such evidence was presented to the District Court, however. Accordingly, we find that, under Russian law, the Government and the Russian Federation should be treated as the same party for the purpose of this confirmation proceeding.

D. *Federal Common Law*

The question of whether a federal court will confirm a foreign arbitration award against a sovereign nation, where one of the sovereign's political organs was a party to the arbitration, appears to be one of first impression. Federal courts have been asked to confirm such awards against a corporation owned or operated by a foreign sovereign under such theories as alter ego, piercing the corporate veil, or agency. The Fifth Circuit's recent decision in *Bridas S.A.P.I.C. v. Government of Turkmenistan*, 345 F.3d 347, is illustrative.

There, an Argentinian corporation (Bridas) entered into a joint venture agreement with a production association formed and owned by the Government of Turkmenistan, which was not itself a party to the agreement. Bridas subsequently initiated an arbitration proceeding against both the production association and the Government of Turkmenistan, alleging breach of the agreement. The arbitrators expressly rejected the argument of the Government of Turkmenistan that it was not a proper party to the arbitration because it had not signed the agreement. The arbitrators subsequently issued an award in favor of Bridas, which successfully brought an action in the Southern District of Texas to confirm the award. On appeal, the Fifth Circuit declined to confirm the arbitration award against the Government of Turkmenistan under theories of agency, estoppel, and third party beneficiary. Nevertheless, the court remanded the case to the district court for further proceedings with respect to whether the production association was the alter ego of the Government of Turkmenistan, instructing the district court to consider, inter alia, the factors used by the Fifth Circuit in determining whether a state agency is the "alter ego" of a state for Eleventh Amendment sovereign immunity purposes.

Likewise, this Court has been asked to confirm domestic arbitration awards under similar theories against nonparties to an arbitration proceeding or agreement. It is this latter line of cases that both the District Court and the Russian Federation cite in support of their conclusions that the Phase I Award should not be enforceable against the Russian Federation. But, as we noted above, analogizing the relationship between the Russian Federation and the Government to the relationship between a corporate parent and a subsidiary belies the reality of the political relationship between the Russian Federation and the Government and is thus inapposite. Analogies, as Cardozo warned of metaphors, "in law are to be narrowly watched, for starting as devices to liberate thought, they end often by enslaving it."

[The court's discussion of cases arising under the Foreign Sovereign Immunities Act and bankruptcy is omitted.]

. . .

In sum, under the federal common-law principles articulated above, no meaningful legal distinction can be drawn between a sovereign and one of its political organs. Accordingly, the Russian Federation has failed to overcome the presumption in favor of confirming the Phase I Award, and it has failed to demonstrate that the Government should be treated as a separate party from the Russian Federation in this context under federal common law.

E.   *International Law*

The distinction made by the District Court between the acts of a sovereign and the acts of one of its governmental organs also finds no basis in international law. An axiomatic principle of international law is that "the conduct of any State organ shall be considered an act of that State under international law, whether the organ exercises legislative, executive, judicial or any other functions, whatever position it holds in the organization of the State, and whatever its character as an organ of the central government or of a territorial unit of the State." Draft Articles on Responsibilities of States for Internationally Wrongful Acts ("Draft Articles"), art. 4(1), reprinted in Report of the International Law Commission on the Work of Its Fifty-Third Session, U.N. GAOR, 56th Sess., Supp. No. 10, at 84, U.N. Doc. A/56/10 (2001). As the commentary to this provision of the Draft Articles explains, "the replies by Governments to the Preparatory Committee for the 1930 Conference for the Codification of International Law were unanimously of the view that the actions or omissions of organs of the State must be attributed to it." "The Third Committee of the Conference adopted unanimously on first reading an article 1, which provided that international responsibility shall be incurred by a State as a consequence of any failure on the part of its organs to carry out the international obligations of the State."

The maxim that the acts of an organ of a sovereign's government are attributable to the sovereign have also been regularly applied in international courts and arbitrations. For example, in *Texaco Overseas Petroleum Co. v. Government of the Libyan Arab Republic*, 53 I.L.R. 393 (1975), the arbitrator rejected the Libyan Government's objections to the tribunal's jurisdiction to arbitrate claims arising out of Libya's nationalization of its oil industry. One of those objections was that the contracts in question had been entered into by the Libyan Minister of Petroleum and thus Libya, "a sovereign State, was not a party to these contracts." Citing to the 1970 draft of the (as yet unfinished) Draft Articles, the arbitrator overruled this objection, concluding that "it [was] incontestable and uncontested that, if the 'Ministry of Petroleum' or any other qualified organ of the Libyan Government . . . had entered into Deeds of Concession, such organ acted as the organ duly qualified and authorized to do so by the Libyan Government." Thus, it was "the Libyan Arab Republic . . . and that State alone—which had become bound by the acts performed by its own organs."

In sum, we hold that regardless of whether principles of Russian law, federal common law, or international law are applied, the Russian Federation and the Government are not separate "parties" for the purposes of confirming and enforcing an arbitral award under the Convention. Accordingly, the judgment of the District Court denying Noga's motion to confirm is vacated.

. . .

■ [The concurring opinion of JUDGE JACOBS is omitted].

NOTES

1. This lawsuit sought to confirm and enforce an arbitral award obtained pursuant to the New York Convention. Confirmation means that a domestic court has reviewed the award and found that no defenses to its enforcement exist under local law. At that point the award becomes a judicially enforceable debt, which provides a legal basis for attachment of assets of the debtor and their forced sale to satisfy the debt. Enforcement requires that assets be identified, attached, and seized. Note that as a result of the Second Circuit decision, Noga overcame one set of defenses, but did not obtain final confirmation of its awards. Furthermore, the opinion did not discuss the identification of assets for enforcement, other than in a note, omitted here, where it reported on intervention by the U.S. government to prevent enforcement against uranium stockpiles belonging to the Russian Federation.

2. *Compagnie Noga* confronts the question of whether an obligation contracted on behalf of one entity (here the Russian government) binds another entity (the Russian state). The courts resolved the question by looking at Russian law, international law, and federal common law. Why should anything other than Russian law apply? Putting the point only a bit differently, suppose that enforcement of an arbitral award under the New York Convention, which the Federal Arbitration Act implements, rests ultimately on federal common law, operating interstitially to resolve issues

not addressed expressly by the Convention or the Act. Why shouldn't the federal common law rule be one of incorporating the law of the place of the contract, unless the contract specifies some other choice? When Noga contracted with the Russian government in the transaction that led to the arbitral award, didn't Noga accept the Russian government as it found it? Noga's argument, which the court adopted, is that under Russian law the government is not a distinct legal entity (in civil law parlance, a legal person). Rather, under Russian law some members of the government have the capacity to enter into contracts that bind the Russian state. Compare the uses of Russian law in the *Films By Jove* case above.

3.   Why would Noga rather have a claim against the Russian state than one against the government? If its claim does run against the Russian state, does it follow that it can enforce its award against any entity that belongs to the Russian state? *First National City Bank v. Banco Para El Comercio Exterior de Cuba*, 462 U.S. 611 (1983), discussed in *Compagnie Noga*, involved a claim by a U.S. bank for compensation based on expropriation of its property by the Cuban state. Banco Para El Comercio Exterior was a separate legal person, but it also was wholly owned by the Cuban state and operated by the Cuban government as an instrument of foreign policy, rather than as a separate commercial enterprise. The Supreme Court stated that in principle the separate legal identity of state-owned enterprises should be respected, but that under the facts of the case "veil-piercing" so as to treat the Banco as interchangeable with the Cuban state was appropriate.

4.   In instances where a claim runs only against a particular state-owned enterprise (with no corporate-veil-piercing) and not against the foreign sovereign that owns the enterprise, it becomes necessary to determine which assets belong to the enterprise, and which to the state. Consider the following case.

Karaha Bodas Co., L.L.C. v. Perusahaan Pertambangan Minyak Dan Gas Bumi Negara

United States Court of Appeals for the Second Circuit
313 F.3rd 70 (2002), cert. denied, 539 U.S. 904 (2003)

■ SACK, CIRCUIT JUDGE.

Respondent-appellant Perusahaan Pertambangan Minyak Dan Gas Bumi Negara ("Pertamina") and non-party-appellant the Ministry of Finance of the Republic of Indonesia (the "Ministry") appeal from an April 26, 2002, memorandum and order issued by the United States District Court for the Southern District of New York insofar as it permits petitioner-appellee Karaha Bodas Company, L.L.C. ("KBC") to execute against a portion of the funds in several Bank of America trust accounts that are listed in the district court's order. KBC appeals the same order insofar as it denies KBC's motion to execute against the remainder of the same funds. The question on appeal concerns the ownership of the funds in the Bank of America trust accounts, which derive from sales of Indonesian liquefied natural gas ("LNG"), and whether such funds can be attached under New York law, as applicable pursuant to the Foreign Sovereign Immunities Act of 1976, 28 U.S.C. §§ 1330, 1602–1611 ("FSIA"). KBC's claim rests on the allegation that all such funds belong to Pertamina, and on the alternative theory that KBC was entitled to rely on Pertamina's ownership thereof. Pertamina and the Ministry respond that under Indonesian law, the funds belong to the Republic of Indonesia.

We agree with the district court's disposition of the ownership question. The district court correctly analyzed the Indonesian law that controls the ownership of the funds and correctly concluded that most, but not all, of the funds belong to Indonesia. Accordingly, we affirm.

BACKGROUND

The Parties

KBC describes itself as "a Cayman Islands limited liability company formed by two American power companies and other investors, and is 90%-owned by U.S. investors." The Ministry, acting on behalf of the Government of the Republic of Indonesia, is a "foreign state" within the meaning of the FSIA, 28 U.S.C. § 1603(a). Pertamina is an oil and gas company owned and controlled by the Republic of Indonesia. Pertamina engages in oil and gas exploration, extraction, processing, marketing, transportation, and distribution. The 1971 statute creating Pertamina, Law 8 of 1971, explains that the company's goals are "to develop and carry out the exploitation of oil and natural gas . . . for the maximum prosperity of the People and the State." The Indonesian government owns all of Pertamina's equity and controls a supervisory board, constituted pursuant to Law 8, that supervises Pertamina's management. Pertamina, for purposes of the FSIA, is therefore "an agency or instrumentality of a foreign state." 28 U.S.C. § 1603.

The KBC-Pertamina Geothermal Energy Contracts

In November 1994, KBC executed two contracts—a "Joint Operation Contract" and an "Energy Sales Contract"—with Pertamina and another Indonesian state-owned entity, Persero, for the development of geothermal energy extraction facilities in the Karaha area of West Java. In these contracts, Pertamina waived "any . . . right of immunity (sovereign or otherwise) which it or its assets now has or may acquire in the future." The contracts did not contain any representations about KBC's right to attach particular assets in case of default or breach. And KBC points to no evidence, either within the contracts' text or in pre-contract negotiations, that Pertamina made any representations regarding its ownership of LNG revenues or its obligation to provide a security interest. Each contract also contained a choice of law clause specifying Indonesian law and provided that disputes would be resolved by an international arbitral tribunal constituted under the Arbitral Rules of the United Nations Commission on International Trade Law.

In 1997 and 1998, Indonesia experienced a fiscal crisis that induced political instability and the eventual collapse, on May 21, 1998, of the regime led by President Mohamed Suharto. In the course of the crisis, on September 20, 1997, the KBC projects were suspended by an Indonesian "Presidential Decree," along with approximately seventy-four other government-related infrastructure projects. In November 1997, another decree permitted the KBC projects to proceed again, but in January 1998, a third decree terminated the KBC projects once more, despite lobbying by KBC and Pertamina, among others.

[KBC invoked its arbitration rights against Pertamina in Geneva and in 2000 received an award for more than $250,000,000. KBC then brought a suit in a Texas federal court to enforce the award. Pertamina filed suit in Indonesia and obtained an injunction from a local court requiring KBC not to take any action to enforce the award anywhere in the world. The Texas court ordered Pertamina to pay KBC $261,000,000 and also barred Pertamina from requesting enforcement of the Indonesian court injunction. Pertamina appealed the Texas decision to the Fifth Circuit. KBC registered the Texas judgment in the Southern District of New York and sought to execute it against deposits held in New York by the Bank of America, among others.]

The Nature of the Disputed Funds

This appeal concerns fifteen trust accounts at Bank of America. These accounts contain funds from the sale of LNG extracted in Indonesia under arrangements called Production Sharing Contracts ("PSCs"), which are governed by Indonesian law.

As mandated by Indonesian law, Pertamina enters into PSCs with private oil and gas contractors for the extraction of Indonesian crude oil and natural gas. The Republic of Indonesia is not party to the PSCs, but it must approve them. Under a PSC, the private contractor (the "PSC contractor") is responsible for all exploration, development, extraction, production, transportation, and marketing operations related to a specified geographic area under Pertamina's management. As part of their compensation, PSC contractors initially receive a share of the oil or natural gas after extraction. They then transfer the remaining oil or gas to Pertamina.

Pertamina transports the gas for domestic sale or for conversion into LNG at liquefaction plants. Pertamina sells LNG to foreign buyers pursuant to long-term sales contracts that contain choice of law clauses specifying New York law as governing the contracts. LNG sales were the "largest single source of Pertamina sales revenue" in the last nine months of 2000. Buyers of LNG remit payment to specified trust accounts in New York. In all such LNG sales, Pertamina, in its own name, purports to transfer title to the LNG, or title to the refined product, to the buyer. Pertamina warrants that it has "good title to the [LNG], free of all liens and encumbrances of any kind." Revenues from sales of natural gas are also sent to trusts in New York. The trusts "distribute the proceeds in accordance with trust agreements and ultimately to the [PSC contractor] in accordance with their respective [PSCs]." However natural gas is sold, and whether or not it is liquefied, proceeds from sales are first paid into trust accounts such as those at Bank of America.

Bank of America is the trustee of the accounts deposited with it. Before making any allocations or distributions, it credits all LNG revenues from a particular project, or subpart of a project, to a general account. The general accounts and other subaccounts are operated pursuant to contractual arrangements known as Trustee and Paying Agent Agreements ("TPAA") that define the trustee's obligations. TPAAs are signed by Bank of America, Pertamina, and relevant PSC contractors, but only Pertamina has authority to direct payment. Like the LNG sales contracts, the TPAAs also contain choice of law clauses specifying New York law as governing.

Before any distribution can be made to Pertamina or the PSC Contractor, the TPAAs specify that production expenses—which include debt service payments, production costs, and trustee expenses—must be paid first. After production payments are made, the "PSC Revenue" or the "Net Operating Income" remains in the general trust account. This remainder is essentially the net profit from the PSC, after costs have been deducted and debts have been serviced.

The PSC Revenue is then divided between Pertamina and the PSC Contractor for a particular project in contractually specified portions known as "Production Sharing Percentages." These payments are made to separate subaccounts or separate line accounts within the general trust account. The funds at issue in this appeal are, thus, Pertamina's Production Sharing Percentage or, in the terms used in the contracts, Pertamina's share of the Net Operating Income.

Pertamina's Production Sharing Percentage is transferred directly to the Republic of Indonesia. Indeed, "Pertamina, at the direction of the Indonesian Government, has issued standing instructions to the Trustee to pay its Production Sharing Percentage to an account of the Government of Indonesia at Bank Indonesia." Evidence submitted by the Ministry and Pertamina suggests that twenty percent of the Indonesian national budget derives from oil and natural gas revenues. The funds are typically used to maintain Indonesia's foreign exchange reserves, and thus to service Indonesia's foreign debt.

The LNG Security Arrangement

One noteworthy feature of the trust arrangements is the mechanism whereby Pertamina borrows funds for the construction of natural gas liquefaction facilities, without requiring a counter-party lender to depend on Pertamina's willingness or ability to assure repayment. For example, the record contains 1997 loan agreements for funds to create a natural gas liquefaction facility. One loan agreement explains that "certain proceeds of liquefied natural gas" that are held in trust accounts at Bank of America are the "*sole* source of repayment." A fixed percentage of gross revenues from LNG revenues in the trust accounts is therefore allocated to loan repayment, and only after loan repayments are complete can other disbursements be made. Through this device, the LNG revenue stream structure protects lenders' interests.

[The district court determined that under Indonesia law Pertamina had a right to only five percent of the funds held in the banks and permitted KBC to attach only that amount.]

III. Execution Against or Attachment of Foreign Sovereigns' Property

Attachment of a foreign state's property in the United States is governed by the FSIA. In relevant part, the FSIA provides that "the property in the United States of a foreign state shall be immune from attachment arrest and execution except as provided in sections 1610 and 1611 of [the FSIA]." 28 U.S.C. § 1609. Section 1610 provides different regimes for sovereign states on the one hand, and their agencies and instrumentalities on the other. First, 28 U.S.C. § 1610(a) provides that any property of a foreign sovereign that is

> used for a commercial activity in the United States, shall not be immune from attachment in aid of execution, or from execution, upon a judgment entered by a court of the United States . . . if

. . . (1) the foreign state has waived its immunity from attachment in aid of execution or from execution either explicitly or by implication, notwithstanding any withdrawal of the waiver the foreign state may purport to effect except in accordance with the terms of the waiver.

Second, § 1610(b), which concerns foreign states' instrumentalities, such as Pertamina, provides in relevant part that:

> any property in the United States of an agency or instrumentality of a foreign state engaged in commercial activity in the United States shall not be immune from attachment in aid of execution, or from execution, upon a judgment entered by a court of the United States . . . if . . . (1) the agency or instrumentality has waived its immunity from attachment in aid of execution or from execution either explicitly or implicitly, notwithstanding any withdrawal of the waiver the agency or instrumentality may purport to effect except in accordance with the terms of the waiver.

Subsection (a) is generally thought to be narrower than subsection (b). While subsection (b) applies to *all* property of the agencies and instrumentalities of foreign states, subsection (a) applies only to the property of foreign states that is "used in commercial activity."

In the appeal before us, sample geothermal energy contracts between Pertamina and KBC state that Pertamina "waive[s] any . . . right of immunity (sovereign or otherwise) which it or its assets now has or may have in the future." Pertamina, through its use of the trust funds to channel LNG revenues, engages in commerce in New York. Under 28 U.S.C. § 1610(b), Pertamina has thus waived its sovereign immunity from attachment in United States courts.

A.   *Attachment Under the FSIA and New York Law*

The FSIA states that when a foreign state is not protected by sovereign immunity, "the foreign state shall be liable in the same manner and to the same extent as a private individual under like circumstances." 28 U.S.C. § 1606. In attachment actions involving foreign states, federal courts thus apply Fed. R. Civ. P. 69(a), which requires the application of local state procedures.

In the instant action, the district court is located in New York state. We therefore apply New York law to determine what assets are "subject to enforcement, and thus available to judgment creditors." "New York procedure for enforcement of judgments is set out in Article 52 of the Civil Practice Law and Rules. The first section of Article 52 describes the assets that New York law has made subject to enforcement, and thus available to judgment creditors." The relevant provision, N.Y. C.P.L.R. § 5201(b), states that:

> Property against which a money judgment may be enforced. A money judgment may be enforced against any property which could be assigned or transferred, whether it consists of a present or future right or interest and whether or not it is vested, unless it is exempt from application to the satisfaction of the judgment.

In New York, then, a party seeking to enforce a judgment "stand[s] in the shoes of the judgment debtor in relation to any debt owed him or a property interest he may own." Nonetheless, a party cannot "reach . . . assets in which the judgment debtor has no interest." A determination of Pertamina's property interest in the disputed funds—i.e., whether Pertamina can "assign or transfer" any of these funds—is therefore dispositive of this appeal.

B. *Ownership of the Disputed Funds*

While the litigants agree that New York law governs what property can be attached, they diverge on what law governs the property rights of the Republic of Indonesia and Pertamina in the disputed funds. KBC argues that under New York law, Pertamina owns the Production Sharing Percentage because Pertamina controlled the allocation of the funds within the trust accounts and retained initial title to the LNG, which it sold to generate the disputed funds. KBC finds no significance in the fact that much of those funds flow to the Republic of Indonesia. In KBC's view, these funds merely represent "various royalties, taxes, and dividends" which "Pertamina is obligated to pay the Government." KBC argues that before those obligations are met, the funds belong to Pertamina. KBC's expert also argues that Indonesian law does not vest the Republic of Indonesia with any ownership interest in these funds.

Both Pertamina and the Ministry argue to the contrary that Indonesian law deprives Pertamina of all but a future property interest, limited to five percent of the Net Operating Income, while the Republic of Indonesia has the exclusive right to the rest of Pertamina's Production Sharing Percentage. They, like the district court, identify Government Regulation 41 as providing the dispositive rule of decision:

> Article 5 (1) The retention (fee) received by Pertamina with regard to the Production Sharing Contract shall be 5% (five percent) of the Net Operating Income of the relevant Production Sharing Contract.
>
> (2) The difference between portions received by Pertamina according to each Production Sharing Contract and the retention (fee) received by Pertamina as intended in paragraph (1) of this Article *shall be the Government's portion.*

Government Regulation of the Republic of Indonesia Number 41 of 1982, Art. 5 (emphasis added). According to Pertamina's expert, "[t]his [provision] means that the Government owns the Percentage Share due to Pertamina under the PSC, but must pay Pertamina the five percent fee," or the Retention.

Pertamina also argues that even the Retention, which equals five percent of the Net Operating Income, cannot be attached. Pertamina contends that before it transfers its Production Sharing Percentage to the Republic of Indonesia, the latter *owns* all the PSC Revenue as a result of Government Regulation 41. Only after the revenue reaches Jakarta does Pertamina receive the Retention. And even in Jakarta, Pertamina is not entitled to the entire Retention. Regulation 41, in Article 5(3), subjects the retention to a sixty percent tax. A second regulation, Government Regulation 73, then mandates payment of a fifty percent dividend to the government. In all, Pertamina actually receives one-fifth of the Retention.

Resolution of this appeal requires that we determine the legal ownership of the PSC Revenues. At the threshold, we must consider which choice of law rule governs the question of ownership.

IV. Choice of Law Analysis

[The court relied on its precedent for the proposition that in cases brought under the Foreign Sovereign Immunity Act, a court must apply the same choice of law rules that a state court in the same forum would apply.]

B. *New York or Indonesian Property Law*

Under New York law, "[t]he first step in any case presenting a potential choice of law issue is to determine whether there is an actual conflict between the laws of the jurisdictions involved." In property disputes, if a conflict is identified, New York choice of law rules require the application of an "interests analysis," in which "the law of the jurisdiction having the greatest interest in the litigation [is] applied and . . . the facts or contacts which obtain significance in defining State interests are those which relate to the purpose of the particular law in conflict."

1. Actual Conflict of Law. In the case at bar, the Republic of Indonesia and the State of New York apply the same general rules to property disputes. The Republic of Indonesia offers the only specific rules—Indonesian statutes and regulations—that determine the respective rights of Pertamina and the Republic of Indonesia in the disputed funds. New York law directs us to apply these Indonesian statutes and regulations. There is thus no actual conflict of law.

Under New York law, the party who possesses property is presumed to be the party who owns it. When a party holds funds in a bank account, possession is established, and the presumption of ownership follows.

Similarly, the Indonesian Civil Code provides that "whoever is in control of movable goods . . . shall be deemed to be the owner of such goods," Indonesian Civ. Code, art. 1977, and the phrase "movable goods" includes cash held in bank accounts.

Pertamina possesses the disputed funds. Under both New York and Indonesian law, we therefore proceed from the presumption that Pertamina owns the disputed funds. It is clear, however, that this presumption may be rebutted by evidence that the Republic of Indonesia actually controlled the disputed funds, or that Pertamina merely held the funds for the Republic of Indonesia, in the manner of a trustee. Under New York law, then, the property rights are determined by the underlying relationship between Pertamina and the Republic of Indonesia.

KBC urges us to apply New York law to this relationship, and thus, to the property rights in the disputed funds. Yet KBC has not pointed to any New York cases or statutes that purport to govern this kind of arrangement. The Republic of Indonesia is a foreign state, and Pertamina is a corporate entity of Indonesia, created by the legislative enactments and executive orders of the Republic of Indonesia. The relationship was created neither by contract nor by any other mechanism familiar to the laws of New York. It was established instead by provisions of Indonesian law uniquely applicable to the relationship itself: Law of the Republic of Indonesia Number 8 Year 1971 and Government Regulation of the Republic of Indonesia Number 41 of 1982. Under New York law, the meaning of these two provisions of Indonesian law determines the property rights of the parties. There is thus no actual conflict between the laws of New York and the laws of Indonesia.

2. *Interests Analysis.* In any event, even if there were such a conflict, we are confident that Indonesian law would govern under the "interests analysis" that would be applicable under New York choice of law rules. [The remainder of the court's discussion of this issue is omitted.]

V. The Property Interests of the Republic of Indonesia and Pertamina in the Restrained Funds

[The court determined that Pertamina had made no representation on which KBC reasonably could have relied to assume that Pertamina, and not the Indonesian government, owned the New York bank accounts.]

B. *The Property Interest Argument*

As described above, the crux of the parties' disagreement about Indonesian law hinges on a provision of Government Regulation 41 [quoted above]. . . . This provision, by using the possessive "Government's," mandates that all of the disputed funds, with the exception of the five percent that constitutes Pertamina's Retention, belong to the Republic of Indonesia. Thus, we agree that most of "the share denominated as 'Pertamina's' share under the PSCs belongs entirely to the Government," with the exception of the Article 5(1) Retention.

KBC responds that "the 'Government's Portion' referenced in [Government Regulation 41] is not a property interest [but] simply a reference to the 'indebted obligations' [already] owed by Pertamina to the Government of Indonesia." KBC contends that Law 8, the statute under which Regulation 41 was passed, creates these "indebted obligations." Article 15 of Law 8 states that Pertamina's deposit of sixty percent of Net Operating Income from PSCs "shall constitute the payment" of corporate tax, various levies, and other contributions. KBC argues that the amount that Pertamina owes to Indonesia in taxes, levies, and contributions is the "Government's portion." The disputed funds are, in KBC's view, owned by Pertamina and owed to Indonesia.

But KBC's interpretation of Article 5 of Government Regulation 41 is inconsistent with the surrounding statutory text. While Article 5(2) identifies in mandatory terms what "shall be the Government's portion," the very next provision imposes a "tax," which it explicitly labels as such. Government Regulation of the Republic of Indonesia Number 41 of 1982, Art. 5(3). The presence of a parallel provision explicitly referencing "tax" obligations suggests that Article 5(2) describes a different kind of obligation. The terminology of Article 15 of Law 8 underscores this inference: It refers to payments that "constitute" corporate taxes, customs levies, and the like, Law of the Republic of Indonesia Number 8 Year 1971, Art. 15, which are distinguished from other obligations.

Further, Article 5(2) of Government Regulation 41 and Article 15 of Law 8 refer to different amounts. The former, which creates the

"Government's portion," refers to the *"difference* between portions received by Pertamina according to each Production Sharing Contract and the retention (fee) received by Pertamina." Government Regulation of the Republic of Indonesia Number 41 of 1982, Art. 5. That is, the Government portion comprises, with respect to each PSC, the total amount of the Net Operating Income, *less* the amount to which the particular PSC contractors are entitled, *less* five percent of the Net Operating Income—a sum that depends upon the exact percentage to which contractors are entitled under the PSC. And, as KBC's counsel explained at oral argument, this percentage varies from contract to contract, so that the "Government's portion" also varies above and below sixty percent of Net Operating Income. Thus, the "Government's portion" is a varying amount.

Article 14 of Law 8, in contrast, refers to a *fixed* "sixty percent of the net operating income from the operations of Production Sharing Contracts prior to the division between the Enterprise and the Contractor." The *fixed* sixty percent that is Law 8's "indebted obligation" therefore cannot be the same thing as the *varying* percentage of the Net Operating Income that is the "Government's portion."[18]

The record also contains uncontroverted evidence that Pertamina's share of the Net Operating Income is transferred directly to the Ministry's account at the Federal Reserve Bank of New York. While this does not prove that the Republic of Indonesia has an ownership interest in such funds, it is consistent with such a conclusion.

We also agree with other Courts of Appeals that have suggested that a foreign sovereign's views regarding its own laws merit—although they do not command—some degree of deference. That Indonesia is a party to the case does not blunt this comity concern. Where a choice between two interpretations of ambiguous foreign law rests finely balanced, the support of a foreign sovereign for one interpretation furnishes legitimate assistance in the resolution of interpretive dilemmas. The Republic of Indonesia, of course, insists that Pertamina's reading of the relevant Indonesian law is correct. We thus conclude that Pertamina does not own any portion of the disputed funds, with the exception of the Retention. Like a trustee, Pertamina possesses the remaining funds but has no ownership interest in them.

C.   *The Retention*

Pertamina also argues that it has no right to the Retention, or, at a minimum, no right to eighty percent of the Retention. We disagree. While

---

[18] Despite this discrepancy, KBC's expert argues that "Article 14 and 15 [of Law 8] were implemented by [Government Regulation 41]." Decl. of Robert Hornick ¶ 27. But as a matter of Indonesian law, government regulations are not implementing mechanisms for legislation. Indonesian law contains "a bewildering variety of types of laws—statutes, regulations, decrees, circulars, etc." Eddy Damian & Robert N. Hornick, *Indonesia's Formal Legal System: An Introduction,* 20 AM. J. COMP. L. 492, 523 (1972). Among the varieties of law enumerated in the aforementioned article are "Government Regulation[s]," "Presidential Decision[s]," "Regulation[s] of the Minister," and "internal memoranda." This plethora of legal instruments in part ensues because the Indonesian executive branch has "considerably more executive law-making discretion than is the case, e.g. in the legal system of the U.S." And under Indonesian law, "[e]ven statutes passed by the House of Representative commonly look[ ] to the executive orders and Presidential speeches for their inspiration and legal base." Given the discrepancy in meaning between Law 8 and Government Regulation 41, we conclude that these rules do not exist in the hierarchal relationship described in the declaration of KBC's expert.

Pertamina may be under an obligation to transfer the Retention to the Ministry's account in New York, this fact does not alter the extant allocation of ownership interests. Pertamina has not identified any Indonesian statute or regulation that grants the Republic of Indonesia ownership rights in the Retention. "[U]nder New York law, a defendant has an interest in . . . funds if any part of the money is within the present or future control of the defendant." As property within Pertamina's control, which only Pertamina controls, the Retention is validly subject to attachment.

NOTES

1.   The court assumed that the question of ownership of the money in the account turned on Indonesian law. Was this necessarily correct? As the bank account was in a New York bank, shouldn't it be governed by New York law? Might the production sharing agreements that led to the creation of these accounts have specified what law would apply to their ownership? Could a bank agree that ownership of funds that it held in New York could be determined by reference to foreign law? Compare the choice of law analysis in *Films By Jove* above.

2.   The court states that a foreign sovereign's views regarding its own laws merit some degree of deference. Why? If the foreign sovereign is an interested party to a lawsuit, shouldn't its views be suspect? Should one make a distinction between longstanding and well-document views, on the one hand, and views arising in the course of litigation, on the other hand?

3.   The funds that KBC sought to attach represented sales from a production sharing agreement (PSA), a structure that we discussed in the previous chapter. One of the reasons for the payment structure used here is to ensure that attachable assets will be located in a jurisdiction with strong legal institutions, in the event of a dispute between the sovereign host and the foreign service-provider under the PSA. KBC thus was an indirect beneficiary of a provision intended to benefit a different foreign entity that was doing business with Pertamina.

4.   *Karaha Bodas* refers to parallel lawsuits in Texas and Indonesia, which contested the validity of the arbitral award on which KBC based its claim. Subsequent to the Second Circuit decision excerpted above, the Fifth Circuit determined that the federal district court in Texas should not have enjoined Pertamina from litigating in Indonesia to contest the validity of the award. The court reasoned that Indonesia had the right under the New York Convention to contest the award, and its choice of Indonesia as the forum for doing so had no practical effect on the Texas litigation. KBC had no assets in Indonesia and it seemed unlikely that any other jurisdiction would give comity to any Indonesian judicial order arising from that Indonesian litigation. *Karaha Bodas Company, L.L.C. v. Perusahaan Pertambangan Minyak Dan Gas Bumi Negara*, 335 F.3rd 357 (5th Cir. 2003).

Pertamina then brought suit in the Cayman Islands charging Karaha Bodas with fraud in the procurement of the arbitral award. The suit did not challenge the award itself, which Pertamina by then had satisfied, but rather sought damages in the amount of the money paid to Karaha Bodas under the award as well as a preliminary injunction preventing Karaha Bodas from disposing the money it had received until the court had resolved the suit. Karaha Bodas responded by procuring an injunction from the Southern

District of New York forbidding Pertamina from maintaining the Cayman Islands lawsuit. On appeal, the Second Circuit affirmed. The Court argued:

> Here, by contrast, the Cayman Islands has no arguable basis for jurisdiction to adjudicate rights and obligations of the parties with respect to the Award. Cayman Islands courts have no power to modify or annul the Award under the Convention; and Pertamina does not even attempt to argue that the Cayman Islands action is one that would be contemplated by the Convention. We conclude that in these circumstances the District Court had power to prevent Pertamina from engaging in litigation that would tend to undermine the regime established by the Convention for recognition and enforcement of arbitral awards. "[C]oncerns of international comity, respect for the capacities of foreign and transnational tribunals, and sensitivity to the need of the international commercial system for predictability in the resolution of disputes require that we enforce . . . agreement[s]" to submit disputes to binding international arbitration. *Mitsubishi Motors Corp. v. Soler Chrysler-Plymouth, Inc.*, 473 U.S. 614, 629 (1985). These considerations also require us to protect the regime established by the Convention for enforcement of international arbitral awards, if necessary by enjoining parties from engaging in foreign litigation that would undermine it.

Karaha Bodas Company, L.L.C. v. Perusahaan Pertambangan Minyak Dan Gas Bumi Negara, 500 F.3d 111, 125 (2d Cir. 2007), *cert. denied*, 555 U.S. 929 (2008).

NML Capital Ltd. v. Republic of Argentina

United States Court of Appeal for the Second Circuit
727 F.3d 230 (2013), *cert. denied*, 134 S. Ct. 2819 (2014)

■ PARKER, CIRCUIT JUDGE

This is a contract case in which the Republic of Argentina refuses to pay certain holders of sovereign bonds issued under a 1994 Fiscal Agency Agreement (hereinafter, the "FAA" and the "FAA Bonds"). In order to enhance the marketability of the bonds, Argentina made a series of promises to the purchasers. Argentina promised periodic interest payments. Argentina promised that the bonds would be governed by New York law. Argentina promised that, in the event of default, unpaid interest and principal would become due in full. Argentina promised that any disputes concerning the bonds could be adjudicated in the courts of New York. Argentina promised that each bond would be transferable and payable to the transferee, regardless of whether it was a university endowment, a so-called "vulture fund," or a widow or an orphan. Finally, Argentina promised to treat the FAA Bonds at least equally with its other external indebtedness. As we have held, by defaulting on the Bonds, enacting legislation specifically forbidding future payment on them, and continuing to pay interest on subsequently issued debt, Argentina breached its promise of equal treatment.

Specifically, in October 2012, we affirmed injunctions issued by the district court intended to remedy Argentina's breach of the equal treatment obligation in the FAA. Our opinion chronicled pertinent aspects of Argentina's fiscal history and the factual background of this case, familiarity with which is assumed. Those injunctions . . . directed that whenever Argentina pays on the bonds or other obligations that it issued in 2005 or 2010 exchange offers (the "Exchange Bonds"), the Republic must also make a "ratable payment" to plaintiffs who hold defaulted FAA Bonds. We remanded, however, for the district court to clarify the injunctions' payment formula and effects on third parties and intermediary banks . . .

In accordance with our October 2012 opinion, the litigation then returned to our Court. Argentina has challenged certain aspects of the amended injunctions, and appeals have also followed from other entities: a group of Exchange Bondholders, styling themselves as the Exchange Bondholder Group ("EBG"); the Bank of New York Mellon ("BNY"), indenture trustee to Exchange Bondholders; and Fintech Advisory Inc., a holder of Exchange Bonds. We further received briefing (but no notices of appeal) from two intervenors: a group of bondholders calling themselves the Euro Bondholders, and ICE Canyon LLC, a holder of GDP-linked securities issued by Argentina.

. . .

Argentina advances a litany of reasons as to why the amended injunctions unjustly injure itself, the Exchange Bondholders, participants in the Exchange Bond payment system, and the public. None of the alleged injuries leads us to find an abuse of the district court's discretion.

I.   Alleged Injuries to Argentina

Argentina argues that the amended injunctions unjustly injure it in two ways. First, Argentina argues that the amended injunctions violate the Foreign Sovereign Immunities Act ("FSIA") by forcing Argentina to use resources that the statute protects. As discussed in our October opinion, the original injunctions—and now the amended injunctions—do not violate the FSIA because "[t]hey do not attach, arrest, or execute upon any property" as proscribed by the statute. Rather, the injunctions allow Argentina to pay its FAA debts with whatever resources it likes. Absent further guidance from the Supreme Court, we remain convinced that the amended injunctions are consistent with the FSIA.

Second, Argentina argues that the injunctions' ratable payment remedy is inequitable because it calls for plaintiffs to receive their full principal and all accrued interest when Exchange Bondholders receive even a single installment of interest on their bonds. However, the undisputed reason that plaintiffs are entitled immediately to 100% of the principal and interest on their debt is that the FAA guarantees acceleration of principal and interest in the event of default. As the district court concluded, the amount currently owed to plaintiffs by Argentina as a result of its persistent defaults is the accelerated principal plus interest. We believe that it is equitable for one creditor to receive what it bargained for, and is therefore entitled to, even if other creditors, when receiving what they bargained for, do not receive the same thing. The reason is obvious: the first creditor is differently situated from other creditors in terms of what is currently due to it under its contract. Because the district court's decision does no more than hold Argentina to its contractual obligation of equal treatment, we see no abuse of discretion.

Argentina adds that the amended injunctions are invalid because a district court may not issue an injunctive "remedy [that] was historically unavailable from a court of equity." How-ever, English chancery courts traditionally had power to issue injunctions and order specific performance when no effective remedy was available at law. As we explained in our October 2012 opinion, the plaintiffs have no adequate remedy at law because the Republic has made clear its intention to defy any money judgment issued by this Court. Moreover, Argentina has gone considerably farther by passing legislation, the Lock Law, specifically barring payments to FAA bondholders. And it is unremarkable that a court empowered to afford equitable relief may also direct the timing of that relief. Here, that timing requires that it occur before or when Argentina next pays the Exchange Bondholders.

II. Alleged Injuries to Exchange Bondholders

Invoking the proposition that equitable relief is inappropriate where it would cause unreasonable hardship or loss to third persons, Argentina, EBG, and Fintech argue that the amended injunctions are inequitable to Exchange Bondholders. But this case presents no conflict with that proposition. EBG argues, notwithstanding our affirmance of the district court's finding that Argentina has the financial wherewithal to pay all of its obligations, that the amended injunctions will harm Exchange Bondholders because Argentina "has declared publicly that it has no intention of ever paying holdout bondholders like NML" and, as a result, neither plaintiffs nor Ex-change Bondholders will be paid if the amended injunctions stand.

This type of harm—harm threatened to third parties by a party subject to an injunction who avows not to obey it—does not make an otherwise lawful injunction "inequitable." We are unwilling to permit Argentina's threats to punish third parties to dictate the availability or terms of relief under Rule 65. Argentina's contention that the amended injunctions are unfair to Exchange Bondholders is all the less persuasive because, before accepting the exchange offers, they were expressly warned by Argentina in the accompanying prospectus that there could be "no assurance" that litigation over the FAA Bonds would not "interfere with payments" under the Exchange Bonds. Under these circumstances, we conclude that the amended injunctions have no inequitable effect on Exchange Bondholders and find no abuse of discretion.

III. Alleged Injuries to Participants in the Exchange Bond Payment System

Argentina, BNY, Euro Bondholders, and ICE Canyon raise additional issues concerning the amended injunctions and their effects on the international financial system through which Argentina pays Exchange Bondholders. The arguments include that (1) the district court lacks personal jurisdiction over payment system participants and therefore cannot bind them with the amended injunctions, (2) the amended injunctions cannot apply extraterritorially, (3) payment system participants are improperly bound because they were denied due process, and (4) the amended injunctions' application to financial system participants would violate the U.C.C.'s protections for intermediary banks. None of these arguments, numerous as they are, has merit.

First, BNY and Euro Bondholders argue that the district court erred by purporting to enjoin payment system participants over which it lacks personal jurisdiction. But the district court has issued injunctions against no one except Argentina. Every injunction issued by a district court automatically forbids others—who are not directly enjoined but who act "in active concert or participation" with an enjoined party—from assisting in a violation of the injunction. In any event, the Supreme Court has expressed its expectation that, when questions arise as to who is bound by an injunction though operation of Rule 65, district courts will not "withhold a clarification in the light of a concrete situation." The doors of the district court obviously remain open for such applications.

The amended injunctions simply provide notice to payment system participants that they could become liable through Rule 65 if they assist Argentina in violating the district court's orders. Since the amended injunctions do not directly enjoin payment system participants, it is irrelevant whether the district court has personal jurisdiction over them. And of course, "[t]here will be no adjudication of liability against a [non-party] without affording it a full opportunity at a hearing, after adequate notice, to present evidence." In such a hearing, before any finding of liability or sanction against a non-party, questions of personal jurisdiction may be properly raised. But, at this point, they are premature. Similarly, payment system participants have not been deprived of due process because, if and when they are summoned to answer for assisting in a violation of the district court's injunctions, they will be entitled to notice and the right to be heard.

Euro Bondholders and ICE Canyon next argue that the amended injunctions are improper or at a minimum violate comity where they extraterritorially enjoin payment systems that deliver funds to Exchange Bondholders. But a "federal court sitting as a court of equity having personal jurisdiction over a party [here, Argentina] has power to enjoin him from committing acts elsewhere." And federal courts can enjoin conduct that "has or is intended to have a substantial effect within the United States.

The district court put forward sufficient reasons for binding Argentina's conduct, regardless of whether that conduct occurs here or abroad. And the district court has articulated good reasons that the amended injunctions must reach the process by which Argentina pays Exchange Bondholders. The amended injunctions do not directly enjoin any foreign entities other than Argentina. By naming certain foreign payment system participants (such as Clearstream Banking S.A., Euroclear Bank S.A./ N.V., and Bank of New York (Luxembourg) S.A.), the district court was, again, simply recognizing the automatic operation of Rule 65.

If ICE Canyon and the Euro Bondholders are correct in stating that the payment process for their securities takes place entirely outside the United States, then the district court misstated that, with the possible exception of Argentina's initial transfer of funds to BNY, the Exchange Bond payment "process, without question takes place in the United States." But this possible misstatement is of no moment because, again, the amended injunctions enjoin no one but Argentina, a party that has voluntarily submitted to the jurisdiction of the district court. If others in active concert or participation with Argentina are outside the jurisdiction or reach of the district court, they may assert as much if and when they are summoned to that court for having assisted Argentina in violating United States law.

Argentina and Fintech further argue that the amended injunctions violate Article 4A of the U.C.C., which was enacted to provide a comprehensive framework that defines the rights and obligations arising from wire transfers. Two sections of that article are at issue: § 502, concerning creditor process, and § 503, requiring "proper cause" before a party to a fund transfer (but not an intermediary bank) may be enjoined.

Section 502(1) defines creditor process as a "levy, attachment, garnishment, notice of lien, sequestration, or similar process issued by or on behalf of a creditor or other claimant with respect to an account." Within the context of electronic funds transfers ("EFTs"), § 502 requires that creditor process must be served on the bank of the EFT beneficiary who owes a debt to the creditor. N.Y. U.C.C. § 4–A–502(4). The Republic argues that the district court impermissibly skirts § 502's bar to creditor process except against a beneficiary's bank because the amended injunctions purport to affect multiple banks and other financial institutions in active concert and participation with Argentina.

Section 502 is not controlling because the amended injunctions do not constitute, or give rise to, "creditor process," essentially defined in the statute as a levy or attachment. The cases cited by Argentina are inapposite because they deal with attachments, and as we have seen, none has occurred here.

Section 503, however, does apply. It provides that only "[f]or proper cause" may a court

> restrain (i) a person from issuing a payment order to initiate a funds transfer, (ii) an [EFT] originator's bank from executing the payment order of the originator, or (iii) the [EFT] beneficiary's bank from releasing funds to the beneficiary or the beneficiary from withdrawing the funds. A court may not otherwise restrain a person from issuing a payment order, paying or receiving payment of a payment order, or otherwise acting with respect to a funds transfer.

N.Y. U.C.C. § 4–A–503. This section "is designed to prevent interruption of a funds transfer after it has been set in motion," and "[i]n particular, intermediary banks are protected" from injunctions that would disrupt an EFT.

Argentina argues that plaintiffs purport to have cause for an injunction only with respect to Argentina, and therefore any transfers not involving Argentina cannot be enjoined. But as discussed above, the district court explained why it had good cause to issue injunctions that cover Argentina as well as the Exchange Bond payment system. Moreover, taking into account § 503's ban on injunctions against intermediary banks, the district court expressly excluded intermediary banks from the scope of the amended injunctions. Nonetheless, Fintech argues that BNY, BNY's paying agents, and DTC all act as intermediary banks and are all bound by the amended injunctions. We need not determine now what entities may or may not act as intermediary banks in an EFT that violates the amended injunctions. Whether or not an institution has assisted Argentina in a payment transaction solely in the capacity of an intermediary bank will be a question for future proceedings.

We note, however, that the record does not support Fintech's assertions. BNY does not route funds transfers originated by Argentina to Exchange Bondholders. Rather, BNY accepts funds as a beneficiary of Argentina's EFT and then initiates new EFTs as directed by its indenture.

Similarly, the clearing systems such as DTC and Euroclear appear from the record and from their own representations to be other than intermediary banks. DTC does not route wire transfers but accepts funds that it then allocates "only to the [participant banks and brokerage houses] who have deposited the respective securities with DTC." Euroclear receives "payments from paying agents" and then "credits such amounts to its account holders." These are not the functions of an intermediary bank under § 503.

IV. Alleged Injuries to the Public Interest

In our October opinion, we considered the dire predictions from Argentina that enforcing the commitments it made in the FAA would have cataclysmic repercussions in the capital markets and the global economy, and we explained why we disagreed. On this appeal, Argentina essentially recycles those arguments. We are mindful of the fact that courts of equity should pay particular regard to the public consequences of any injunction. However, what the consequences predicted by Argentina have in common is that they are speculative, hyperbolic, and almost entirely of the Republic's own making. None of the arguments demonstrates an abuse of the district court's discretion.

The district court found that Argentina now "has the financial wherewithal to meet its commitment of providing equal treatment to [plaintiffs] and [Exchange Bondholders]." However, Argentina and the Euro Bondholders warn that Argentina may not be able to pay or that paying will cause problems in the Argentine economy, which could affect the global economy. But as we observed in our last opinion, other than this speculation, "Argentina makes no real argument that, to avoid defaulting on its other debt, it cannot afford to service the defaulted debt, and it certainly fails to demonstrate that the district court's finding to the contrary was clearly erroneous." Moreover, and perhaps more critically, Argentina failed to present the district court with any record evidence to support its assertions.

Argentina and amici next assert that, by forcing financial institutions and clearing systems to scour all of their transactions for payments to Exchange Bondholders, the amended injunctions will delay many unrelated payments to third parties. But the financial institutions in question are already called on to navigate U.S. laws forbidding participation in various international transactions. Indeed, the record in this case appears to belie those concerns and suggests that payment system participants know when Exchange Bond payments are to arrive, because each is identified by a unique code assigned to a particular Exchange Bond. In this context, we view Argentina's concerns as speculative. In any event, a district court always retains the power to adjust the terms of an injunction as unforeseen problems or complexities involving entities such as the clearing systems present themselves.

Also unpersuasive is Argentina's warning that we should vacate the injunctions because future plaintiffs may "move against multilateral and official sector entities" like the IMF. As we have observed, this case presents no claim that payments to the IMF would violate the FAA. A court addressing such a claim in the future will have to decide whether to entertain it or whether to agree with the appellees that subordination of "obligations to commercial unsecured creditors beneath obligations to multilateral institutions like the IMF would not violate the Equal Treatment Provision for the simple reason that commercial creditors never were nor could be on equal footing with the multilateral organizations." Speculation that a future plaintiff might attempt recovery affecting the IMF simply provides no reason to withhold relief here.

Next, Argentina and various amici assert that the amended injunctions will imperil future sovereign debt restructurings. They argue essentially that success by holdout creditors in this case will encourage other bondholders to refuse future exchange offers from other sovereigns. They warn that rather than submitting to restructuring, bondholders will hold out for the possibility of full recovery on their bonds at a later time, in turn causing second-and third-order effects detrimental to the global economy and especially to developing countries.

But this case is an exceptional one with little apparent bearing on transactions that can be expected in the future. Our decision here does not control the interpretation of all *pari passu* clauses or the obligations of other sovereign debtors under *pari passu* clauses in other debt instruments. As we explicitly stated in our last opinion, we have not held that a sovereign debtor breaches its *pari passu* clause every time it pays one creditor and not another, or even every time it enacts a law disparately affecting a creditor's rights. We simply affirm the district court's conclusion that Argentina's extraordinary behavior was a violation of the particular *pari passu* clause found in the FAA.

We further observed that cases like this one are unlikely to occur in the future because Argentina has been a uniquely recalcitrant debtor and because newer bonds almost universally include collective action clauses ("CACs") which permit a super-majority of bondholders to impose a restructuring on potential holdouts. Argentina and amici respond that, even with CACs, enough bondholders may nonetheless be motivated to refuse restructurings and hold out for full payment—or that holdouts could buy up enough bonds of a single series to defeat restructuring of that series. But a restructuring failure on one series would still allow restructuring of the remainder of a sovereign's debt. And, as one amicus notes, "if transaction costs and other procedural inefficiencies are sufficient to block a super-majority of creditors from voting in favor of a proposed restructuring, the proposed restructuring is likely to fail under any circumstances."

Ultimately, though, our role is not to craft a resolution that will solve all the problems that might arise in hypothetical future litigation involving other bonds and other nations. The particular language of the FAA's *pari passu* clause dictated a certain result in this case, but going forward, sovereigns and lenders are free to devise various mechanisms to avoid holdout litigation if that is what they wish to do. They may also draft different *pari passu* clauses that support the goal of avoiding holdout creditors. If, in the future, parties intend to bar preferential payment, they may adopt language like that included in the FAA. If they mean only that subsequently issued securities may not explicitly declare subordination of the earlier bonds, they are free to say so. But none of this establishes why the plaintiffs should be barred from vindicating their rights under the FAA.

For the same reason, we do not believe the outcome of this case threatens to steer bond issuers away from the New York marketplace. On the contrary, our decision affirms a proposition essential to the integrity of the capital markets: borrowers and lenders may, under New York law, negotiate mutually agreeable terms for their transactions, but they will be held to those terms. We believe that the interest—one widely shared in the financial community—in maintaining New York's status as one of the foremost commercial centers is advanced by requiring debtors, including foreign debtors, to pay their debts.

NOTES

1. The enforcement of sovereign debts based on bonds presents special complications. Bondholders are dispersed and difficult to organize. States such as Argentina that face liquidity problems typically offer new obligations with new features in return for the bondholder's waiver of its right to enforce the old bond. The difference in nominal value between the old and new obligations is described as the bondholders' "haircut," *i.e.*, the discount they have given Argentina in return for new assurances as to ultimate payment. Not everyone accepts the deal, and those bondholders who hold out will continue to assert their rights.

In bankruptcy, a debtor can solve this holdout problem by having the court impose a deal on all similarly situated creditors. But sovereigns, of course, cannot put themselves in bankruptcy. The IMF put forward a proposal in the early 2000s that would have created something like a sovereign bankruptcy process, but the idea went nowhere.

2. A judgment creditor goes after the debtor's assets. In the case of sovereign debtors, this can be hard. Sovereigns generally have few assets that they own outright outside their own territory, and those that do generally enjoy immunity from attachment or execution under international or local law (*e.g.*, diplomatic premises, military equipment, deposits belonging to the sovereign's central bank). State-owned enterprises may have extraterritorial assets, but as the *Karaha Bodas* case indicates, the enterprise will not be liable for its owner's debts, any more than the owner is liable for the enterprise's debts.

3. The holdout bond creditors in *NML* enforced their judgment not only by going after Argentina's assets, but also going after persons receiving money from Argentina. As a normal rule a creditor cannot claim money to which another person is entitled. Here, the creditor did not try to claw back the money that the other bondholders received, but rather sought to block any payment to them unless and until Argentina paid the creditor on equal terms. These bond creditors could assert this right because their bond contract entitled them (in the view of the courts that interpreted the contract) to equal treatment with the other bondholders. In effect, their contract gave them a veto over payments to those bondholders who found the haircut acceptable.

Many judgment creditors seeking payment from foreign sovereigns may not have similar rights to equal treatment. Are there other ways for them to assert veto rights as a way of pressuring the sovereign debtor to settle?

NOTE ON PREJUDGMENT ATTACHMENT

In addition to enjoining relitigation of a claim in other jurisdictions, does a court have the power to order a party over which it has jurisdiction to make available assets located outside the jurisdiction for enforcement of an arbitral award? If so, may it take steps before confirming an award to make sure that a potential debtor not hide its assets or otherwise take steps to frustrate enforcement?

In the case of the United States, the Supreme Court has interpreted the federal rules of civil procedure as not providing the authority for protective orders that would limit a potential debtor's power to dispose of its assets in advance of a determination of its liability. *Grupo Mexicano De Desarrollo v. Alliance Bond Fund*, 527 U.S. 308 (1999). That decision did not preclude the several states from developing such prejudgment remedies, and *Grupo Mexicano* left open the possibility that a federal court could exercise those powers given state courts with respect to claims based on state law.

In the British Commonwealth, the law of prejudgment remedies is much more developed. The leading case is *Mareva Compania Naviera SA v. International Bulkcarriers SA*, [1975] 2 Lloyds Reports 509. A court, if convinced both that the plaintiff has a strong likelihood of success and that the defendant has both the capability and inclination to move assets out of the jurisdiction to frustrate enforcement of a judgment, may enjoin the defendant from doing anything that would interfere with the plaintiff's ultimate ability to collect on its judgment. In some cases, a court will issue such an injunction even if the underlying litigation that will generate a judgment is taking place in another country.

The use of such injunctions in support of enforcement of an arbitral award, rather than a court judgment, also is permitted. A rather extreme case involved a dispute between Exxon Mobil and Venezuela, following adoption of Venezuelan legislation in 2007 that, the company argued, resulted in the expropriation of its investment in that country. It sought an order from a British court freezing the worldwide assets of Petroleos de Venezuela S.A., the state oil company. A judge initially granted the request as an emergency matter. After full briefing and argument, another judge dissolved the injunction. It gave primary weight to the absence of any connection to the United Kingdom with respect to either the dispute or the defendant company:

> In my view it is apparent from the cases cited earlier, and is sufficient for present purposes, that this court will only be prepared to exercise discretion to grant an application in aid of foreign litigation for a freezing order affecting assets not located here if the respondent or the dispute has a sufficiently strong link here or, . . . there is some other factor of sufficient strength to justify proceeding in the absence of such a link. This way of putting the matter does not assume that presence of the respondent here will necessarily be sufficient to warrant the exercise of discretion in favour of an

applicant . . . There will always need to be a careful examination of the justification for any part of the proposed order which would tend to run counter to principles of comity with courts in other jurisdictions.

. . .

The major difficulty confronting Mobil in this regard is that affidavits and affirmations by senior officers of PDV have been lodged which state expressly that it has no office, conducts no business operations, and has no bank accounts, real property or other assets of any kind in England and Wales. Mobil is not content to accept these assurances. However, there is no reason whatever to think that those who have given these assurances have sought to deceive the court or have misunderstood the ordinary meaning of the words used.

The court made clear, however, that the fact that the injunction was intended to secure enforcement of an arbitral award, rather than a judicial judgment, was not dispositive. *Mobil Cerro Negro Limited v. Petroleos de Venezuela S.A.*, Case No: 2008 Folio 61, [2008] EWHC 532 (Q.B.).

NOTES

1. The *Mareva* injunction is a powerful tool in the hands of plaintiffs. Not only does it increase the odds that an eventually prevailing party will collect what will be due, but it ties up funds that defendants may need to conduct their business operations. A defendant may settle for more than it otherwise would to regain the use of its assets. The judge's dilemma thus should be clear: Do nothing and leave meritorious claims unsatisfied, or intervene and force defendants to buy off claimants for what might be more than fair value. And remember that because the injunction issues before the judge has heard all the evidence (and in some cases before it has heard from anyone other than the plaintiffs), the risk of error about the actual merit of the claim is great. Given the concerns in both sides, it may not be surprising that countries with strong legal institutions take very different approaches to the problem.

2. What is more interesting, that a British court eventually withdrew the world-wide injunction or that the injunction initially issued? Note that Mobil did not seek to protect the court's jurisdiction: Any claim against PDV's assets would result from an award in one of the several arbitral proceedings. Arbiters typically do not have the authority to enjoin parties or otherwise to control their behavior outside the narrow confines of the disputes submitted to arbitration. Is it appropriate for courts to exercise their powers to protect the interests of potential arbitral claimants?

3. Note that one of the arbitral mechanisms that Exxon Mobil had invoked was the International Center for the Settlement of Investment Disputes (ICSID). The right to arbitrate under the New York Convention typically rests on a contractual commitment. The right to invoke ICSID arbitration normally arises as a result of a provision in a bilateral investment treaty (BIT) between the host state and the investor's home state. ICSID arbitration thus can have a somewhat greater tendency to incorporate issues of broad public policy, such as the line between legitimate governmental regulation and illegitimate expropriation.

PROBLEMS

A.   Petro America plans to enter into a joint venture agreement with Rosneft, a state-owned company, to develop an oil field. Draft contractual language regarding dispute resolution. Consider the possibility of waivers, guarantees, structure of dispute settlement, choice of forum and choice of law, as well as any other issues that might affect dispute settlement.

B.   Drawing from cases and notes from Chapters 3 and 4, as well as from this chapter, consider how to solve the following problem for your client, a major U.S. manufacturer, which sells into Ukraine through a distributor. The distribution agreement provides that title to the goods passes to the distributor upon delivery at the manufacturer's facility in Budapest, Hungary. The distributor then makes arrangements to import the goods to Ukraine, but a corrupt group within the Ukrainian police seizes the goods on the pretext that they were being imported without paying proper customs duties and value-added tax and that the distributor was bribing Ukrainian customs officials to facilitate the illegal scheme. In reality, the corrupt group plans to sell the goods on the black market and pocket the proceeds. The U.S. company no longer has any legal rights to the goods, so it cannot challenge the actions of the police in a Ukrainian court, and the distributor will not cooperate and, in any event, is under criminal investigation in Ukraine. Worst of all, the goods were sold to the distributor on credit, and the distributor is refusing to pay for the confiscated shipment.

What recourse does the U.S. manufacture have to recover it goods since its legal remedies are limited? What counsel can you provide?

INDEX

References are to Pages

343